Meta-Emotion
How Families Communicate
Emotionally

Meta-Emotion
How Families Communicate
Emotionally

by

John M. Gottman
Lynn Fainsilber Katz
Carole Hooven
University of Washington

LEA LAWRENCE ERLBAUM ASSOCIATES, PUBLISHERS
1997   Mahwah, New Jersey

Lawrence Erlbaum Associates, Inc., Publishers
10 Industrial Avenue
Mahwah, NJ 07430

Cover design by Kathryn Houghtaling

Library of Congress Cataloging-in-Publication Data

Gottman, John Mordechai.

Meta emotion : how families communicate emotionally / John Mordechai Gottman, Lynn Fainsilber Katz, Carole Hooven.

p. cm.

Includes bibliographic references and index.

ISBN 0-8058-1995-9 (cloth : alk. paper). — ISBN 0-8058-1996-7 (paper : alk. paper)

1. Communication in the family. 2. Emotions in children. 3. Parenting.   I. Katz, Lynn Fainsilber. II. Hooven, Carole. III. Title.

HQ728.G633 1996

155.4'124—dc20   95-49700
                                                                CIP

Printed in the United States of America
10 9 8 7 6 5 4 3 2 1

Dedicated to the work and to the memory

of

Dr. Haim Ginott

He led the way

since feeling is first
who pays attention
to the syntax of things
will never wholly kiss you;

wholly to be a fool
while Spring is in the world

[...]

then laugh, leaning back in my arms
for life's not a paragraph

and death i   think is no parenthesis

Gottman: Where do you think babies come from?
  Moriah (daughter, 4 years old): From vaginas.
Gottman: Mommies make them all by themselves?
  Moriah: Um hmm.
Gottman: How do they do it?
  Moriah: I don't know.
Gottman: Don't you need daddies to make babies?
  Moriah: No.
Gottman: Then what are daddies for?
  Moriah: To play with, to give love, and to keep their children safe.

Contents

Foreword **xi**

Acknowledgments **xvii**

PART I: THE EMOTIONAL LIFE OF FAMILIES

Introduction to the Concept of Meta-Emotion **3**

Chapter 1   Research on Parenting and Meta-Emotions **9**

Chapter 2   Popular Parenting Guides: Introducing Ginott **14**

Appendix 2.1   Life Space Interviewing in More Detail **35**

PART II: MEASUREMENT AND CONCEPTUALIZATION

Chapter 3   The Selection of Development Outcomes **39**

Chapter 4   The Meta-Emotion Interview **45**

Chapter 5   An "Emotion Regulation Theory" **86**
of Meta-Emotion, Parenting, and Child Outcomes

Appendix 5.1   How Specifically Might Meta-Emotion **106**
and Parenting Affect a Child's Development?

Appendix 5.2   Necessary Concepts From Child Physiology: **117**
                A Brief Review of Research

Chapter 6   Designing a Family Psychophysiology   **123**
                Laboratory: The Methods of Our Study

Appendix 6.1   More Detail on Measures and Coding   **132**

Chapter 7   The Internal Structure of Parents' Meta-Emotions   **140**

Chapter 8   Validity of the Meta-Emotion Interview   **143**

PART III: PARENTING, META-EMOTIONS, AND CHILD OUTCOMES

Chapter 9   Parenting, Parental Meta-Emotions,   **149**
                 and the Child's Peer Relations

Chapter 10   Parenting, Parental Meta-Emotions,   **152**
                 and the Physical Health and Negative
                 Affectivity of Children

Chapter 11   Parenting, Parental Meta-Emotions,   **155**
                 and Childrens' Academic Achievement
                 at Age 8

PART IV: MECHANISMS, PROCESS MODELS, AND THE PARENTS' MARRIAGE

Chapter 12   How Might Meta-Emotions Have Their   **163**
                 Effects? Preliminary Tests of Our Theory

Chapter 13   Parenting, Meta-Emotion, and the Parents'   **190**
                 Marriage

Chapter 14   The Effects of Marital Conflict and Buffering   **214**
                 Children From Marital Conflict

PART V: EXTENSIONS

Chapter 15	Meta-Emotion and Gender	**229**
Chapter 16	When Parents Feel Emotionally Out of Control	**236**
Chapter 17	Meta-Emotion, Emotional Expressiveness, and Parental Social Class	**259**
Appendix 17.1	Vagal Tone and the Inhibition of Expressiveness	**268**
Appendix 17.2	Child Temperament	**270**
Chapter 18	Discussion and a Research Agenda	**272**
Chapter 19	Emotion Metaphors	**306**
Appendix A	Methodology for the Vagal Tone Computations	**323**
	References	**333**
	Author Index	**355**
	Subject Index	**360**

Foreword

Haim Ginott, to whom this book is dedicated, was a clinical psychologist, child therapist and parent educator whose books *Between Parent and Child*, *Between Parent and Teenager*, and *Teacher and Child* revolutionized the way parents and teachers relate to children. The communication skills that he advocates in these books help adults enter into the world of children in a compassionate and caring way and teach them how to become aware and respond to children's feelings. As he said, "I'm a child psychotherapist. I treat disturbed children. Supposing I see a child in therapy one hour a week for a year. Her symptoms disappear; she feels better about herself, gets along with others, even stops fidgeting in school. What is it that I do that helps? I communicate with her in a unique way. I use every opportunity to enhance her feelings about herself. If caring communication can drive sick children sane, its principles and practices belong to parents and teachers. While psychotherapists can cure, only those in daily contact with children can prevent them from needing psychological help."

Most of us are unaware that words are like knives; that we need to be skilled in the use of words. How would Jane feel if the surgeon came into the operating room right before the anesthesiologist put her under and said, "Jane, I really don't have much training in surgery but I love being a surgeon and I use common sense?" Jane would probably panic and run for her life. But there is no exit for children. Unlike a surgeon who is careful where he cuts, parents and teachers use words carelessly. They make many painful incisions until they hit the right spot, heedless of the open wounds they leave behind. They perform daily emotional operations on their children without training.

Were he alive today, Haim Ginott would be most appreciative of the research in this book, which confirms his anecdotal findings. As stated in chapter 5, there is evidence that from the beginning of a child's life, parents' interaction with a child has implications for the child's ability to self-regulate, focus attention, share intersubjective meaning, form the essential affectional bonds with parents and be able to interact with a changing environment. As children develop, the child's developing emotion regulation abilities are directly influenced by parenting and by the way parents talk to children about their emotion.

The book confirms Haim Ginott's findings of the importance of relating to children in an empathic and caring way, as stated in chapter 5: "parenting, which involves being affectionate, enthusiastic, engaged, responsive to the child..." is helpful in healthy development of children. But not many parents know how to relate to children in a "Scaffolding/Praising way." That is where Haim Ginott came in. He tried to teach parents and teachers how to express anger, criticize, praise, acknowledge and reflect feelings, and respond to hurt and disappointment in a way that does not damage a child's emotional well-being. He showed them how to be authoritative without being authoritarian and how to respond rather than react to children's anger and pain.

He used to say that children need to feel understood, because when they feel understood, they feel loved. By acknowledging their complaints, by accepting all their feelings, be they negative, positive, or ambivalent, and by reflecting their feelings to them, a parent can make a child feel understood and loved. Suppose a child complains by saying, "I hate Grandma. She brought the baby a present but she didn't give me anything." A parent could respond by reflecting the child's complaint and by acknowledging the child's feelings: "Grandma brought a present for the baby but not for you. No wonder you're upset. You think that if she loved you as much as the baby she would have brought you a present too. Why don't you tell her how you feel?"

When Haim Ginott finished *Between Parent and Child*, he offered the book to McGraw-Hill, the firm that had published his *Group Psychotherapy with Children* in 1961. But a young psychologist who was asked to review the book did not think it had anything new to offer and, therefore, it was rejected. He then submitted the book to the Macmillan Publishing Company. The editor at Macmillan was a father of two young children, but he was not interested in Ginott's work. He gave the book to his wife who, while reading it one evening in bed, laughed so appreciatively that the editor became curious. When she told him how helpful the book would be in bringing up their children, he felt compelled to accept the book for publication.

Two years later (1967) a young reporter, Phyllis Feinstein, wrote an article in *The New York Times* Magazine section entitled "Childrenese—A Language for Parents," describing the empathic communication skills that Haim Ginott developed in his book. The producer of the "Today" show was intrigued and invited him to talk about his ideas on the morning program. The response was so overwhelming that he was asked to return 34 times. The sales of the book sky-rocketed; it became a best seller and stayed on the best seller list for more than a year. Eventually the book was translated into 30 languages, including Chinese, and has sold more than 3 million copies. When *Between Parent and Teenager* was published in 1969, it, too, became a best seller. In 1972 Ginott published *Teacher and Child*. In 1973 he died of cancer at age 51.

It was gratifying to watch the warm response young parents, especially mothers, gave to learning the communication skills that would help them respond empathically to their children, skills that Haim Ginott advocated in his books. They welcomed the idea that finding it difficult to bring up children and not always knowing what to say and do did not mean that they needed psychological help in order to become more caring and effective parents. At that time, most psychologists felt that poor parenting was the result of parents' psychological problems rather than lack of skill, misinformation, or poor parental models.

Often when parents brought *Between Parent and Child* to their psychotherapists, the psychotherapists would denigrate it by calling it a cookbook that they should not need for bringing up their children, that it was contrived and manipulative. They encouraged parents to be spontaneous, to listen to their instincts, to be natural. Unfortunately, most parents could not distinguish impulsivity from spontaneity. They did not know how to examine their natural reactions to their children, to separate that which helps from that which can hurt, and their therapists did not know how to help.

As chief psychologist at the Jacksonville, Florida Child Guidance Clinic, Haim Ginott treated emotionally disturbed children and adolescents. This intensive experience with troubled children sensitized him to children's emotional needs and to the needs of their parents. He came to realize that the traditional model of offering psychological treatment to these parents may help them personally but did not necessarily teach them how to relate to their children in a more compassionate way. Thus, in the early 1950s, he began experimenting with parent education and guidance groups as an alternative to psychotherapy for parents. Eventually, he expanded his parent guidance groups to include parents of healthy children who wanted to learn how to be more caring and effective with their children, to become aware of how they felt about their own feelings and thus become more understanding of their children's anger and hurt.

Before he became a psychologist, Haim Ginott was an elementary school teacher in Israel. He was a graduate of the David Yellin Teachers College in Jerusalem. But after teaching for a few years he realized that he was not sufficiently prepared to deal with "live" children in the classroom. As he would say: "I tried to teach them to be polite and they were rude; to be neat and they were messy; to be cooperative and they were disruptive." It was then that he decided to come to the United States, to Columbia University Teacher's College, but Columbia's education courses were not helpful either. Like most teachers, he knew that he came to the profession with the best of intentions, to function in the classroom humanely as well as effectively. He wanted to learn how to discipline without humiliating; how to criticize without destroying self-worth; how to praise without judging; how to express anger without hurting; how to acknowledge feeling, not argue against it; how to respond so that children would learn to trust their inner reality and develop self-confidence.

Haim Ginott's early experience as a teacher left him with an appreciation of the problems that confront the well-intentioned adults who interact with children. It influenced his development as a parent counselor and child therapist. He became aware of the importance of empathy, not only for the child but also for the adult, and the latter's need for practical help.

His development as a clinical psychologist and child therapist was influenced by his teacher, Virginia Axline, who had been a student of Carl Rogers. As a graduate student assistant to Axline he learned the Rogerian technique of how to communicate empathy by acknowledging and reflecting feelings. It was a skill that he used with children who were in treatment with him, and he also taught this skill to parents. Acknowledging and reflecting feelings was the primary tool that both Axline and Rogers used in treating children and adults. But Haim Ginott realized soon after he started treating disturbed children that he needed to develop a more varied set of tools for communicating with his young patients. The children would get angry and he had to respond to their anger; he got angry and he had to learn how to express his anger; how to criticize, praise, and say no without inflicting hurt or doing damage to the child's emotional well-being. As a result he experimented until he came up with specific communication skills that he found therapeutic in treating disturbed children, which he shared in his books with parents and teachers.

The philosophy that guided him was part of the Hippocratic Oath: At first: Do no damage, and the dictum: Deal with the situation, not the person. When things go wrong, do not blame the person but look for a solution. State the problem and the possible solution. "Ohhh ...the vase broke. We need to pick up the pieces." Not: "You're so clumsy! Look what you did! How am I going to replace this expensive vase? You're like a bull in a china shop!" Neither response will bring back the beautiful vase, but by concentrating on the mishap and not on the perpetrator, the parent has protected the child from feeling guilty and from developing an image of himself as being clumsy.

Parents, Haim Ginott felt, need to discard their language of rejection and learn a language of acceptance. They even know the words. They heard their parents use them with guests and strangers. It was a language that was protective of feelings, not critical of behavior. When a guest accidentally breaks a valuable object, rarely do parents say anything negative directly to the guest. Just the opposite. They make sure that the guest does not feel bad about the accident; they reassure the guest: "It's all right. I know exactly where to get another one like it." Haim Ginott tried to encourage parents and teachers to treat children as guests; to be as aware as they are of hurting their guests' feelings when they respond to children.

But many parents and teachers were confused when they listened to Haim Ginott or read his books. They could not decide whether he was strict or permissive. They were concerned that if they started to relate to children in a caring way they would have to sacrifice setting limits and setting standards, that the children would become undisciplined.

Haim Ginott was both strict and permissive. He was strict when it came to behavior. There was acceptable and unacceptable behavior. Parents and teachers had to decide for themselves what behavior they would or would not tolerate. But he was permissive when it came to feeling, because neither children nor adults can help how they feel. He used to say: "Birds fly, fish swim and people feel." That is how we are. It is therefore not in anyone's best interest to make children feel uncomfortable or, even more serious, guilty for the way they feel.

"What is the goal of parenting?" he would ask. "When all is said and done, we want children to grow up to be decent human beings, a person with compassion, commitment and caring."

How, then, does one go about humanizing a child? Only by using humane methods. By recognizing that the process is the method, that the ends do not justify the means and that in our attempt to get children to behave in a way that is acceptable to us we do not damage them emotionally.

Over the years many parents and teachers studied with Haim Ginott. They contributed to his understanding, providing many of the anecdotes in his books that illustrate his principles of communication. They, on the other hand, benefited from his wisdom, his warmth, and his humor. Although English was not his native tongue, he loved the English language. He loved it as a poet, using it sparingly and with precision. Raised in a verbal Jewish tradition, Haim Ginott often made his points through jokes, parables, and anecdotes. He was in great demand as a speaker where his message, expressed with caring, humor, and enthusiasm, easily seduced his audience.

A story is told about a rabbi who died at the age of forty-nine. When the family returned from the funeral the eldest son said: "Our father had a long life." Everyone was aghast. "How can you say that of a man who died so young?" The son responded: "Because his life was full; he wrote many important books and he touched many lives."

That is my consolation.

Alice Ginott

Acknowledgments

The research that has formed the basis of this book could not have been possible without the continuous support for more than a decade of the National Institute of Mental Health, through its dedicated, supportive, and highly professional staff, and also through research grants MH42484, titled "Marital discord, parenting, and child emotional development," and MH35997, titled "Friendship formation among children," an NIMH Merit Award to extend research in time, and Research Scientist Award K2MH00257 awarded to John Gottman. We are now able to replicate this research and to extend to the study of newlywed couples as they become parents and interact with their infants; this makes it possible to study the marriage before children arrive, and to follow the children as they develop from infancy.

We have been blessed with a very active, dedicated, and creative group of students and staff. These people include Lauren Bush, Jim Coan, Holly Collier, Don Goldstein, Vanessa Kahen, Kim McCoy, Erin Moline, Sonny Ruckstahl, Regina Rushe, Joann Wu Shortt, Karen Walker, Beverly Wilson, and Kathy Zelis. Kim McCoy designed the Oral History Interview coding system and Vanessa Kahen designed the parent-child interaction coding systems. Our fabulous programmer and great friend Catherine Swanson has been a superb member of our team for a decade and has helped us with our thinking as well as with our computing. Sybil Carrere has been a great force for mustering our creative energies, finding direction, and helping us to communicate with and nurture one another.

This work would not have been possible without the enormous help and support of the Center for Human Development and Disabilities (CHDD) of the University of Washington, its talented director, Michael Guralnick, and the Instrument Development Laboratory, particularly Bill Moritz, Tim Myers, and Alan Ross. Both the University of Illinois and the University of Washington and their respective Psychology departments have been great contexts for research and for helping us build our laboratory.

Our laboratory was initially graciously constructed by our collaborator Robert Levenson, whose encouragement and patience were essential in getting us trained in psychophysiology. Others teachers have helped in the process including John Cacioppo, Louis Tassinary, John Simpson, Loring Rowell, and Steve Woods. A constant source of encouragement and a great guide was our good friend Steve Porges.

John Gottman would like to thank his wife, Julie, for all her intellectual camaraderie, for her encouragement and support, for the many hours together thinking about how to best raise their daughter, Moriah, for agreeing to run the parenting groups together and for all the fun that turned out to be, and also for drawing Figure 18.2.

None of this would have been possible without the continuing daily support of the backbone of our laboratory, Sharon Fentiman.

John Gottman
Lynn Fainsilber Katz
Carole Hooven

PART I

THE EMOTIONAL LIFE OF FAMILIES

Introduction to the Concept
of Meta-Emotion

This chapter introduces our concepts of " meta-emotion" and "meta-emotion struc-ture," and provides some historical context for the evolution of these ideas in our laboratory.

HISTORY AND PREFACE

For the past 20 years, our laboratory has had two lines of research. We have been studying children's friendships and children's peer relations since 1972 (e.g., Gottman, 1983; Gottman & Parker, 1986). We have also been studying the social interaction processes related to marital satisfaction (Gottman, 1979), to longitudi-nal change in marital satisfaction (Gottman & Krokoff, 1989), and, more recent-ly, to marital dissolution (Buehlman, Gottman, & Katz, 1992; Gottman, 1993; Gottman, 1994; Gottman & Levenson, 1992). Much of this latter work emerged from a continuing collaboration with Robert Levenson that began in 1979, when Gottman and Levenson decided to study the role of emotion in marriage using methods of social psychophysiology. These methods proved to be quite produc-tive (e.g., Gottman, 1994; Gottman & Levenson, 1985, 1988, 1992; Levenson & Gottman, 1983, 1985).

In 1984, Gottman decided to try to bring his work with Levenson on marital psychophysiology and his research on children's friendships and children's social development together into a single series of studies. The idea was to build a new family psychophysiology laboratory, to study the linkages between the marital, parent–child, and child–peer systems, extending the work that Levenson and Gottman had employed in studying marriage. To accomplish this task, it was necessary for Gottman to become a psychophysiologist and also to learn about parent–child relationships. It also required designing and building a new laboratory, which could not have happened without the critical assistance, guidance, and technical help of Robert Levenson. Lynn Fainsilber Katz, then a graduate student at the University of Illinois, joined the project at its inception. Gottman and Katz wrote the grants that eventually funded the work. In 1985, Levenson came to the University of Illinois and put together a family psychophysiology laboratory. Levenson guided Gottman in this first entry and later development as a psychophysiologist, a process that took about 5 years. Gottman's training was assisted by his NIMH Research Career Development Award, by informal instruction by Stephen Porges, by membership in the Society for Psychophysiological Research, and by formal instruction in John Cacioppo's National Science Foundation's training program in psychophysiology during the summer of 1987. The Family Psychophysiology Laboratory was completed in 1985 and our first study began in 1986.

For the past decade, our laboratory has been studying the relationship between the parents' marriage, parent–child interaction, and the emotional-social development of children. We have suggested that these linkages are mediated through the development of emotion-regulation abilities in the child (Gottman & Katz, 1989; Katz & Gottman, 1991). By emotion-regulation abilities we had a specific set of abilities in mind, namely the child's ability to inhibit inappropriate negativity, the child's ability to self-soothe, and the child's ability to focus attention in the service of an external goal. Steve Porges was then at the University of Illinois, and his thinking about regulation in the cardiovascular system was an important influence. In fact, Porges and Gottman team taught a course on time-series analysis to graduate students that introduced them to the measurement of vagal tone by spectral time-series techniques.

The area of parent–child relations was new to us. As fledglings in this area, we decided to build on Philip and Carolyn Cowans' balanced approach to parenting, much of which had been guided by the work of Diana Baumrind. This collaboration was made possible by the NIMH Family Research Consortium, which was set up in 1980 by Joy Schulterbrandt. In selecting a theoretical basis for our studies, building on the work of the Cowans and Baumrind, we decided to focus on the emotional life of families and the development of emotional regulation in children. The focus on emotional regulation was inspired by Eleanor Maccoby's (1980) seminal book on social-emotional development.

This book presents the results of our initial work with meta-emotion. We are excited by these results, but we offer this work only as our initial, exploratory work with meta-emotion. Clearly replication is necessary, and experiments are needed to test the path analytic models we have developed from our correlational data. This book explores our initial study, which includes meta-emotion, generates some theory, and in Chapter 18 proposes a research agenda. We think that the research agenda is as important as our initial findings. We hope that other researchers will find these ideas interesting and stimulating, and we offer them in the hopes that others will join us in investigating this exciting new area of a family's emotional life.

Much of our laboratory's initial work was designed to parallel the work of Carolyn and Philip Cowan. In the design of our studies, we added to the Cowans' approach a social psychophysiological emphasis, an emphasis on the parents' marriage, an emphasis on emotion regulation in children, and an emphasis on children's relationships with other children.

Before the first study in 1984 was launched, Gottman visited Robert Levenson, who was then on sabbatical in Paul Ekman's laboratory, and Ekman introduced him to Hochschild's (1983) book, *The Managed Heart*. This book inspired Gottman to think of the idea of meta-emotion, and to the development of a "meta-emotion interview" in conjunction with Lynn Fainsilber Katz (Katz and Gottman, 1986).

In this first study we planned for our family psychophysiology laboratory, each parent was to be separately interviewed about their own experience of sadness and anger, their philosophy of emotional expression and control, and their attitudes and behavior about their children's anger and sadness. Their behavior during this interview was audiotaped and later coded with a meta-emotion coding system designed by a central member of our laboratory staff, Carole Hooven, a coauthor of this book. Initially, the goal of the meta-emotion interview was to examine each parent's feelings about being emotionally expressive, but this idea was later expanded.

In pilot work for our first study of the effects of the parents' marriage on children, we discovered a great variety in the experiences, philosophies, and attitudes that parents had about their emotions and the emotions of their children. One pair of parents said that they viewed anger as "from the devil," and that they would not permit themselves or their children to express anger. Their child was quite docile in her interactions with her parents but appeared quite angry and bossy in her interactions with her best friend. A similar negative view toward anger was echoed by other parents. Some parents in our study said that they put their children in Time Out for being angry, even if there was no child misbehavior. Other parents felt that anger was natural, but ignored the experience of anger in their children. Other parents encouraged the expression and exploration of anger. There was similar variety with respect to sadness, and the information we gathered about sadness was not redundant with the information we gathered about anger. Some parents minimized sadness in themselves and in their children, saying such things as, "I can't afford to be sad," and "What does a kid have to be sad about?" Other parents thought that emotions like sadness in themselves and in their children were important and viewed themselves as emotion coaches of their children about the world of emotion. In our pilot work there also appeared to be gender differences: Fathers seemed less likely to be aware of their own sadness or to assist when their children were sad; fathers who were oriented toward emotion seemed more interested in their children's anger than in their sadness. Mothers seemed to be more concerned with their children's sadness than fathers. These were our initial impressions.

We decided to focus on studying parents' feelings about feelings, which we called their meta-emotions. The notion of meta-emotion we had in mind paralleled the area of metacognition, which referred to the executive functions of cognition (Allen & Armour, 1993; Bvinelli, 1993; Flavell, 1979; Fodor, 1992; Nelson, 1992; Olson & Astington, 1993). Metacognitions are thoughts about thinking. In social interaction research, the term "metacommunication" referred to communication about communication. We began to also use the term meta-emotion structure to refer broadly to similar executive functions of emotion, ones that included concepts, philosophies, and metaphors about emotions, as well as emotions about emotions. Concepts similar to meta-emotion have been discussed by Salovey and Mayer (1990) in their ideas about emotional intelligence, and by Mayer and Gaschke (1988) in their state and trait meta-mood scales.

What we mean by the meta-emotion structure construct, specifically, is the parent's awareness of specific emotions, their awareness of these emotions in their child, and their coaching of the emotion in their child. Emotion coaching refers to a set of processes that include such elements as talking to the child about the emotions, helping the child to verbally label the emotions being felt, accepting the child's emotions, discussing the situations that elicited the emotions, and having goals and strategies for coping with these situations. In chapter 4, we delineate the five components of an emotion coaching meta-emotion structure. If this construct of emotion coaching is to be useful, it should relate to how the family actually functions, and our goal is to test this notion in this book. At that time we did not expect the concept of meta-emotion to become the centerpiece of our work. That result was entirely serendipitious. The data led us to modify our initial theorizing and to realize that we had a particularly appealing and parsimonious theory and set of initial findings. Once we made meta-emotion the centerpiece of our work, this became a data set that said yes to almost all the theoretical questions we asked of it in building our theoretical model. Lynn Fainsilber Katz's thinking was instrumental to the development of the theoretical models. We also wish to acknowledge the help and feedback of Stephen Porges in building our theoretical model. He took a look at our initial results the same year he gave his spectacular presidential address on the vagus nerve and vagal tone to the Society for Psychophysiological Research, in Atlanta, in 1994.

DEFINITIONS

Meta-Emotion

By meta-emotion, we mean emotion about emotion. The idea is analogous to metacognitions, which are cognitions about cognition (see Nelson, 1992). Researchers have searched for uniformity with respect to emotion, thinking that, for example, the emotion of anger is the same for most people, but they have tended to overlook how people feel about a particular emotion such as anger. Some people are ashamed or upset about becoming angry, others feel good about their capacity to express anger, and still others think of anger as natural, neither good nor bad. Any experiment that involves the induction of emotion will also involve meta-emotions, even if they are not studied; hence, in emotion induction experiments, meta-emotions are not controlled. Thus, the effects of inducing the emotion of anger may vary across subjects, not only because anger is not induced uniformly across people, but because people's emotions about their own anger vary so much. A good paradigm to take as an example is the startle experiment (Ekman, Friesen, & Simons, 1985; Landis & Hunt, 1939). In a startle experiment the experimenter will fire off a high intensity stimulus, like a gunshot, behind the subject's head. After displaying a startle response, people will have various emotions to having been startled (Ekman, personal communication; Sutton & Levenson, personal communication.) Some laugh with pleasure, some laugh with embarrassment, some become afraid, some are disgusted, and some become angry. This latter emotional response is a meta- emotion: Quite simply, it is an emotion about an emotion. (We ignore here the issue of whether the startle is a reflex or an emotion.) This discussion is clearly not limited to the startle experiment. Whenever we elicit emotion, we are also dealing with emotions about having experienced or felt the emotion. We always engage the person's meta-emotion structure, whether we study it or not.

Meta-Emotion Structure

What do we mean by meta-emotion structure? By a meta-emotion structure we mean an organized and structured set of emotions and cognitions about the emotions, both one's own emotions and the emotions of others. Thus, a meta-emotion structure is an organized set of feelings and concepts about emotion, and this idea includes the idea of an emotion philosophy. For example, one parent may be disgusted by his or her 5-year-old's anger and believe that children of that age should not express anger, that it is destructive and bad. Another parent may view his or her 5-year-old's anger as acceptable, and as an important moment for talking about the child's emotions and understanding what the child is feeling.

We analyze people's metaphors about emotion (Lakoff & Johnson, 1980) as one way of getting at people's concepts about meta-emotion. We are only beginning this study. An example may help clarify the importance of this idea of meta-emotion metaphors. One father in our research referred to sadness as if it were a limited resource, like how much money one has. He thought that his children should not "waste" their sadness on trivial things but instead "invest" their sadness only in important things. For this father it was a sin for his child to be sad about missing mom one morning, because that was wasting sadness on a trivial, unimportant, everyday event. If his daughter's pet had died, he would have thought it would be a wise "investment" of sadness to express sadness about that event, but merely missing mom was showing poor judgment on the child's part on what to "spend" this valuable and limited resource on. This "limited resource" metaphor for sadness led this father to act disapproving some of the time, perhaps most of the time, when his daughter was sad, but other times to be compassionate and understanding of his daughter's sadness. Would his daughter understand his concept, would she see only his disapproval, or would she see only his compassion at moments selected by him? At any rate, it seemed clear that his metaphor for sadness was likely to have a profound effect on his parenting and on his relationship with his daughter. In our research this metaphor is an example of a pattern of meta-emotions, and an organized set of thoughts about these patterns of meta-emotions, and we refer to each of these various patterns as a meta-emotion structure.

1

Research on Parenting and Meta-Emotions

This chapter is a brief review of the literature on parenting research. We think that meta-emotion is not an independent dimension but, rather, it is contextualized within a network of parenting dimensions, and we suggest two parenting dimensions that will be employed in our model building.

Because we think that our meta-emotion variables are embedded in a set of variables that describe parenting, this chapter briefly reviews the parenting research literature. We do not attempt to provide a thorough review of this large literature. Rather, we offer this review with the goal of outlining the kinds of variables that have been considered to date. Our purpose, in part, is to convince the reader that there is something new in considering meta-emotion as part of parenting, despite the fact that we believe that meta-emotion variables do not stand alone but are contextualized in a web of variables that describe parenting.

Parenting has been classified and studied primarily in terms of the predominant parental affects toward the child and predominant parental discipline techniques. What we think is missing is how the parent feels about and relates to specific emotional displays by the child, and how this might relate to the parent's feelings about his or her own emotions. This area of family functioning is likely to be more general than the parents' predominant affect or the parents' discipline techniques.

In early multidimensional parenting research that employed factor analysis, two major independent dimensions emerged. Maccoby and Martin (1983) pointed out that these variables emerged despite the initial theoretical bases of the investigations that derived them, rather than because of the theories; these orthogonal dimensions seem to have been born from the myriad of variables considered. They are: (a) a *permissive/restrictive dimension*, which refers to the amount of autonomy parents permit their children to have, and (b) a *warm/cold-hostile dimension,* which refers to affect (Becker, 1954; Schaefer, 1959). Restrictive parents characteristically make many demands on their children, set limits, and monitor their children to insure that they meet these demands. Permissive parents characteristically make relatively few demands and give their children much greater freedom in exploring, making decisions for themselves, and so on. Warm parents characteristically display affection and approval. Hostile parents are characteristically critical and likely to belittle and punish their child, while restricting the amount of affection they give.

Becker (1964) created a 2 × 2 table of permissive versus restrictive as one factor, and warmth versus hostility as the other factor. Becker noted that specific kinds of child outcomes had been related to each of the four cells of his table. The warm and restrictive cell tended to have positive child outcomes, the warm and permissive cell tended to have generally positive outcomes with the exception of compliance, the hostile and restrictive had social withdrawal, quarreling, and shyness, with self-aggression as child outcomes, and, finally, the hostile and permissive cell tended to have noncompliance, aggression, and delinquency as child outcomes.

Later, Baumrind (1967, 1971, 1987) distinguished three parental styles: (a) authoritarian (restrictive and cold), (b) authoritative (restrictive and warm), and (c) permissive. Authoritarian parents characteristically impose many demands and limits and expect strict obedience, usually without giving the child an explanation. Authoritative parents also set limits on their child's behavior, but are considerably more flexible, providing explanations and lots of warmth. Permissive parents characteristically make few demands, encourage emotional expression in the children, rarely exert firm control, and are warm. Baumrind identified three groups of preschool children: (a) energetic-friendly, (b) conflicted-irritable, and (c) impulsive-aggressive. Authoritative parents tended to have children in the energetic-friendly category (self-reliant, self-controlled, cheerful, friendly, able to cope well with stress, cooperative with adults, curious, purposive, and achievement-oriented). Authoritarian parents tended to have children who at 8 to 9 years old were conflicted-irritable (fearful, apprehensive, moody, unhappy, easily annoyed, passively hostile, vulnerable to stress, aimless, sulky, and unfriendly). Permissive parents tended to have children who at 8 or 9 years old were impulsive-aggressive (rebellious, low in self-reliance and self-control, impulsive, aggressive, domineering, aimless, and low in achievement). The children of authoritative parents rated high in both social and cognitive skills, but children of permissive parents were relatively unskilled in both. The male children of authoritarian parents were most likely to withdraw both academically and socially. These patterns tend to persist into adolescence.

How powerful are these relationships? One recent answer is provided by the Cowans' project on the transition to parenthood, which is described in their recent book (Cowan & Cowan, 1992). Theirs is a rich and complex longitudinal study, the only one on the transition to parenthood that has also included an intervention study. Their coding system for marital and parent–child interaction is largely based on Baumrind's work (we also used the Cowan coding system in our research). In the Cowans' study, parent–child interaction was evaluated when the children were in preschool. Two years later, their kindergarten teachers rated the children on the Cowans' Child Adaptive Behavior Inventory (CABI) and the children's academic achievement was also tested using the Peabody Individual Achievement Test (PIAT). The marital relationship was assessed by examining the amount of warmth and coldness the parents generated toward one another when they were interacting in the laboratory with their child, as well as with the Locke–Wallace test of marital satisfaction. They also used Main's Adult Attachment Interview.

What were their results? Cohn, Cowan, Cowan, and Pearson (1992) used a structural equation modeling method called "soft modeling" and reported that there was strong relationship between the marital, parental, and teacher's ratings of child externalizing and internalizing problems on the CABI. The father's model accounted for 62% of the variance in externalizing problems whereas the mother's model accounted for 29% of the variance in externalizing problems. For internalizing problems, the father's model accounted for 30% of the variance, and the mother's model accounted for 56% of the variance. For academic achievement, the father's model accounted for 19% of the variance and the mother's model accounted for 37% of the variance. These are impressive levels of prediction, and they also represent independent validation of the predictive power of Baumrind's constructs.

One problem with Baumrind's sample is that there was a restricted range on these dimensions; most parents were warm and accepting. Other research has found that the combination of permissive and rejecting is a good predictor of delinquent and antisocial behavior (Patterson, 1982), whereas the combination of restrictive and rejecting is predictive of withdrawn and inhibited behavior and other internalizing disorders. Subsequent to this work, the two dimensions have been further differentiated. The work of Ainsworth and her colleagues (Ainsworth, Bell, & Stayton, 1971) has added a parental responsiveness dimension, which is related to but not identical with the warmth/hostility dimension. Responsiveness emphasizes the temporal linkage of the parent's behavior with the child's. The dimensions of parental affect and parental control have been modified over time. Other dimensions have emerged that classify the predominant parental affects toward their children (e.g., calm detachment versus anxious emotional involvement, Becker, 1964). Other dimensions related to the permissive dimension that emerged were democracy versus autocracy and emotional involvement versus detachment (Maccoby & Martin, 1983). The attachment literature and the infancy literature have both suggested that parental responsiveness is a positive dimension of parenting and perhaps it is in the contexts of face to face play with infants and in the Ainsworth Strange Situation. However, the work of Patterson and his colleagues (e.g., Patterson, 1982) suggests that temporal linkage and responsiveness can either be healthy or unhealthy for the child's later development. In the coercive process the parent is responsive to the child's misbehavior, switching from authoritarian to indulgent when the child escalates the irritability of his or her aversive behavior. There is temporal linkage in the coercive process, but it is predictive of later antisocial behavior. Also, the coercive process that the Patterson group identified as one precursor of later child antisocial behavior involves a dynamic temporal switch from authoritarian (cold and restrictive) to cold and permissive when the child escalates the intensity of his or her aversive behavior. This temporal pattern does not fit neatly into any of the static cells of the Becker 2×2 table, or into Baumrind's categories of parenting. Furthermore, such extreme parenting as the pattern that has been described as "parental rejection" and abuse has been found to play a consistent role in the development of antisocial behavior in children (e.g., Myers, Alvy, Arrington, & Richardson, 1992; Simons, Robertson, & Downs, 1989; Whitbeck, Hoyt, Simons, & Conger, 1992).

The permissive/restrictive dimension has undergone further modification as well. Baumrind and Black (1967) identified four orthogonal dimensions: the consistency of the discipline, the presence or absence of maturity demands, restrictiveness, and the encouragement of independent contacts. Other studies have identified the amount of engagement of the parents as a dimension of importance.

Maccoby and Martin (1983) classified parental discipline techniques into power assertive and love-oriented. The power-assertive techniques rely on physical punishment, yelling, shouting, forceful commands, and threats. The love-oriented techniques rely on showing disappointment, isolation, withdrawal of love, praise, contingent giving of affection, and reasoning. Brody and Shaffer (1982) reviewed studies on parental discipline and divided discipline strategies into power assertive versus induction. The power-assertive technique teaches children to avoid negative consequences whereas the induction technique is relatively nonpunitive and teaches children to understand why they need to follow rules, why their transgressions are wrong, and how to change their behavior. Brody and Shaffer concluded that power-assertive parents have children who scored low on tests of moral development, whereas induction parents have more altruistic children.

PARENTING AND META-EMOTION

To summarize and to simplify, we see that parenting has been classified and studied (quite productively) primarily in terms of: (a) the predominant parental affects toward the child, and (b) predominant parental discipline techniques. What we think is missing is how the parent feels about and relates to specific emotional displays by the child, and how this might relate to the parent's feelings about his or her own emotions. The theme of this volume is that we suspect that this area of family functioning is likely to be more general than the parents' predominant affect or the parents' discipline techniques.

In the next chapter we continue to examine parenting by studying the popular parenting guides and the child clinical literature.

2
Popular Parenting Guides: Introducing Ginott

In this chapter we review popular writing on parenting advice. In some ways this literature is similar to the parenting research literature, and in some ways it is far richer and more complex. We review the history of this writing and explore its major influences. The seminal work of Haim Ginott is introduced in this chapter. We briefly review research on the effects of spanking children, and on the effectiveness of parent training.

In this chapter, we show that an examination of popular parenting guides can enrich our theorizing about parenting and how it contextualizes meta-emotion. There appears to be a bewildering array of popular parenting advice books. However, we show that there really are only a few traditions represented among these many books, and that most of the other books are repetitions of the advice in a few classics.

We were surprised to find that in some ways, the parenting guides were a mirror of the child development research on parenting. In the popular parenting press we found the same emphasis on discipline rather than emotion as we found in the parenting research literature. For example, in reviewing the research literature, in one computer search of the ERIC database we conducted, we found 1,412 references to "parent and discipline" and only 69 references to "parent and emotion." Similarly, when we went to our local university book store and perused the popular parenting guides we were surprised to find how many of them ignored the child's emotions. Instead, most parenting guides address themselves to parents who feel out of control, to those whose major issue is obtaining compliance, obedience, and respect from their children.

For example, the famous Dreikurs (1964) program (over 500,000 books sold, reads the current cover) speaks to adults who share the following views of children today:

> Distraught parents crossly say "no more," and then yield to the screaming. Harassed fathers dig into their pockets and spend more than they had intended. Spankings are administered in public. Finally mothers impatiently drag resisting children by the arms and they will arrive home wondering why they went. In restaurants children often display deplorable behavior . . . In all such public places we hear angry, demanding storming, screaming children answered by weary, resentful, desperate parents. At home, our children show a deplorable lack of cooperation. Many refuse to accept any responsibility for helping with home tasks. They are noisy, inconsiderate, boisterous and unmannerly. They sometimes show a colossal lack of respect for their parents or any other adult. They frequently insult us and we take it. Our children are defiant and we stand helpless . . . One grandmother stated in despair, "Children just don't mind any more!" This unruly, defiant behavior has become so common that it is accepted as normal "Children are like that." . . . headlines give accounts of children in trouble. Potentially delinquent behavior appears at earlier and earlier ages . . . Many parents are becoming increasingly upset and bewildered. (pp. 4–5)

In many ways we found the parenting advice literature to be far richer and more complex than the parenting research literature. These advice books talk about much more complex questions than have been researched. An example is how to parent children when they are having nightmares, for example, Brett's (1988) *Annie Stories*. Advising a parent to be "authoritative," or "warm," or focusing on discipline techniques is of little use in this and other everyday complex situations that parents encounter. Doris Brett is a poet who wrote what she called *The Annie Stories*. Brett's own daughter was having nightmares in which she was chased by a tiger. In the stories Brett wrote and subsequently read to her daughter, a mother gives a fictional child called Annie (who, like Doris Brett's daughter was also having nightmares) a special invisible dream ring. Annie then uses the dream ring when she's having a nightmare. She faces the tiger in the dream and asks the tiger why she is chasing her. The tiger replies that she is lonely and wants to make friends. Annie scolds the tiger and says that this is no way to make friends, but Annie and the tiger then become friends, and in subsequent scary dreams Annie often calls on the tiger to be her ally in facing danger. Brett's book teaches parents how to help preschool children deal with their fears while the nightmare is occurring. Parents learn to use their preschool children's natural tendency to rely on pretend play and fantasy, and to imitate the actions of heroes and heroines in stories. Parents are taught the art of storytelling and tailoring the stories they tell their children to their own children's nightmares. This is only one example of how the parenting advice books are far richer than the parenting research literature.

What historical traditions underly the various parenting advice books? A number of popular childrearing advice books converged in the 1920s and 1930s to attempt to change parents who felt out of control and who might unwittingly adopt an authoritarian mode of raising their children. These books suggested a new approach to discipline that could change the nature of parenting.

The effort was heightened after World War II, when it was commonly thought by psychologists that the authoritarian childrearing patterns ascribed to the German family were, in part, responsible for producing leaders who believed in racial domination, who were capable of genocide and bent on total world domination, and who could use propaganda to lead an obedient, mindless, and immoral people to play the role of cogs in an evil machine of war.

These ideas led to the classic study of the "authoritarian personality" (Adorno, Frenkel-Brunswick, Levinson, & Sanford, 1950). After World War II, the idea was that if these childrearing patterns could be altered, the horror of Nazi Germany might never be repeated. They started out to study the roots of anti-Semitism, but they felt the need to expand their study, first to racism, and then to what they called "ethnocentrism," which is a prejudice against all outsiders. With violent conflicts between ethnic groups proliferating at an alarming rate around the world today, with disastrous consequences for children and families, their work seems highly relevant.

What did this classic study find? In their interviews, did the authors of *The Authoritarian Personality* report a family pattern that accompanied prejudice? Indeed they did. Prejudiced subjects reported that their families were systematically different from the families of nonprejudiced subjects. As reported by the interviewees, the families of prejudiced subjects:

> were more harsh and threatening in disciplining children.
> had a cold and dominating father.
> had fathers who demanded passive submission from their sons, but also aggressive and rugged masculinity;
> adhered to rigid sex roles.
> made a distinct separation of the sexes within the family.
> saw home discipline as more arbitrary (by the child).
> based family relationships on dominance and submission.
> had parents who were distant and not affectionate.
> had parents who emphasized obedience and highly conventional behavior.
> had parents who were intolerant of internal child impulses.
> had parents who were intolerant of disobedience.
> had parents who did not stress spontaneity, imagination, and creativity.
> stressed duties and obligations over free-flowing affection.
> emphasized the exchange of material goods as opposed to affection.
> had a lack of mutuality in the area of emotion.

had parents who valued child fear and self-negating submission to them.

had children who reported having complied, but with feelings of victimization and resentment.

had children who described themselves as overconforming and also as having an underlying destructiveness and resentment of authority, customs, and social institutions.

had children who had less freedom from parents, particularly in decision-making.

The fascinating combination of conformity and obedience to authority, and a potential for antisocial behavior is the dialectic that this work suggests. Also, the prejudiced subjects had what the authors called an "externalized view of other people," appreciating those higher than them in the social hierarchy who conformed to conventional local standards, and condemning those who deviated, which suggests a dynamic for the prejudice. If one's own status is insecure, anyone deviant is a target for aggression, and that aggression reaffirms one's own tentative sense of inclusion.

Is there further empirical evidence that this picture of the harsh and cold family has implications for the way children develop? Indeed, this study has continued to have reverberations in current research that consistently links these patterns of child rearing to social class (e.g., de-Boeck, 1976 in Belgium; Goldenberg, 1971 for U.S. teachers; Graudenz, Kraak, & Haver, 1976; Jordan, 1970; Kohn, 1969; Steinhausen, 1972). In addition to the research we summarized in our last chapter, and the research we just referred to, a recent study by Franz, McClelland and Weinberger (1991) of a 36-year prospective study (based on the Sears, Maccoby, & Levin, 1957, sample) reported that having a warm and affectionate father or mother was significantly associated with adult accomplishment, as assessed by a long and happy marriage, children, good relationships with friends, higher levels of generativity, work accomplishments, lower levels of strain, and more effective ways of dealing with conflict.

Historically, the great popular work that attempted to counter and to change this authoritarian pattern of child rearing was initiated by Rudolf Dreikurs (1964). The Dreikurs program owes much of its inspiration to the pioneering work of Alfred Adler, *The Education of Children* (English translation, 1970, with introduction by Rudolf Dreikurs), and it represents a radical departure from the commonly held authoritarian ideas exemplified by the Biblical motto "spare the rod and spoil the child." Instead, it proposes the idea of democratic rather than authoritarian means of child rearing, and that the use of both rewards and punishments be abandoned in favor of "natural and logical consequences." The work has had a major impact. It also attempted, in part, to have parents become aware of how children felt, to avoid humiliating their children, and making them feel powerless.

Dreikurs (1964) suggested that "a misbehaving child is a discouraged child"

(p. 36), and that problem children have one of four possible "mistaken goals" of the discouraged child. These mistaken goals arise from an escalating dynamic in which parents and children are somehow missing each other. The mistaken goals are: (a) the child's desire for undue attention, (b) the mutual parent–child struggle for power, (c) the intensification of the power contest, which leads to the child's mistaken goal of retaliation and revenge, and (d) finally, the child's attempt to demonstrate complete inadequacy (which is probably being communicated by the parents in their disappointed rages, mockery, and insults). Dreikurs then suggested a program for structuring the family's life that can avoid these problems and, in their place, set up democratic problem-solving processes that facilitate cooperation.

He also suggested ways around problems such as the milder power struggles. However, he really had little real advice once a power struggle has defined the parent's interaction with the child. Many current books on parenting continue to echo Dreikurs' ideas, with little innovation.

All of these new approaches to democratic parenting also attempted to shift the emphasis from parental control to understanding children in all their developmental stages. One offshoot of this approach (one that added relatively little to Dreikurs) was the incredibly popular approach to raising children popularized by Benjamin Spock. Later, during the Army-McCarthy House Committee on Un-American Activities hearings, Spock was to be blamed for advocating a laissez-faire style of childrearing that McCarthy called "communist." These absurd charges did nothing to hurt the sales of Spock's books. However, despite the popularity of Spock's parenting guide, this was not the only approach developed during this era.

THE WORK OF HAIM GINOTT

Another important writer who entered the scene of popular parenting guides in the mid-1960s was Dr. Haim Ginott. Dreikurs' work is an interesting contrast to Ginott's. Ginott's very influential work included only three books, cut short by his premature death by cancer on November 4th, 1973. Although Ginott fit into the trend away from authoritarian parenting, in our view his work represents a major departure and innovation because it is the first parenting guide to focus entirely on the processes of parent–child interaction, to focus on the child's emotions, and to attempt to alter parents' views of the emotional world of the child. Ginott ran parenting groups in the community. Ginott was also a superb observer, and he learned a great deal from his parents. Although he was influenced by psychoanalysis, his works are primarily the result of his vast experience with parents and children.

Ginott's work plays a central role in our book because we think that our results on meta-emotion represent the first prospective longitudinal data to suggest that Ginott's ideas were essentially correct.

We would like to briefly review some of the Ginott's ideas because we think they represent a clarity of vision and understanding of children that surpasses all other previous writers. After his book on group psychotherapy with children (recently re-issued, Ginott, 1994), he published his groundbreaking book, *Between Parent and Child*.

Ginott's Focus on Emotional Communication Between Parent and Child

Ginott's first chapter is interesting to think of in relation to Dreikurs' work. It is titled "Conversing With Children." Ginott begins with a question asked by 10-year-old Andy, who asked his father, "What is the number of abandoned children in Harlem?" His father began by giving his son a long lecture on social problems, only to realize later that Andy's question was a personal question, not an intellectual one. Ginott (1965/1994) wrote,

> His questions stemmed not so much from sympathy for abandoned children as from fear of being abandoned. He was looking, not for a figure representing the number of deserted children, but for reassurance that he would not be deserted. (p.22)

First Ginott suggested that the most important thing a parent can do is *listen*, and to listen for the emotion behind the words. This requires knowing something about children at various stages of development, for instance, what their concerns and fears are. As an aid toward this listening, chapter 8 of Ginott's work discusses some common sources of anxiety in children: fear of abandonment, denial of autonomy, friction between parents, interference with physical activity, and death. Second, Ginott suggested that parents feel differently about a child's emotions. Dreikurs suggested that parents feel differently about their child's misbehavior (recall that Dreikurs said that a misbehaving child is a discouraged child). In contrast, Ginott suggested that parents feel differently about the moment-to-moment interactions they have with their child, that what matters is emotion, that they look for it, listen to it, and respond genuinely and empathically with real understanding.

It is very interesting that Ginott did not suggest that this listening is a social skill and attempt to provide social skill training. Instead, he assumed that most parents already have this skill, and he proposes a way to feel about and respond to the child's affect, and a strategy for reading the child's emotions. Rather than concentrating on the parents' behavior, Ginott assumed that parents have all the right emotions and he proposed a way they can sense the child's feelings. We return to this idea later.

Ginott also suggested a "new code of communication" in which there are only two principles, that the messages preserve both the child's as well as the parent's self-respect, and that statements of understanding *precede* statements of advice. The principles can be applied to mitigate the kind of power struggles Dreikurs later discussed. However, as we mentioned earlier, Dreikurs suggested ways of structuring family interaction to avoid power struggles, but there is little suggestion of what the dynamic is that sets them up in the first place. Ginott provided the missing dynamic in Dreikurs' program.

An example from Faber and Mazlich (1980) may help. Suppose a parent is driving on a hot summer day with a child, and gets caught in unrelenting bumper-to-bumper traffic. The child says, "Dad, I want some cold milk." Dad says very sweetly, "Honey, there's nothing I can do until we get home. Then I'll get you some milk." Not mollified, the child repeats the request more insistently: "I want some cold milk now!" Dad repeats himself, explaining why he cannot get the milk now. This exchange continues, with the child escalating, adding whining and crying as the exchange continues. Eventually the father is upset and threatening. An oppositional struggle has erupted. All this, Ginott said, might have been avoided if the father had originally said something like "Yeah, cold milk sounds great. I wish I had some myself right now." The child, whose feelings are understood, would have said "Yeah," and the father might have added "Some ice cream would be nice too," and the child might have continued "Yeah, an ice cream sundae." Dad: "Yum."

Ginott said that when a child is in the midst of strong emotion he or she can not listen to anyone, and he or she certainly can not process good advice. The child wants us to understand, to understand the feelings and thoughts going on inside at this very moment. Ginott (1965/1994) wrote:

> When a child tells us "The teacher spanked me," we do not have to ask him for more details. Nor do we need to say, "What did you do to deserve it? If your teacher spanked you, you must have done something. What did you do?" We don't even have to say, "Oh, I am so sorry." We need to show him that we understand his pain and embarrassment and feelings of revenge. How do we know what he feels? We look at him and listen to him, and we also draw on our own emotional experiences. We know what a child *must* feel when he is shamed in public in the presence of peers. We so phrase our words that the child knows we understand what he has gone through. Any of the following statements would serve well: "It must have been terribly embarrassing." "It must have made you furious." "You must have hated your teacher at that moment." (p. 27)

Ginott pointed out that a child's feelings do not disappear when he is told not to feel that way, or that it's not nice to feel that way, or that he has no proper justification for feeling that way. Ginott noted the common mistakes that parents make, to rush in and judge, to rush in with advice and solutions, and also just to rush.

Ginott's approach is so radically different from approaches that emphasize external configurations such as family rules, or a list of consequences parents can apply to child misbehavior, or a way to structure family meetings so that the rules are democratic and not authoritarian, and so on. The difference is that Ginott's methods engage the parent with the *processes of the child's emotional world.* Once this process begins the parent is on a whole new course with the child.

Ginott discourages parents from telling children what *they ought to feel,* because it makes them distrust what they do feel. Statements like "You don't mean what you say. You love your little brother," or "This is not you. This is the devil in you acting up," or "If you mention that word 'hate' one more time you'll get the spanking of your life," or "You don't really hate your brother. Maybe you dislike him. You should rise above such feelings" convey to the child that she not trust her emotions, but instead rely on what parents tell her she is feeling.

This acceptance of a child's feelings does not imply that parents have to accept all of a child's *behavior.* Ginott suggested that although all feelings are real and acceptable, not all actions are, and parents must set limits. The process of going from feeling to action, from emotion to motion, is part of what a parent does when problem solving with a child during a moment of strong child emotion.

Ginott's Approach to Praise and Criticism: How Criticism Becomes Engraved in Stone Inside the Child's Mind

Dreikurs advised parents to encourage their children, but not to reward or punish them. Dreikurs' motivation in giving this advice to parents is that praise and punishment creates unnecessary hierarchy instead of democratic processes.

Ginott had different advice and different reasons for his advice. Ginott's rule for praise is "[When using] praise, deal only the child's efforts and accomplishments, *not* with his character and personality . . . [and] mirror for the child a *realistic* picture of his *accomplishments,* not a Madison Avenue image of his personality (p. 45)." When Jim cleans up the yard, Mother does not tell Jim what a perfect angel he is. Instead she says, "The yard was so dirty. I can't believe it could be cleaned up in one day." Jim is proud of his accomplishment instead of being given an impossible image to have to live up to (and one he must disconfirm, because it isn't true). Ginott suggested that the praise be the parent's genuine emotional reaction, not contrived. He suggested it not be global, but specific; for example, words like "you always" preceding the praise are to be omitted.

About criticism, Ginott (1965/1994) wrote "Constructive criticism confines itself to pointing out what has to be done, entirely avoiding negative remarks about the personality of the child (p. 51)."

The Lasting Effects of Parental Contempt.

Ginott's (1965/1994) knowledge of children led him to some surprising recommendations. He pointed out how quickly children will internalize a negative view of themselves a parent communicates, either directly ("You'll break it. You're always breaking things." "You're clumsy.") or indirectly with a look of contempt or disgust. He suggested that these moments are times when the parent should try to repair the internalized self image conveyed to the child, or it will become a self-fulfilling prophecy. The child will work to live up to the parent's negative self image of him or her. We return to this point of Ginott's when we discuss our results on the effects of intrusiveness, mockery, and criticism during a parental teaching task when the child is 5 years old, and its ability to predict destructive consequences for the child at age 8 (see chapters 10–12, in this volume). This idea of Ginott's turns out to be very important in our results. Meanness by parents toward children is an extreme of these more subtle everyday communications that may have a similar negative result. We suggest that it be broken out as a principle:

> Children will internalize global parental disapproval as contempt, and contempt as their own characteristic trait of failure.

The Parent's Anger

In recent years it has become common to suggest that anger and its expression are destructive (e.g., Tavris, 1982), that anger is related to spousal violence (e.g., Walker, 1984), and that it is the expression of anger that is predictive of coronary artery disease (e.g., Siegman & Smith, 1994). However, we dispute this negative view of anger in this book, and suggest instead that *it is contempt and defensiveness, not anger that is destructive in family relationships*. Surprisingly, Ginott agreed with us. He did not suggest that a parent avoid becoming angry toward a child. Indeed, he suggested that a parent's anger and *specific* displeasure can become the very type of emotional communication that can be the basis of effective discipline:

> Resolutions about not becoming angry are worse than futile. They only add fuel to the fire. . . . There is a place for parental anger in child education. In fact, failure to get angry at certain moments would only convey to the child indifference, not goodness . . . 1. We accept the fact that children will make us angry. 2. We are entitled to our anger without guilt or shame. 3. Except for one safeguard, we are entitled to express what we feel. We can express our angry feelings provided we do not attack the child's personality or character. (pp. 56–58)

Here Ginott predicted two of our own major findings, which we discuss later. The effects of parental anger depend, in part, on how the parents feel about their anger, that is it depends on their meta-emotions about anger. The effects also depend on the anger not being expressed as contempt (mockery, derision, insult). Ginott suggested that the expression of anger be specific, direct, a statement of our inner feelings ("I feel angry"), perhaps with a reason for our anger, and a statement of what we would wish for ("When I see the shoes and the socks and the shirts and the sweaters spread all over the floor, I get angry, I get furious. I feel like opening the window and throwing the whole mess into the middle of the street") (p. 58).

Responsibility: Chores and Values

Ginott pointed out that it is a goal of most parents that their children become responsible people, and they approach this goal by thinking that the children need to take some responsibility for things around the house. So parents typically give children a list of household chores, the children don't do them, don't do them well or regularly, the parents nag, and a power struggle begins. Ginott pointed out that if the parent were completely successful in this endeavor, the child would end up being obedient, perhaps polite, but not responsible.

> Yet a child may be polite, keep himself and his room clean, do his assignments with precision, and still make irresponsible decisions. This is especially true of children who are always told what to do and who therefore have little opportunity to exercise judgment, to make choices, and to develop inner standards. (p. 80)

He also noted that when given the opportunity to make choices, children can be expected to make many bad choices. They need to learn our values (like caring about how other people feel), and they learn these values largely from the way we treat them and how parents treat one another, not through lectures.

Instead, Ginott suggested that responsibility is fostered by giving children a voice in *some* matters that affect them, and a choice as well. He then discussed specific domains such as food, clothes, homework, music lessons, allowance, friends and playmates, and pets. In each case he informed the reader of the limitations and needs of children.

Discipline: Permissiveness and Limits

Ginott began by sympathizing with the modern parent, who is anxious and uncertain, even when right. He compared this state to our grandparents, whom he described as confident, even when wrong. He suggested that children can sense this anxiety, that parents have needs, and that parents should not let their children become tyrants. He defined good permissiveness as accepting the childishness of children (a clean shirt will not stay clean very long when a child is climbing trees) and overpermissiveness as accepting undesirable acts. The approach he suggested is handling feelings and behaviors differently. He suggested setting limits on acts, but not on feelings: "We set limits on acts; we do not restrict wishes" (p. 111). He contrasted the old and his new approach to discipline:

There is a vast difference between the old and the new approach to discipline. In disciplining a child, parents used to stop undesirable acts, but ignored the urges that brought about the acts. The restrictions were set in the midst of angry argument and were often incoherent, inconsistent, and insulting. Furthermore, discipline was administered at a time when the child was least able to listen, and in words that were most likely to arouse his resistance. More often than not, the child was left with the dooming impression that not just a specific act had been criticized, but that as a person he was no good. The modern approach helps the child with both his feelings and conduct. The parents allow the child (under conditions to be discussed later) to speak about what he feels, but limit and direct undesirable acts. The limits are set in a manner that preserves the self-respect of the parent as well as that of the child. The limits are neither arbitrary nor capricious, but educational and character-building. (p. 113)

Once again, the emphasis in Ginott's approach to discipline is based on a recognition of the child's needs and limitations, of the parent's needs, and of dignity. Dreikurs had the same ideas in mind. Ginott spelled out principles for how to interact with the child when a spontaneous situation arises that calls for discipline. Dreikurs' rules and family meetings are a good idea and they help build cooperation and a democratic family process, but so much is conveyed in the moment-to-moment interaction when emotions are hot, and here Ginott stepped in to offer parents a road map.

Following Fritz Redl, Ginott suggested "zones" for discipline. The "yellow zone" includes behavior that is not sanctioned but is tolerated for specific reasons such as leeway for learners and leeway for tough times, but the "red zone" covers conduct that can not be tolerated at all and must be stopped (e.g., wanting to cut off the cat's tail to see what is inside). Ginott noted that when a child is allowed behavior in the red zone, his or her anxiety mounts. The parent is the child's ally here in allowing him or her to cope with undesirable and unsafe impulses (e.g., hanging off a moving truck, carrying a switchblade knife).

Ginott talked about how to set limits and how to enforce them. He suggested that the limit be set so it explains what constitutes unacceptable behavior and what substitute will be accepted, that this be done in a manner that preserves the child's self-esteem and to be specific, dealing with a specific event and not a developmental history. When a child asks for something we have to deny, we can at least allow the child the satisfaction of having the wish for it. Ginott suggested that children's motor activities should not be over restrained, that a higher motor activity is a characteristic of childhood. For persistent disobedience, Ginott suggested that parents express their genuine anger (not their contempt), and that they enforce consequences (much like Dreikurs). He suggested that parents should never permit their children to hit or kick them, because these acts are harmful for both parent and child. The child should be encouraged to express feelings in words. On the issue of spanking we quote Ginott extensively, because this remains an issue today:

Spanking, though in bad repute, is a popular method of influencing children . . . Frequently it is not planned, but occurs in a burst of anger when we have reached the end of our endurance. . . . What is wrong with spanking is the lesson it demonstrates . . . It dramatically tells them "When you are angry—hit!" Instead of displaying our ingenuity by finding civilized outlets for savage feelings, we give our children a taste of the jungle. One of the worst side effects of physical punishment is that it may interfere with the development of a conscience. Spanking relieves guilt too easily: the child, having paid for his misbehavior, feels free to repeat it. Children develop what Selma Fraiberg calls a "book- keeping approach" to misconduct . . . A child who asks for punishment needs help managing his guilt and anger, not compliance with his request. (p.125)

Because we wanted to educate ourselves about the research findings on spanking, we conducted a review of the literature, and offer the reader the following brief summary of current research on the issue of spanking.

SPANKING

The issue of spanking has received some research attention. In the United States a recent survey (Graziano & Namaste, 1990) found that 93.2% of college students were spanked as children, with only 10.6% reporting physical punishment severe enough to cause welts or bruises. These students reported that 90.7% of the parents were angry when they spanked. In fact, in the United States, a survey of practicing psychologists found that most recommended the use of spanking children, most spanked their own children, and half approved of school personnel spanking children; there were no age, sex, or educational differences among those surveyed with respect to these approval ratings for spankings. The situation is completely reversed in Sweden. Very few college students in Sweden reported having been spanked, nor did they approve of it (Deley, 1988; Gelles & Edfeldt, 1986). What are the effects of spanking on American children? Larzelere (1986) reported a positive linear relationship between spanking and aggression in the family. His was a national representative U.S. sample of 1,139 parents. However, for preadolescents and adolescents there was a minimal effect of aggression toward parents when parents used reasoning frequently. The combination of low levels of reasoning and high levels of spanking created a dramatic increase of aggression toward parents. Roe (1980), in a study of 10-year-old Greek island children, found that spanking and fear of their fathers was characteristic of low empathic subjects (assessed by the Feshbach and Roe Situational Test). However, subjects whose fathers were away most of the year score high on empathy, even though spanking is common for mothers as well as fathers. The results are explained by the typically very positive relationship these children have with their mothers and the distant, ambivalent relationship they have with their fathers. The suggestion is that spanking within the context of a warm relationship is not as deleterious. Support for this hypothesis comes from a study conducted by Larzelere, Klein, Schumm, & Alibrando (1989) in a retrospective study of the effects of spanking, as reported by college students. The negative effects of spanking on self esteem and fairness were enhanced when positive communication was minimal with the parent, and when the spanking was seen as being caused by a parent-centered motive. The authors suggested that the effects of spanking are enhanced when it is a replacement for positive communication. Spanking does not seem to be necessary when it has been studied in research. Interventions with conduct problem children tend to spontaneously result in a reduction of parental use of spanking when other alternatives are available (Webster-Stratton, 1990). Spanking does not seem to be necessary to obtain compliance with time-out methods, when compared to the use of a physical barrier (Roberts, 1988; Day & Roberts, 1983).

THE VIEW FROM CHILD PATHOLOGY: FRITZ REDL'S LIFE SPACE INTERVIEWING TECHNIQUES

Nothing occurs in a vacuum, and Ginott mentioned Redl in his first book. Redl had developed a technique for helping delinquent boys in a live-in milieu that he eventually called "life space interviewing." The method is relevant to our discussion because the interview deals with children's strong emotions, and its techniques are probably useful for parents of normally developing children. In fact, Redl's (1966) study on the life space interview discussed this idea. He suggested that:

> The . . . assumption that being normal and healthy also means being free from the danger of being overwhelmed by the complexities of life is a naive illusion . . . Take any child, no matter how well endowed, how healthy, how wonderful, even in the best conceivable classroom. At some time during some phase of his life he will find himself in two kinds of predicament in which he will need the adult at hand to stand by . . . *The first predicament is of a child overwhelmed by internal confusion or conflict from within . . . The second predicament involves the child overwhelmed by experiences and events from without.* (pp. 62–63)

Redl gave examples of the second predicament: the child's first disappointments, the friend who betrays him or her, an admired hero or heroine who ridicules the child, becoming a sibling, the loss of a friend, the trauma of divorce, or a death in the family.

One of us (Gottman) was trained extensively in the Life Space Interview at the University of Colorado Medical Center, while on a clinical child postdoctoral fellowship. Firsthand experience suggests that these techniques are quite powerful and can be used effectively by parents. Everyone at the school for emotionally disturbed children (ages 6 to 12) was trained in the techniques: the busdriver, the receptionists, the teachers, the trainees, psychologists, social workers, and psychiatrists. Furthermore, they all needed the training, because it is not a standard method, and training is rarely available. Although Redl (1959) stated that more research needs to be done on this interview, in the intervening 35 years, to our knowledge, there has been none.

What is the technique? How does it differ from standard forms of child therapy? How can parents use it with normally developing children?

The Technique

Life space interviewing differs from most child therapy in that the child does not need to recreate or recall a salient event in the therapist's office. The interview happens on the spot, when the child's emotion is hot. The actual interview is usually quite brief, about 15 to 30 minutes. Usually the interviewer has been there to see the precipitating event (as is the parent in most cases), or the interviewer has been briefed by a teacher or other staff member. Experienced children sometimes ask for an interview. Over the course of several years, children may have hundreds of Life Space Interviews. Redl began his discussion with the case of Johnny:

> A group of children is just about ready to go out on an excursion it has anticipated with eagerness for quite a while. [There is] some delay at the door because of a last minute search for shoes, footballs and so forth . . . irritability mounts . . . two of our youngsters get into a flare-up, which ends up in Johnny's getting socked, more vehemently than he can take, furiously running back to his room, cursing his tormentor and the world at large and all educators in particular . . . We find him just about to soak himself in a bath of self-pity. . . . (p. 42)

The person who conducts the interview, Redl said, can decide on one of two goals, although it is possible to go back and forth between the two goals in one interview. The first goal is *emotional first aid*. The interviewer may want to be with Johnny in his misery, assist him in disentangling the complex web of emotions he feels trapped by, help him get over it, and perhaps get him back into the activity he withdrew from. On the other hand, a second goal may emerge, exploiting this event to help the child learn about emotions. This event with Johnny may give the long awaited opportunity to help him come to grips with an issue in his life, pointing out the similarity with previous incidents, to see how his provocation gets other children infuriated, and so on. As Redl (1959) wrote, "In short, half an hour later our interviewer may be driving after the rest of the group with a somewhat sadder but wiser companion at his side" (p. 43). Clearly, the two goals are not mutually exclusive.

Gottman's experience with the technique suggests that children learn, over time, how to benefit from it, and become active collaborators in the interview. How can life events be "exploited" (Redl's term) in the interests of the child's emotional growth? Redl's methods evolved from the very difficult group of children he was working with, and they need not be relevant to most parents who have normally developing children. Children who have antisocial disorders have unique characteristics, explicated in the earlier volume called *Children Who Hate* (Redl & Wineman, 1951). The fascinating part of the Life Space Interview is how well it dovetails with Ginott's messages about making an emotional connection with a child right on the spot, when emotions run high.

ANOTHER VIEW FROM PATHOLOGY: SOCIAL LEARNING AND OTHER BEHAVIORAL APPROACHES TO THE NONCOMPLIANT AND ANTISOCIAL CHILD

Another tradition that has produced many parental advice books is the behavioral and social learning tradition in family psychology. Perhaps the most influential of these books was Patterson and Gullion's (1971) *Living With Children,* and Forehand and McMahon's (1981) *Helping the Noncompliant Child.* These books initially focused on the noncompliant child in middle childhood. However, recently, Webster-Stratton (1993) wrote a book for parents summarizing her research at her Parenting Clinic at the University of Washington with younger noncompliant children, aged 3 to 8. Webster-Stratton's effectiveness data for her videotaped parent training program is impressive (e.g. Webster-Stratton, 1994).

Patterson and his colleagues at the Oregon Social Learning Center (OSLC) have programmatically developed an empirically based model of the development of antisocial boys, beginning with ineffective parenting. This work represents a high point in methodological sophistication and care in the development and testing of constructs and models. The model they have developed of "ineffective parenting" involves a negative reinforcement pattern in which the parent's command for the child to comply or stop some aversive behavior is met with the child increasing the aversiveness of his behavior until the parent eventually backs down and is rewarded by the child's de-escalation. The model was detailed in Patterson's (1982) book *Coercive Family Process.* This escalation of aversive behavior is viewed by the OSLC group as excellent training for the child's noncompliance and aggression in school, and they have found evidence for a cascade of negative events including his impatience, lack of attention and self-regulatory abilities, his eventual academic failure, his rejection by peers, his subsequent depression, his wandering, the lack of parental monitoring of where the child is after school and at night, his eventual inclusion in a deviant peer group, which eventually shapes him to commit deviant acts (e.g., Dishion, Patterson, Stoolmiller, & Skinner, 1991; Patterson, Crosby, & Vuchinich, 1992; Patterson & Forgatch, 1985; Snyder, Dishion, & Patterson, 1986). The pattern of misbehavior includes lying, stealing, fire setting, and eventual adjudication for criminal acts. The model has recently been expanded to include depression in these children and school failure (e.g., Patterson & Stoolmiller, 1991), and "late starters," a group of children who begin the antisocial sequence later and drop out earlier, a pattern Patterson has detailed in his famous "chimera" research (Patterson, 1993). The OSLC group has also developed an effective parent training program for therapeutic intervention (e.g., Patterson & Narrett, 1990; Stoolmiller, Duncan, Bank, & Patterson, 1993); the program even has significant effects on the untreated siblings of the targeted children (Arnold, Levine, & Patterson, 1975).

Like the Patterson group, the Forehand group has included eminent researchers (McMahon, Stoneman, Brody). They have also tested the effectiveness of their intervention (e.g., Church, Forehand, Carvin, & Holmes, 1990; Forehand, Breiner, McMahon, & Davies, 1981; Forehand, Furey, & McMahon, 1984; Williams & Forehand, 1984). Their work is quite impressive. Long, Forehand, Wierson, and Morgan (1994) reported the results of a 14-year followup of the children they treated when they were 2–7 years old. At the termination of treatment these children no longer differed from a healthy community group of children (an excellent comparison group); in young adulthood, 14 years later, they still remained no different from the comparison sample. This is exemplary work.

Note, however, that the social learning tradition has focused on parent training with respect to reward and punishment, instead of the moment-to-moment emotional interactions with the child, which was the focus of Ginott's and Redl's approaches.

SUMMARY

There is a vast array of popular parenting guides in bookstores today, and it is hard to organize these books into some set of traditions. However, most of them are quite redundant and present very little that is new and we think that they can be traced to three main sources of the parenting advice books: (a) Dreikurs as an offshoot of Alfred Adler and the response to authoritarian parenting, particularly its impetus following World War II, (b) Haim Ginott's work on the emotional life of children and parent–child interaction around emotional exchanges, and (c) writing on the deviant child, from an analytic position (Redl), and from a behavioral tradition (Patterson; Forehand & McMahon). Each one of these beginnings has spawned distinct types of advice books.

There was a fourth source of popular parenting advice, and this came from the work of Arnold Gesell. Beginning in the 1940s, a series of publications began appearing from the Yale University Clinic of Child Development. Gesell started attempting to inform parents about what to expect from the normal child from birth to five (Gesell, 1940), from five to ten (Gesell, 1946) and from 10 to 16 (Gesell, 1956). This series of books spawned the fourth type of parental advice book, one that discusses what to expect and the variety to expect in normal child development.

CRITIQUE

The contribution of the writers who started these streams of popular advice books for parents must be enormous. Today most parenting guides available in book stores are, in fact, repetitions of the advice given by the writers we have mentioned, usually with very little additional information, and, also unfortunately, often without giving credit to the original sources. Books have stolen their contents (by "stolen" we mean not giving credit where it is due), and so there appears to be a vast proliferation of ideas, when this is actually not the case. The actual number of ideas in the parenting advice books is rather small, all stemming from the same basic big five: Adler, Dreikurs, Ginott, Gessel, and Redl.

Are all these books equal in their validity? We briefly critique them here. Dreikurs suggested that parents and children be equals, and, on this basis recommends that parents abandon the use of rewards and punishments, because whosoever dispenses these is in a position of greater power. Instead, he recommended the use of natural, or, failing that, logical consequences of child misbehavior. However, this is somewhat a word game. Whoever dispenses the *consequences* is also in a position of greater power, and surely Dreikurs does not suggest that the children mete out consequences for parental misbehavior.

Ginott's stand on parental power is more straightforward and not constrained by principles of supposed democracy. Parents decide what behavior is and is not acceptable. However, Ginott added, all feelings are acceptable. The child's feelings require respect and genuine empathy. But, not all actions are acceptable, and the child learns the parents' morality by being given choices and being able to evaluate the choices made against standards the parents set. Emotional communication itself becomes the vehicle through which values are transmitted to the child. Not only by what the parents say, but *by how they treat one another and the child.* The example is based on interaction; that is, the process is everything.

Dreikurs and his followers emphasized family rules. In contrast, Ginott would say that each family is a unique collection of individuals, in a unique situation, and a particular subculture, and it must create its own rules that are suitable for establishing positive, respectful, and empathetic emotional communication.

Many famous and influential books, such as Dr. Spock's, added very little or nothing to these seminal books. The vast array of parenting advice books boils down to the few original writers we have mentioned, represented by four traditions (Adler and Dreikurs are one tradition). Often, the books that follow add very little in content, however, some more recent books are particularly noteworthy. We are especially interested in the stream of books that have followed the Ginott tradition, because these focus on emotional transactions within the family. The most important are four books. Three are by Faber and Mazlich (1974, 1980, & 1987). They acknowledge Ginott's contribution; in fact, they were students in one of his parenting groups. Their writing is superb, clear and lucid, and it is a faithful rendition of Ginott's ideas, often quoting "the master" and illustrating his wisdom and his ability to work with parents. The fourth is by Levant and Kelly (1991), and it is based on Levant's work with fathers. This is a great contribution, because overwhelmingly, parent training has been conducted exclusively with mothers. Levant and Kelly suggested that the fathers they worked with have lots of trouble even reading their children's emotions, let alone knowing what to do once they do read them. Levant and Kelly break down the skills they try to teach fathers into very small components, and this is very helpful.

Three other major programs have emerged. They are Gordon's (1970) Parent Effectiveness Training (PET), Dinkmeyer and McKay's (1976) Structured Training for Effective Parenting (STEP), and Gilmore and Gilmore's (1978) Self Esteem Method (SEM). These programs appear to us to have emerged from the various traditions we have outlined, most being a stew combining ingredients from each of the founding writers. The STEP program seems to be more purely Adlerian and Dreikursian. The SEM program seems more like Ginott, and the PET program seems to have borrowed from them all.

The scientific evaluation of these popular press parent training programs is discussed in the following section. We hope we have given the reader a historical perspective that integrates research, clinical work, and popular press advice, and draws from all of these in building a case for our subsequent presentation of our own work on meta-emotion. None of the approaches we discussed relate the parent's own emotions and the parent's meta-emotions to the emotions of the children. Also, none of the parenting guides is very sensitive to the developmental periods of the child. The way we talk to a child about emotions depends very critically on the child's level of development, and the cognitive capabilities the child has for symbolic representation (e.g., problem solving). We hope to address both of these limitations in this book.

BRIEF EVALUATION OF PARENT TRAINING

The term "parent training" is very broad, and it represents many kinds of programs. The important distinctions to be made have been specified in an excellent review by Barclay and Houts (1995). They made two important distinctions. First, they distinguished between whether the training program was preventive and aimed at all parents, or whether the program was aimed only at parents whose children were already somehow considered problematic. Second, they distinguished the developmental stage of the child, breaking the programs down into four stages of child development: (1) infancy (birth to 2); (2) early childhood (2–6); (3) middle childhood (7–12); and, (4) adolescence (13–18).

These distinctions are quite critical. Most intervention programs or general parental advice programs are aimed at everyone, and they must be evaluated very differently from programs aimed at one particular type of problem (e.g., childhood depression, anxiety, noncompliance, or antisocial behavior). Unfortunately, in general, the programs aimed at specific problems have set out much stricter research criteria for judging effectiveness, and they have met these criteria. In contrast, the more general programs, aimed at preventing a wide class of possible deleterious child outcomes, have settled for much softer criteria, subject to many biases (such as reliance on parental report), and they often have not met these softer criteria. There are several important methodological problems that many researchers have observed. First, parents often report improvement and satisfaction with the intervention even when there has been no observable behavior change in the children, and second, parents continue to base their evaluations in treatment of their child on negative and not emerging positive behavior (e.g., Furey & Forehand, 1983, 1986; Patterson, 1982; Scaife & Frith, 1988). Apparently parents are grateful for the researchers' attention, or they don't want to hurt the researchers' feelings. Thus, we must greet the available data with hearty skepticism if the parent training program has not carefully examined child outcomes using methods other than parental report. Although the behaviorally based programs of Patterson have been well researched, they have been developed primarily for the noncompliant boy in middle childhood and adolescence. They have not been evaluated for effectiveness as preventive programs aimed at all children.

Nonetheless, despite all these caveats, there is reason for being encouraged. As Barclay and Houts (1995) summarized, "The general efficacy of parent training is typically not disputed" (p. 195). Unfortunately, as we have noted, many of these parent training programs rely only on parental reports of change. Yet, despite the fact that there are generally few well-designed studies with a control group and long-term followup of the children in each developmental period, to the extent that these programs have been evaluated, within their limited array of measures, they have generally been found to be effective.

Parent training programs, in general, have the content listed below for each developmental stage. As Table 2.1 suggests, the results of parent training programs are generally viewed as quite effective, particularly if we suspend our skepticism about whether the programs affected the children. Some studies nevertheless do find a lack of effectiveness (e.g., Gordon & Rosen, 1984; Sirbu, Cotler, & Jason, 1978), but that is not the overall conclusion.

For example, a meta-analysis of 26 studies of Parent Effectiveness Training (Gordon, 1970) reported an overall effect size of 0.33 standard deviation units compared to a group of alternative treatments. These are quite modest effect sizes. There were significant effects on parents' knowledge, attitudes, and behavior, and on children's self esteem, and effects endured up to 26 weeks after treatment.

Specific comparisons of different theoretical approaches (e.g., Dreikurs vs. Ginott) are usually not available. However, Esters and Levant (1983) compared STEP and SEM to a wait list control group. Recall that STEP is primarily Adlerian (Dreikurs), and that SEM focuses more on teaching children to attend to

TABLE 2.1
General Evaluation of Parent Training Programs

Developmental Stage	Content	Results
Infancy	Responsiveness to baby Education about development How to take care of and play with baby	Generally quite positive for parent and baby.
Early childhood	Family rules, reflective listening Problem-solving skills Providing structure, consequences	Improvement in parent–child interaction.
Middle childhood	Structure, discipline, social learning principles, consequences, mild punishment (time out), understanding and accepting child's feelings, I-messages	Generally these various programs were effective
Adolescence	Includes list for middle childhood as well as clarifying values, structured problem–solving, contracting, regular discussion of anticipated problems	Very few studies ($N = 4$) but results generally positive

children's feelings (Ginott). The children were low-achieving rural youth. The outcome measures were children's self-esteem and their grade point average (GPA). Both interventions significantly increased the children's GPA, but only SEM had a positive effect on their self-esteem. In general, the effectiveness of STEP has been mixed (e.g., Brooks, Spearn, Rice, & Crocco, 1988; Levi, Buskila, & Gerzi, 1977). Myers et al. (1992) reported positive results with a program called the "Effective Black Parenting Program" on reducing parental rejection, improving parent–child relationships, reducing child behavior problems, and increasing social competencies.

WHAT'S NEW SINCE GINOTT: OUR PLAN FOR THIS BOOK

In the remainder of this book, we show that there are several major changes that have taken place in the thinking and research on families and child development in our field that make it possible to extend Ginott's seminal work.

Ginott's work started in the 1960s, and his participants in his parent groups were mothers. This fact created two major limitations in his work. First, we have learned about the importance of fathers since Ginott began writing, and we see how important fathers can be, exerting potentially positive or negative influences on their children, depending on how they parent. Second, Ginott ignored the marriage, and we see that developmental and family psychology has now discovered the critical importance of the parents' marriage on the developing child.

Third, we see that the parents' own emotional life and meta-emotion structure is critical. Hence, we can extend the idea of parents interacting with their children's emotions to the parents first interacting with their own emotions, and with their emotion philosophy. Herein may lie the beginning point of entry for changing the family system. Meta-emotions will turn out to be central to the individual's psychology, as well as that of the marriage, and the parent–child system.

Fourth, we have recently learned a great deal about the child's regulatory physiology and in this book we explore how it may relate to the child's developing ability to focus attention, regulate emotion, and be able to engage the world cognitively and socially without being overwhelmed and disorganized.

These, and the application of longitudinal empirical data represent the extensions of Ginott's work that we explore in this book. In the following chapters we discuss our own methods.

Appendix 2.1
Life Space Interviewing in More Detail

We include a brief summary of Life Space Interviewing for the interested reader. There are several techniques, although they are examples, and the interview is not limited to them:

1. *Reality Rub-In.* Some youngsters have trouble reading the meanings of events they are in, and others distort these meanings and cues in systematic ways. Some of Redl's young patients perceived things correctly, but had what he called "alabi-ing skills" in deluding their own consciences and retelling themselves the events so that they are blameless, and so that they believe their own accounts in a space of a few minutes.

2. *Symptom Estrangement.* Some children have learned how to benefit from their dysfunctional behavior and receive secondary gains, and are not interested in accepting the idea that there is anything wrong with what they just did. The interviewer, over time, tries to pile up evidence that what they did (what he calls "their pathology") didn't really pay; in time, they are inclined to let go of their symptoms, and the interview succeeds in "alienating their egos from their symptoms" (Redl, 1959, p. 44–45).

3. *Massaging Numb Value Areas.* Many of the children in Redl's group were very sensitive to losing face. Admitting, even to the interviewer, that they hunger for love or that some other positive motive was operating in their behavior would result in a loss of face. Redl said that even for such youngsters the appeal to certain codes of "fairness" within a fight-provocation ritual was quite acceptable to them. In this way, areas of positive values may be kindled.

4. *New Tool Salesmanship.* The interviewer can suggest that there are other defenses than the ones they are using. In this way the interviewer can use many of the child's life experiences to suggest that there are alternative reactions to these same messes. Even the simple alternative of finding an adult to talk things over with is acceptable. These alternatives are introduced without inducting shame and a loss of face to the child.

5. *Manipulation of the Boundaries of the Self.* Some children are vulnerable to emotional contagion from other children, and even manipulation by them. Redl gave the example of one child who was being used to act out by two other children, who enjoyed manipulating him in this way. After many interviews the child was better able to avoid getting sucked into the acts of this clique.

PART II ————————————————

MEASUREMENT AND CONCEPTUALIZATION

3

The Selection of Developmental Outcomes

In this chapter we summarize our rationale for selecting the child developmental outcomes we chose to study. They represent a particular set of research goals, the most important of which is understanding linkages between the emotional life of families and the child's peer relations.

OVERVIEW

There are five classes of developmental outcomes of interest to us, that we present in decreasing order of importance. A major goal of the research program we undertook in 1985 was to discover family linkages when the child was in preschool to predict the child's peer relations during middle childhood. First, our most important set of outcomes concern the child's peer relations. Second, we discuss the child's negative affectivity as an important outcome variable. Third, we discuss the development of behavior problems. Fourth, we discuss the child's physical health, and fifth, we discuss the child's ability to focus attention and the child's academic achievement.

CHILD–PEER RELATIONS AS OUR MAJOR DEVELOPMENTAL OUTCOME

As we review in chapter 5, the ability to interact successfully with peers and to form lasting peer relationships are important developmental tasks. Children who fail at these tasks, especially in the making of friends, are at risk for a number of later problems (Parker & Asher, 1987).

The peer context presents new opportunities and formidable challenges to children. Interacting with peers provides opportunities to learn about more egalitarian relationships; to form friendships with agemates, negotiate conflicts, engage in cooperative and competitive activities, and learn appropriate limits for aggressive impulses. On the other hand, children are typically less supportive than caregivers when their peers fail at these tasks. Although parents are likely to do a lot of the work at making communications clear, peers are less likely to do this work if it is unilateral. Hence, the peer context is likely to be somewhat tougher for a child with communication skill deficits.

The regulation of negative affect appears to be particularly critical for effective peer interactions. For example, there is a negative relationship between the expression of negative affect and peer sociometric ratings (Sroufe, 1979, 1984; Troy & Sroufe, 1987; Urban, Carlson, Egland, & Sroufe, 1991). Children who expressed more negative affect were seen as less desirable playmates by other children. Emotion regulation abilities and the coordination of interaction may be skills that children from maritally distressed homes have difficulty mastering. Cassidy, Parker, and Butkovsky (1992) examined the relationship between fathers and children's ability to sustain a "bout" of rough-and- tumble affectional play and young children's peer relationships. There was a significant positive relationship, demonstrating that the affectional system has serious implications for developmental outcome.

Young children acquire important skills about playing with others and the repair of negative affect in the parent–child setting. The acquisition of these skills has powerful implications for children's relationships. MacDonald (1987) compared the dyadic interactions of parents and their sons who were classified as popular or rejected by peer sociometric ratings. Popular boys and their parents (popular dyads) were able to maintain longer bouts of physical play and showed more positive affect than rejected boys and their parents (rejected dyads). Physical play is an especially useful setting for looking at regulation processes because of the potential for overstimulation and the need for mutual regulation. Children typically express their displeasure when their optimal level for stimulation is exceeded. MacDonald found that the frequency of overstimulation was much higher in the rejected dyads than the popular dyads, especially for boys and their fathers. Parents of rejected children were less able to keep the stimulation within the child's optimal level. Children in these dyads were more likely to try to avoid and to make negative responses to stimulation.

Carson (personal communication, 1993) used sequential analyses to investigate the nature of these relationships. He found that Child Negative Affect was followed by Parent Negative Affect more often in the rejected dyads than the popular dyads, especially for fathers and sons. In the rejected dyads, Parent Negative Affect was also more likely to be followed by Child Negative Affect when children interacted with their fathers. In contrast, popular dyads were more likely to have sequences of negative affect by father followed by child neutral or positive behavior. It appears that these popular children had learned how to diffuse or regulate the negative affect of their fathers.

Parenting is therefore likely to play a role in children's social competence with peers. Cowan and Cowan (1992) reported that greater discrepancy between couples' expectations about the division of labor and roles before the baby's birth and their actual behavior and roles after the birth was predictive of declines in marital satisfaction. Children's academic and peer relationship problems were also predicted by the degree to which parent's expectation were violated. Greater discrepancy was related to more aggressive behavior, shyness, a decreased ability to concentrate in school, and lower reading and math scores.

Teacher Ratings of Children's Peer Relations at Age Eight

What teachers are rating when they assess a child's peer relations at age 8 is likely to be quite different than what gets measured in the dyadic best friend context. As we discuss in chapter 5, the child's social competence with peers in middle childhood is based on a different set of social skills than in the preschool period. As we discuss in chapter 5, there is an important theoretical challenge in predicting peer social relations across these two major developmental periods, (i.e., from preschool to middle childhood). Major changes occur in peer relations in middle childhood. Children become aware of a much wider social network than the dyad. In preschool, children are rarely capable of sustaining play with more than one other child (see for example, Corsaro, 1979, 1981). However, in middle childhood, children become aware of peer norms for social acceptance, and teasing and avoiding embarrassment suddenly emerge (see Gottman & Parker, 1986). Children become aware of clique structures, and of influence patterns as well as social acceptance. The correlates of peer acceptance and rejection change dramatically, particularly with respect to the expression of emotion, and that is of the greatest interest to us. One of the most interesting changes is that the socially competent response to a number of salient social situations such as peer entry and teasing is to be a good observer, somewhat wary, "cool" and emotionally unflappable (see Gottman & Parker, 1986). Thus, the basic elements and skills a child learns through emotion coaching (labeling, expressing one's feelings, and talking about one's feelings) become liabilities in the peer social world in middle childhood. Thus, the basic model linking emotion coaching in preschool to peer relations in middle childhood can not be a simple isomorphic transfer of social skills. Instead, it becomes necessary to identify a mechanism that makes it possible for the child to learn something in the preschool period that underlies the development of appropriate social skills across this major developmental shift in what constitutes social competence with peers.

NEGATIVE AFFECTIVITY AND BEHAVIOR PROBLEMS AS IMPORTANT DEVELOPMENTAL OUTCOMES

Watson and Clark (1984) suggested the concept of "negative affectivity" as a disposition to experience negative emotion states. They suggested that perhaps a number of seemingly diverse personality and mood scales might actually be measuring the same thing. Among these they listed trait anxiety, neuroticism, ego strength, general maladjustment, repression–sensitization, and social desirability, and they reviewed studies using measures such as the Beck Depression Inventory, Eysenck Personality Inventory, and the Multiple Affect Adjective Check List. They suggested that perhaps some people are simply "more likely to experience discomfort at all times and across situations, even in the absence of overt stress. They are relatively more introspective and tend differentially to dwell on the negative side of themselves and the world" (p. 465).

Indeed, there is evidence that this may be the case among children as well. For example, Ollendick and Yule (1990), in a study of 327 British and 336 American children found depression closely related to anxiety. Similar evidence of the comorbidity of a variety of symptoms were reported by Tannenbaum, Forehand, and Thomas (1990), and by Stark, Kaslow, and Laurent (1993). However, Rothbart, Ahadi, and Hershey (1994) found that there were two factors, with internalizing components of negative affectivity (fear and sadness) related to prosocial traits, whereas irritable components of negative affectivity (anger and discomfort) were related to antisocial traits.

Other research has suggested that disorders such as antisocial personality have a developmental trajectory that includes aggression, poor attentional abilities, peer rejection, school failure, depression, and a drift toward a deviant peer group (Patterson & Stoolmiller, 1991). Hence, there is some evidence of comorbidity in the development of children's behavior problems, and that this comorbidity may be related to negative affectivity.

EMOTION REGULATION

Recently, the area of the development of the child's ability to regulate emotion (variously conceptualized) has blossomed as a research area. Maccoby (1980) suggested the reconceptualization of research on such areas as the development of inhibition and impulse control. Garber and Dodge (1991) presented current research on the child's ability to regulate emotion. In our research, we measured the child's ability to regulate emotion with parental reports. We used the Down-Regulation scale of the Katz–Gottman Emotional Regulation Questionnaire, assessed when the children were 8 years old variable; this variable was called DOWN REGULATION in our diagrams. This variable assesses the extent to which the parents have to exert external control the child to reduce the child's level of activity, negative emotion, inappropriate behavior, and misconduct.

PHYSICAL HEALTH AS A DEVELOPMENTAL OUTCOME

Recently psychologists have reawakened an old interest in pediatrics, exploring the psychological concomitants of infection and immune functioning in children, as well as the classical psychological interest in psyhosomatic disorders (e.g., Weiner, 1977). Bakal (1992) recently wrote about the relationship between psychology and health and psychoimmunology, and Karoly (1988) put together a handbook on child health assessment. Although this is a relatively new field, Gottman and Katz (1989) reported a relationship between the child's physical health and family variables. This interest in physical health and immune functioning has been a part of our laboratory's research for some time. This interest is currently largely exploratory.

ACHIEVEMENT AS A DEVELOPMENTAL OUTCOME: RELATIONSHIPS BETWEEN SOCIAL-EMOTIONAL AND COGNITIVE DEVELOPMENT

Despite the fact that recent theorizing in cognitive psychology has largely ignored emotion, this has not always been the case. The notion that arousal influences task performance has a long history in psychology. The Yerkes–Dodson law (1908) predicts an inverted-U function between arousal and performance. This law proposes that performance should be lowest at very low and very high levels of arousal and increase with moderate levels. Although there have been many methodological critiques of this "law," including the difficulty of defining arousal in a unidimensional way, as well as the difficulty of disproving the hypothesis, Kahneman (1973) showed that, in general, physiological arousal increases with task difficulty. He suggested that task difficulty is based on the degree of mental effort or attentional capacity required by the task. There also appears to be more evidence favoring the law when the increased arousal has been produced by aversive stimulation than by incentives (see Eysenck, 1982, for a review).

Other emotional factors influencing academic performance have also been studied, including anxiety, depression, learned helplessness, and expectancy, to name a few. Clearly, emotions affect cognitive performance (see Lewis, 1993 for a study of this in infants 12 to 23 weeks old), and academic performances have emotional effects (Sullivan & Lewis, 1989; Telegina & Pigarera, 1992). However, if we search for developmental studies that have examined aspects of emotional development that affect cognitive development, the literature is limited. Haviland and Kramer (1991) studied affect and cognition relationships developmentally in the diaries of Anne Frank and concluded that passion preceded and facilitated the development of abstract thoughts during adolescence. In a parent training study by Feldman, Case, Rineover, and Tower (1989), mothers increased their affection, praise and imitations of infant vocalizations, with a concomitant increase in the infant's cognitive development; however, Nurcombe, (1984) found no such effects in a similar program. Feshbach and Feshbach (1987) conducted a 2-year longitudinal study of 8–9 year-olds, and found that for girls measures of empathy at age 8–9 were strong predictors of achievement in reading and spelling at ages 10–11.

Damon (1983) noted that contemporary theories of cognitive development sample from a limited range of human thought. He wrote:

> The primary empirical base for Piaget's model, as well as for information-processing approaches, is the child's solitary attempt to master physical, logical, or scientific tasks in a laboratory setting. It is still an open question whether models that draw mainly upon such restricted data will be appropriate for describing the development of human cognition in all its forms. Of all the many manifestations of thinking during the day-to-day lives of children and adults, scientific problem solving is only a part, and for most persons a minor and unusual part. (p. 103)

Do thinking and problem solving that take place every day within the social and emotional arena affect cognitive and intellectual growth? The question has been the subject of surprisingly little research.

Hollos and Cowan (1973) and Hollos (1975) compared the behavior of children living in environments with a great deal of social interaction versus living in an atmosphere with little social interaction. They found that children in the two environments did not differ in logical operations, but did differ in role-taking ability; children from more isolated environments were lower in role-taking skills.

Perret-Clermont (1980) asked the question, what characteristics of social interactions are likely to facilitate intellectual growth? She suggested that, contrary to an imitation perspective, that conflict and its resolution should be the basis for cognitive development. Her experimental data provide some support for her contention.

In summary, there is evidence to suggest that it is reasonable to expect effects on cognitive development of different conditions of emotional-social development.

4

The Meta-Emotion Interview

In this chapter we describe the meta-emotion interview, the variables we derived from it, and we present our qualitative analysis of this interview. We introduce the distinction between emotion dismissing and emotion coaching families.

In our study, each parent was separately interviewed about their own experience of sadness and anger, their philosophy of emotional expression and control, and their feelings, attitudes, and responses to their children's anger and sadness. Their behavior during this interview was audiotaped. A brief summary of the meta-emotion interview questions follow. Note that the interview is semi-structured, so the interviewer is free to probe for as long as necessary to make things clear and specific. The interviewee is encouraged to engage in long monologues, and to wax philosophical and poetic. Now that we have a coding system for the interview, the interviewer is encouraged to cover aspects of the interview that would make the job of coding easier. The interviewer probes responses that are unclear, asking for examples, obtaining clarification, trying to obtain examples of what the subject would say, what the child might say, and so on. For example, one father said he responded to his daughter's needs when she was sad. The interviewer probed and the father said "I respond to her needs, I ask her, 'Do you need to eat something? Do you need to go outside? Do you need to watch a video?' Like that." This clarifies a vague statement like "I respond to her needs."

WHAT WE ASK IN THE META-EMOTION INTERVIEW

The following is an outline of our meta-emotion interview.

Introduction

I: We would like to ask you some questions about how you feel about your feelings. For example, how you might feel about different kinds of feelings like surprise. Now some people don't ever like being surprised. They hate surprise birthday parties, if you make a surprise party for them, boy, they'll just turn around and go the other way. Thanks guys but no thanks. On the other hand, some people love to be surprised and love surprising others. They will take their families on a surprise vacation and go on a little trip and not tell anybody where they're going just to surprise them or, you know, they'll make birthday parties, surprise parties for their spouses, or bring surprise gifts home or whatever but it's a feeling that they like and they really enjoy. They want to have more of it in their lives and they go out of their way to have it. So, there's no right or wrong about this. People are just different. What I am going to be asking you today is about your own feelings about your feelings, how you feel about being happy and being angry etc. And also about how it relates to how you're raising ___, how you react to his or her feelings, how you view his or her feelings, and so on. Ok? Any questions? So we're going to start off with the feeling of sadness. What we want to know is, how do you feel about being sad? Why don't you tell me a little bit about your own reactions to being sad.

Part One: The Interviewee's and the Child's Sadness

I: What about feeling sad?

I: What would you look like, what would I see if I saw you sad? Could I tell you were sad? What would be going on inside? What would you be feeling about being sad? What would you be thinking? Does this way you feel about sadness have a history? Tell me the story of that. What do you do to get over feeling sad? How does sadness work in your life? What role does it play? Could you tell if your dad was sad? Your mom? How were your parents about sadness, how did they treat you, what was it like for you in your family?

I: What about ___ (the child)? What do you do, well, let me start out with this question, how do you react to ___ when (s)he's being sad? Can you tell that (s)he's sad? Can you tell subtle signs? Like what does (s)he do when sad or a little blue? How do you respond? What do you think about the sadness? What are your reactions, thoughts, feelings? What might you do? What would your goals be in this situation? Does this relate to anything in your past? Tell me the story of that. When (s)he gets sad, what does that bring

46

out in you? What do you think you are trying to teach ___ about sadness? What are your goals, what would you be trying to accomplish? What, if anything, are you trying to teach your child? Can you give me a recent example, or a vivid example of one time that ___ was sad, and what happened, who said and did what (try to get a play-by-play account of what happened).

Part Two: The Interviewee's and the Child's Anger

I: What about feeling angry?

I: What what would you look like, what would I see if I saw you angry? Could I tell you were angry? What would be going on inside? What would you be feeling about being angry? What would you be thinking? Does this way you feel about anger have a history? Tell me the story of that. What do you do to get over feeling angry? How does anger work in your life? What role does it play? How were your parents about anger, how did they treat you, what was it like for you in your family?

I: What about ___ (the child)? What do you do, well, let me start out with this question, how do you react to ___ when (s)he's being angry? Can you tell that (s)he's angry? Can you tell subtle signs? Like what does (s)he do when angry or irritated? How do you respond? What do you think about the anger? What are your reactions, thoughts, feelings? What might you do? What would your goals be in this situation? Does this relate to anything in your past? Tell me the story of that. What do you think you are trying to teach ___ about anger? What are your goals, what would you be trying to accomplish? What, if anything, are you trying to teach your child? Can you give me a recent example, or a vivid example of one time that ___ was sad, and what happened, who said and did what (try to get a play-by-play account of what happened). When (s)he gets angry? What does that bring out in you?

Part Three: Hard and Easy Emotions for the Interviewee

I: O.k. What we'd like you to do is, look at this list of different feelings and pick out the one that you'd like to experience the most.

I: Are there things you do, you know, again on a daily basis to make sure that you feel ___, that you feel ___ towards people to sort of maximize that feeling?

I: O.k. What about the feeling of that list that you don't like the feeling very much of. Which one do you like the least?

I: Are there things you do, you know, again on a daily basis to make sure that you don't feel ___ that you're not feeling ___ toward people to sort of minimize that feeling?

I: O.k. Now we're going to look at this next list. And I want you to tell me, of those emotions, which do you think that you have the most trouble calming yourself down or soothing yourself, sort of getting over that feeling, which do you have the most trouble getting over?

I: What, what do you do to get over it? What do you try to do?

Part Four: The Interviewee's Perceptions of The Child's Emotion Regulation Abilities and Problems

I: What about ___, what feeling does (s)he have the most trouble getting over?

I: O.k. Um, do you see ways in which (s)he tries to get over that emotion?

I: O.k. If you could sum it up, I know you've probably said some of this already, but if you could sum it up, can you maybe describe a philosophy about the world of feelings, how to approach that, how to work with feelings, what they're for, what they're about?

OUR META-EMOTION DIMENSIONS

We started by studying three dimensions of meta-emotion for *sadness* and for *anger*, for each parent. The dimensions were: (a) awareness of one's own emotion, (b) awareness of the child's emotion, and (c) coaching the child's emotion. We now briefly define each dimension. Each scale is made up of a sum of specific items on the meta-emotion coding system.

Awareness of one's own emotion is being able to talk about the emotion in a differentiated manner (differentiating various types and intensities of the emotion), particularly that the subject experiences this emotion, has no problem distinguishing this emotion from others, answers questions easily, without hesitation or confusion, talks at length about the emotion, and shows interest and excitement about this emotion.

Awareness of the child's emotion is noticing when the child has the emotion, having no problem distinguishing this emotion from others, being descriptive of the child's emotion, having insight into the child's experience of the emotion, being descriptive of some part of the remediation process (e.g., what makes child feel better), knowing the cause of the child's emotion, being able to talk at length and easily about the child's experience, and being interested in the child's experience.

Coaching the child's emotion involves helping the child to verbally label the emotions being felt, showing respect for the child's experience of this emotion (i.e., accepting the emotion), when the child is upset, the parent talking to the child, intervening in situations that caused the emotion, at times comforting the child during the emotion, teaching the child appropriate rules for expressing the emotion, educating the child about the nature of the emotion, teaching the child strategies for dealing with the emotion, and for soothing the intense levels of the emotion.

We devote some space in the remainder of this chapter to giving the reader a qualitative feeling for what these interviews were like, and what we examined in these interviews. Chapter 16 discusses the meta-emotion dimension of *Dysregulation,* or feeling out-of-control with respect to an emotion. Dysregulation is a dimension that assesses the fact that there is difficulty for the subject in controlling and regulating this emotion, that the emotion occurs often, is difficult to get over, has been a problem or concern, that the subject thinks this emotion can be dangerous, and has needed help with this emotion in the past.

QUALITATIVE ANALYSIS OF THE META-EMOTION INTERVIEW

In the following sections, we give the reader examples of how people responded to our questions in the meta-emotion interview. The responses were varied, often rich in both detail and metaphor, and sometimes poignantly personal. Many people had given a lot of thought to how they felt about their preschool child's emotions, and how this related to their own emotions and lives. The excerpts and the way we organize them give the reader a sense for what we are coding, and how distinct meta-emotion philosophies may be derived from how people talk about their emotions.

To organize these materials, we describe three different kinds of families with respect to their child's sadness or anger. The first kind of family is *dismissing or disapproving* of their child's emotion. This kind of family often finds their child's negative emotions difficult, and they respond by distancing themselves in some way from their child's emotional experience. The second kind of family is the *coaching* family. They are actively engaged in their child's emotion, and also regard emotional moments as teaching opportunities. The third type of family is basically positive about sadness or anger, but is unable to structure their child's experience in ways that teaches the child about the emotion. We call this type *high in acceptance, but low in coaching.* We think they are a permissive family in the sense of Ginott: accepting of feelings in general, but not limit-setting or problem solving when it comes to emotion.

RESPONDING TO SADNESS

The Disapproving Family or Dismissing Family

Some families are less comfortable than others with their child's sadness and they find ways to distance themselves from their child's experience. When talking about emotion, these families often either show disapproval of their child's sadness, or they dismiss their child's sadness as a trivial event. Disapproving families tend to be noticeably critical and unempathic when describing their child's experience, which is different than the dismissing families, who tend to seem somewhat disengaged, or disrespectful, of their child's experience.

Disapproving of Sadness

Some families are disapproving of their children's emotionality and view emotion as a behavior that needs to be controlled. They view their sad child from a critical distance, noticing what is wrong with the sad behavior rather than focusing on the sadness itself. For the following father, his son's sadness demands a disciplinary response.

> (Father 182)
> **F:** And so he's down, but then usually when he's sad, he turns into a real brat after a while and then it's kind of the thing that you try to rationalize with him after a while, you have to almost discipline him because he gets a little bit out of control.

This father is involved in his son's sadness but he is involved in controlling it. Interestingly, this same father has difficulty describing his own sadness, and even confuses it with other emotions, a tendency we describe as "low awareness of his own sadness." When initially asked about sadness, he was certain he did not experience it.

> **F:** No, I don't think I'm, ah, ever sad. I may be mad, I think there's a . . . but sad, I don't think I'm very often very sad.
> **I:** So you don't think you ever, it's not that you don't show it, you just don't feel it?
> **F:** Yeah that's true. I really don't think I ever feel it. I might be down, you know, I guess that could go along kind of with being sad, but, I don't know, ah, just being in that kind of bad mood or something. When I've been looking for, when I change careers or change jobs, I don't know if I'm really sad or just, um, here again, I'm not the most enthusiastic person in the world.
> **I:** So you said maybe you don't feel down sometimes.
> **F:** Discouragement, I guess that can be related to sadness, so, you know, that does happen from time to time.
> **I:** Can others tell?
> **F:** Yeah, I show it in the sense that sometimes I might be drinking more than I (laughs) normally do. That's ah, I think one of the biggest things. This other way is, um, you know, if I'm down, then I might actually start to be

real nitpicky at home and start yelling about things that normally wouldn't probably bother me.

Another parent views her daughter's sadness as manipulative, and therefore she also views sadness with disapproval.

> (Mother 144)
> **I:** Does R get sad?
> **M:** She does and she don't. She does it more for attention. I can't tell when she really gets sad.
> **I:** How does she get sad when she does it for attention?
> **M:** She just sits and cries and pouts. When she don't get her way.
> **I:** How can you tell that's just for attention?
> **M:** Just, when I end up giving her what she wants, then she's happy (laughs). As far as really being sad, I've only seen her a couple of times. She's more concerned that she is sad.

This mother is suspicious of the child's motives for sadness, and sees it as designed to manipulate her. She sees sadness as a demand for something, and responds with some annoyance and a criticalness of her child's expression. Because she cannot distinguish an attempt to manipulate her from genuine sadness, she rejects all sadness from her child.

Dismissing of Sadness

Often families are more dismissing than disapproving of their child's sadness. These dismissing families can be sensitive to their children's feelings and want to be helpful, but their approach to sadness is to ignore or deny it as much as possible. They seem to hope this strategy will make the emotion go away more quickly. They often convey a sense that a child's emotion is something a parent is forced to deal with, but is not interesting or worthy of attention in itself.

They may describe sadness as something to get over, ride out, look beyond, or not dwell on. They often use distractions when their child is sad to move the child along, and even use comfort, albeit within specified time limits. They prefer a happy child, and often they do not present a clear or insightful description of their child's emotion experience. Their problem solving revolves around what made their child sad or what it takes to get over sadness rather than with the emotion itself. They do not see the emotion as beneficial or as any kind of opportunity.

In the following interviews a father and mother both respond to their daughter's sadness by emphasizing the importance of her not remaining sad. The father focuses on a myriad of distractions; the mother is more inclined to belittle the cause of the sadness. At the same time that they dismiss their child's sadness, both parents also convey affection in the concern they show that their child not be unhappy.

(Father 128)

I: How do you react when she is sad?

F: I pamper her.

I: What do you do?

F: I just hold her, carry her around. I ask her if she needs anything. Ah, if she needs, mostly ask if she needs anything, or I just talk to her.

I: What do you talk about?

F: Hmmmm? "What do you want?" Well, back to needs again, uhhh, "You want to watch television?" "Can we get you a movie or anything like that?" "You want to go upstairs?" "You want to go outside?" Just, I don't know. Just work with her and see what she answers back with cause then you find out. Most of the time she isn't sad either, she's happy unless she's sick. She just got over being sick a couple of days ago or yesterday, and Wednesday she was sort of down in the dumps, but ah, she's usually never sad.

Here we see that the father's statement that he responds to his daughter's needs requires more probing by the interviewer. His idea of responding to her needs is to distract her from the emotion, to ask her which distraction she needs.

In the following interview, the mother focuses on showing her daughter she has no reason to be sad by laughing it off. She sees her daughter's being sad about a book as silly and views the sadness as unimportant and trivial.

(Mother 128)

I: How do you react to her when she's sad?

M: She is such an emotional child. (Laughs). It depends on, on, like what she's sad about, like a lot of times, she gets, she'll read a book that has a sad ending or a sad middle and she'll start crying, and she gets very upset about it. And I try, you know, I try to laugh a little bit and say, you know, "Come on it's just a book," you know, "You can't go by that," and try to get her out of it a little bit and stuff.

Another parent described how he set limits on his son's sadness. The reference to "alarm clock" in this excerpt comes from earlier in the interview where the father says that when he gets depressed, after a while an alarm clock goes off and tells him "Enough!" Then it's time to stop being depressed and he just shakes it off.

I: What happens when R gets sad?

F: Well, he gets, uh (pause) he frets a lot, really, ah kicks toys and just kind of, you know, it, well, you know it doesn't do much good. (Laughs) Um, he gets over-sensitive as far as, you know, any kind of "Well, don't do that," or, "Won't you please," or ah, just any kind of, you know, you're trying to communicate, and he over-reacts a lot. . . . You know, it's just like the alarm clock again. There, you know, this is good, lets let him do that, lets let him feel that, but then it gets to the point, where hey, it's, you know, time to bring him out of it. And a lot of times he doesn't want to.

I: What happens?

F: Then I get frustrated of course. You know, life has to go on, you know, you can't stay static.

This father lets his son express some sadness, but at a certain point "an alarm goes off." He views staying with an emotion as being stuck, or being "static." The father becomes impatient, he's had enough, and he thinks it's time to change his son's feeling. Again, for this father, sadness is not an emotion to explore or learn from, but rather one to beware of getting stuck or "static" in. The emotion spells a kind of death, a dangerous state of no forward movement. In the following excerpt we see that he does not view his child's sadness as an opportunity for the child's learning, but as a state to be avoided.

I: What are you trying to teach him about being sad?

F: I don't really think that I'm trying to teach my children anything so much as to let them find things and then hopefully modify, you know, ah how they use that . . . ah, loses his favorite stuffed animal, that's sad . . . but ah, to make light of it or to make less light of it at that period, to shape his feelings toward sadness or towards anything.

Sometimes parents dismiss their child's emotional experience in ways that tend to dismiss the child. They suggest a child's sadness isn't important enough to get terribly concerned over. They may laugh at their child or use unflattering examples when describing their sad child. They may invalidate their child's reasons for responding emotionally. The father in the next excerpt suggests that because his child is young her feelings of sadness are probably a result of her lack of understanding and immaturity; therefore her sadness is not worth really giving too much attention.

(Father 118)

F: I classify myself as a realist in the scheme of life, you know, there's, I try to look at things and see them as at least as close as I can find to what they are. She's sad. What am I going to do? Am I going to go tickle her chin or cheer her up? I don't know if that's really what you need to do. I think a lot of times people need to work out their own problems.

I: Is that what you encourage her to do?

F: I don't have much reaction to it at all. She's not sad that much. She pouts but you're talkin' a four year old also. She's four and a half. Ah, their reactions are not adult reactions, they're likely to get upset about something and therefore become sad by it because of lack of understanding of the situation probably more so than anything else.

Interestingly, we again see a connection between this father's view of sadness in his child and his view of sadness in himself. This same father describes his own experience of sadness as a depressed mood, which he dismisses as an utterly useless time for him.

(Father 118)
A depressed mood to me is a useless time. It's when you're doing nothing constructive whatsoever. You're feeling sorry for yourself if nothing else.

It was also difficult for him to describe his own sadness. He went on to describe himself as unemotional in general, again an aspect of what we describe as "low sadness awareness."

(Father 118)
You'll find that I'm very cold in this whole thing . . . I don't react the way most people (do).

The following excerpt shows a father who also dismisses typical childhood causes for sadness. We referred to this father earlier in the book when we mentioned parental metaphors about their children's emotions. He implies his child's usual reasons are not important enough for the emotion of sadness. They are a "waste" of the emotion. The father appears to have a metaphor of sadness as a finite precious resource like money that is not to be wasted. This metaphor has profound implications for his thinking. He is the judge of when it is "wasteful" to spend sadness and when it is wise, and it places this father in a position of selective approval and disapproval of his child's sadness emotions. We wonder what having this metaphor conveys to his child.

(Father 123)
F: Well, C. will break a toy or he'll lose something and he'll get upset or he's sad about something and I ask him what he's talking about, *saving sadness for major things be to sad over*, you know, like losing a toy or tearing a page in the book or something like that *is not something to waste your time being sad on*. You *save sadness* for, you know, one of the things we could be sad for is flat dogs, the death of a pet or something like that. For flat dogs or something like that C would, that's not something to waste your time being sad on [italics added].

Another father showed qualified empathy for his son's sadness, but distinguished sadness he disapproved of from sadness he could understand, but tolerate only briefly. He portrayed his son's sadness as a time of "being a brat" or "moping around." This father tries to get his child out of the mood, as if the mood itself were harmful, as if sadness retards progress (he thinks his child needs to "just press on"). The father also has the developmental theory that his child could not understand reasoning about the emotion.

(Father 170)
F: I understand that. He misses his mom and you try to cheer him up. But, like I said, if he's just being sad because he's being a brat then it doesn't bother me. (Laughs). He's got to learn not to do that so I try to show him that by saying, hey, it's not going to get you anywhere. But if he's genuinely in a bad mood for one reason or the other, I go ahead and give him a hug and a kiss and get him back on his feet again. It brings me down a little ways if he's just moping around. That's not fun.
I: Do you think there's something that you're trying to teach him, something you're teaching him about how to handle being sad, what it means to be sad?
F: Yeah, I suppose by being all casual about it, if he's upset, throw him on the ground and roll him around and tickle him and say, don't worry about it and just press on. Don't let it drag you down. *I don't know, at this stage it's not like I reason with him* [italics added].

Thus, this father's policy is to teach his son to "carry on," to not let sadness get him down or get in the way. He wants his son to change his sad mood by ignoring the sadness he actually feels. He also demonstrates this philosophy of "moving on" when his son comes to him because of a problem with his friends. Notice that his meta-emotion structure about sadness precludes his coaching his child about a very specific peer relationship even, dealing with aggression. He simply counsels his child to forget about it and "go on."

(Father 170)
F: Yeah, Not to really worry about it. If he comes in and says one of his friends took his toys, I'll just say, well, don't worry about it, he'll bring it back, you know. Or, you know, *he says, "he hit me." Don't worry about it, he probably didn't mean it, it was probably an accident. Just to take it lightly, don't dwell on it,* but I don't sit there and say, you shouldn't be upset. That's fine, he can be upset all he wants, but just teach him to roll with the punches and get on with his life [italics added].
I: so it's OK to feel sad but don't wallow in it.
F: Right. Definitely and that, at this point at his age there's nothing you can't really sit down and say it to him, I think it's through my actions, I'll give him a quick hug and a kiss ok, fine, lets go out and play now.

It is very interesting to us that this child's mother responded in a similar way to questions about her child's sadness.

> (Mother 170)
> **M:** I usually give him a hug. I usually try to get him over it.
> **I:** How do you do that?
> **M:** Um, maybe give him ice cream or something that he would enjoy. Ah, I guess *I do try to make him forget about it, cheer him up,* I mean it's ok if he's sad, but still I think, I guess I don't want him to experience it too much. I don't know [italics added].

Like her husband, her approach is to "move along," and to try to change the sad mood to a cheerful one. She shows a somewhat different approach when she discusses the sadness of her adult friend who is going through a divorce. In this discussion she encourages her friend to express and accept her feelings.

> **M:** And I thought, if he's going through a divorce, she should be upset and heck don't try to hide it. I mean don't drag everybody else down with you but, don't pretend to the world that everything's OK when actually it's not. Sadness to me it's fine, don't get everybody involved but then don't shut yourself off from it either. If you're sad, you're sad, work through it and you know, go on. Just accept it and deal with it and go on because if you don't deal with it then I think if you keep all of your emotions inside then it starts affecting you, later on it will come back.

This mother talks about "working through the sadness." What does she mean by this? Again, it turns out that she sees sadness as something one simply gets through with the passage of time. There's nothing that can be done actively to deal with being sad, it's simply a "ride," one that eventually completes itself and is gone.

> **I:** So when you say deal with it, how do you deal with it?
> **M:** Just let it *ride itself out*, just if you're sad, feel it, just um do whatever, ah this is hard [italics added].

Still, even with a friend, the metaphor of movement—moving beyond the sadness—prevails. In the adult case one moves beyond by not resisting, by letting sadness wash over her. She thinks that it's a matter of mental hygiene to express sadness, as there may be future repercussions if you don't. It is difficult for this mother to say the same thing about her son because sadness in a child suggests to her that her child is not well-adjusted. She demonstrates a common theme among parents dealing with sadness: it is their own feelings of discomfort about their child's sadness that prevent them from tolerating it for long.

I: How do you feel when he's sad?

M: It makes me sad because you want to think that your kids are very happy and well adjusted and it's just, I don't like to see him upset. *I want him to be very happy all the time* [italics added].

Again we see the theme that sadness is a resource not to be idly wasted on trivial events, that it's okay for a child to be sad about something really important like the death of animal.

I: So when he's sad you feel like it's OK for him to be sad to feel it but you don't want him to.

M: *I just don't want him to dwell on it* I guess. Um, I don't think I have never really seen him sad that often. It's not something I guess, you know, if you've had an animal that's been killed or something, that would make a child very sad but he, um, I guess he hasn't experienced that that much.

Part of parents' discomfort with a child having a strong emotion like sadness is that they are not sure what their task is when the child has a strong emotion. They see only the demand to fix things, and the demand is at times too overwhelming. They cannot see that just understanding or empathizing with the emotion is the primary task. In the following excerpt a mother is uncomfortable with her child's sadness because she feels it demands something of her she cannot provide. She feels that she cannot change the event which caused her child's sadness, a broken toy, and she conveys a sense of being as mystified by the breaking of the toy as is her child.

M: The toy was, it was a plastic green tractor and it broke and he's been playing with it ever since he was like 16 months.

I: It was one of his oldest and most favorite toys.

M: You know, it's something he's been so enthusiastic about and I have never been able to figure it out but it broke.

I: What did he do?

M: He just says, mommy, it broke and I say, well, I can't do anything, you know, he just kind of went, oh. It's something, I don't know, he hasn't, it's still in his toys because I haven't thrown it out. (Laughs). I don't have the heart to yet.

I: How did you respond to him knowing that he was feeling sad?

M: Well, I just told him that *there was nothing I could do to fix it* [Italics added]. And you know, everything would be OK because he's got so many other toys and trucks and you know, well, he's picked up another toy I think in the place of this and that's because him and his daddy watched the movie Jaws and I found this jaws like, it looks like this shark, this purple like thing, you move the mouth and it opens up and you shut it and he's more or less kind of plays with that.

This mom felt very bad about the toy having broken, but she was unaware of the idea that all she needed to do in this situation was to be sad together. Instead, she experienced her child's sadness as a demand that she reverse time and make the toy whole again.

Some parents teach their children directly to minimize sadness by focusing a philosophy of "realism" where life goes on, and there's no reason to be sad. In this practical approach there just isn't a lot of room for negative emotion.

(Mother 125)

M: One thing I teach J. and all my kids is not to feel sorry for themselves because, you know, one of my philosophies is that you're here, you're breathing, you've got a chance to get it together, you know. Um, I don't, even though I said his sadness is usually when he's not feeling so well, I'll give him a hug and I'll try to brush it off because he'll say, the hurt is gone now, you know. I feel like (pause) *let's not wallow in this*, you know. It's all going to be better. It's all past, you know, it's a big thing now but tomorrow it won't be a big thing. And, I mean I, talk to him. I don't just, you know go boohoo and all that, I don't talk like that. I just talk to him [italics added].

In the next excerpt, a father takes this philosophy a bit further, and dismisses the importance of his own involvement in his child's sadness altogether. In his attempt to be reassuring to his child he invalidates her feeling entirely, telling her it is absurd to feel sad about anything. In his view she has no valid reason to be sad.

(Father 126)

F: I'm not trying to teach her about sadness, *I'm trying to teach her about what she's sad about, there's no reason to be sad about it.* That's what I'm trying to teach her. I was just telling her everything would be all right. But, you know, she's kind of cute in a way, but you know, but the only thing you can teach a kid about being sad is just, there's no reason, there's nothing to be sad about.

F: Everything will be OK, when it's all over with. Later you'll be OK [italics added].

In Contrast: The Coaching Family

What we call *the coaching family* may not seem altogether different from some of the previous families. The coaching family shows the same concern for their child's pain seen in many dismissing families; in fact, they may seem harsher at first glance because they additionally show the same concern for appropriate behavior seen in some disapproving families. However, there are important differences. In contrast to dismissing and disapproving families, the coaching family values the emotion in a way that allows them to share sadness with their child. They can tolerate spending some time with sadness. These parents are available for sadness and they are willing to "dwell a bit." They often state that they see their child's sadness as a time for intimacy with the child, and they see much of the task as one of intimacy.

They even take valuing the emotion a step further and see sadness as a time for some proactive teaching with their child. From some coaching parents we heard an eagerness to share sadness with their child, because they feel it is important to them to be part of this experience in their child's life. In the following excerpt we can see the enormous contrast with a dismissing approach in a father who actually welcomes a time when his child feels sad and sees it as an important time for him to be a father.

(Father 121)
I: How does it make you feel when you see L. sad?
F: It makes me feel like a parent if that's an answer to your question. It's the time to be there. Ummm, because you have to be there for all things. But that's one of the times when I feel that I'm more like I'm L.'s dad. 'Cause it's one of the things that's more important for her.

Or perhaps this parent is proud to see his child can be sad because the ability to feel sadness is an important part of who they want their child to be. In the following excerpt a mother articulates this well by talking about *how important it is to her that she be able to feel sad as part of being empathic.*

(Mother 139)
I like it when I see them getting upset because, you know, not upset, but if they see a sad show like that, Alex was on TV, I don't know if you know it, but it was real sad because the girl died, you know. I kind of like to see that they've got some feeling in them. You know, little tears will well up in their eyes or something like that. *I like that because it makes me feel like she's got a heart, she cares about people, she cares about more things than just herself.*

In the following excerpt, the parent can value time with his child in sadness, even though it's uncomfortable at the same time to see his child sad. Instead of viewing his child's sadness as something to be changed, he sees it as an opportunity for feeling close to his child.

(Father 184)
I: How do you respond to D. when he is sad?
F: I guess pretty, um, I mean I feel very close to him when he's sad. When I see him sad about something, I want to sit down and talk to him.

I: Um-hmm.

F: You know, it gives me the *opportunity to do something.* Even if he'll feel sad after getting a punishment, we'll talk to him about getting in touch with the feeling.

I: OK

F: I find myself being drawn toward him.

I: Umm-hmm

F: I have a hard time seeing them unhappy or frustrated.

I: It makes you feel?

F: I think there's this tendency for parents to want things to be good.

I: Yeah. I wondered if you might label yourself as feeling sad if you see him sad.

F: I guess I don't know. I guess I'd feel bad, the word I was thinking earlier was empathetic.

I: Um-hmm

F: I guess I share the feeling.

So for this father there is a clearly defined task when his child is sad, in marked contrast to dismissing parents, who are very confused about what their task is (and think it may be to have to fix everything). This child's mother is also very conscious and respectful of her son's approach to dealing with his sadness. Some of her concern with cheering up and moving on remind one of the more dismissive approach, but the thoughtfulness she shows and time she takes to be with her son's sadness make her a coaching mom. It's where her emphasis is. In the following excerpt this mother offers a kind of manual on how to help her child when he is sad and she finds it insignificant.

(Mother 184)

M: Sad. I share it, you know, unless it's, you know, and then I'm sure that there's times when he's sad that I just can't relate because it seems so insignificant to me so I will think and I will have to come down to his level and realize that this is something that makes a kid sad and what I try to do is remember my own childhood and I'll try to share that with him, you know, "I remember when I felt that way."

I: Uh-huh.

M: Such and such happened, you know, and I'll relate the story which usually helps cheer him up to hear about somebody else especially his mom.

I: Yeah.

M: When I was a kid, he loves "when I was a kid" stories. So that will make him start feeling better probably because he feels like it's OK to be sad, you know.

I: Yeah

M: Because you felt that way too and you're a grown up so it must be OK.

I: That gets into our next question. What do you think you are trying to teach D. about sadness?

M: Well, I think that I try to teach him that it's OK to be sad, that you need to talk about it and that D. likes to be, likes to work out things himself so with him and the other kids I encourage him to talk about it more but I have to respect his space and I do that and usually he will want to talk about himself and his feelings when I'm around.

I: Um-hmm

M: And what I usually do is I ask him, you know, is there something I can do for you? Um, if you want to be left alone, he should let me know how he's feeling at that time. But I think, I also try to communicate with him, OK it's blown away now, it's over with we've dealt with it and let's get on, you know, with our lives.

Some coaching parents make sure children have opportunities to experience sadness. This mother is very interested in her son's experience and of serving as a guide.

(Mother 129)

M: I'm conscious of my children, being sure they experience it. Uh, in stories, umm, something's coming up, I can't pull it out of my brain, but something's coming up about it . . . a book we read recently about some, a lost something, or a dog that died or something like that. And John gets real affected by these kinds of things. He cries, and, "I don't want that to happen," you know.

I: Well, you just said that you want him to experience the sadness, but you really don't want him to cry?

M: No, that's OK with me if he cries. Now, my older son will bop right through it. He might feel sad for a couple of seconds and, um, he doesn't really slow down enough to let it affect him too much, but John will stop and cry.

I: Is it the intensity that bothers you?

M: No, he just feels, he just really feels it. And I don't know if he takes it personally like, "Why doesn't that happen to me?" or I don't know what it is that's going on with him, but he'll cry, and um, so I don't want him to do this everyday, but I want him to do it enough so that he can understand I can feel sad and then feel happy again or this is why I feel sad and maybe I shouldn't have felt sad because it wasn't me personally but it's something with him that, um, I'm conscious of the sadness in him. The way he responds to a sad situation.

I: How does it make you feel to see him like that?

M: Oh, let's see. Oh it kind of tugs at my heart because his feelings are right out there, you know. And, ah, I'm proud of him that he can feel that. Um, I'm not worried about it. I don't think it's anything abnormal.

I: Do you get sad with him at all?

M: A little bit, yeah, but of course, I'm *conscious of leading him through it* [italics added].

Some families talk directly of seeing and using the teaching opportunities inherent in sharing their child's emotion. In the following family both parents strive to understand and help their son with sadness. This mother makes an effort to respond to her child's emotion because it is important to her philosophy of emotion and of parenting. She reveals that part of the task of the coaching parent is to find out why the child is feeling sad.

(Mother 108)

M: I think the thing Eric and I have learned from the Bible that when the other person is sad we're sad with him or when another person is happy, we're happy with him. That you're sharing in that and that kind of thing. So I think it's the kind of thing you share and when Josh was sad, I want to relate to that. I think often times when children are sad, we don't, we don't really empathize with their sadness. It may seem so trivial to us and we don't really let them go through that process of being sad. We just say, "Oh, you're going to be OK," you know.

I: Um-hmm

M: But they're hurting and, so J.'s sad, I try really hard to understand why it's that way. Why are you feeling sad. And, um, him being just a little boy, I think you can't expect too much out of him. But *I try to find out why he's feeling that way*. Some kid might of hit him or someone made fun of him or something. But my feelings toward him are my goodness, my heart just goes out to him. I just stop everything else at the moment and really empathize with him and try to support him and help him feel better.

Some parents link their coaching of their child's sadness with their own experience and expression of sadness, as with the following mother. Although this mother is cautious about who she shares her sadness with outside her home, she also values sharing sadness with intimate friends and family, and *the intimate aspect of sadness* is what she wants to teach her daughter.

(Mother 121)

M: I think sadness is real important. I think that if you don't feel sadness at some point whether it's in your life or during the week or anything, I think you're missing a big part of the importance of life. Umm, L. is a lot like me. We are both very sensitive, and umm, you know we can get sad watching "Highway to Heaven." Umm, we watched it together the other night, and we both sat there crying. And, I think "Highway to Heaven" is a real good show for her to watch, and I think that it allows her to learn how to express those feelings of sadness, you know because the kitty didn't get out of the house before it burned down. Umm, I think that's real important that you go through that stage.

I: Umm-hmm.

M: Everything isn't always happy and umm, happy-go-lucky you know.

M: I think that when L's going through sad times in her life, I think that it's a real important bonding stage between parent and child, especially when they're younger. Umm, it's important for me to be able to teach L., when *you're sad, come and talk to me. You know, I want to know, I want to talk to you, I want to know how you feel.* And, you know, sitting here saying, you know, "Well, I close myself off when I'm sad," I do, but yet I don't. You know, L will come up and say, you know, "Mommy what's wrong? Why aren't you smiling?" or, you know, "What's wrong?" And, I'll tell her. You know, "Well, such and such happened at work," or, umm, you know, "I ran over my toe with a chair" or something like that. You know, I do tell her and "Well, why?" and I try to explain it to her, you know, I don't want to completely shut her out 'cause I want her to know what my feelings are too [italics added].

The expression of empathy is critical to the coaching parent. We see this expressed very clearly by the following mother:

(Mother 108)

M: When, ah, hmm, boy, I don't think you can ever say. (Laughs.) I mean it depends on the situation, like obviously if there's a death in the family of someone who meant so much to you and you miss them terribly, that's going to take longer to really, you may never really get rid of that sadness. It may always be with you, it's just not obvious. But other things that come along, I think it's relative with what you're sad about. Um, ah, that's one thing that Eric and I have learned, you know, from the Bible, that when the other person is sad, we're sad with him or when another person is happy, we're happy with him. That you're sharing in that together and wanting the best for the other person and love things the best and that kind of thing. So I think it's the kind of thing you share and when J. was sad, I want to relate to that. I think often times when children are sad, we don't, we don't really empathize with their sadness. It may seem so trivial to us and we don't really let them go through that process of being sad. We just say, "Oh, you're going to be Ok," you know.

This empathy does not always come easily to this mother:

And I had to learn about children and why they are the way they are. They're not adults and so I don't know, with J. I have to try really hard to think about if it were me and I was a little person and it happened to me, how would I feel and everything and forget my adult judgment that knows that life goes on because a little kid doesn't feel that way at the time. But, I guess that's it.

The next step after empathy that this mother articulates is trying to understand why he feels the way he does:

> **I:** Um-hmm.
> **M:** But they're hurting and, so J.'s sad, I try really hard to understand why he's sad and what he's thinking and at the same time how I can relieve that sadness if possible or how to help him work through it. Let him talk about it. Things like that.

Avoiding Derogation.   Coaching parents clearly express the care they take in being critical of their children, making sure that they avoid using negative trait labels, or expressing their complaints in a destructive manner. For example, one mother said:

> (Mother 108)
> **M:** I think there's a lot of people that do walk around with chips on their shoulders and they'll just get angry about anything and, you know, they're really, they're wasting a lot of time in their life. But, um, (pause) I try very hard with my children, if I get angry at them, I really try to bite my tongue and to be careful not to say something that I wish I hadn't and never to attack them, their personal character. I mean, um, attack what they did (laughs) or, you know, the consequences of what they did or something like that but not to attack them. I don't know, anger is all right, it's just a matter of how you utilize it and not to use it to hurt somebody.

High Acceptance But Low in Coaching

Some families are very accepting about their child's sadness, but they do not help their child understand or learn from this emotion. They accept and value the experience, they do not criticize or constrain their child's expression, but they stop short at explaining or teaching. This type of family has a lot of empathy and may stress the importance of allowing their child to feel what he or she has to feel. They often respond to the questions in a very feeling way, and in their description and voice tone they may join their child in pain. At the instructional level, they may not have given sadness a lot of thought, nor have seen this emotion as a way to teach their child something valuable about life. Some feel that there's something else they want to be doing; some struggle in the interview with the meaning of their child's emotion experience, and seem genuinely puzzled about what they could do or what there is to teach a child about sadness.

In the following excerpt, this mother actively joins her daughter in acting sad, believing that it will help her daughter feel less alone and more normal. At the same time, there is a humorous quality to the sad act she describes with her daughter that suggests she does not really take this interaction seriously.

(Mother 138)

I: What's she like when she's sad? Does she get sad?

M: She gets sad. She tells me, she goes "Mommy, I'm sad."

I: OK, so she's got the label and everything.

M: I say, "Why are you sad?" (In a whiny, sympathetic voice).

I: You say it that way? (Laughs)

M: (Laughs). I try to just like she's doing, you know, even grin and she'll start telling me what the problem is and I forget what, and I can't even give you an instance. But I know there was one time I told her, I said, "Oh, Jennifer, well that makes me sad too." (Laughs.) And I let her know that, that it was OK for her to feel sad. You know I didn't want her to think like she had some strange, alien feeling or something like that. You know, it was just normal, and I said sometimes you feel sad, sometimes you feel happy and it's OK.

Another mother shares her son's sadness, but when she thinks of what there is to learn from it she focuses on the comfort of love and she does not go beyond comforting.

(Mother 134)

I: How do you feel when B. is sad?

M: Oh it hurts.

I: You get sad with him?

M: Ah, well, if he's sad like over his toy I can empathize and I empathize, but if you know, another child is mean to him, and it hurts his feelings and he gets upset over it, that hurts me too because that's something that it's harder to heal than things like with a toy.

I: OK.

M: I get sad with him.

I: By upset you mean upset, sympathetic or upset, sad right with him.

M: Yeah.

I: Is there something you are trying to teach B. by the way that you respond to him when you're feeling sad? Is there something you would like him to know about sadness?

M: Yeah. I try to let him know that I love him no matter what, and think that we think the world of him, and um, when different things have happened, you know, we both try to explain that. That's kind of the way life is at times.

Even though the idea of coaching is very simple, many parents struggle to find a way to relate to their child's sadness and don't know what to do beyond being understanding. In the next excerpt, the mother wants to be more involved in her son's experience of sadness, but she is not sure how to proceed. Her efforts so far at interpreting his feelings to him have not been successful. We would say that she is higher in accepting than in coaching of sadness. However, she is actively seeking a way reach her son when he's sad, and her lack of success may be constraining her confidence in articulating a philosophy about sadness. She is genuinely struggling for some way of going beyond comforting him, but doesn't know what to do.

I: When you see J. sad, how do you respond to him?

M: I have empathy, and um, I think I'm pretty matter of fact. Um, he brushes off his sadness. He's very explicit. He'll say no, I'm angry or I'm mad or I'm sad and it's usually he might be more mad. Somebody did something to him and I thought he was sad but then he says he feels mad.

I: Umm-hmm.

M: But there's a sadness there too so, I just know I have to be careful not to repeat too much to him, feedback too much to him. It's better to just hug him and say how are you now, or if I say I'm sorry that that happened he'll say, he'll get very agitated and say, you know, I didn't ask you to say I'm sorry! That kind of thing, you know, I'm really not quite sure what he wants me to do. I think if I listen and say, Mmmmm, that might be better because the minute I give any interpretation he turns off his feelings.

Her idea that perhaps she should say she is sorry, or perhaps that she should interpret his feelings has been unsuccessful.

I: Um-hmmm.

M: I guess I'm just beginning to realize that.

I: Um-hmmm.

M: I knew something wasn't working but I didn't know what to do. And I'd like to say, hmmm.

I: Empathize on what he feels.

M: Um-hmmm. But he does share, he'll come home and say I had a happy day. I had sort of happy day, I had a bad day at school, he'll tell me. But I better not ask too much, he'll tell me, and I think I didn't know what to do until now, Mmmmm. (Laughs.) So . . .

M: Oh it just makes him respond to the question, No you don't understand. It's kind of what he's feeling or sharing, I know it doesn't work. It doesn't work.

I: Umm-hmm. Well I have a question you may or may not have thought of before but what do you think you're trying to teach J. about sadness, about feeling and expressing sadness?

M: That, um, it's real and it's OK. Um, that there are things you can do about it. Um, but mainly just that it's OK.

I: To feel and express it.

M: Yeah. If you want to express, that it's going to be OK. I don't know what else to say.

RESPONDING TO A CHILD'S ANGER

The Dismissing or Disapproving Family

Families who are uncomfortable with the expression of negative emotion tend to disapprove of anger in their children more often than they disapprove of sadness. Sadness is more often dismissed than disapproved of when it is painful for a parent, while the more apparent quality of anger may provoke disapproval along with dismissal. For example, we were surprised to find that there were quite a few families we interviewed who actually used Time Out when their child was angry, not for misbehavior, but only for the expression of anger.

Disapproving of Anger

As with sadness, families who disapprove of anger tend to be critical and unempathic when describing their child's emotionality. The following mother thinks about what her disapproval is teaching her son about anger. She has a view of her son's temperament and is worried that he will turn out to be like her husband.

(Mother 170)
I: What about with N., does he get mad?

M: He's got a bad temper. Sometimes, oh, I don't know, with him, I tend to try and stop it because he is gonna have a bad temper like his dad and I guess I'm trying to teach that he shouldn't go all out with it and I really don't know how to teach him because he'll, you know, kick and holler for a while and then I'll spank him to try to calm him down.

I: Umm-hmm.

M: And that may be the wrong thing to do, you know, I don't know, but I really don't want him to have a really bad temper.

I: Umm-hmm, so you try to get him to stop being angry by spanking him and putting a limit on it?

M: Or talking to him, yeah, if I've had like a bad morning or something, usually I'll give him a whack or something, send him to his room, that's really not the right way to deal with it, I don't think, I should try to talk to him but, you know, it depends on the situation.

I: Is it hard to talk to him when he's angry?

M: Ah, sometimes because he's just, you know, going on and on and he's not hearing what I'm trying to say and that's when I, you know, get in your room and when he calms down we can talk it out.

I: Um-hmm.

M: But he's gonna have a bad temper I can tell.

I: Do you think there's something you're teaching him about being angry and feeling angry and showing that you're angry to other people?

M: I guess really I'm teaching him that it's not right to show it because I do tend to tell him to calm down or whatever and go to your room and when you settle down you can talk to me.

A father who disapproved of his son's sadness felt the same way about his son's anger.

(Father 182)

I: When he's angry, how do you respond to him?

F: Um, when he gets angry it just depends on the, um, you know, when it's a temper tantrum which he still throws a lot of them, you know, you just let him throw them basically. Um, but then when he starts getting a little destructive like he throws temper tantrums and then starts throwing things, then (laughs) then it's a little different. Then just say, "Hey, cool it or you go upstairs or you get spanked and go upstairs," you know. You try to say, "Hey, you're not going to get your way all the time, kid, sorry." Unfortunately, he thinks he can get his way all the time.

I: Could you sum up what you are trying to teach him about anger?

F: You know, it's all right in a sense, but most of the time in his case it's not.

The following father showed his disapproval of his son's anger by responding to queries about anger with descriptions of punishments. He offered no insight into what his son is trying to express via anger. In his view, anger is a situation to control with spankings or time out. We begin this excerpt with a description of how unproductive anger has been in this father's own life.

(Father 135)

F: . . . But when you do express your anger, are you being more productive toward, um, how should I say this? Toward your own situation, in life, for instance, like, I can be angry at my wife and sometimes, no not sometimes, all the time, it's not good. She doesn't want me to be angry at her. And, so, my being angry may help me, you know, at that point in time. But it's really going to be damaging to me as far as, she's gonna give me a lot of negative feedback from that. Not necessarily getting angry again, but I've had a lot of long term feedback from that one angry that helped me at that point. I, I'm not really sure that being angry really is a good and productive thing. Um, I guess it's what I'm trying to say is that I realize there is this emotion, anger, and we all use it or disuse it or abuse it, and, um, I really, I..

I: What about R. when he's angry? How do you feel when he gets angry?

F: Oh, I laugh a lot, I guess. Really, you know, kids are pretty funny when they're angry. Little tiny, you know, creatures, um, being willful like that. You know, "I'm gonna hurt you," and, "By golly!" It's really pretty funny. So I guess, more than anything else I'm kind of laughing inside, you know, chuckle, chuckle.

I: Do you show them that you're laughing?

F: I try not to ah, because, nobody needs to be ridiculed. Ah, then again sometime I think maybe I do let it peep through a little bit. I try to be good-natured more than anything else. I think somehow I try to, that's what I try to project, you know, good humor and consciousness I hope. So, you know, sometimes, it's good to, you know, have somebody poke at you when you're being angry. You know, you're not such a big stuff after all. You look pretty silly. Ah, sometimes, but a lot of times you got to go with the flow. I think, you know, I can't give you a pat answer for anything.

I: No, it's been very helpful. How does R. get out of anger?

F: Basically send him, we have time out for R. and that seems to work real good. Um, spanking doesn't work good for R., never did. You know, we tried it. There are times when spanking is more therapeutic for the parent than it is for the child, I think. Ah, like my younger son, J., spanking works. Ah, you know you say, "No," so many times. He's not going to listen, and if you pick him up and give him a spank, he knows, "Whoops, I really did cross that line." And you don't have to spank him hard or anything else, just the physical, you know, I did spank you, that is enough.

You know with R. it never did work. He pulled in and sulked, ah, you had to be more logical with R. You know, "Time out because you did this wrong," or, " You are not being acceptable right now." And especially anger, ah, it works great for him. You just put him in his room, let him calm down, give him five minutes, and he's ready for try something else again. And it works great.

I: Is there something that you are trying to teach him about anger or you are teaching him about being angry?

> **F:** I don't know if I really want to answer that or if I can. I'm sorry. It draws a blank on me. Teach him. You now, I, like I said, I'm really not. . . .

This father's disapproval is very apparent. His response to his son's anger is intended to eradicate anger. However, in addition to being disapproving, this response to anger is also an example of what we call a dismissive attitude toward emotion: an attitude that denies the importance of the child's experience of anger. When a parent is humorous or mocking of his child's experience, the parent is unlikely to make an effort to explore what the experience means to the child. The words and tone of voice often convey that the parent really does not want to be bothered with this child's emotion.

Dismissing Anger

What we find in a dismissing attitude toward anger is a sense that the child's anger, aside from dealing with the behavioral intrusions, is not important to the parent. These parents may belittle the child's experience or expression, suggesting that a child's anger is not to be taken seriously. They may show little interest in what the child is communicating, or in instructing their child regarding the nature of this emotion. Perhaps their child's anger makes them very uncomfortable, so they teach their child that anger is something you "do alone in your bedroom." This child may feel abandoned, physically or emotionally, when he or she is angry, and through that abandonment the child learns that anger will make him or her very lonely.

In the following excerpt, a mother minimizes the importance of her daughter's anger by making fun of her anger, both in the interview situation and, apparently, to the child herself.

> (Mother 141)
>
> **M:** I really have this thing. She's really cute. (Laughs). And, um, I just love her so much that even when she's angry I just kind of smile and of course it depends, you know, there are times when she's being completely ridiculous and I point that out to her usually. I just say, you know, can it or lighten up. (Laughs). Those are two of my favorite phrases to use with her. Um, I guess what I do wrong there, what I'm embarrassed about is I don't always take her seriously because she's so little and her face gets all (laughs) red and I tend to think of her as this little doll and, you know, isn't that funny. Obviously it's not funny to her, um, and then at other times, you know, I, I try to just gloss over it. I'm not, again, I'm not taking it seriously. I think that I don't handle it well. I think that my husband is much better. He diffuses her anger. I mean, he puts her onto something else or starts changing the subject or gets her interested in something else.

This same mother has difficulty dealing with her own anger. Note the use of "explosion metaphors" in her discussion of her own anger:

> **M:** Um, for me personally, anger tends to cloud my judgment and I do things that I regret.
>
> **I:** Um-hmm.
>
> **M:** And I don't like being angry. I don't like the way it makes me feel and I don't like the things that it makes me do. Ah, of course I'm responsible for my own actions and I have nobody to blame but myself and I think that anger is normal. Human beings become angry. I mean things do not go your way and it's not abnormal *to explode* sometimes when you're feeling angry. But I also think sometimes it comes from, ah, the more negative parts of life that would be selfish, or, for me it's just that I'm being selfish or I'm being, you know, just irritable, sleepy, often when I'm very tired or I'm very hungry, those are the two worst times for me, those are the times when I'm usually angered and, you know, it reminds me of those killer bees, (laughs), you know, and I just think, you know, I'm not accomplishing anything here and if I'd really just eaten a little snack, I probably would have handled this a little bit differently.
>
> **I:** You talked about how anger makes you do something. What is it that anger makes you do?
>
> **M:** Well, there will be times when my kids, they won't misbehave, maybe I have a legitimate complaint, but instead of handling it smoothly and with equanimity, the way I would if I weren't say hungry or tired or irritable for whatever reason, I yell. Ah, I, I just, you know, I yell. I raise my voice to a loud (laughs) extreme and all that really happens is that I probably make them disgusted with me or maybe they chew me out. I don't think I'm dealing with them as effectively [italics added].

Because this mother feels she's not good with her own anger, she is unsure of her ability to deal with her children's. She abdicates responsibility to her husband, and prefers to maintain a humorous stance when faced with her daughter's anger.

The following excerpt is the case of a father who has struggled with anger throughout his life, and has a difficult time taking his daughter's anger seriously. Here is what this father said about himself:

(Father 128)

> **I:** What emotions are still hard for you?
>
> **F:** Anger, I would say anger 'cause I can still have a violent moment. And I can, you know, go out and do something. That's probably my worst. If I've ever get to that point, if I, I'll rubber bank and stamp if anger finally got me I was so mad at something I'd go out and probably would hurt somebody. I wouldn't hurt S. I'd go out at the source, find out who it was.

I: How do you make sure that you don't feel angry that often if it's something you don't like to feel?

F: Ah, that's a hidden secret in my head. Um, I really don't know. I'm just saying that the intelligent half of my head talks to it. It says, "All right asshole, don't screw up." Talk, you know, "You're gonna go out, and you're gonna do something dumb, you're gonna get in all kinds of trouble, embarrass your family, and slow down and stop." I never, I guess I never let my mind get angry anymore. That's all. It's just that they do something dumb or they or I do something dumb, most of the time if I do get angry, it's because of me. I'll do something stupid.

And here is how he speaks of his 4-year-old daughter's anger.

F: (laughs) J. being mad? Ahh, when's the last time..I laugh.

I: You think it's cute?

F: I think, yeah, it is.

I: Uh-huh.

F: She, she, she'll, "Gosh darn it." And she'll walk away like a little midget human. It's so funny.

I: (Laughs). Well how does she react to when she watches you laugh?

F: Huh?

I: What does she, what do you think she thinks when she watches you laugh?

F: She gets embarrassed. Yeah, she'll go, she's got a shy streak in her about a mile thick. She'll go, "Daddy!" And then that's it.

In the following excerpt, a mother has no idea what to do with her own anger, so she can't deal with her son's anger. First she talks about her own experience with anger.

I: If, if you were angry with someone not in your family, somebody, a friend at work or something, how would you handle that?

M: (Sigh). I would probably just have to shut it up inside, and, if it was a close friend, I would probably raise my voice, you know, if I wasn't in a public place. If I were in a public place, I would probably deal with it later, just sort of, you know, try and calm myself down and then, you know, certainly talk about it later. Probably, you know, talk about it in a heated manner. Go home and talk to John, just sort of, you know, maybe, you know, stomp around the room and, you know, get angry like that.

I: And that, then you feel that, that gets it out of your system? And it's pretty much done then?

M: Yeah. Yeah, I think so.

When she speaks of her son's anger, it's as hard for her to provide details of what his anger is like as it is to describe how she responds to it. She initially shows a low awareness of her son's anger.

I: OK, let's talk about M. again. How do you respond to him and how does it make you feel when you see him angry?

M: I think it depends if, I think it's different from the crying, I think sometimes I get mad at him, and I'm not quite as free with support, I don't think. That, 'cause his anger can make me very mad sometimes depending on, you know, the reason for it. I don't know, maybe I do, I don't let him get rid of it. You know, I can't, if I could think of a specific instance, maybe I could think of how I deal with it. I can't think of anything right now. I can't think of how I've dealt with his anger.

I: Does he throw a tantrum?

M: Usually he still just cries. Ummmm

I: What kinds of things make him mad?

M: Ummm, mostly his little brother stealing his toys, or biting him, for good reason. But they, they like to quarrel a lot and most of the time, since it's M. who would go up to his room and stay there, you know, if they're mad at each other, I'll just separate them, you know, or if M. has done something, or if Rudy had done something to make M. angry, you know, I don't know, I think I let him deal with it. You now when I'll send him to his room, I'll hear toys being thrown, (laughs) screaming, yelling, and threats. (Laughs).

I: And so it's like, it's OK if he does it there then . . .

M: I think I let him deal with it by himself because I, you know when he gets angry sometimes it makes me mad and it seems to set us both off really badly, so. . .

In the following excerpt the father is somewhat dismissive in his "hands off" approach; he finds his daughter's anger amusing, and isn't particularly engaged in helping her work with it.

(Father 151)

F: IImm, I don't know, it doesn't, I would not be as coddling to her as when she's sad or hurt or something. Ah, anger, I don't want to, I never try and squelch her, I never say, you know, you have no reason to be angry, I'll say don't yell, OK, so you're mad, go ahead and be mad but don't, you know, affect others.

I: Umm-hmm.

F: Or just times when she gets really mad and goes and tries to, sometimes she'll do something that she normally would not do that would not necessarily hurt Jessica but to really bug her, just do something to annoy her.

I: Umm-hmm.

F: Just to be doing something against somebody else. And, ah, that I won't allow. I'll snag her. Otherwise, if she's angry and she wants to stomp around a little bit, and not, you know, not start (laughs) kickin the cat or throwin dishes on the floor or if she wants to vent her anger a little bit, I don't stand in her way. I don't say, oh good, now kick this (Laughs).

I: Yeah.

F: But I don't, I don't really say, you know, sit still and smile, you know (Laughs).

I: It's OK to feel it and only certain ways are OK to express it.

F: Yeah, it's ah, however you feel you should get it out would be, I would imagine she would choose the easiest and most releasing way to do it, and all I keep my eye on is how far she goes and that she doesn't affect somebody else. And affect their right to sit around without being poked in the eye or something. I wouldn't want to have that happen.

About his own anger that father confesses:

F: I just, I have a problem when someone hits that certain area, I have a problem with keeping my composure.

I: So if you did lose your composure, what would you do?

F: I, ah, depending on the degree, I have fairly recently, I guess a year, it may be something that happens every four to six months, you know, I usually can't get through a time longer than that where somebody says something where I react and rattle off some stuff to let them know my distaste for what they're doing, you know.

I: Right.

F: Um, and in the past, I've gotten really, you know, I've had people say really, in a way I removed myself from the position to a certain extent. I don't leave myself open to be in that position but I have had people at various times say just totally obnoxious, insulting, low type of stuff and I've gotten violent against them. Ah, and it just, it's something like, it's not a pre-meditated, if I sit there and plan how I'm going to hurt somebody, you know. It's like, if they say something really ignorant and I just (snaps fingers) POW!

I: And you actually hit them?

F: I might, you know, I have in the past back when I was much younger. (Laughs.) And didn't know I could go to jail for it (laughs) no, but, I ah, I've learned just I guess from maturity or something to keep my temper down.

The Coaching Family

Compare these dismissing and disapproving families to the coaching family. Especially when it comes to anger, the coaching family is quite different than the they use with anger, coaching families are willing to get involved and they are able to remain connected with an angry child. They can be present for the emotion as well as the situation. Rather than abandon their child when he is angry, they use this emotion experience to teach. They are able to teach what is acceptable behavior, and to distinguish this behavior from feelings, which are always acceptable. They find their child's anger interesting.

In the following excerpt, the mother is aware of the different facets of her daughter's anger, and it is obviously because she is really paying attention and thinking about it.

(Mother 121)

M: Ummm, L. is still learning as far as anger goes. She's learning with sadness, too, but anger is for a four year old just so much more exciting than it is to sit down and cry. Ummm, maybe because it shows them a lot more different things; it shows destruction; it shows, ummm, "Oh, boy I sure do feel better after I did that." Or, you know, it's just really neat to see what mommy and daddy's reaction is to all of these different things too, you know, to stomping down the hall, or throwing your food on the floor, or something like that. So I don't think she and I are alike in anger at all.

They make distinctions about which are appropriate behaviors, and are able to find things they like about their child's anger.

(same mother)

M: Ummmm, when she shows the anger of breaking the crayons because the white crayons doesn't work on white paper, ummm, that part of it I don't like. When she is angry at me because she doesn't like the way I'm talking to her, then, I like that because that shows she's learning. "Don't talk to me, L., I don't like that tone of voice. You hurt my feelings when you talk to me like that." I like that, ummm, it shows that she's maturing, she's growing up, and but more importantly, that she's listening and comprehending what I say to her. So that part of it I like, umm, you know, and there's the side that I have to turn my head and hold my cheeks so that I don't laugh at her, you know she's getting angry which is "Humph!" crossing her arms and stomping down the hall, you know, I think that's cute, but . . .

I: Can you summarize for us what it is you are trying to teach L. about anger and feeling angry?

M: There's different ways to, there's different types of anger, and there are different ways to express each type. And you have to be able to know how to do it. But to do, to express the anger in a constructive manner and not to be destructive with it.

Coaching families show respect for their child's emotionality. The anger is not unimportant because it is a child's anger.

(Father 144)

I: How do you respond to G. when she is angry?

F: I just let her, you know, anger usually doesn't last for a while. Usually when she's angry she has a reason to be. And we talk about why, you know. She has this friend she plays with, a boy, I mean, I don't watch them but she comes in crying and stuff and she's really mad. And I usually say that *she, you know, has every right to feel that way*. You know, you just talk about it. I mean I don't try to say you shouldn't be mad.

I: Umm-hmm. Just find out what is making her mad.

F: Right. And why and stuff like that.

I: Does it make you feel any particular way when you see her angry?

F: Not, like when she's sad I really want to cheer her up. When she's angry I get like I say, it's usually a pretty quick thing. I mean, I don't, I can't protect her from being angry, you know, why she's angry and how to deal with it. How to go back out and deal with this little boy or whatever it is that's making her angry, you know.

I: So . . .

F: So I don't have that protective feeling towards anger as I do towards sadness.

I: I have the same question that I asked earlier. What is it you think you're trying to teach her about anger and expressing anger?

F: Again it's just a natural fact of life. It's natural to feel that way. You know, whatever's making you angry, ah, if you want to keep on being angry about it, *you've got to deal with it one way or the other*. You know, you can walk away from it, you can confront it, whatever. That's what I want to teach her. There's some things that when you're angry it's best to walk away and forget it and there's other situations that it's best to confront [italics added].

Coaching families are able to be present when their child is angry. The father in the following excerpt sounds like he wants to be a place his son can come to when the child feels angry.

(Father 124)

F: I think first I should try to find out what's going on, you know, and if I couldn't make any kind of a judgment call about it at all you now, I'd just try to just be there, just kind of hang out so that whatever he wanted to do, you know, if he needed somebody to be there that I would be there.

F: Well, I think, yeah I, I think that if I've done something that he disagrees with, and we have a big argument, ummm, and he gets me to listen to his point of view, then that probably makes him feel a lot better because it gets resolved on his, on the terms that he wants it resolved on, rather than me saying, you know, "No, shut up. I don't want to hear this." You know, it rather than me giving him an order and saying, "I just don't want to listen to this," then *he gets to tell me what's going on at which time I learn what's going on, you know, then we settle it like two people rather than, you know, the guy and his dog.*

I: So you're really respectful of his anger and you say, "That's OK, you can have that. Let's talk about it."

F: Yeah, I respect him a great deal. I think he's a real neat person. Yeah. I think sometimes I lose sight of that, though, because he's also a child. You know, he's ummm, he's a lot more volatile than I am, you know, and so sometimes I tend to think it's just the emotions of the moment tend to carry me away, too. And so I'll get real emotional.

I: When he's getting emotional.

F: Sure. Sure. Yeah, sure. Umm-hmm. Yeah, I find that I'm a lot more, I'm a lot more free with my emotions with the kids but then that seems to be where they're coming from too, you know. They don't hold back anything, there aren't any rules.

I: Right.

F: Which is sort of neat. I sort of enjoy that.

What Does High Acceptance but Low Coaching of Anger Look Like?

A family that accepts anger but does not coach it tends to have a "hands off " philosophy about their child's anger. They may believe that managing anger is merely a matter of hydraulics; once released, the anger is over and done with, it is handled. Or they may espouse a philosophy of free expression but without having anything else in particular to teach about anger. In that case they may remain present but stay uninvolved, as a kind of minimal presence.

In the following example (#165), the mother is accepting of her son's anger, but she lets him go off on his own to work it out:

M: He never strikes out, you know, physically, he just goes off on his own.

She then explains that she is just like him:

I: No tantrums?

> **M:** No not tantrums, he doesn't throw himself down, he'll just cut you off. And I let him go, you know, I'm a loner when I'm angry so I figure maybe he's the same. He needs time, and then he'll come back and you never know a thing happened.

There is a kind of dismissing quality to her letting him go off on his own, and when asked about what she is trying to teach him, she says, "Oh, if I could just teach him to roll with the punches and accept people for what they are."

Another parent (#127) talked about being pleased that her child expressed his anger toward his older brother. However, this mother said that when her child is angry she does not intervene:

> **M:** [I want him to know] that there are gonna be a lot of things in life that are going to make you angry or that are not going to be the way you want them to be, but you just have to accept it. Be able to go on and try to do the best that you can.

So this mother engaged in no problem solving with her son, even though she accepted her son's anger, and even welcomes it because her philosophy is that one needs to learn how to endure even in the face of a frustrating world. The father of this child expressed a similar philosophy about anger. He is accepting of its expression:

> **F:** I'm sort of glad to see it, ah, because he's never really done that much of it, he's never really, his brother used to push him around when he was little, when he was younger (laughs) and, ah, and I'm glad to see he does it every once in a while.

He encourages the expression of his child's anger, saying that "because a lot of times when I'm angry I don't always say, ah, I keep it to myself a lot." But there is no problem solving with the child that follows this encouragement of the expression of anger.

Another father (#102) also described being accepting of his child's anger but not following up this acceptance with problem solving. He leaves the problem solving to his son:

> **F:** [Anger is] just something you have to learn to live with. He usually, like I said, he usually goes off by himself when he gets mad. I don't know if that's teaching him anything or not. I guess it is . . . I guess he teaches himself on that.

Distinguishing Anger and Sadness

We found in our families that an emotion philosophy may be emotion specific. Several parents remarked on how they responded differently to anger than sadness, and it does seem true that families often had different philosophies about the two emotions. As one father in the anger coaching section mentioned, he wanted to protect his daughter from sadness, but with anger he finds he can tolerate the emotion. With anger he problem solves to find out what there is to learn about the experience, but not because he wants to spare his daughter the emotion.

Some parents had a difficult time with some emotions in their children and found that portion of the interview very poignant. In the following excerpt the father mentions comforting his daughter, and seems very empathetic of his daughter's sadness. His voice sounds sad and it is difficult for him to articulate his thoughts about the emotion. He mentions earlier in the interview that he can't talk to his wife about his feelings, and that a lot of his own sadness is related to his marriage.

(Father 144)
I: What's R. like when she gets sad?
F: She kind of quiets down.
I: Is that what you do too when you're sad?
F: Yeah, the same way.
I: Is she kind of like her dad in that way?
F: Yeah.
I: How does it make you feel when she's sad?
F: Bad, I don't, (pause) I, I stop and think about it.
I: Uh-huh. Do you let her know that you can tell she's feeling sad?
F: Yeah. I try to talk to her. Tell her everything will be all right.
I: Um-hmm.
F: And I don't like to see her that way.
I: Does it make you sad to see her sad?
F: Yeah, I try to talk to her, tell her everything will be all right.
I: Umm-hmm.
F: And I don't like to see her that way.
I: Does it make you feel sad to see her sad?
F: Yeah, cause it makes me do a lot of thinking of why she's sad.
I: Uh-huh. Does that, it sounds like that makes you sad too.
F: Yeah.
I: OK. So this is going to be a real tough question that I'm going to ask you, most people don't think about this. Responding like you do to R.: letting her know that you see that's she's sad, trying to help her through that even

though you feel kind of sad yourself, can you see that maybe you're trying to teach her something about sadness, how to cope with sadness?

F: Well, in a way, yeah.

I: What's that? What are you trying to teach her?

F: Just, ah, well, I don't know; (laughs) it's hard to explain.

I: Sure, this is tough stuff.

F: Things will be all right. I think, you know, just trying to teach her that things will be all right if she's just got to hold on and sadness will go away sooner or later.

For some parents the distinction is between an emotion they respond to emotionally or one they do not.

(Father 118)

I: How does D.'s anger make you feel?

F: I've always been of the opinion personally that you get treated the way you treat people and vice versa.

I: So when she gets mad, you get mad at her.

F: Basically.

I: But, that wasn't the same with sadness though. When she gets sad, you didn't necessarily get sad.

F: But I'm a little cold you see.

I: With sadness, but not with anger.

F: Well, OK but they're not the same, they're not even close to the same emotions in my book.

For another father, the distinction is between an emotion he is teaching about, and one that he isn't.

(Father 123)

F: I don't know, you know, gee, I've slipped, we were talking about sadness before and as far as something like sadness I think that maybe I am trying to teach him something but as far as anger, I don't think there's ever, I don't know if I'm actually trying to teach him anything other than to just work through it, you know.

I: And working through it would be?

F: You know, the problem solving bit, why am I angry? What do I have to do to alleviate this condition? Or what must I do or what must I say to so and so.

I: Umm-hmm.

F: I don't know if there's anything I can honestly say like with sadness I would like to teach him a specific lesson but with anger I don't know if I'm trying to teach him any specific lesson about anger.

We often shared moments with parents as they gained insight into their responses to emotion within the interview process. Sometimes it was the insight of actually distinguishing an emotion, of discovering that they did experience it, like the father working on his awareness of sadness at the beginning of the chapter. Another parent, like the mother who ponders her son's sadness at the end of the sadness section, uses the interview experience as a time to explore what she would like to be doing with her son, what works and what doesn't when she responds to his sadness. In the following excerpt the mother had a moment of illumination regarding how she was responding to her son's emotion. She hadn't realized how different the messages were that she was conveying to her son about the acceptability of sadness versus anger. We close the chapter with her new insight:

(Mother 124)

M: Yeah, I'm just sort of realizing that maybe there is some kind of a double standard between letting him cry, that's OK, but anger, maybe, you know, "Don't have it," you know, "Go upstairs, get rid of it and then come down and be pleasant," you know. I can deal with the crying, you know, I can say, "Poor Max," and stroke his head, but when he's mad I don't say "Poor Max," and stroke his head, I say, "Take it somewhere else. I don't want to hear it." I don't know. It's kind of interesting.

I: Do you have an idea of what you'd like to teach him about it that may be different from what you actually do?

M: I don't think I've ever really thought about it. Maybe if you ask me in a week, I would have thought about it more, but, I just, I don't think I ever realized that I, I did different ways of, because they are similar emotions in some ways, you know. And I'm doing completely different things.

ARE THE META-EMOTION VARIABLES COGNITIVE OR EMOTIONAL?: ADDRESSING AN ANONYMOUS REVIEWER

In an anonymous review of our work, we encountered the criticism that our meta-emotion variables are not really emotions about emotions but cognitions about emotion. The major point we want to address involves our use of the term *meta-emotion,* which the reviewer thought ought to refer only to a particular emotion about an emotion (e.g., feeling guilty about anger), and the reviewer did not think that our use of the phrase "meta-emotion philosophy," which we designed to suggest that we were interested in cognitions about emotion as well as emotions about emotion, was adequate to deal with this limitation. The reviewer suggested that the two major variables we eventually extract from the coding of the interview for model building, namely, awareness and coaching, are not related to emotion but to something else, something purely cognitive.

Perhaps we can add some clarity here that might better address this anonymous reviewer's concern. It is important to point out that our meta-emotion interview pulls for all kinds of feelings and thoughts about the parent's own emotions about anger and sadness, the parent's reactions to the child's emotions about anger and sadness, the parent's responses to the child's anger and sadness, and the parent's reasoning about these responses (e.g., what the parent is trying to teach the child when responding to the child's anger, and so on). All of these are part of the interview. They often cannot be summarized with a single word like "guilt," but they are emotional responses to the child's anger or sadness.

We categorized all of these responses into the two global variables for each parent, awareness and coaching. The reviewer wrote that "it is cognitive, not emotional." Here we urge the reader to consider what the items on the meta-emotion coding system are tapping when they measure variation on these two variables. Remember that we are categorizing everything a parent is saying about the emotions of anger and sadness in themselves and their children, so we are categorizing emotion metaphors, emotion phrases, attitudes they express about an emotion or a child expressing that emotion, and so on.

OUR EMOTION COACHING
SUMMARY VARIABLE

High on This Variable

Examples of Emotion-Related Statements Parents Made. "I feel close to my child when he is sad." "When Jason is sad, it makes me feel like a real Dad, now my heart just goes out to him." "When Harriet is sad, I take some time to be with her and experience this feeling." "When my child is sad I let her know that I understand." "When my child gets sad, we share this together." "When Markie is sad, I want to know what he is thinking." "It makes me want to hold him close." "I feel affectionate." "I feel love even when he's upset and angry at me."

Examples of Emotion Metaphors and Concepts Parents Expressed. "Anger gives me energy and drive." "I think that sadness can be good and even productive." "Sadness tells you to slow down." "When I am sad, I know something is missing from my life." "Anger is just like clearing your throat, just clear it and go on." "In my view, attending to sadness is cleansing." "I want her to be sad like in the movies. It means she can feel and emphasize." "I often have the good cry, and I think she does that too." "Getting angry can be a relief, like a storm that finally happens."

Low on This Variable

Examples of Emotion-Related Statements Parents Made.   As we noted, this includes parents who are either *disapproving* of the child's emotion or *dismissing* of the child's emotion. Taken from the interview, this reflects comments like, "Seeing my child sad makes me uncomfortable." "I think that sadness is OK as long as it's under control." "A child's anger deserves a time out." "I get annoyed when my child acts sad." "Children often act sad just to get their own way." "She looks cute and silly when she's angry, like a little midget." "I warn him about not developing a bad character." "Her shouting scares me." "Molly gets into these *black moods.*"

Examples of Emotion Metaphors Parents Expressed.   "When people get angry they are just relieving themselves on others," and other disapproving examples that had to do with loss of control, humiliation in public, metaphors of fire, pressure, heat, and other explosion and violence metaphors for anger, and generally defeat, hopelessness, and pathology concerns about sadness.

AWARENESS VARIABLE

Only people who are aware of emotion and can differentially talk about nuances of emotion and emotion intensity find emotional expression to be acceptable. If the low awareness reaction to negative emotions needs to be a specific emotion paired to anger and sadness it would be **fear.** People low in awareness and coaching see these emotions as toxic and dangerous. Let us be specific and discuss each of our two variables in turn:

High on This Variable

These parents tended to believe that one should not stifle body's emotions, that it was good to pay attention to emotion, healthy and positive, that emotions are always there, a part of life, and it is best to be aware of them. They said things like it is best to get anger or sadness "out of your system" by becoming aware of it and then being able to deal with it. They believed that it was important to recognize smaller and less intense expressions of emotion to prevent them from escalating. They should speak in a differentiated manner about each emotion and the bodily sensations of each; for example some parents talked about the "delicious" aspects of sadness in some romantic movies but the awful grief that accompanies an important loss. These parents often described the physical sensations that accompanied an emotion, for example, "Sometimes I get so mad that my stomach is in knots."

Low on This Variable

This State Was Often So Aversive for Them That They Tended to Prefer Not to See It at All, So They Wouldn't Have to Deal With It. That is what we are tapping into with this variable. That is probably the essence of being low on the awareness variable. For example, one parent said, "When he gets on my nerves like that, I just tune him out," and "He's not sad much. It hurts me to see him sad though. I have to go out for a run." Many parents who expressed discomfort with their child's negative affect tended to view it as toxic and believed that it was their role to get the child out of the negative mood as quickly as possible also said that they and their children rarely showed the emotion, or to prove that they could survive the negative mood, that they can "roll with the punches." They seemed to be at a loss when asked to describe how they could tell when they or their children had the emotion, seemed unaware of what might make a child feel sad or angry, and what might be done about it. The often expressed the philosophy that the way to cope with negativity was to emphasize the positive aspects of life and to substitute a positive emotion for the negative emotion. They said that negative emotion must simply be endured, that the passage of time alone will solve emotional problems, that to get over a negative emotion just get on with life's routines, ignore the emotion and just go on, that anger or sadness meant loss of control, that feelings are private not public and that it is embarrassing to be sad or angry, and better not to be aware of it. These parents were often most aware of the demand component of a child's emotion (that they fix the world and make it perfect so that their child will not have this awful emotion).

Summary

As can be seen, these variables represent highly emotional reactions and metaphors to anger and sadness, even if their names "awareness" and "coaching" don't sound very emotional.

SUMMARY

Emotion-coaching parents are doing the following five things.

1. The parent is aware of the child's emotion.
2. The parent sees the child's emotion as an opportunity for intimacy or teaching.
3. The parent helps the child to verbally label the emotions the child is having.
4. The parent empathizes with or validates the child's emotion.
5. The parent helps the child to problem solve.

First, the parent is aware of the child's emotion. This generally means being aware of relatively lower intensity emotions. A child does not have to be weeping for a parent to detect the signs of sadness, nor be enraged for the parent to detect the signs of anger. It appears to be important to emotion-coaching parents to connect with their children when their children are being emotional before the negative emotion escalates to a high intensity.

Second, emotion-coaching parents see the child's negative emotion as an opportunity for intimacy or teaching. This is in marked contrast to emotion-dismissing parents, who see the child's negative emotion as an unreasonable demand that they fix the world so the child will never be unhappy, who see the negative emotion as toxic, to be changed as quickly as possible, and whose major lesson is that their children should minimize, endure, and get over the negative affective state quickly.

Third, the emotion-coaching parent empathizes with the child's emotion, is understanding and accepting about it, and communicates a genuine understanding of why having this emotion at this time in this situation makes sense to the parent. Ginott wrote about how this communication of validation needs to be dramatically different to be effective for the teenager, compared to the younger child. In this empathizing, the parent may soothe the child, calm the child, and use affection. It needs to be emphasized that it is not easy to do this empathizing when the parent is actually the target of the negative affect. Thus, this part of emotion coaching may require the parent to be nondefensive.

Fourth, the parent helps the child to verbally label the emotions that he or she is feeling. This need not involve standard labels (angry, afraid, sad), but they involve putting the feelings into words ("You felt that the way the teacher treated you was unfair").

Fifth, the parent helps the child problem solve. In this problem solving, emotion-coaching parents often set limits ("It's OK to be angry, but it's not OK to hit your brother") and describe appropriate behavior and consequences for inappropriate behavior. At times the will also help the child decide what they would wish would happen in this situation (goals), and what might work to accomplish these ends (strategies).

As we see in subsequent chapters in this book (and, amazingly, as Ginott also emphasized), emotion coaching is embedded in a constellation of parenting variables that involve: (a) avoiding derogating and insulting the child, or using negative trait labels, and (b) using authoritative (warmth, limit setting, structuring) and responsive parenting practices, practices we will call "scaffolding praising."

5

An Emotion Regulation Theory of Meta-Emotion, Parenting, and Child Outcomes

Written with Beverly Wilson

This chapter lays the cornerstone for the models we work with in this book. It builds the theoretical foundation for the work, introducing our major variables for meta-emotion, parenting, the child's regulatory physiology, the concept of emotion regulation as we use it, and the developmental outcomes we have studied. Because we have selected a social psychophysiological approach to studying families, we construct an "Emotion Regulation Theory" of emotion in families and its linkages to child peer social competence and other developmental outcomes.

In this chapter, we discuss the theoretical model that has guided the design of our research and data analysis. We attempted to construct a theoretical model that was parsimonious and integrated behavior, thought, and physiology. We also sought a model that would make it possible for us to analyze linkages across systems, including marital, parent–child, and child–peer systems, and to generalize across child cognitive and affective domains. We also wanted a theory that was useful in discussing developmental change. With this tall order for a theory, we began reviewing a variety of literatures.

BUILDING A MODEL

We discuss the selection of variables from four domains: (a) meta-emotion, (b) parenting, (c) child regulatory physiology, and (d) child emotion regulation abilities in creating a model that can predict and understand the child outcomes we have selected for study. In this section we want to introduce this discussion as a conceptual path model that states our major expectations and predictions. We then discuss the selection of variables for this modeling.

Parenting and Meta-Emotion Structure

As we discuss, there is evidence that from the beginning of a child's life, parents' interaction with the child has implications for the child's ability to self-regulate, focus attention, share intersubjective meaning, form the essential affectional bonds with parents, and be able to interact with a changing environment. Evidence suggests that the parents' early emotional interactional style with their infants affects the very basic propensities that children have in approaching and exploring a novel stimulus or withdrawing, and in the formation of attachment. As children develop, the child's developing emotion regulation abilities are directly influenced by parenting and by the way parents talk to children about their emotions.

We expect that the parents' meta-emotion structure will be related to the three dimensions of parenting that we discuss. The first parenting dimension, which we call Derogation, is a negative style of parenting that involves being critical, mocking the child, and being intrusive in a parental teaching task. We expect that parents who have a coaching meta-emotion structure will be less likely than other parents to be critical, intrusive, or mocking with their children. The second dimension of parenting, which we call Warmth, shows warmth toward the child, as well as the parents' warmth toward one another when they are with the child. The third dimension of parenting, which we call Scaffolding/Praising parenting, involves being affectionate, enthusiastic, engaged, responsive to the child, and positive in structuring a learning task. We expect that the parental meta-emotion structure relates to these three dimensions of parenting, but we were not sure at the outset how it would relate, and we had two separate hypotheses about the potential relationship.

Child Regulatory Physiology

As we discuss, we expect that both parenting and meta-emotion variables will affect the child's regulatory physiology, particularly the child's basal vagal tone and the child's ability to suppress vagal tone. This regulatory physiology is central to our thinking in building a balance systems theory.

Emotion Regulation

We expect that parenting and the child's regulatory physiology will affect a child's ability to regulate emotion, particularly to down-regulate negative emotions. These variables will then affect child outcomes. This conceptual model is summarized as Fig. 5.1.

We now review research from each of the four domains of process variables and discuss the selection of variables for the model.

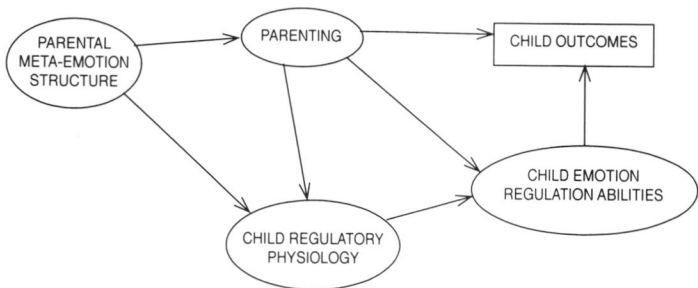

FIG. 5.1. Summary model for how parental meta-emotion structure might influence child outcomes.

PARENTING AND PARENTAL
META-EMOTION STRUCTURE

The History of Childhood

We now know that the way we believe that children should be treated is the result of a long historical evolution. deMausse's (1974) essay titled *The Evolution of Childhood,* was an extensive review of multiple historical sources on the way society urged parents to treat children. The history of childhood is replete with practices that today are horrifying, such as the sale of children, the common and standard sexual use of children by adults; the abandonment of children to a wet nurse for the child's first 3 to 5 years of life; food deprivation; tying up, hitting, and swaddling as punishment for crying infants; using alcohol, opium, and swaddling as a technique for keeping children immobile; and the general belief that beating and flogging were good practices for child discipline (which lasted up to the 1800s). Probably the most upsetting aspect of deMausse's history is his chronicling of the steady practice of neglect and physical brutality and abuse toward children throughout the centuries, replaced in the 1800s by psychological forms of cruel punishment like locking children in dark closets.

One can find examples in history of affectionate relationships between parent and child. We can cite Hesiod's (1993) work from ancient Egypt entitled *The Days,* which contains affectionate advice from an industrious uncle to a lazy nephew or Rawson's (1991) edited book on family life in aristocratic pre-Christian ancient Rome to find some exceptions to deMausse's overall summary. However, although some historians have criticized deMausse's review, his findings have not been disputed.

Today such parental practices are considered illegal and deviant. Children are protected by law from such treatment, which, fortunately, we now consider as abuse. However, it is important to point out that many families today live under extreme conditions of poverty and stress in which many life transitions (moving, change of job, change of primary relationships) are typical. In these and other families, such as families with antisocial or rejecting parents (e.g., Myers, Alvy, Arrington, & Richardson, 1992; Simons, Robertson, & Downs, 1989; Whitbeck, Hoyt, Simons, & Conger, 1992), the neglect or abuse that children experience can be extreme. Charlotte Patterson's (1991) classic paper (Patterson, Vaden, & Kupersmidt, 1991) documented the amazing amount of monotonic prediction these cumulative stresses on families can have in predicting a child's rejection by peers and general preparation for failure when the range of families in a sample is extreme.

We need to point out the extremely important fact that our sample is quite normal and does not contain these extremes in family stress or poverty, or deviations in parental personality that would make the prediction of child outcomes a much easier task. Hence, we have a restricted range of parenting types in our sample, which should work against us in attempting to predict variation in child outcomes.

Meta-Emotion and Parenting

Theoretically, we think our measures of parental meta-emotion structure are embedded within a web of measures that tap parent–child interaction. We expect that parents' meta-emotion structure is not independent of their parenting (see chapter 8). Hence, in our models we include meta-emotion variables along with parenting variables.

We need to be more specific about our description of parenting, and, for heuristic purposes, within the restricted range of families in our samples, we begin by discussing our three dimensions of parenting behaviors. We begin with everyday, mundane negativity. Inherent in the literature on parenting is the idea that small things in everyday parenting can be quite harmful for children (or serve as indices of more harmful types of parenting), akin to what J. Reid has called "nattering" (see Patterson, 1982). Ginott wrote strongly about this in his discussion of the importance of understanding and validating the child's emotions, and avoiding contempt and disapproval. Thus, in our measurement of this negativity in parent–child interaction, we include three variables: parental intrusiveness, criticism, and mockery, derived from our Kahen coding systems. We call this type of parenting Derogatory. In a teaching task, as some of the parents in our laboratory instruct their children, they mix in a blend of frustration, taking over for the child as soon as the child has trouble with the task (which we call "intrusiveness"), criticism, and derisive humor (mockery, humiliation, belittling the child). Usually, these are behaviors displayed by parents whose desire is not to inflict harm. Most of the parents in our samples do not beat their children.

Most are not particularly violent. However, as we show, their behavior is none-theless dangerous to their children's development. In fact, we think that *this dimension of parenting represents the micro-social processes characteristic of parental rejection.*

As we noted earlier, we also wish to measure two kinds of positive parenting. The first is the kind of warmth that Baumrind and others described, and which we reviewed in chapter 1; like others, we refer to this dimension of positive parenting as Warmth. The second dimension of positive parenting involves a positive structuring, responsive, enthusiastic, engaged, and affectionate parenting during the teaching task in our laboratory. This type of positive parental response goes beyond warmth to include the responsive style that attachment theorists have identified, a dimension that we call Scaffolding/Praising parenting. It is a dimension similar to Baumrind's Authoritative parenting, but it also contains codes for responsiveness and engagement, similar to those introduced by the attachment theorists. This type of positive parenting was observed in the context of parents obtaining information from the child (asking the child questions about a story the child had just heard) and the context of parents teaching the child something new. We have called this positive form of parenting *Scaffolding/Praising* because it is, in part, similar to the general scaffolding concept (see Choi, 1993; Kirchner, 1991; Pratt, Kerig, Cowan, & Cowan, 1988; Vygotsky, 1987). However, the pattern of behaviors also goes beyond traditional definitions of scaffolding. Here is what we noticed about the Scaffolding/Praising parenting pattern: Parents high on the Scaffolding/Praising dimension provide structure for the task, stating the goals and procedures of the game simply, in a relaxed manner, with low information density. They then wait for their child to act, and comment primarily when the child has done something right, acting like a "cheering section" at a football game, giving praise and approval. Parents low on this Scaffolding/Praising dimension, on the other hand, provide little structure for the learning situation for their children, they give information rapidly, with high density, and enthusiastically, appearing to excite and confuse the child. Then they wait to comment until their child has made a mistake; they are then usually critical of the child's performance.

What is the relationship between meta-emotion and the Derogation, Warmth and Scaffolding/Parenting dimensions? When we began, we had two working hypotheses. The first hypothesis was that a Coaching meta-emotion structure might be nested within a web of Warm parenting, including warmth, and co-warmth (between parents), or perhaps nested within a web of positive parenting variables we call Scaffolding/Praising. The second hypothesis was that meta-emotion performed its major function by inhibiting parental Derogation, particularly, as Ginott noted, that understanding and validating the child's emotions serves to avoid criticism, contempt, and disapproval of the child. Both hypotheses seemed reasonable to us.

Emotion Coaching Meta-Emotion Structure

As we described qualitatively in chapter 4, in our pilot work we noticed that there are those parents who are aware of the emotions in their lives, particularly the negative emotions, can talk about them in a differentiated manner, accept these emotions in themselves and their children, are aware of these emotions in their children, and assist their children with their emotions of anger and sadness, acting like an emotion coach. In our qualitative discussion of the interview, we described a parental meta-emotion structure we called an emotion-coaching structure. This was a meta-emotion structure in which parents valued their children's emotional expressions, had a high degree of awareness of their own emotions, and assisted their children with their emotions, acting like an emotion coach.

We hypothesize that these parents have a greater ability than other parents to maneuver in the world of emotions, they are more comfortable with the world of emotions, and they are better able to regulate emotions. We expect that these parents will not avoid conflict in their parent–child relationships, nor in their marital relationships, and they will not have a negative view of conflict. We also expect them to be better at coping with stress, we expect them to be more affectionate with their children and less autocratic than other parents. It is our hypothesis that a coaching parental meta-emotion structure is different from parental warmth, that it adds something extra. We are not sure how it might interact with Derogation and Scaffolding/Praising parenting to affect child outcomes. Very concerned, generally positive and warm parents can be oblivious to the world of emotion in their own lives and of children's emotions as well. For example, Faber and Mazlich (1987), in their book *Siblings Without Rivalry* quote a father in one of their groups. This man said that he was worried about all their emphasis on emotion; that emotion was exactly what he wanted to see *less of* in his family. At the end of a day, when he came home from work, both his wife and his children were highly charged and emotional, and he just wanted far less emotion from everybody in the family. He said he was especially concerned about their idea of encouraging children to express their emotions. Because they lacked the adequate self control of adults, eventually things would escalate and then children would be emotional all the time. This man had a meta-emotion structure that linked expressing emotion with being out of control, and he felt that children did not express emotion unless they were out of control. He certainly did not see part of his role as a father to detect and empathize with his children's emotional expressions. In fact, in his view if he did this he would be encouraging a loss of control in his children. There is probably nothing bad or cruel in this man's concerns. But his concerns are a reflection of a particular meta-emotion structure, one that is not oriented toward emotion coaching. Far less extreme examples than complete disapproval of emotional expressions abound in our interviews with parents who are quite good at being warm and setting limits with their children (see chapter 19 on emotion metaphors). An emotion-coaching meta-emotion structure is something additional that these parents bring to their roles as parents. We expect that warmth and limit setting may be correlated with emotion-coaching meta-emotion variables, but we think that they are not the same dimensions of parenting. Hence, we had two hypotheses at the outset.

Hypothesis #1: Meta-Emotion Is Related to Warmth and the Scaffolding/ Praising Dimension.   On the one hand, we could expect that a coaching meta-emotion structure would imply either that parents are Warm, or that they are Scaffolding/Praising, or both. To measure parental warmth, we have employed the Cowans' observational system, which codes parental coldness and parental warmth, both toward the child, and toward one another (called "co-parenting" warmth and coldness). To measure the Scaffolding/Praising dimension, we used our laboratory's Kahen engagement and affect coding systems. We proposed that an emotion-coaching meta-emotion structure entails parenting that goes beyond the idea of warmth. Thus, to summarize, we hypothesize that a coaching meta-emotion structure entails another step beyond parental warmth, that is, we suggest that it entails (but is not the same as) Scaffolding/Praising parenting. For this variable, we computed the sum of the following five variables selected from the Kahen Engagement and Affect Coding Systems, which we have called Scaffolding/Praising: three positive engagement codes: (a) Engaged, which consisted of parental attention toward the child, (b) Responds to Child's Nccds, in which parents responded to a child's question or complaint; and (c) Positive Directiveness, in which parents issued a directive in a positive fashion. The sum also included two positive affect codes: (a) Affection, which consisted of praise and physical affection, and (b) Enthusiasm, which was coded as cheering and excitement at the child's performance. We omitted the father's enthusiasm code from this sum, because we found that, for the father alone, our enthusiasm code was significantly correlated with his criticism. This was not the case for the mother.

The hypothesis that this form of positive parenting should be related to a coaching meta-emotion structure is implicit in the writing of Ginott. However, we also propose an alternative hypothesis.

Hypothesis #2: Meta-Emotion Inhibits Derogation, but It May Be Unrelated to Positive Parenting.   Most of the examples from Ginott's books, as well as Faber and Mazlich's books have to do with the importance of emotion coaching in avoiding escalating negativity, frustration, disapproval, and increasing emotional distance between parents and children. It appears to have been first suggested as a mechanism for obtaining extensive relief from spiraling negativity. Hence, it is entirely reasonable to hypothesize that the major effect of a coaching meta-emotion structure will be inhibiting parental negativity. To measure this form of negativity we used the codes of our Kahen coding systems that tap parental intrusiveness, criticism, and mockery of the child.

Another reason we suggested this hypothesis came from our increasing awareness of the father's role in the emotional life of his children, and the impact of this involvement on the marriage as well as the children. We expect that the father's involvement with the child's emotions will turn out to be very important in our data. The importance of fathers has been pointed out for some time by several writers, most notably Parke (1981), Lamb (1981, 1986, 1987), and Levant (1988). Recently, we were struck by an example from Schwartz's (1994) book about peer marriages, in which she compared a father who was emotionally involved with his children to a more traditional father. The traditional father typically asked the children about their day at dinner, saying, "Children, how was your day?" and they answered in chorus, "Fine." That was the end of that conversation, and the father seemed puzzled that his wife quietly fumed about how little her husband knew about his children's lives. This lack of knowledge was symptomatic of this father's general lack of emotional involvement in the family. In contrast, at dinner, an emotionally involved father's question was specific and detailed, revealing his knowledge of his children's everyday life names of their friends, their immediate thoughts and concerns. The involved father knew the names of his children's friends, what the children did every day, what their concerns were, and so on. In short, he knew quite a lot about his children's social and emotional worlds. Fathers of this sort do not get their knowledge of their children's emotional worlds without quite a lot of time and active involvement with the children when they are having emotions. As Schwartz (1994) suggested, the father's active involvement with his children's daily lives and emotions is related to the quality of his involvement in the marriage as well. For these reasons, we do not expect parental meta-emotion structure to be limited to the parent–child system, but to be related to the parents' marriage as well (see chapter 13).

CHILD REGULATORY PHYSIOLOGY

In building our Emotion Regulation theory, we need to discuss two opponent processes in the child's autonomic nervous system, which we call the vagal "brake" and the sympathetic "accelerator." Crudely speaking, the vagal brake slows many physiological processes down, such as the heart's rate, whereas the sympathetic accelerator acts to speed them up. Each of these processes influence emotion regulation. They are discussed in more detail in Appendix 5.1. Briefly, there are two classes of opponent physiological processes, those mediated by the parasympathetic nervous system (PNS), primarily through the X-th cranial, or "vagus nerve" (so called because it is the "vagabond" nerve that travels throughout the body, innervating the viscera), and those mediated by the sympathetic nervous system (SNS), typically measured either by heart rate reactivity, or stress-related endocrine responses (e.g., adrenaline secretion). Research by Porges and his colleagues on the PNS indicates a strong association between high vagal tone and good attentional abilities, and there is evidence that these processes are related to emotion regulation abilities. Evidence for this contention has come from various sources (e.g., Fox, 1989; Fox & Field, 1989). Also, the suppression of vagal tone appears to be a necessary physiological state for sustained attention. Research on the SNS indicates that endocrine secretion of catecholamines and cardiovascular reactivity are related to both attention and behavior and to the resiliency of children by directing the allocation of these resources.

Porges (1984) reviewed evidence that suggests that a child's baseline vagal tone is related to the child's capacity to react and to self regulate. Porges' research in the early 1970s (Porges, 1972, 1973) demonstrated a link between heart rate reactivity and spontaneous base-level heart rate variability. Initially the demonstration was that among college students baseline heart rate variability was related to heart rate reactivity and to reaction time (higher variability was related to faster reaction times). This was extended to newborn infants' heart rate variability and their reaction to simple visual and auditory stimuli (Porges, Arnold, & Forbes, 1973); newborns with greater heart rate variability had shorter latency responses and only the infants with high heart rate variability responded to the stimuli as the illumination was lowered. Because heart rate variability is related to many factors other than the functioning of the vagus nerve (respiratory, blood pressure changes, thermoregulatory influences), Porges and his colleagues developed a more precise measure of the tonic functioning of the vagus ("vagal tone") by using only that portion of heart rate variability that is related to respiration (known as respiratory sinus arrhythmia). It is well-known that the heart rate increases when we inhale and decreases when we exhale, and this induces a rhythmic respiratory component into heart rate variability, which can be extracted statistically with the methods known as time-series analysis (e.g., Gottman, 1981; Williams and Gottman, 1981).

Porges (1984) showed that baseline vagal tone is related to reactivity as well as to regulatory processes. During circumcision, infants with a higher vagal tone showed larger heart rate accelerations and lower fundamental cry frequencies (Porter, Porges, & Marshall, 1988). Behavioral reactivity and irritability on the Neonatal Behavioral Assessment Scale were also associated with higher basal vagal tone. DiPietro and Porges (1991) found that vagal tone was related to reactivity to gavage feeding. Fox (1989) found that infants who had higher basal vagal tone were more likely to cry during mild arm restraint than infants lower in vagal tone.

However, this relationship of basal vagal tone to reactivity is also usually associated with greater regulatory abilities as well. Linnemeyer and Porges (1986) found that infants with higher vagal tone were more likely to look longer at novel stimuli. Richards (1985, 1987) found that infants with higher basal vagal tone were less distractible. Infants with higher vagal tone habituate to novel stimuli more rapidly than infants with a lower vagal tone (Huffman, Bryan, Pederson, & Porges, 1988). Hofheimer and Lawson (1988) found that basal vagal tone with premature infants was significantly correlated with the percentage of focused attention they exhibited while with the mother; the high vagal tone infant's higher reactivity may predispose the infant to receive greater caretaking responses and this ability to maintain attention when with the mother may also predispose these infants to be able to elicit more face-to-face positive interaction from the mother as well. Huffman et al. also found a relationship between higher vagal tone and greater soothability, little soothing was required and distress was easily relieved. Fox (Fox, 1989; Stifter & Fox, 1990; Stifter, Fox, & Porges, 1989) also found that the same infants who at 5 months had higher basal vagal tone were more reactive at 5 months to mild arm restraint, by 14 months they were better at self-soothing, higher in exploring a potentially scary novel stimulus, and more likely to approach a stranger. Soumi and his associates found that there were two kinds of male monkey who leave the troop. One type of male, higher in basal vagal tone, who is far less socially isolated than the another type leaves the troop early, usually in the company of other male friends, and enters a new troop quite directly. The other type of male is more tense, more of a loner, leaves later, and if he successfully enters a new troop at all, enters more indirectly, by first linking up with more marginal members (e.g., Rasmussen, Fellowes, Byrne, & Suomi, 1988).

Although there is evidence that infants with high vagal tone are more facially expressive in response to mild arm restraint, the relationship between vagal tone and emotional expressivity may change with the development of emotion regulation abilities. Maccoby (1980) suggested that the preschool years are the major period for the development of emotionally expressive control, and it may be the case that children in this age range with higher vagal tone are *less* emotionally expressive than children with lower vagal tone. We see later that this is indeed the case with our data.

However, there is another dimension of vagal tone that needs to be considered, namely, *the ability to suppress vagal tone*. In general, vagal tone is suppressed during states that require focused or sustained attention, mental effort, focusing on relevant information and organized responses to stress. Thus, the child's ability to perform a transitory suppression of vagal tone in response to environmental, and particularly emotional demands, is another index that needs to be added to the child regulatory physiology construct. Some infants with a high vagal tone who were unable to suppress vagal tone in attention-demanding tasks exhibited other regulatory disorders (e.g., sleep disorders). Porges (1991) wrote:

> Three studies have been conducted with infants who exhibit regulatory disorders . . . First, these infants tend to have a high vagal tone, and second, they tend to exhibit a defect in their ability to suppress vagal tone during attention-demanding situations. It appears that these "fussy babies" are highly reactive to not only the

environmental stimuli but also to visceral feedback . . . Other populations with attentional deficits also exhibit an inability to suppress heart rate variability or vagal tone during task demands. (p. 124)

For example, in comparing hyperactive children to retarded children, Porges, Walter, Korb, and Sprague (1975) found that the retarded children do not suppress vagal tone and they have a lower baseline heart rate variability, whereas hyperactive children were more likely to have normal levels of baseline heart rate variability but a deficit in suppression during task demands. Huffman, Bryan, Pederson, and Porges (1992) used the Garcia-Coll Behavioral Responsiveness Paradigm (BRP) with 3-month-old infants. Infants who suppressed vagal tone during the BRP were rated by their mothers as having longer durations of orienting, more frequent laughing and smiling, and greater ease in soothability as compared to infants who failed to suppress vagal tone. Porges, Doussard-Roosevelt, Portales, and Suess (1994) found that 9-month-old infants who had lower baseline vagal tone and less vagal tone suppression during the Bayley examination had the greatest behavioral problems at 3 years of age, as measured by the Achenbach & Edelbrock Child Behavior Checklist. Measures of infant temperament derived from maternal reports (Bates, 1980) were not related to the 3-year outcome measures.[1]

Sympathetic Nervous System

We have not discussed the sympathetic branch of the autonomic nervous system, but we think that it is important to measure this branch as well (see Appendix 5.1). Stresses are known to increase adrenal responses through either the sympathetic nervous system, which gives rise to increased secretions of the catecholamines (dopamine, norepinephrine, and epinephrine) or the hypothalamic-pituitary-adrenocortical axis, which gives rise to increases in cortisol (see Gunnar, Connors, Isensee, & Wall, 1988; Larson, Gunnar, & Hertsgaard, 1991); also, the adrenal medulla and adrenal cortex are known to interact (Axelrod & Reisine, 1984). The catecholamines are secreted by the adrenal medulla in response to direct stimulation from preganglionic sympathetic neurons; cortisol is secreted by the adrenal cortex in response to pituitary-hypothalamic secretions, as well as by feedback from the adrenal medulla. Kagan and associates (e.g., Kagan, Resnick, & Snidman, 1988) found support for the contention that behaviorally inhibited children are higher in baseline heart rate, lower in basal heart rate variability,

---

[1]Porges and Doussard-Roosevelt (in press) point out that we must be cautious about expecting the suppression of vagal tone to always be the appropriate vagal response to external demands. In the neonatal intensive care unit the appropriate response to gavage feeding turned out to be increases in vagal tone, consistent with the support of digestive processes (DiPietro & Porges, 1991). Premature infants who increased vagal tone during gavage feeding had significantly shorter hospitalizations.

and higher in cortisol secretions. We (Gottman & Katz, 1989) have found that children who experience chronically high levels of stress in their lives due to having unhappily married parents will be elevated in stress-related urinary hormones, such as adrenaline, and that this chronically high level of stress will negatively affect both their physical health and their peer play. These sympathetic responses will interact with the parasympathetic nervous system. Porges (1991b) wrote:

> Under some conditions, however, psychological factors may elicit major changes in autonomic tone and disrupt ongoing homeostatic processes . . . and when vagal tone is withdrawn from the periphery and the excitation of the sympathetics is maintained for long periods, normal central nervous system functioning may be compromised. (p.118)

In our research, we collected a 24-hour urine sample and assayed this sample for the stress-related hormones, the catecholamines (epinephrine, norepinephrine, and dopamine), and cortisol.

EMOTION REGULATION ABILITIES AND DEVELOPMENT

The ability to regulate emotion is probably learned by infants, to some degree, through interactions with parents. Some writers have suggested that these abilities are also, to some extent, temperamental. Rothbart and Derryberry (1981) suggested that individual differences in reactivity and self-regulatory processes underlie much of an infant's affective, cognitive, and social behavior. Reactivity refers to the threshold, intensity, and latency of an infant's reactions to changes in the environment. Individual differences in reactivity may also influence interactions with caregivers (Porges, 1991b). For example, irritable reactive infants may initiate more interactions with caregivers than more placid infants. In addition, infants who are more reactive to both negative and positive events may provide caregivers with more information about their optimal level of stimulation and preferred modes of interaction (Rothbart & Derryberry, 1981).

The development of physiological homeostasis, which develops in the very first few months of life, is considered a crucial task for infants because it enables them to shift their energy and attention from the inner to the outer world. It also provides an optimal state for the reception of sensory and social information. This state has been referred to as one of alert inactivity (Stern, 1985). During these times infants are physically quiet, yet alert and apparently able to take in information from the outside world. Infants who are highly reactive yet are able to modulate their reactivity should be better able to benefit from experiences in their environment. For example, infants with high vagal tone are more reactive to stimulation than infants with low vagal tone, yet are able to modulate this reactivity (Fox, 1989).

As we mentioned earlier, Fox (1989) found that infants with high vagal tone were more reactive to both negative and positive stimulation than infants with low vagal tone. At 5 months, infants with high vagal tone were also more likely to use emotion regulation strategies when they encountered aversive situations (e.g., having their arms held down to their side). Other studies indicate that infants with high vagal tone look at novel stimuli for longer periods of time, are less distractible, and have greater attentional abilities than infants with low vagal tone (Huffman, Bryan, Pederson, & Porges, 1988; Linnemeyer & Porges, 1986). Thus, once in a state of alert inactivity, infants with high vagal tone may be more able to take advantage of relevant information from their environment. To achieve this optimal state, however, infants must first develop means to modulate their reactivity.

Learning to modulate reactivity may be influenced by individual differences in latency to peak arousal state. For some infants reactivity builds rapidly after the presentation of a stimulus, whereas for others it builds more slowly (Rothbart & Posner, 1985). An infant whose reactivity builds too rapidly may have less time to practice self-regulatory behaviors. Stern (1985) proposed that coping and regulatory strategies are acquired in the space between the initial threshold for peak arousal and the point at which behavior becomes disorganized (e.g., when the infant cries). In highly reactive infants, this window may be very small. Thus, these infants may have fewer opportunities for learning and practicing these abilities. These infants and their caregivers also experience fewer opportunities to learn early signs of the forthcoming distress. This decreases the probability that appropriate changes in the level of stimulation can be made before behavioral disorganization occurs. These events may be experienced by some young children with cardiovascular reactivity and may interfere with their acquisition of effective regulatory strategies.

As we noted earlier, basal vagal tone has been associated with both reactivity and self-regulation. Newborns with high vagal tone are highly reactive, more irritable, and initially have greater difficulty soothing themselves then those with low vagal tone; at 3 months, infants with high vagal tone are high in reactivity but they are also more easily soothed than infants with low vagal tone; 5-month-old infants with high vagal tone are more likely to employ selective attention strategies to calm themselves when distressed than infants with low vagal tone. These infants divert their attention to objects or other things in the environment when exposed to stressors. At 14 months they were also more likely to approach novel objects and people with less apparent apprehension or stress. Rothbart and Posner (1985) suggested that the ability to attend selectively to stimuli in the environment provides multiple strategies for dealing with physiological arousal. Thus, the attentional abilities of young infants with high vagal tone may provide a protective function for these infants. It may be that early in life, infants with high vagal tone are more likely to elicit both care and positive affectional interactions from their caregivers via their higher reactivity and higher ability to sustain attention. Frequent and effective soothing episodes and positive affect with caregivers in combination with the high vagal tone of these infants may aid in the development of a more optimal organization of the central nervous system. The resulting system should allow infants to quickly respond to both positive and negative events and return to a less aroused state. Second, the suppression of vagal tone also appears to be a necessary physiological state for the promotion of sustained attention. In general, individuals with low vagal tone are less able to suppress or modulate their vagal tone to meet immediate challenges in their environment. Thus, it appears that two physiological variables, basal vagal tone and the ability to suppress vagal tone in response to attentional demands may prove useful in our theory as indices of the child's developing emotion regulation skills.

During the first 2 to 3 months of life, the infant's major task is one of achieving physiological homeostasis. Attentional and other emotion regulatory processes play a central role in this process as they provide multiple strategies for self-soothing and should increase the ability of infants to be soothed by others. Caregivers play a vital role by helping infants achieve this state before they are able to do this for themselves. In the way caregivers interact with their infants, they can influence the child's basic regulatory abilities, and, in part, lay the groundwork for later abilities the child will have in self-soothing, repairing interaction, and focusing attention. In addition, some infants are more physiologically able to accomplish this task. Highly reactive infants who are unable to regulate their reactivity may be at particular risk for later problems. On the other hand, high vagal tone is related to high reactivity and the ability to regulate this reactivity (Fox, 1989); the child's ability to suppress vagal tone in response to environmental demands for attentional shifts or sustained attention may also be an index of the child's developing emotion regulation skills. These infants self-soothe more easily and utilize more emotion regulation strategies such as selective attention when distressed. Once physiological homeostasis is more stable infants can turn their attention toward the social world.

THE EMOTION REGULATION THEORY: OUR HYPOTHESES

Precisely how do we think that meta-emotions affect the functioning of families and act to affect child outcomes? What do we propose as the mechanism? We are particularly drawn to theories that attempt to integrate behavior and physiology, and so our theorizing is oriented toward approaches that have emphasized the importance of balance and regulation, the developing children's abilities in the regulation of emotion (Garber & Dodge, 1991), in the development of children's abilities to self-soothe strong, potentially disruptive emotional states (Dunn, 1977), focus attention, and organize themselves for coordinated action in the service of some goal.

The Challenge in Finding Linkages Between Family and the Peer Worlds: The Development of "Emotional Intelligence"

It is now well-known that the ability to interact successfully with peers and to form lasting peer relationships are important developmental tasks. Children who fail at these tasks, who are rejected by their peers, and especially those who are unable to make friends, are at risk for a number of later problems (Parker & Asher, 1987). The peer context presents new opportunities and formidable challenges to children. Interacting with peers provides opportunities to learn about more egalitarian relationships than parent–child relationships; to form friendships with agemates, negotiate conflicts, engage in cooperative and competitive activities, and learn appropriate limits for aggressive impulses. It provides opportunities for learning that friends can be sources of great fun and adventure as well as comfort in times of need. Even very young children are able to obtain this kind of comfort in times of stress from their friends. For example, Kramer and Gottman (1992) found that the quality of young friendships among 3-year-olds were the best predictor of adjustment to becoming a sibling. On the other hand, children are typically less supportive than caregivers when their peers fail at these tasks.

In our research, the quality of the child's peer relationships forms our most important class of child outcome measures. A major goal of the research we undertook was to predict peer social relations in middle childhood from variables descriptive of the family's emotional life in preschool. We should explain what the theoretical challenge here is in predicting peer social relations across these two major developmental periods, from preschool to middle childhood. Major changes occur in peer relations in middle childhood. Children become aware of a much wider social network than the dyad. In preschool, children are rarely capable of sustaining play with more than one other child (see for example, Corsaro, 1979, 1981). However, in middle childhood, children become aware of peer norms for social acceptance, and teasing and avoiding embarrassment suddenly emerge (see Gottman & Parker, 1986). Children become aware of clique structures, and of influence patterns as well as social acceptance.

In middle childhood, some of the correlates of peer acceptance and rejection change dramatically, particularly with respect to the expression of emotion. One of the most interesting changes is that the socially competent response to a number of salient social situations such as peer entry and teasing is to be a good observer, somewhat wary, but basically to be cool and emotionally unflappable. The child in middle childhood being teased needs to act as if he or she had undergone an emotion-ectomy, and, indeed a major concern of children in this developmental period is avoiding embarrassment (see Fine, 1987; Gottman &

Parker, 1986). Thus we can see that the basic elements and skills a child learns through emotion coaching (labeling, expressing one's feelings, and talking about one's feelings) become liabilities in the peer social world in middle childhood, if they were to be simply transferred by the child from the home to the school. Thus, we think that the basic model linking emotion coaching in preschool to peer relations in middle childhood can not be a simple isomorphic transfer of social skills model. Instead, it becomes necessary to identify a mechanism operative in the preschool period that makes it possible for the child to learn something in the preschool period that underlies the development of appropriate social skills across this major developmental shift in what constitutes social competence with peers.

Thus, there is a major challenge in being able to make linkages from the family's affective world to the child's peer world. The challenge is that, as the child develops, many of the child's peer social competencies become precisely the opposite of what children specifically learn in emotion coaching with parents. Even in the preschool period, entry into a peer group is successful to the extent that children do not call attention to themselves and their feelings, but instead watch the peer group, understand what they are doing, and quietly and non-intrusively do what they are doing, waiting to be invited in. These skills of observing, waiting, watching, and not expressing one's emotions and discussing them are even more important in middle childhood, when teasing becomes central. Any theory we develop has to contend with the problem that the specific skills children learn in emotion-coaching interactions with parents are precisely the wrong skills for succeeding with peers, and this is even more the case in middle childhood. Hence we propose that a social learning or modeling theory of the development of social competence will not do. It is doomed to failure.

What do we offer as an alternative? We suggest that instead of a social skills theory for making developmental predictions and linkages from the family to the child peer system, a set of general abilities underlie the development of social and emotional competence with peers, and that these abilities form the basis of what Salovey and Mayer (1990) called *emotional intelligence*. While Salovey and Mayer's idea of emotional intelligence is a very long list of skills, we thought that the link in making these predictions would be much simpler, it would be the child's ability to regulate emotions and to self-soothe and focus attention during salient emotionally trying peer situations. We expect that we will observe that the child's peer social competence will hold primarily in the inhibition of negative affect (Guralnick, 1981), particularly aggression, whining, oppositional behavior, fighting requiring parental intervention, sadness, and anxiety with peers. Being teased in middle childhood is the ultimate proving ground for the child's ability to inhibit negative affect.

Children's peer social competencies include the ability to resolve conflict, to find a sustained common ground play activity, and to empathize with a peer in distress (e.g., see Asher & Coie, 1990; Berndt & Ladd, 1989; Eisenberg & Strayer, 1987; Gottman, 1983; Gottman & Parker, 1986; Shantz & Hartup, 1992).

To see how these very basic skills of emotion regulation might operate and underlie the more complex social skills that have been described as the child's peer social competence, consider children's peer social skills at age 5, in which most of the child's interaction occurs in dyads. In one transcript of a play session in our research, two 4-year-olds got into a conflict in which the boy wanted to play Superman and the girl wanted to play house. After shouting their wishes back and forth a few times, he calmed down and suggested that they pretend this was Superman's house, she had also calmed down and thought this was a great idea, and their compromise resulted in an enjoyable pretend play session for both children. It takes a lot of skill to be able to self-soothe in this situation and to both suggest and to accept a creative compromise.

What is different about children who can and cannot do this? We think there is a fundamental set of abilities that have to do with understanding one's own emotions, being able to regulate them, being able to soothe one's self physiologically, focus attention, listen to what one's playmate is saying, being able to take another's role and empathize, being able to engage in social problem solving, or as Asher has suggested, relating one's goals to one's strategies. These are the skills children learn with emotion-coaching parents, but they are not applied isomorphically to the peer world. They involve the child knowing something about the world of emotion, her own as well as others. This knowledge arises only out of emotional connection being important in the home.

Hence, in middle childhood, we suggest that the child who has been emotion coached by parents has developed a general set of skills that appear to have nothing to do with expressing and understanding one's own feelings. However, they have to do with the ability to inhibit negative affect, with being able to self-soothe, with being able to focus attention (including social attention) and with being able to regulate one's own emotions. In middle childhood these abilities are manifest by inhibiting displays of distress and inhibiting aggression when teased and instead acting emotionally unflappable, and in being able to enter an ongoing peer group with ease and awareness instead of with the lumbering bravado of the socially rejected child.

We think that it will eventually turn out that these emotion regulation abilities are, to some extent, temperamental, but that, to a greater extent, we think that they are shaped by parents beginning in infancy (see Appendix 5.1). This shaping begins in parents' ability to deal with an infant's distress with affection and comfort (Dunn, 1977) and continues into the face-to-face play with the infant in the first year of life (Gianino & Tronick, 1988; Stern, 1985). This thinking is consistent with many current theorists writing about social and emotional development in infancy and the role of face-to-face interaction of infants and parents, work we review in this chapter. Hence, we predict that there will be pathways from our meta-emotion variables to the child's physiological responses during emotion-arousing situations in the laboratory parent–child interaction, emotion-eliciting films).

Cognitive and Emotional Development May Be Linked

Other researchers have suggested that linkages exist between social and cognitive development (see Overton, 1983). We suggest that emotion regulation abilities in children are fundamental to the development of cognitive competencies in school. The Emotion Regulation Theory places attentional processes as the central mediator between emotional regulation and the development of cognitive competence. The vagal tone variables have been found to underlie the deployment of attention. The major link between emotional and cognitive abilities may be found in the domain of attention deployment, which we see as one component of emotion regulation (for a review, see Wilson & Gottman, 1995). There is evidence that attentional processes mediate between risk and psychopathology in children (Kellam, 1994). We know that attentional processes organize experiences from the earliest moments of life. They play a central role in the establishment of physiological homeostasis and emotion regulation abilities (Rothbart & Derryberry, 1981). It is quite probable that attentional abilities form a necessary precondition for much subsequent cognitive and social advancement. For example, a major developmental shift that occurs at around 9 months of age is the infant's ability to share attention of an object with a parent, and we see the emergence of social referencing (e.g., see Stern, 1977; Walden, 1991). Attentional processes may also affect important sources of socialization and support for infants. This may occur in the caregiver–infant and peer systems as well as academic settings later in life.

We expect that an emotion-coaching meta-emotion structure will predict the development of superior cognitive skills of the child (through superior vagal tone and greater ability to focus attention). Because we think that this superior cognitive performance is mediated by the parents' meta-emotion structure, we predict that the relationship between the parents' meta-emotion structure and the child's achievement at age 8 would hold over and above preschool measures of intelligence. Thus, we predict that two preschool children of equal intelligence will differ, in part, in their ultimate achievement in school as a function of the parents' meta-emotion structure. In this chapter, we examine the relationship between the parents' meta-emotion when the child is of preschool age and the child's subsequent academic achievement at age 8.

Child Regulatory Physiology

We predict that the parents' emotion-regulation abilities will relate to similar abilities in the child. We expect this emotion-coaching meta-emotion structure to be related to more positive and less negative parent–child interaction. We assume that more positive and less negative parent–child interaction will be reflected in lower levels of child stress and superior functioning of the parasympathetic branch of the autonomic nervous system. These will be displayed by the child's physiology. In this chapter we briefly review the selection of two indices of the child's physiology: (a) a higher child basal vagal tone, and (b) a better ability to suppress vagal tone when required, which are indices of the tonus of the parasympathetic branch of the autonomic nervous system (Izard, Porges, Simons, & Haynes, 1991; Porges, 1984). Later we see that these indices are related to other indices of lower general physiological arousal such as a lower baseline heart rate and lower skin conductance levels. The sympathetic branch of the autonomic nervous system also plays a role in our theorizing. We predict that when parents have an emotion-coaching meta-emotion structure, we expect to find in the children lower levels of stress-related hormones (both catecholamines and cortisol) in a 24-hour urine sample. We also expect that the meta-emotion variables, as well as the physiological variables, will be related to child physical health.

We posit that through the mechanism of lower levels of physiological stress in the child, the child will be better at focusing attention and self-soothing. Toward this end, we examine the child's performance on the Stroop Interference Test, which assesses attentional competence and the ability to inhibit impulsive responses (e.g., see Lufi, Cohen, & Parish, 1990) and attention deficit disorder (e.g., see Grodzinsky & Diamond, 1992).

We measure the child's emotion regulation ability with a questionnaire that asks parents to tell us how much they have to "down-regulate" the child's emotions, that is how much the child is out of control.

We propose that an emotion-coaching meta-emotion structure will also buffer the child against the development of child psychopathology. In our study we examined the correlates of the parents' meta-emotions with the longitudinal development of child behavior problems on measures such as the Child Behavior Checklist (Achenbach & Edelbrock, 1983, 1986).

We think that part of the result of a parental emotion-coaching meta-emotion structure is a superior ability in the regulation of emotion by parents in the service of the management of stress (Fox, 1989). Because of the connection between the management and stress and physical health (e.g., see Barnett & Marshall, 1993), we also expect this emotion-regulation ability to be reflected longitudinally in higher parental physical health.

We recognize that our correlational studies can not test the theory we have proposed. However, we expect the correlational data to provide some insight into the potential validity of this theory and to suggest some directions for future research.

MAKING THE MODEL SPECIFIC

To return to our model, we can now be far more specific, and we have several variables for each of our concepts. For the meta-emotion structure we select from the meta-emotion variables we describe in this chapter. For the parenting construct we have two kinds of variables: Hypothesis 1 suggests variables from the

Cowans' Coding System that make up the Warmth construct (warmth and co-warmth), and from the Kahen systems, the variables that make up Emotional Engagement construct; Hypothesis 2 suggests measuring Derogation from the KEACS system using criticism, intrusiveness, and mockery. For the child physiology construct we have two parasympathetic variables—basal vagal tone and the suppression of vagal tone. For the sympathetic nervous system, we have the urinary secretion of the catecholamines, and the hypothalamic-pituitary-adrenocortical axis' secretion of cortisol. For the child emotion regulation construct we designed the Katz–Gottman measure of how much the parents must emotionally down-regulate the child. The child outcomes we have selected are described in the section preceding chapter 12; they include, child–peer relations as measured by teacher and parent ratings and by observations of peer play with a best friend (which gives a nearly optimal profile), child negative affectivity (which includes child behavior problem ratings at age 8), child physical health at age 8, and child academic achievement at age 8.

SUMMARY OF EMOTION REGULATION THEORY

We have proposed a model that what develops that is central to the prediction of child outcomes, particularly related to child peer relations, is the child's regulatory physiology and the child's ability to inhibit negative affect (negative emotional down regulation). We have suggested that parental interaction with children that is emotion-coaching, Warm, non-Derogatory, and Scaffolding/Praising, are the logical candidates through which children acquire the ability to suppress vagal tone when engaging with the world cognitively or affectively by self-soothing, inhibiting negative affect and focusing attention. In effect, we suggest that parents are helping children develop these regulatory skills by a particular kind of interaction with their children during emotional moments. In Fig. 5.1, there are four domains of variables in the model for predicting peer social competence in middle childhood, as well as other developmental outcomes (cognitive, affective, and physical health). These are: (a) emotional awareness and emotion-coaching, (b) three parenting variables, warmth, derogatory parenting, and authoritative/responsive parenting, (c) two child regulatory physiology variables, basal vagal tone and the ability to suppress vagal tone, and (d) negative emotion down regulation.

Appendix 5.1
How Specifically Might Meta-Emotion and Parenting Affect a Child's Development?

In this section we attempt to fill out the reasoning for the pathways described in Fig. 5.1. We put together a theory that reflects our thinking about how the emotional life of a family can affect the child's emotional development. Thus, although our discussion includes warmth, coldness, structuring, discipline, and maturity demands, in a climate of respect and responsiveness, we think these qualities of parenting form the backdrop for the family's meta-emotion structure and that, taken together these concepts form an operational definition of what Ginott was talking about.

Tronick's (Gianino & Tronick, 1988) mutual regulation model of face-to-face play between mothers and infants suggests that an infant needs to regulate her level of physiological arousal so that she is psychologically available for play. Fox (1989) showed that some infants do this in a variety of ways, using distraction and other means for self-soothing. Fox has discovered that the physiological precursor of an infant's eventual exploration of a novel stimulus or approach to a stranger is baseline vagal tone at 6 months.

We suggest that the most fundamental part of emotion regulation abilities has to do with the deployment of attention, and that through these skills both a child's cognitive and social-emotional development will be affected. There is evidence that attentional processes mediate between risk and psychopathology in children. Kellam (1994) found that problems in concentration played a central role in the development of shy and aggressive behavior and poor achievement in first-grade boys and girls. The ability to regulate attention is a part of the more general abilities in emotion regulation that children develop. We think that parenting plays a central role in the child's developing emotion regulation abilities.

EMOTIONAL REGULATION AND EARLY INFANT–CAREGIVER INTERACTIONS

Beginning in the first months of life, infants and their caregivers engage in cycles of attention and withdrawal (Brazelton, Koslowski, & Main, 1974). At around 3 months, most of these face-to-face interactions involve a great deal of joy, play, and positive affect for most parents; they are largely emotional exchanges. They form a basis for the development of affectional bonds (Cohn & Tronick, 1989; Tronick & Gianino, 1986). These interactions are also characterized by reciprocal gazes, vocalizations, facial expressions, and body gestures that proceed in a turn-taking manner. The caregiver–infant relationship is an important and supportive setting for learning a number skills necessary for establishing and maintaining effective social engagement with others, such as conversations and play. These skills include turn-taking, the regulation of levels of stimulation during engagement, and learning about the emotions of self and others.

Turn-Taking

An important skill needed for social interactions is turn-taking. During early interactions with their infants, caregivers typically watch for signals, such as eye contact or smiles, before engaging their infants (Brazelton, Koslowski, & Main, 1974). Caregivers then direct some behavior toward their infants, such as smiles, vocalizations, or physical play. They wait while their infants respond to these behaviors. Pauses in the infant's behaviors serve as a signal for the onset of additional caregiver behaviors. The infant's cycles of attention and inattention form the basis for these judgments. Sensitive caregivers use these states to draw infants into periods of engagement that become more mutually regulated as the weeks pass. Caregivers also make adjustments in these interactions based on individual differences in the reactivity, tolerance for stimulation, and attentiveness of their infants. For example, mothers of Down syndrome infants talk more rapidly when interacting with their infants (Buckhalt, Rutherford, & Goldberg, 1978). Down syndrome infants, on the other hand, vocalize more randomly and leave shorter pauses between their vocalizations (Jones, 1977, 1980). These mothers may be adjusting their responses to fit into the spaces provided by their infants. As infants mature, parental responsibility for maintaining states of engagement decreases and infants begin to take a more active role in regulating interactions.

Mutual Regulation

Infants have different tolerance levels for excitement during interactions. When they become overstimulated and need to calm down, infants engage in what Tronick (1989) called, "self-directed" regulatory behaviors. These behaviors include looking away, sucking the thumb, or looking at the hands and lower the level of stimulation and consequently their arousal lowers as well. They also serve as signals to caregivers that they need to reduce their level of stimulation and wait until the infant is ready to re-engage. Infants use "other-directed regulatory behaviors", such as smiles or eye contact, to signal their renewed desire to interact (Tronick, 1989). Successful experiences with regulating sources of stimulation help infants feel a sense of control over their arousal levels in social situations.

In normal caregiver–infant interactions, about 30% of the time is spent in this kind of coordinated interaction (Tronick, 1989). Transitions from coordinated to miscoordinated states and back again are frequent events. In fact, these experiences may help to build stress tolerance in infants; they may learn to maintain interactions despite moments of stress. Tronick (1989) suggested that successful transitions from miscoordinated to coordinated states and recovery from negative affect challenge infants to expand and elaborate their regulatory repertoires. Although some conflictual or miscoordinated interactions occur in all infant–caregiver dyads, a high proportion may adversely influence the development of effective regulatory patterns.

Expectations, Attention, and Regulatory Patterns

Infants who habitually experience miscoordinated states, such as infants with unresponsive caregivers, exhibit difficulties in their regulatory patterns. Researchers have investigated the effects of chronic miscoordinated states by using the "still-face" paradigm (Cohn & Tronick, 1983). Mothers are asked to maintain a frozen yet neutral expression while seated in front of their infants. Most infants initially react to this situation by signaling that they want mother to interact with them. When these attempts fail, infants express distress followed by self-directed regulatory behavior. Infants build up expectancies about the consequences of their behavior in these situations. Thus, previous experiences with success or failure at repairing miscoordinated states influence the regulatory behavior of infants. Infants who have experienced a high degree of success are more likely to use other-directed regulatory behaviors to elicit their mother's attention (Gianino & Tronick, 1988).

Infants in chronically miscoordinated dyads, such as depressed mothers and their infants, repeatedly engage in self-directed regulatory behavior. Normal interaction patterns are disrupted and infants employ self-regulatory behaviors in an automatic, inflexible, and indiscriminate way. Because this pattern is used defensively in anticipation of negative affect, it may result in a passive, "depressive" pattern of responding. This atypical pattern has been dramatically demonstrated by Field, Healy, Goldstein, and Perry (1988), who reported that the regulatory patterns and interaction style of infants of depressed mothers did not vary with the responsiveness of different social partners. The regulation of negative affect becomes the infant's primary goal. In extreme cases, the result may be disengagement from people and objects because these take too much regulatory capacity (Field, Healy, & LeBlanc, 1989; Tronick, 1980; Tronick & Field, 1986).

Hence, parental psychopathology influences sensitivity to infant signals. The presence of familial stressors, such as marital discord, may also adversely affect this ability (Fendrich, Warner, & Weissman, 1990). Elizabeth Fivaz-Depeursinge (personal communication, 1991) reported that unhappily married couples consistently overstimulated their infants in triadic play situations (i.e., mother, father, and infant). When their infants became distressed, these parents also failed to appropriately soothe them. Consequently, these infants were less able to organize their gaze in the play situation and looked away from their parents more than infants of happily married parents.

Social interactions present many regulatory challenges for infants. Patterns of attention play a central role in these interactions. Through the use of attention deployment strategies, infants are able to regulate their own level of arousal. These strategies also serve a communicative function. They tell caregivers that they need to adjust the level of their stimulation. The sensitivity and responsiveness of caregivers to these signals is a key element in the infant's ability to acquire effective regulatory patterns. Social interactions also provide infants with opportunities for learning about the emotions of self and others.

Early Socialization of Emotional Expression

A large component of face-to-face interaction involves the modeling or imitation of infant affective expressions by their caregivers. An infant's ability to benefit from these experiences is grounded in the ability to attend selectively to these signals. Parental modeling appears to be selective for the socialization of the more positive emotions (Malatesta & Haviland, 1982). In normal interactions, mothers model the more positive affects of their infants. This modeling is associated with increases in positive affect in dyadic interactions over time.

In a recent study, Malatesta and her colleagues (Malatesta-Magai, 1991; Malatesta, Culver, Tesman, & Shepard, 1989) examined the modeling behavior of mothers of full-term and preterm infants. Mothers of full-term infants modeled most of the affective behaviors of their infants except for pain expressions (Malatesta-Magai, 1991). Mothers of preterm infants, on the other hand, revealed a different more selective pattern. They showed higher levels of modeling interest but were more likely to ignore infant anger, sadness, and surprise. Maletesta noted that preterm infants are more easily overstimulated, more irritable, and show shorter gaze time. The tendency to ignore anger and sadness may be the mother's way of reducing the angry, irritable behavior of these infants. The avoidance of sadness may be due to the perceived frailty of these infants. By ignoring the less acceptable affective expressions of their infants, mothers may be attempting to reduce these behaviors. However this technique appears to be ineffective in some cases. At 22 months, children who had experienced maternal ignoring of sadness and anger displayed more sadness and anger during a reunion after maternal separation than children whose mothers did not ignore these expressions.

By responding to some emotions and not others, caregivers attempt to socialize the affective expressions of their infants. Infants may learn to express emotions within a certain range of acceptable affective expressions because of these experiences. Conversely, certain emotions, especially anger and sadness, may be less malleable. These emotions serve as powerful signals that something needs to be changed. Not responding to these signals over a period of time may be indicative of less sensitive caregiving.

Sharing States of Attention

At about 9 months, infants shift from regulating their experiences to intentionally sharing them with others. Parents also seem aware of this shift in their infant's abilities and increasingly address the subjective experiences of their infants (see Stern, 1985). Intersubjectivity involves the sharing of internal experiences between the self and others. These early experiences include attempts to share attentional focus, intentions, and affective states.

Early signs of intersubjectivity can be seen in infants' responses to attempts to redirect their attention to various objects and events. In the second half of the first year, infants are able to visually follow the line of their mother's gaze to a particular target (Scaife & Bruner, 1975). At about 9 months, they are also able to shift their attention from a pointing hand and follow an imaginary line from the pointing finger to the target with their gaze (Murphy & Messer, 1977). Infants visually check their mother's face during these encounters to confirm that they have correctly identified the target. Infants also begin to use gestures to redirect the attention of their caregivers at about this same time.

At about 9 months, infants point and use other body gestures to communicate their needs and desires. Many of these early attempts to redirect the attention of caregivers involve a desire for an object or event. An infant who spots her bottle on the kitchen counter may point toward the bottle. While doing this, she may also alternate her gaze between her mother and the desired object. This type of "intentional communication" (Bates, 1979) by infants indicates that they understand that internal states can be shared with others. Affective expressions often accompany many of these events.

The sharing of affective states is the primary means of communication for preverbal infants. Requests for objects are often accompanied by changes in the infant's facial expression and/or tone of voice. Infants also learn to differentiate between the positive and negative affective signals of caregivers. As infants gain the ability to move further away from familiar adults, attention to signals from the caregiver provides an important source of emotional regulation. Studies of social referencing indicate that by 10–12 months, infants actively reference their caregiver's emotional responses in ambiguous situations. Infants then modify their own affective responses and behavior based on these signals (Klinnert, Emde, Butterfield, & Campos, 1987; Campos & Sternberg, 1981). The marital satisfaction of fathers strongly influences whether or not infants will socially reference to them (Dickstein & Parke, 1988); infants do not reference unhappily married fathers, but they do reference unhappily married mothers. Emotion regulatory processes such as attention play a central role in the early development of intersubjectivity. In fact, intersubjectivity is a complex problem of shared and coordinated attention between two people. Caregivers and infants use their attentional focus to indicate and verify that they understand each other, to help in communicating their needs and desires, and to share the affective states of the other. The development of intersubjectivity enables children and their caregivers to experience a new level of interrelatedness. Children who experience attentional difficulties, especially in the shifting of attention may miss many of these early experiences of interrelatedness.

REGULATORY PROCESSES AND PEER RELATIONS

In early interactions, responsive parents watch their infants for signs that indicate their readiness to interact or need to disengage. Parents initially take a dominant role in these interchanges and make appropriate adjustments to aid their infants. As children mature, most parents decrease the level of their own directiveness and expect more from their children. Nevertheless, throughout development, parents continue to play a supportive, helpful role in caregiver–child interactions. However, when interacting with peers, the responsibility for engaging, repairing, and maintaining social contact shifts to children. They must be alert to opportunities for social engagement with others, attend to cues and feedback, and modify their behavior based on this information.

From Object Play to Social Interaction

At about 6 months of age, infants begin to spend more time attending to objects in their environment. The ability to shift attention from object to object and from objects to potential social partners is a necessary skill in peer relations. Object play also often mediates early social behavior; 88% of interactions between infants from 12–24 months involve nonsocial objects (Mueller & Brenner, 1976). What begins as object play often leads to the discovery of interpersonal contingencies. Difficulties in shifting attentional focus may limit this important avenue for peer contact. In addition, shifts in attentional focus also aid the older child's peer interactions. Once a joint activity is established, children still need to monitor the behavior of their playmate. Monitoring of the play environment also helps children anticipate and prepare for changes in this environment. Children who become engrossed in object play and fail to appropriately monitor the activities of playmates, will miss feedback from peers about their behavior. These children should be less able to maintain their joint activity than children who attend to the cues of others. Not only do these children miss opportunities available in extended social play, but their peers may come to perceive them as unpredictable or even unrewarding play partners. Research in our laboratory indicates that children with high vagal tone are more able to maintain a joint activity with their best friend [Stanley (aka Wilson) & Katz, 1991]. The superior attentional and emotion regulation abilities of these children may be responsible for this association.

As children mature and their social interactions increase in complexity, difficulties associated with attentional problems would be expected to compound. One complex but necessary social task is entering into the play activities of others. The ability of children to enter the ongoing activities of others has received much interest over the past ten years. Successful entry serves as a prerequisite for further social interaction. Young children are frequently presented with the need to enter a new playgroup, because interactions episodes between young children typically last less than five minutes (Corsaro, 1979, 1981). Entry also appears to be a difficult and potentially stressful task. Dodge, McClaskey, and Feldman (1985) reported that the entry situation is frequently identified by clinicians and teachers as being especially problematic for children. The play interactions of young children are quite fragile and easily disrupted, therefore, children tend to protect their interactions by discouraging the initial attempts of others to enter their play (Corsaro, 1979). Consequently, entering children must frequently deal with disputes over access to the group and their activities. They must also handle rejection from the group, as more than 50% of all initial attempts fail (Corsaro, 1979). Research with normally developing children indicates that successful entry is related to the ability to grasp the group's "frame of reference" (Putallaz, 1983).

Phillips, Shenker, and Revitz (1951) suggested that the most important task for entering children is one of determining the frame of reference common to the groups' members and then establishing themselves as somehow sharing in this frame of reference. In general, high-status (i.e., popular) children are more successful at these tasks (Dodge, Schlundt, Schocken, & Delugach, 1983; Putallaz, 1983; Putallaz & Gottman, 1981; Putallaz & Wasserman, 1989).

Thus, at least two tasks are important to successful entry. First, the child must attend to the group's activities to assess their frame of reference and then incorporate this information into the entry attempt. Second, the child must have strategies for handling initial rejections to their entry requests. These initial experiences are stressful and may generate negative affective responses in the entering child. An inability to calm one's self after strong affect may lead to less organized and adaptive behavior. Children may act aggressively toward the group or withdraw completely. Each of these responses will decrease the probability of successful entry.

Children with good attentional abilities should be better able to selectively attend to relevant information concerning the group's current activity. In addition, selective attention provides a number of avenues for the regulation of positive and negative emotion. Therefore, children with good attentional abilities should be better able to calm themselves after rejection and reorganize their behavior to continue this task. In a recent dissertation in our laboratory, Wilson (1994) studied retarded and normal male children's behavior during an analogue peer entry situation. In this situation, the other children were the confederates of the experimenter and were following the same script for each child. This permitted Wilson to assess such responses of the entering child as the child's latency to respond when the other children asked the entering child for a play object within his reach. The design of this study was also unique. When they were preschoolers, the children had been studied in Dodge–Coie groups of unacquainted 6-person peers for 10 sessions, and the success of their naturalistic attempts to gain entry into the play of their peers was observed and coded. Subjects were either high or low in their success at gaining entry. Wilson also studied these children in a set of attentional tasks, and she recorded heart rate during these tasks as well as during peer group entry. This was a complex study with many interesting findings. Wilson found that basal vagal tone was predictive of sustained attentional abilities for the retarded subjects only. She found that the subjects' performance on the cognitive attentional tasks predicted their performance on the social attention measure she used during the analogue entry situation, and it related to success in naturalistic entry.

The ability to attend to relevant social cues and to regulate one's emotions continues to be important as children engage in play. The ability to successfully coordinate play is a particularly complex task. Children typically negotiate concerning roles, ownership of toys, and changes in activities. Attending to the affective signals of others and modifying behavior appropriately based on these cues, enables children to maintain their play activity despite periods of disagreement and stress. As children's ability to communicate with others increases they also begin to use language to regulate their affective states and social relationships.

LANGUAGE AND WHAT IT ENTAILS
FOR EMOTION REGULATION

In this section we discuss how language facilitates children's emotion regulation abilities. With the development of self-talk, children have at their disposal a new and powerful tool for soothing negative affect during challenging situations. Self-talk can be used to direct one's attention toward relevant aspects of a problem and away from irrelevant factors (i.e., negative cognitions). Vygotsky (1962) proposed a developmental progression in children's use of language. Children first use language to establish and maintain contact with others. At about 3 or 4 years they begin to use egocentric speech, talking to themselves as they engage in activities. Language begins to provide a new means of solving problems at this point. Vygotsky observed that children tend to talk to themselves at a much higher rate (almost double) when confronted with frustrating situations. In the following example a child is getting ready to draw and finds that there is no paper or pencil of the color he needs.

> The child would try to grasp and to remedy the situation in talking to himself: "Where's the pencil? I need a blue pencil. Never mind, I'll draw with the red one and wet it with water; it will become dark and look like blue." (Vygotsky, 1962, p. 16)

At this point the child uses overt speech, but eventually this will no longer be necessary and language will go underground. He or she can then talk to himself as a means of calming down and solving problems more effectively. For example, confronted with an unfamiliar challenging situation, children may tell themselves that everything will be right and that they can figure things out. Alternately, young children may engage in negative self-talk. As described earlier, negative cognitions about one's ability may distract children from their primary task and subsequently impede their performance. These negative cognitions may compete for the attentional capacities of these children.

At this point in a child's development, some parents begin to talk to their child about their own internal thoughts and feelings. For example, Fivush (1991) asked mothers to discuss with their children four specific past events in which their 3-year-old children experienced happiness, sadness, anger, and fear. She found that mothers discussed the emotions of sadness and anger differently with sons and daughters. Conversations about sadness were longer and emphasized the causes of sadness more with daughters than with sons, and mothers were more concerned about comforting their sad daughters than their sad sons. Conversations about anger with sons were longer than with daughters. Daughters were encouraged to resolve anger by reestablishing the damaged relationship and all emotions were placed in more of a social interactional framework for daughters than was the case for sons. We believe that this kind of interaction will be important in shaping the child's abilities to self-regulate using language.

Symbolic Representation

The ability to symbolically represent internal states such as emotions also provides children with new ways to regulate these states. Preschool children typically bring emotional themes into their fantasy play. Situations that are upsetting can be explored and acted out in fantasy, thus enabling them to understand and cope with them (Gottman, 1986). The following episode involves two cross-sex friends aged 4 and 5. Eric pretends to be a skeleton. The "skeleton" voices Eric's concern about people not liking him.

E: (Screams) A skeleton, everyone, a skeleton!
N: I'm your friend. The dinosaur.
E: Oh, hi dinosaur. You know, no one likes me.
N: But I like you. I'm your friend.
E: But none of my other friends like me. They don't like my new suit. They don't like my skeleton suit. It's really just me. They think I'm a dumb dumb.
N: I know what. He's a good skeleton.
E: (yelling): I am not a dumb dumb.
N: I'm not calling you a dumb dumb. I'm calling you a friendly skeleton. (Gottman, 1986, p. 160)

Fantasy play provides a safety valve for expressing fears and other concerns because these feelings belong to the pretend character (Gottman, 1986). By rehearsing these fantasy scenes the child is able to examine different ways of dealing with the emotions. The parents' help in teaching a child to label an affective state may enable children to divert their attention from any physiological arousal caused by the state and focus on understanding and dealing with possible causal factors.

There is evidence of linkages between the family system and the child–peer system (e.g., Booth, Rose-Krasnor, & Rubin, 1991; Bhavnagri & Parke, 1991; Cassidy, Parker, & Butkovsky, 1992; Cohn, Patterson, & Christopoulos, 1991; Gottman & Katz, 1989; Ladd & Hart, 1992; MacDonald & Parke, 1984; Pettit, Harrist, Bates, & Dodge, 1991; Putallaz, Costanzo, & Smith, 1991). Friends also play an instrumental role in this process by providing an new source of solace and understanding beyond the caregiver system. In the preceding example, Eric's friend reassures him that he is liked, that he is "a friendly skeleton." Children who choose to talk about feelings and concerns with friends may have different developmental histories than children who do not. Children who encounter sensitive interactions with caregivers and have been encouraged to express their feelings may be more likely to transfer these skills to the peer realm.

The relationship between emotion language and self-control has been investigated experimentally. In a study of normal 5-year-old children, Greenberg, Kusche, and Speltz (1991) assessed the ability to tolerate frustration and to engage adaptively while waiting to open a gift. The researchers also assessed the quality of the parent–child attachment relationship by observing the child's reunion behavior after a 3-minute separation from the mother. Another variable of interest was the child's ability to identify appropriate emotional reactions to a series of situations related to attachment. This was assessed via a semi-projective task containing photographs of events such as a parent leaving on vacation. This variable, labeled *emotional openness,* was significantly related to the children's ability to tolerate frustration and to cope adaptively during the waiting period. Emotional openness and the ability to tolerate frustration and to cope adaptively were positively associated with the attachment ratings of these children. Children with more secure attachments were more able to tolerate frustration and cope adaptively.

This study supports the hypothesis that the development of emotion-related language skills is related to the ability to tolerate frustrating events. The fact that these variables are also related to the quality of the attachment relationship highlights the role of caregivers in this process.

Thus, there is evidence that sensitive and responsive parenting during the preschool period, involves the ability to notice the affective states of children and help them learn to label and cope with these states (Greenberg et al., 1991). In addition, parents who engage in verbal joint planning, negotiating and anticipatory guidance with their children help them learn more effective ways of dealing with emotions. When caregivers discuss and make plans with their children before stressful events occur such as separations, this gives the children a sense of self-efficacy and enables them to move toward greater autonomy. It also provides a model of ways that they can anticipate and regulate their emotional responses to related stressful events.

A coaching parental meta-emotion structure will make sure that these kinds of interactions occur with the child as he or she develops from infancy to the preschool years, when many children can clearly articulate what they are feeling. We suggest that parental attention to the emotional world of children will strongly affect the child's development of emotion regulation skills, including attentional skills, and self-regulatory skills. We suggest that these skills form the basis of successful child outcomes through their effects on the child's physiology, and on attentional and emotion regulatory processes.

Appendix 5.2
Necessary Concepts From Child Physiology: A Brief Review of Research

THE VAGAL "BRAKE" AND THE SYMPATHETIC "ACCELERATOR"

The autonomic nervous system controls internal organs such as the heart and glands and has, what may crudely be considered, two largely antagonistic branches, the sympathetic nervous system (SNS) and parasympathetic nervous system (PNS). These branches work together to maintain a state of homeostasis inside the body. Although the two systems are not always antagonistic (e.g., see Berne & Levy, 1987; on the synergistic effects of the PNS and SNS in myocardial contractility), the basic function of the sympathetic branch is to mobilize the body to meet emergency situations, while the parasympathetic's is to conserve and maintain bodily resources. The activity of the parasympathetic branch usually works to counteract that of the sympathetic. The result is a complex and highly interrelated system of control.

The chief nerve of the parasympathetic nervous system is the X-th cranial nerve, the vagus nerve, which, among other things, stimulates digestion and acts as a brake on the heart. For example, during initial exercise, rapid heart rate increases of up to 100 beats per minute (BPM) are due to the releasing of this vagal brake. After that, the SNS cuts in and heart rate increases higher than 100 BPM are obtained. The releasing of PNS inhibition cannot speed the heart beyond its intrinsic pacemaker rhythm, usually about 110 BPM. High levels of cardiovascular arousal indexed by increased heart rate involve "releasing" the vagal brake and "stepping on" the SNS accelerator. Further increases in cardiac output (CO) are obtained by increasing dimensions of myocardial contractility (roughly how hard the heart contracts; e.g., ejection fraction), which is mediated mostly by the SNS (see Berne & Levy, 1987).

Vagal Tone

Under most conditions, the vagus nerve acts tonically on the heart, firing frequently so that the heart beats at a rate below that of the atrial pacemaker cells. So the vagus maintains a basal *tonus,* called vagal tone. If the vagus is cut or frozen temporarily, the heart would beat at about 105–110 BPM, the intrinsic rhythm of the heart. Vagal input to the heart is interrupted on a rhythmic basis with each successive respiratory cycle. Heart rate increases during inspiration and decreases during exhalation. This repetitive turning off and on of parasympathetic stimulation to the heart due to respiration is known as *respiratory sinus arrhythmia* (RSA). When there are greater parasympathetic influences on the heart, larger transient accelerations in heart rate occur after interruptions of vagal influences. This results in greater amplitude of RSA (Porges, personal communication, 1992).

Porges et al. (1980) developed a time-series algorithm of RSA, which he equated with vagal tone. The analyses attempts to partial out variability in heart rate due to RSA from variability due to other factors such as blood pressure, thermoregulatory processes, and movement. Pharmacological, surgical, and electrical stimulation studies confirm that Porges' index of vagal tone provides a reliable index of the parasympathetic nervous system's influence on the heart (McCabe, Yongue, Porges, & Ackles, 1984; McCabe, Yongue Ackles, & Porges, 1985; Porges, 1986; Yongue et al., 1982). Although there is some controversy about whether computations of vagal tone need to include respiratory measures, there is also evidence that most computations of vagal tone are highly correlated (Grossman, Van Beek, & Wientjes, 1990). Our computations of vagal tone do not employ the Porges algorithm but actually compute the area under the curve in the appropriate respiratory ranges of the spectral density function of the interbeat interval time-series.

Vagal Tone, Development, and Risk

We know that, in general, vagal tone increases monotonically during development and then decreases with old age (Gellhorn & Loofbourrow, 1963; Larson & Porges, 1982). The myelination process may account for some of the increase early in development (Sachis, Armstrong, Becher, & Bryan, 1982). Vagal tone also appears to index the integrity of the CNS; high risk neonates (i.e., preterm infants) have significantly lower vagal tone than full-term infants (Porges, in press). Furthermore, vagal tone effectively places preterm infants on a continuum of clinical risk; healthier preterms have higher vagal tone (Porges, 1983). Vagal tone begins to show moderate long-term stability by the second half of the first year of life (Fox, 1989). Unfortunately, at this point in time researchers know very little about the factors involved in the stabilization process of vagal tone. It is assumed that maturation of PNS areas are involved in this process (Porges, personal communication, 1992). We also know that vagal tone decreases when physical health is compromised and during periods of stress. Recent work by DiPietro, Larson, and Porges (1987) indicated that at 1–2 days of age, breast-fed infants have higher vagal tone than bottle-fed infants. DiPietro et al. suggested that nutrition (i.e. colostrum) may be the key factor in this association, but social experiences during feeding may also be implicated. The breast-feeding experience offers a potentially rich context for social and tactile experiences (Dunn, 1977). Caregiver responses during the first months of life may also have a more profound influence on brain development because this is a period of rapid neurological growth. The ability to benefit from these early experiences may also be related to the attentional abilities of infants.

Heart Rate Variability, Vagal Tone, and Attention

Research over the past 20 years has consistently found a strong association between heart rate variability and attentional processes. Lacey (1967) noted that heart rate decelerates and stabilizes (periods between beats become more constant) during periods of attention. Although Lacey did not use heart rate variability as a dependent variable, Porges and Raskin (1969) later quantified and examined these data. They found that regardless of the direction of the specific heart rate response (i.e., heart rate increases or decreases), heart rate variability was always suppressed during attention.

Based on subsequent research, Porges and his colleagues constructed a two-component model of attention (Porges, 1976, 1980). The first component is reactive and involuntary. It consists of an organism's initial reaction to an external stimulus, based on stimulus characteristics such as intensity and novelty. This passive form of attention is associated with directional heart rate responses and may be mediated by either sympathetic excitation or vagal inhibition. The second component consists of an organism's voluntary and sustained response to a stimulus. This active form of attention is characterized by a reduction in heart rate variability, respiratory, and motor inhibition (Porges, 1991b). This second component is mediated by the parasympathetic nervous system.

Subsequent studies with infants, children, and adults have found a strong association between vagal tone and attentional abilities. Linnemeyer and Porges (1986) observed the behavior of 6-month-old infants as they engaged in a visual recognition memory task. Infants with high vagal tone looked at novel stimuli longer during test trials and displayed better recognition memory than infants with low vagal tone. Vagal tone has also been associated with sustained attention and faster reaction time during a stimulus-search task in school-aged children. Porges and Humphreys (1977) assessed physiological response patterns related to vagal tone and the allocation of attention in retarded adolescents and nondelayed children of equivalent mental age. The retarded subjects exhibited low resting levels of heart rate variability (suggestive of low vagal tone). Significant group differences in heart rate variability patterns also emerged as subjects engaged in cognitive tasks demanding sustained attention. The retarded adolescents did not suppress heart rate variability during the task. This atypical pattern indicates deficits in parasympathetic control over the heart and suggests a physiological concomitant of developmentally delayed children's attentional difficulties. Thus, evidence indicates a clear and reliable relationship between active attention, the suppression of heart rate variability, and vagal tone.

A logical question at this point might be why would a system (the PNS) that is associated with maintenance, recovery, and homeostasis be suppressed during attentional processes? Heart rate variability is a sign of healthy functioning and decreases in heart rate variability and vagal tone occur with illness, stress, and aging (Porges, 1985). Porges (1991b) suggested that "heart rate variability is a marker of the efficiency of the neural feedback mechanism and may index the health status of the individual's capacity to organize physiological resources to respond appropriately" (p. 208). The actions of the autonomic nervous system are ergotrophic (related to life support and work) and trophotropic (related to growth). The parasympathetic system is critical for both of these functions. Ergotrophic functions include physical work, stress, and intense emotions. Porges (1991b) noted that attentional processes are also ergotrophic and that sustained attention is particularly costly to organisms. Normal homeostatic processes are, therefore, disrupted during these periods. The ability to subjugate homeostatic needs to attend appropriately to relevant aspects of the environment is an adaptive function needed for continued survival (Porges, 1991).

The suppression of vagal tone appears to be a necessary physiological state for the promotion of sustained attention. In general, individuals with low vagal tone are less able to suppress or modulate their vagal tone to meet immediate challenges in their environment. For example, the retarded subjects studied by Porges and Humphreys (1977) exhibited low basal vagal tone and an inability to suppress vagal tone during attention-demanding tasks. This general finding has also been replicated with adults and infants (e.g., Porges & Raskin, 1969; Richards, 1985).

Researchers have identified two anomalous groups that do not fit this general pattern, hyperactive children and regulatory-disordered infants. Hyperactive children have normal resting levels of vagal tone, yet are unable to suppress their vagal tone during attention-demanding tasks. Medication given to these children not only increases their ability to attend, but is paralleled by a suppression in heart rate variability (Porges, Walter, Korb, & Sprague, 1975). Regulatory-disordered infants have high vagal tone and are highly reactive to certain types of stimulation. They also show deficits in physiological organization, fail to establish normal sleep–wake cycles, and are rated as being highly irritable and difficult. Although these infants have high vagal tone, their responses to attention-demanding tasks are extremely heterogeneous (Degangi, DiPietro, Greenspan, & Porges, 1991). Many of these infants have a difficult time regulating their autonomic nervous systems to support attention and information processing. It is interesting that the regulatory disordered infants studied by Degangi et al. had higher vagal tone than normally developing infants with high vagal tone. At this point, however, it is unclear how this may influence their regulatory and attentional abilities. Research with these two anomalous groups of children may further illuminate the precise physiological processes necessary for attention.

Hence, research indicates that the vagal brake is clearly important in attentional processes. What of the sympathetic accelerator? The role of the sympathetic nervous system in the stress response has been recognized for some time (Cannon, 1914). As we have already discussed, high levels of arousal, especially arousal associated with anxiety, have detrimental effects on attentional processes. In the following section we will explore the hypothesis that individual differences in cardiovascular reactivity and Type A behavior pattern impact attentional processes and lead to reduced resiliency.

The Sympathetic Accelerator

The sympathetic branch of the autonomic nervous system is much more diffuse anatomically than the parasympathetic branch. There is no main nerve in the sympathetic nervous system analagous to the vagus. One way that the activity of the sympathetic nervous system is assessed is by measuring stress-related endocrine secretion (in blood or urine), primarily the catecholamines. Another way is through the measurement of cardiovascular reactivity. The secretion of adrenaline and related catecholamines is largely mediated by the sympathetic nervous system through its innervation of the adrenal medulla.

Cardiovascular reactivity (CVR) appears to be an individual difference variable which emerges early in childhood and is quite stable across time (Downey, Cresan, & Berenson, 1989; Matthew, Rakaczky, & Stoney, 1987). Individual differences in CVR have been studied in research on Type A and Type B personality.

Research with children suggests that they see Type A peers as being less fun to play with and the cause of interpersonal problems (Whalen & Henker, 1986). Observations of their behavior in class and during structured group tasks indicates that they are more likely to talk, make noise, disrupt others, and engage in negative contact with peers. Work by Kurdek and Lillie (1985) also indicates that Type A boys may lack a number of social cognitive skills, such as knowledge about friendships. Type A behavior in children is associated with depression (Treiber, Mabe, Riley, & Carr, 1989). Caregiver variables may be involved in the evolution of Type A Behavior Pattern (TABP) in children. Type A sons tend to have fathers who have high expectations of them yet perceive that they are not reaching these goals (Kliewer & Weidner, 1987). Type A sons are also more likely to have Type A fathers (Bracke, 1986; Weidner, Sexton, Matazarro, & Periera, 1988). Hence, not only might these fathers encourage Type A behavior by communicating excessively high goals and dissatisfaction with their son's achievements, but they may serve as role models of the Type A behavior pattern.

Adults classified as being Type A also exhibit this pattern of high expectations and negative cognitions concerning achievements. O'Keefe & Smith (1988) reported that some Type A males (i.e, those rated by the Framington Scale) exhibited a pattern of high expectations, high levels of self-criticism, and dissatisfaction with their accomplishments. These males tended to have low expectations of success and were likely to generalize their failures. Type A fathers may be as critical of their children as they are of themselves.

6

Designing a Family Psychophysiology Laboratory: The Methods of Our Study

This chapter describes the methods we used, which come from a "social psycho-physiological" approach to studying families, with a heavy emphasis on observational methods and longitudinal research. We explain the initial rationale we had for studying marriages, their longitudinal courses, and their effects on children's emotional and social development, with particular emphasis on the child peer system.

OVERVIEW

We began our study in 1986. We wanted our study to be a longitudinal prospective study in which we would follow families through important life transitions and see whether a family's meta-emotion structure affects children's psychological adjustment over time. We also wanted to begin with the youngest preschool age children (ages 4–6) who could sit still enough for the relatively long time periods necessary for us to obtain good physiological measures. Our goal was to follow the children through their transition to elementary school, as this can be a difficult transition for children and families. Our central hypothesis was that children from families with emotion-coaching meta-emotion structures would show better academic abilities, social adjustment, and emotional well-being both before and during this transition. Families were recontacted when the children were approximately 8 years old, which coincided with their entry into second grade.

Procedures consisted of laboratory sessions and home interviews for both parents and children. We also asked parents to complete questionnaires about their marriage, their child's social and emotional adjustment, and basic demographic information (i.e., income, education, occupation). All laboratory sessions involved the measurement of physiological states (e.g., heart rate) and observation of interpersonal interaction. The physiological measures were synchronized with our observational data from marital and parent–child interaction, so we could understand how interaction between families members affects bodily states.

Our interest in obtaining good physiological recordings from children led us to the first of many challenges. One of the basic tenets of physiological data collection is that you cannot obtain good recordings from subjects when they are moving. Hence our challenge: how to keep 4–5 year old children seated! To do so, we designed a laboratory centered around an outer space motif. Children were dressed in space suits, and were seated in a mock-up Apollo space capsule. Our research assistants, who were in the next room, conversed with the children via intercom and referred to themselves as "Mission Control." We even conducted a count-down and blast-off to keep children involved in the outer space theme.

The decision to use the space capsule theme grew out of a mini-study we conducted at Chuck-E-Cheese Pizza Time restaurant. We found that the most popular two toys that children in this age group gravitated toward were a space capsule and video games. Both of these procedures were used in our study.

INITIAL CONTACT WITH FAMILIES

Families were recruited from advertisements in the classified ads section of the local city newspaper. In selecting families, we were looking for married couples who had a 4–5-year-old child and who varied widely in marital satisfaction. Fifty-six families met these criteria and participated in the study; approximately half of the families had a male child and half the families had a female child. We employed a telephone version of the Locke–Wallace (Locke & Wallace, 1959) marital satisfaction scale (Krokoff, Gottman, & Roy, 1988) to ensure that couples had a wide range of marital satisfaction in our study, because it is well known that marital satisfaction can affect parenting and child outcomes. Couples also completed the paper-and-pencil version of the Locke–Wallace Marital Satisfaction Inventory (Locke & Wallace, 1959) before they came to the laboratory. The mean marital satisfaction score was 111.1 ($SD = 29.6$).

Families meeting our criteria were then visited in their homes by a research assistant. We met with the couples first and conducted the *Oral History Interview*. The oral history interview is a semi-structured interview conducted in the couple's home, in which the interviewer asks a set of open-ended questions. The interviewer asks about the history of the couple's relationship; how they met, how they courted and decided to get married, about the good times and the bad times in their marriage, their philosophy of what makes a marriage work, and how their marriage has changed over the years. This interview places the couples in the role of experts as couples tell us what makes a marriage work. We find that couples enjoy reminiscing about their marriage, and this interview provides a wonderful opportunity for us to establish rapport. Moreover, we have found that variables obtained from this interview predicted divorce and marital stability with 94% accuracy (Buehlman, Gottman, & Katz, 1992). Six dimensions from the oral history interview that were predictive of marital dissolution were examined (Buehlman, 1996). They included: Fondness/Affection, Negativity Towards Spouse, Weness versus Separateness, Conflict is Handled Through a Discussion of Emotional Issues, Chaos, and Glorifying the Struggle (see Appendix 6.1 for detailed descriptions).

In our next home visit, we met with the child. The main purpose of this visit was to acquaint the children with the laboratory procedures. We reasoned that some children might be reluctant to have the physiological sensors necessary for physiological monitoring placed on their bodies, and that prior familiarity with these procedures would allay any fears they might have. Our assistants showed the children photographs of our space capsule and other children participating in the procedures. Photographs obtained from NASA depicting real astronauts were also shown, including ones of astronauts having their hearts and body processes monitored. We explained that like real astronauts, they too would have sensors placed on their body that monitored their hearts beating and other important bodily processes. We also attached a sensor to the child's body to show them what the hook-up procedure would be like once they came to the laboratory and how the sensors would feel. Children also got to color a space capsule of their choosing and keep their art work to help remind them of their upcoming experience in our laboratory. One of the peak events in the visit was when children met "Space Puppy," the stuffed animal who would accompany them into outer space. By the time they came to the laboratory, most children were prepared and eager for their adventure as astronauts. We also used the home visit to obtain an assessment of intellectual functioning using the Block Design, Picture Completion, and Information Subscales of the Wechsler Preschool Scales of Intelligence (WPPSI, Wechsler, 1974).

VISITS TO THE LABORATORY

Meta-Emotion Interview

Each parent was separately interviewed about their own experience of sadness and anger, their philosophy of emotional expression and control, and their feelings, attitudes, and responses to their children's anger and sadness. Their behavior during this interview was audio-taped (see chapter 4 for a more detailed description of the interview). The audio tapes of the meta-emotion interview were coded using a specific checklist rating system that codes for parents' awareness of their own anger and sadness, their own regulation of anger and sadness, and their awareness and coaching of their child's anger and sadness (see Appendix 6.1 for more detailed information).

Marital Interaction

To obtain a picture of how different couples resolve conflict, we asked married couples to spend 15 minutes discussing two problem areas in their marriage. The problem areas for discussion were determined from each spouse's ratings on the Couple's Relationship Inventory (Gottman, Markman, & Notarius, 1977). This questionnaire consists of 10 general areas in which couples typically report disagreement (e.g., money, communication, in-laws), and each spouse indicates the extent and length of the disagreement. Based on each spouse's ratings, and through the course of a play-by-play interview in which each spouse articulated their version of the problem (Gottman, 1979), two top problems were selected for the interaction task. Problems were selected for discussion if they were areas in which the spouses had differing perspectives, rather than areas in which both spouses recognize that they are living with a problematic situation (e.g., both agree that they do not have enough money). Videotapes of marital interaction were obtained and used for later observational coding.

The marital interaction was coded for problem solving behavior and emotional communication using the Rapid Couple Interaction Scoring System (RCISS, Krokoff, Gottman, & Hass, 1989) and Specific Affect coding systems (SPAFF, Gottman, 1994; see Appendix for detailed discussion of coding systems). In both the coding of specific emotional communications and problem solving, we were interested in those variables that we have previously found to be predictive of marital dissolution (Gottman, 1993a, 1993b, 1994; Gottman & Levenson, 1992), because we reasoned that processes that are detrimental to the health of the marriage would also be detrimental to the child's psychological well-being. On the SPAFF, these codes included disgust, contempt, belligerence, stonewalling, and defensiveness. On the RCISS, they included stonewalling, defensiveness and contempt. We also included two SPAFF codes that reflected positive interaction between spouses; these were affection and validation.

Parent–Child Interaction

Parents interacted with their children while the children were seated in the space capsule. The parents were informed that the child had previously heard a story, and they were to find out what the story was. After they got as much of the story as they could, they were instructed to teach the child how to play a video game. In order to make this procedure somewhat more challenging for the parents, the story that the children heard did not follow normal story grammar and was read in a monotone voice, and so the story was only mildly interesting for the children. Also, the video game was turned on while the parents were asking the child about the story, creating a conflict between the goals of the parents and children: The children wanted to play the video game, whereas the parents wanted to find out about the story. We reasoned that this task mirrored common everyday situations in which parents want the child to do one thing and the child wants to do another. The interaction, which was adapted from Cowan and Cowan (1990), lasted 10 minutes.

The parent–child interaction was coded for negative and positive parenting using the SPAFF and Kahen Coding systems. Using the SPAFF codes, the total amount of time father, mother, and child spent in the affective states of affection, excitement, anger, and the blends of whining/anxiety and sadness/anxiety were computed. The Kahen Engagement and Affect coding systems enabled us to determine the amount of intrusiveness, mockery and criticism parents expressed toward their child. The Cowan and Cowan (1982) coding system was also used to tap parental warmth, coldness, and limit-setting, and the degree to which parents were warm or cold toward each other while interacting with their child in the role as co-parents (see Appendix for detailed information).

CHILDREN'S FACIAL EXPRESSIVENESS

Children's Reactions to Emotional Films

We were also interested in the amount of positive and negative affectivity that children display spontaneously while viewing films designed to elicit emotion. To examine this question, children were shown segments of emotion-eliciting films. Each film clip was preceded by a neutral story and an emotion induction film clip of an actress who acted out the emotions of the protagonist in the upcoming story. The function of the emotion induction was to direct the child to identify with the protagonist and to experience the specific emotion in question. The emotion elicitation was not very successful: instead, we obtained a range of facial expressions of emotion in each film. Hence, we will refer to the films by their titles instead of by the emotion they were intended to induce. The child viewed clips from six films: (1) Fly fishing, (2) from the Wizard of Oz the flying monkey scene, (3) from Charlotte's Web the scene where Charlotte dies, (4) from Meaning of Life the restaurant scene, (5) from the Wizard of Oz when Toto is taken away, and (6) Daisy. Facial expressiveness was coded using Ekman and Friesen's (1978) Emotion Facial Action Coding System. Facial expressions of anger, disgust, sadness, fear, and happiness were coded.

Directed Facial Action Task

We were also interested in individual differences in children's ability to pose cross-culturally universal facial expressions of emotion. Following Ekman, Levenson, and Friesen (1983), we asked children to move specific facial muscles that corresponded with specific emotional expressions. Children posed facial expressions corresponding with the emotions of happiness, anger, disgust, fear, and sadness. Children's success at making these faces were coded using a modified version of the Ekman and Friesen's (1978) Facial Action Coding System.

CHILD'S PHYSIOLOGICAL FUNCTIONING

Autonomic Assessment

We were interested in obtaining an index of the child's sympathetic and parasympathetic nervous system activation. Two main physiological processes were monitored to obtain these measures. We looked at the child's heart rate and how much they were sweating under resting or baseline conditions, during parent–child interaction, and while children were watching the films. Children's heart rate gave us several measures, including mean levels of interbeat interval (i.e., time between heart beats) at baseline, interbeat interval variability, and the change or reactivity of heart rate variability in different situations (e.g. from baseline to parent–child interaction). Vagal tone was also computed as an index of parasympathetic activation of the heart.

We also measured how much the child was sweating, or the child's skin conductance level (SCL), as an index of sympathetic nervous system activation. Skin conductance level is a measure that is sensitive to changes in levels of sweat in the eccrine sweat glands located in the hand. Mean skin conductance level during baseline was computed as an index of general sympathetic nervous system arousal.

Child's Stress-Related Hormones

General physiological arousal was also measured by examining stress-related hormones in the child's urine. We collected a 24-hour sample of urine from the child, usually on a Sunday when the children were at home all day and could better comply with our request. We sheepishly called this our "Sunday Pee Procedure." A 24-hour sample was necessary to control for variations of hormones within a day. Assays were conducted to determine urinary catecholamines dopamine, norepinephrine, and epinephrine, as well as cortisol concentrations. Although it is an oversimplification, the catecholamine hormones are generally responsive to acute and chronic stressors related to both hostility and active coping whereas cortisol is responsive to sadness, depression, separation anxiety, loss, and passive coping (Gunnar, 1989; Henry, 1986; Henry & Meehan, 1981; Henry & Stephens, 1977; Kagan, Reznick, & Snidman, 1988).

PEER INTERACTION HOME VISIT

One of the major goals of our research was to attempt to predict from family variables collected during the preschool period the children's social competence with peers during middle childhood. Toward this end, the peer interaction home visits were included to assess the child's social competence in dyadic interaction. Each child was audiotaped at home in one 30-minute dyadic play session with a peer the mother identified as the child's best friend (regardless of gender). Because play with a best friend likely involves social processes that are less likely to occur with an unacquainted peer, this procedure provides an estimate of the highest level of social competence that a child can attain.

The audio tapes were coded with the MACRO coding system (see Gottman & Parker, 1986). Two main sets of peer variables were expected to be related to the family's meta-emotion style: the amount of negative affect during peer play and the overall quality of the play (see Appendix 6.1 for more detailed information).

FOLLOW-UP ASSESSMENTS AT AGE 8

Overview

Families were recontacted 3 years later for follow-up assessments when the children were on average 8 years old ($M = 96.9$ months; Range $= 82–110$). Ninety-five percent of the families in the initial sample and 86% of the children's teachers at follow-up agreed to participate in the Time-2 assessments. Time-2 assessment consisted of parent and teacher ratings of child outcomes, couple's reports of considerations of marital dissolution and marital satisfaction, and couple's physical health.

Marital Outcomes

Marital Dissolution and Satisfaction. We conducted telephone interviews to ask couples about their thoughts about marital dissolution. Interviews were used since couple's thoughts about marital dissolution predict actual dissolution (Booth & White, 1980; Gottman & Levenson, 1992). Interview questions were aimed at assessing whether couples had separated or divorced during the intervening three year period or had any serious considerations of separation or divorce. Each spouse was interviewed individually and was asked the following five questions: "In the last three years, have you seriously considered separation?", "In the last three years, have you seriously considered divorce?", "In the last three years, have you and your spouse separated?", "If so, how many months have you been separated, or how long was your separation period?", and "In the last three years, have you and your spouse divorced?". Questionnaires were also distributed to obtain information about their current satisfaction with their marriage. As at Time-1, couples completed the Locke-Wallace Marital Satisfaction Inventory.

Physical Health. The health of adults was assessed to test hypotheses about whether adults who have a more emotion-enhancing meta-emotion structure would be more physically healthy than adults who dismiss or deny emotion. The Cornell Medical Index (e.g., Klonkoff & Landrine, 1992) and the Krokoff Health Index were used for this purpose. The Krokoff Health Index asks each spouse to report on the health of their partner. One advantage of this method is that it attempts to control for the well-known reporting bias that males tend to under-report illness.

Child Functioning

Five general categories of child functioning were examined at age 8: (a) Academic achievement and attentional abilities, (b) Peer relations, (c) Negative affect and behavior problems, (d) Emotion regulation abilities, and (e) Physical Illness.

Child Academic Achievement and Attentional Abilities. Children were individually administered the Peabody Individual Achievement Test (PIAT-R) as a measure of academic achievement (see, Costenbader & Adams, 1991). They were administered the mathematics, reading recognition, reading comprehension, and general information tests. To assess their attentional abilities, they were also given the Stroop Interference Task. This test has three sections, one section in which the names of colors written in black ink (W), one section in which there are colored X's (C), and one section in which the names of colors are written in ink different than the color name (CW). The CW section is the most taxing of the child's attentional abilities, and has been used as an assessment of attention deficit hyperactivity disorder (Lufi, Cohen, & Parish, 1990). The CW score was used as our measure of attentional skills.

Peer Relations: Observational Measures and Teacher Ratings. As at Time-1, peer interaction with a best friend was audiotaped and later coded for negative peer play and quality of play . Teachers also completed the Dodge Peer Aggression Scale, which contains items that measure the degree to which the child uses overt aggression with peers.

Negative Affect and Behavior Problems. To give us some idea about the amount of negative affect displayed by children in an average week, mothers filled out a questionnaire about their child's emotions in the past week, checking the specific emotions they observed their children to display (Izard, 1982). The total number of negative emotions for the week were computed. Mothers also completed the Child Behavior Checklist (CBCL; Achenbach & Edelbrock, 1986). The CBCL is a well-established measure that consists of ratings of academic performance, general adaptive characteristics and 112 behavior problems. Total number of behavior problems were computed as outcome measures. Subscales tapping aggression and social withdrawal were also used. Teachers completed the Child Adaptive Behavior Inventory (CABI; Cowan & Cowan, 1990). The CABI consists of 91 items that are less pathological in nature than most current measures of behavior problems, and thus may be sensitive to more subtle behavior problems. Total score and the subscales of antisocial behavior and negative peer engagement were examined.

Emotion Regulation Abilities.   Mothers completed the Katz–Gottman Emotion Regulation Scale (Katz & Gottman, 1986) to report the degree to which their child requires external regulation of emotion by adults. The Down Regulation subscale, which measures whether parents find that they need to help them calm down and focus attention when the child gets upset, was used in this study.

Child's Physical Health.   Child illness was assessed by parental report using a version of the Rand Corporation Health Insurance Study measures (see Gottman and Katz, 1989): The following true–false items were summed: "In general, would you say that this child's health is excellent, good, fair, or poor?," "The child's heath is excellent," "The child seems to resist illness very well," "When something is going around this child usually catches it," "This child has had a nosebleed in the past 30 days."[1]

---

[1]Reliability coefficients computed for the child physical illness items yielded an alpha of .82.

Appendix 6.1
More Detail on Measures and Coding

META-EMOTION CODING SYSTEM

The audiotapes of the meta-emotion interview were coded using a specific checklist rating system that codes for parents' awareness of their own anger and sadness, their own regulation of anger and sadness, and their coaching with their child's anger and sadness. For each dimension the coding manual was quite detailed and specific. The awareness score was a sum of 12 subscales: experiencing the emotion, being able to distinguish the emotion from others, having various experiences with the emotion, being descriptive of the experience of the emotion, being descriptive of the physical sensations connected with this emotion, being descriptive of the cognitive processes connected with this emotion, providing a descriptive anecdote, knowing the causes of the emotion, being aware of remediation processes, answering questions about the emotion easily, without hesitation or confusion, talking at length about this emotion, and showing interest or excitement about this emotion. Coaching was a sum of 11 scales: showing respect for the child's experience of the emotion; talking about the situation and the emotion when the child is upset; intervening in situations that give rise to the emotion; comforting the child; teaching the child rules for appropriate expression of the emotion; educating the child about the nature of this emotion; teaching the child strategies to soothe the child's own emotion; involvement in the child's experience of the emotion; confidence about how to deal with this emotion; having given thought and energy to the emotion and what he or she wants their child to know about this emotion (goals); and, using strategies that are age and situation appropriate. The range of interobserver reliabilities, computed as correlations across scales for independent observers of this coding was 0.73–0.86.

We were also interested in parent's feeling of being out of control with respect to the emotions of sadness and anger. To measure this construct, we summed together the following items from the meta-emotion coding system: has difficulty regulating the intensity of the emotion; the emotion occurs often; the emotion is difficult to get over; the emotion has been a problem or concern; the person thinks the emotion can be dangerous; and the person has needed help with the emotion. Separate variables indexing parent's report of feeling out of control were computed for sadness and anger.

OBSERVATIONAL MEASURES OF TIME-1 MARITAL INTERACTION

Problem Solving Behavior

The marital interaction was coded using the Rapid Couple Interaction Scoring System (RCISS, Krokoff, Gottman, & Hass, 1989), which employs a checklist of behaviors that are scored for the speaker and nine behaviors that are scored for the listener on each turn of speech. RCISS behavioral codes can be scored in terms of underlying positive–negative dimension. The data are also coded each turn at speech and later summarized into the following scales: (1) Complain/criticize; (2) Defensiveness; (3) Contempt; (4) Stonewalling, a set of behaviors that describe the listener's withdrawal; (5) Positive presentation of issues; (6) Assent, simple agreements and positive vocal listener backchannels; (7) Humor; and, (8) Positive listener. We also computed, for each spouse, the overall cumulated speaker slopes for the variable Positive minus Negative. Overall Cohen's kappa reliability was 0.71, with a range of 0.70–0.81. The four negative scales of the RCISS are used here, as well as the overall level of positive minus negative speaker codes; this latter index was found to be predictive of marital stability in Gottman and Levenson (1992).

Affect

Marital interaction was also coded in real time using the Specific Affect Coding System, (Gottman, 1996; SPAFF). SPAFF is a gestalt coding system in which coders consider the verbal content, voice tone, context, facial expression, gestures, and body movement of the spouse they are coding. This system codes 16 emotions and emotional behavior patterns at both high and low levels of intensity. In addition to Neutral there are ten negative codes: (1) Anger, (2) Disgust, (3) Contempt, (4) Sadness, (5) Tension, (6) Whining, (7) Defensiveness, (8) Domineering, (9) Belligerence, and (10) Stonewalling. There are five positive codes: (11) Affection, (12) Humor, (13) Interest, (14) Joy, and (15) Validation. Emotions were coded separately for both husband and wife and done in real time. Scores reflect the percentage of time over the 15-minute interaction that each code was used. Codes were collapsed across intensity level for all analyses. Reliability for SPAFF codes was computed using interobserver correlation coefficients. Only those behaviors that have been found to predict marital dissolution in other studies (e.g., Gottman and Levenson, 1992) were analyzed; these codes are husband and wife contempt, belligerence, and defensiveness, and their sum (a variable we called hostility).

Facial Expressiveness

To examine the relationship between meta-emotion structure and facial expressiveness, we coded the marital interaction using Ekman and Friesen's (1978) Emotion Facial Action Coding System (EMFACS). Using this coding system, we can examine specific emotional expressions as well as non-emotional expressions that serve to control facial expressions (e.g., chin boss contractions). We obtained measures of the frequency of anger and sadness facial expressions, as well as measures of overall expressivity and emotional control.

CODING OF ORAL HISTORY INTERVIEW

Oral History Coding System

The oral history interview was coded on seven dimensions (Buehlman, 1991):

1. Fondness/Affection (husband and wife) is a dimension that rates couples according to how much they seem to be in love or fond of each other. This includes compliments, positive affect, and reminiscing about romantic, special times;

2. Negativity Towards Spouse (husband and wife) assesses the extent to which spouses are vague or general about what attracted them to their spouse, the extent to which they express disagreement during the interview, the display of negative affect towards one another during the interview, and the extent to which they are critical of their spouse during the interview;

3. Expansiveness versus Withdrawal (husband and wife) is a dimension that categorizes each spouse according to how expressive they are during the interview. The dimension separates individuals who are expressive and expansive from those who are withdrawn;

4. We-ness versus Separateness (husband and wife) codes how much a spouse identifies his or her self as part of a couple versus emphasizes his or her individuality or independence;

5. Gender stereotypy (one score per couple) assessed how traditional a couple's beliefs and values were. Couples were coded on how gender stereo-

typed they were in emotional expression, responsiveness, and traditional male or female roles;

6. Couples were also rated on how they reported dealing with conflict. They were rated on the following dimensions:

   (a) Volatility (one score per couple) are those that are intense both in positive and negative ways. Both spouses have extreme feelings toward each other. They fight a lot but they are still very much in love with one another.

   (b) Chaos (one score per couple) is a dimension that codes couples who report that they have little control over their own lives. These couples may have had unexpected problems and hardships come up within their relationship that they were not prepared to deal with. They have a laissez-faire attitude that life is hard and must be accepted as hard.

   (c) Glorifying the Struggle (one score per couple) is a dimension for couples that have had hard times in their marriage but have gotten through them and are proud of the fact. The difficult times have helped them grow stronger and closer to each other. They glorify their marriage as being the most important thing in the world to them;

7. Marital disappointment and disillusionment (husband and wife) tells us which couples have given up on their marriage. Couples who feel defeated or depressed about their marriage fall into this category. They often say that they do not know what makes a marriage work and will often mention unfilled needs or expectations that they had about marriage in general.

Overall reliability for the oral history Coding System was 75% agreement between coders. Intercorrelations for individual dimensions ranged between .71 and .91.

OBSERVATION CODING OF PARENT–CHILD INTERACTION

Parenting was coded using the Kahen Engagement Coding System (KECS), the Kahen Affect Coding Systems (KACS), and the Cowan coding system (Gottman, in press). The KECS consists of 7 parental engagement codes including 3 positive, 3 negative and 1 neutral code. The three Kahen positive engagement codes were: (a) Engaged, which consisted of parental attention toward the child, (b) Positive Directiveness, in which parents issued a directive statement that began in a positive way (e.g., "move to your right"), and (c) Responds to Child's Needs, in which parents responded to a child's question or complaint. The three negative engagement codes were: (a) Disengaged, in which parents were not attending to the child, (b) Negative Directiveness, in which parents issued a directive statement that began in a negative way (e.g., "don't move around so much"), and (c) Intrusiveness, which involved physical interference with the child's actions (e.g., grabbing the joystick). The KACS also consists of 7 parental affect codes. The three positive affect codes were: (a) Affection, which consisted of praise and physical affection, (b) Enthusiasm, which was coded as cheering and excitement at the child's performance, and (c) Humor, which involved parental laughter or joking. The three negative affect codes were: (a) Criticism, which involved direct disparaging comments or put-downs of the child's behavior or performance, (b) Anger, in which parents were visibly frustrated by the child's actions or demonstrated disappointment, annoyance, or irritation toward the child, and (c) Derisive Humor, in which parents used humor at the child's expense (e.g., through sarcasm or by making fun of the child). Parent–child interaction was coded continuously in real time with coding synchronized to the original parent–child interaction. The total number of times each variable occurred in the 10-minute parent–child interaction session was recorded and totals across time were calculated for each of the 14 parent–child interaction variables. This index is therefore an estimate of the frequency of the parenting behavior within a 10-minute period. Mothers and fathers were coded by independent observers. Engagement and affect dimensions were also coded by independent observers. Reliability was calculated across coders using a correlation coefficient. Because total number of seconds within each parent code was the variable computed and used in all data analyses, the appropriate reliability statistic is a correlation coefficient rather than Cohen's kappa or percentage agreement. For the KECS, the mean correlation was .96, with a range of .86–.99, and for the KACS the mean correlation was .93, with a range of .84–.97. We computed the sum of derisive humor, intrusiveness, and criticism for both parents to form our Derogation variable. The Kahen systems were also are used to measure the Authoritative/Responsive dimension, which consists of parental affection, engagement, positive structuring, responsiveness, and enthusiasm; we computed the sum of these variables across parents, omitting the father enthusiasm code because for fathers alone, enthusiasm was significantly correlated with his criticism.

The parent's behavior during the parent–child interaction was also coded using the Cowan and Cowan (1987) coding system. This coding system codes parents behavior on dimensions of warmth-coldness, presence or lack of structure and limit setting, whether parents back down or not when their child is noncompliant, anger and displeasure, unresponsiveness or responsiveness, and whether or not parents make maturity demands of their child. The behavior of parents toward each other during their interactions with their child (their co-parenting) is also coded on dimensions of warmth, cooperation or competition, anger, disagreement, responsiveness, pleasure in co-parenting, clarity of communication, and amount of interaction. For the purposes of this study, only the warmth dimension (parenting and co-parenting) was of interest. For the parenting dimension, coders rated the overall degree of warmth and the highest level of warmth and coldness exhibited by each parent. For the co-parenting dimension, coders rated the overall degree of warmth and the highest level of warmth and coldness exhibited by the couple toward each other. Warmth is defined as the sum of all the warmth variables minus the sum of all the coldness variables. Reliability between observers was variable. For the warmth variable we created the inter-reliability was .64.

Parent–child affective interaction was also coded using the SPAFF coding system. The total amount of time father, mother, and child spent in the negative affective states of whining, sadness, anxiety, and the blend of whining and anxiety for the child and the totals summing across all family members was computed. Cohen's kappas were computed for the entire coding system and the average kappa was 0.69, with a range from 0.52–0.85.

PEER INTERACTION

The Rapid Macro (R-MACRO) peer interaction coding system (Gottman, 1983) was used to code best friend peer play. The R-MACRO consists of 43 specific behaviors (21 positive and 22 negative) that index children's coordination of play. For example, there are codes indexing the ability to repair conversation included skill at clarifying messages and conflict management; conversational skills are indexed by children's success at information exchange, self-disclosure, and gossip and their ability to explore similarities; connected interaction consisted of negative parallel play, positive parallel play, common ground success and connected interaction; solitary play or disrupted interaction is indexed by children's tendency to monologue, to disrupt play by departing from the play area, or to require parental direction of play; negative and positive affect codes include: Anger, Crying, Bossiness, Affection, Sympathy, Sharing, Laughter, and Joy/Excitement. Totals for individual codes were calculated by summing the frequency of each code's occurrence across all 3 minute periods. Reliability was calculated across coders using a correlation coefficient. The mean correlation was .72, with a range of .60–.88.

CHILD PHYSIOLOGY

Autonomic Physiology

We computed one index of vagal tone as the amount of variance in the interbeat interval (related to the heart rate: Heart rate = 60000/interbeat-interval) spectrum that was within the child's respiratory range; we used a spectral time-series analysis. This measures respiratory sinus arrhythmia, a measure of parasympathetic nervous system tonus, which has been found to index attentional processes and emotion regulation abilities (Porges, 1984). We also computed mean levels of interbeat interval at baseline, interbeat interval variability (a measure of vagal tone, Izard, Porges, Simons, & Haynes, 1991), and the reactivity of heart rate variability from baseline to the mean of the parent–child interaction (an index of the child's ability to modulate vagal tone, DiPietro, Porges, & Uhly, 1992), and mean skin conductance level during baseline (first visit to the lab). These were designed as indices of the amount of the child's chronic physiological arousal, and the parasympathetic functioning of the child. In addition to their relation with attentional measures and measures of recognition memory and attention to novel stimuli in 6 month old infants (Linnemeyer & Porges, 1986), and regulatory competence (DeGangi, DiPietro, Greenspan, & Porges, 1991), vagal tone measures are related to socio-emotional competence. For example, vagal tone measures have been found to relate to facial expressivity in 5 month old infants (Stifter, Fox, & Porges, 1989), to general developmental well being (DiPietro, Porges, & Uhly, 1992), to the ability to cope with mildly frustrating situations and stressful events (Fox, 1989), and to the initial entry to preschool (Fox & Field, 1989). The computation of vagal tone has included spectral and cross-spectral analysis (with respiration) and the computation of heart period variability; generally these measures are developmentally stable, related to one another and function well (Grossman, Van Beek, & Wientjes, 1990; Izard, Porges, Simons, & Haynes, 1991).

For our physiological variables we selected as an estimate of the child's baseline vagal tone the vagal tone when the child was listening to a neutral story about fly fishing, a variable we called BASE VAGAL. The child's ability to withdraw vagal tone was estimated as a difference between this estimate of basal vagal tone and the child's vagal tone during an exciting film clip taken from the *Wizard of Oz* (the scene when the flying monkeys kidnap Dorothy), a film clip designed to elicit a strong emotional response; we call this second variable DELTA VAGAL; DELTA will be abbreviated as DEL. This second variable indexes the child's ability to suppress vagal tone when engaging with a strong emotional stimulus that includes an environmental demand for changing attentional focus, or regulating emotion; in our case the engagement with the environment involves the demands for an emotional response being elicited by the emotional film, as well as the demands to focus attention on the Atari video game the child played immediately after each film clip standing for a difference in vagal tone from the baseline film to the exciting film conditions. However, the order of the films was randomized.

Further mathematical information about the computation of the vagal tone variables can be found in Appendix A at the end of this volume.

DEMOGRAPHIC INFORMATION

Parents also completed a questionnaire asking about the family's income level, occupational status and average education level (in years) for husband and wife. To assess income level, couples were asked to indicate the range within which their joint incomes fell. Families were then assigned a score ranging from 1–14, depending on their income level, with a higher score indicating greater income. Families were also classified according to their occupational status as either blue or white collar, using criteria outlined in Krokoff, Gottman, and Roy (1988).

7

The Internal Structure
of Parents' Meta-Emotions

This chapter explores the internal structure of our meta-emotion variables, particularly the relationship between the parents' awareness of their own emotions and their awareness of their children's emotions, as measured from the interview.

How do the parents' feelings about *their own emotions* relate to how they will act when their child is experiencing a strong emotion? Here we ask questions related to the first issues parents must face, namely the emotional baggage parents bring into the parenting role. We ask, "Is there any relationship between how the parents view their own emotions and whether they will coach the child when the child is sad or angry?"

One of the reasons why we think that this question is of some practical importance is that all parenting books appeal to the parent's sense of duty, guilt, or obligation to encourage the parent to acquire new parenting skills. Tying the parent's own emotional life to parenting can provide a more "narcissistic" or personal growth motivation for being interested in exploring one's own parenting.

PARENTAL META-EMOTIONS
AND COACHING THE CHILD'S
SADNESS AND ANGER

The Father

The father's awareness of his own sadness was significantly correlated with his awareness of his own anger, $r = 0.53$, $p < .001$.

TABLE 7.1
Internal Structure of the Meta-Emotions

	Father		Mother	
	Coaching		Coaching	
	Sadness	Anger	Sadness	Anger
Father sadness				
Awareness	.28*	.50***	.29*	.32**
Father anger				
Awareness	.20	.30*	.14	.15
Mother sadness				
Awareness	.07	.18	.37**	.13
Mother anger				
Awareness	−.06	.15	.23*	.28*

*$p < .05.$ **$p < .01.$ ***$p < .001.$

The Father's Meta-Emotions About Sadness.   Table 7.1 shows that the father's awareness of his own sadness was significantly related to his coaching of his child with both anger and sadness; interestingly, it was also related to his wife's coaching of the child with anger and sadness. The more fathers are aware of their own sadness, the more likely they are to coach their children's emotions, and also the more likely their wives are to coach their children's emotions.

The Father's Meta-Emotions About Anger.   Table 7.1 shows that the father's awareness of his own anger was significantly related only to his coaching of his child with anger, but not with sadness, and it was unrelated to his wife's coaching of the child with anger and sadness.

The Mother

The mother's awareness of her own sadness was also significantly correlated with her awareness of her own anger, $r = 0.48, p < .001.$

The Mother's Meta-Emotions About Sadness.   Table 7.1 shows that the mother's awareness of her own sadness was significantly related to her coaching of her child with sadness; it was unrelated to her coaching of the child with anger or to her husband's coaching of the child with anger and sadness.

The Mother's Meta-Emotions About Anger.   Table 7.1 shows that the mother's awareness of her own anger was significantly related to her coaching of her child with both anger and with sadness; it was unrelated to her husband's coaching of the child with anger and sadness.

TABLE 7.2
Correlations Between Awareness of One's Own Emotions and
Awareness of the Child's Emotions

	Awareness by Same Parent of Child's	
Awareness of Own	Sadness	Anger
Father sadness	.50***	.54***
Father anger	.74***	.75***
Mother sadness	.39*	.32*
Mother anger	.63***	.55***

$^*p < .05.$ $^{**}p < .01.$ $^{***}p < .001.$

SUMMARY

The largest correlations in Table 7.1 suggest that if the father is aware of his own sadness he is likely to coach his child's anger, whereas if the mother is aware of her own sadness she is likely to coach her child's sadness. Perhaps this represents a division of labor in parental coaching.

How Is Awareness of One's Own Emotions Related to Awareness of the Child's Emotions?

In this section, we ask whether parent's awareness of his or her own emotions is related to the parent's awareness of the child's emotion, separately for anger and sadness. As Table 7.2 shows that, based on the coding of the subject's responses to the meta-emotion interview questions, for both mother and father, the parent's awareness of their own emotion is significantly correlated with the parent's awareness of that emotion in their child. This suggests the interesting hypothesis that one vehicle for increasing the parent's awareness of the child's emotions may be through self-awareness of the parent's own emotions.

Validity of the Meta-Emotion Interview

This chapter asks whether the information we obtained from parents' self reports about their parenting is, in fact, actually related to the ways they parent, as observed in our laboratory.

What is the validity for the meta-emotion variables derived from the interview? Respondents during the interview are talking about their interaction with their children in the interview. Is there any relationship between their coded responses and their actual behavior with their children? We use the accuracy criterion of observations of actual parent–child interaction. Unfortunately, we do not yet have data on how parents actually talk to their children during everyday emotional interactions, so instead we substituted our standard laboratory parent–child interaction. We expect the correlations during this task to be statistically significant, but we do not expect them to be measuring the same thing as the variables tapped by the meta-emotion coaching variable.

We employ our three dimensions of parenting as validity criteria. Warmth is based on the Cowans' Coding system, the Derogation and Scaffolding/Praising dimensions are based on the Kahen systems (KEACS). The KEACS assesses communications of intrusiveness, which is taking over when a child is trying to learn something new, criticising, mocking, or derision, and conveying to the child a sense of his or her own incompetence. In using these systems, our major interest is whether or not the parents are intrusive, use derisive humor or mockery, or are critical of their child during the child's learning of the video game; we computed the sum of these codes. The Cowans' Coding System assesses warmth and coldness toward spouse and child; we computed the sum of these variables minus the parental and co- parent coldness variables. The KEACS

TABLE 8.1
The Meta-Emotion Variables, Awareness of One's Own and the
Child's Emotion, Coaching the Child With That Emotion, and the
Three Dimensions of Parenting

	Derogation	Warmth	Scaffolding/Praising
Father sadness			
Awareness own	−.22	.10	.15
Awareness child	−.11	.28	−.13
Coaching	.03	−.09	−.01
Mother sadness			
Awareness own	−.31**	−.05	.36**
Awareness child	−.45***	−.17	.32**
Coaching	−.33**	−.12	.20
Father anger			
Awareness own	−.27*	.29*	.07
Awareness child	−.46***	.12	.20
Coaching	−.30*	−.05	.28*
Mother anger			
Awareness own	−.16	−.05	.25*
Awareness child	−.32**	.09	.21
Coaching	−.26*	.14	.21

$^*p < .05.$ $^{**}p < .01.$ $^{***}p < .001.$

systems also are used to measure the Scaffolding/Praising dimension, which consists of parental affection, engagement, positive structuring, responsiveness, and enthusiasm; we computed the sum of these variables across parents.

Table 8.1 is a summary of the relationship between the parents' meta-emotion variables for sadness and anger and the three parenting dimensions. The father's awareness of the child's sadness was related to parental warmth. Eight of the twelve meta-emotion variables were significantly related to less parental Derogation, and 4 of the 12 variables were related positively to more Scaffolding/ Praising parenting. Thus, there is evidence for the validity of the meta-emotion variables. Even though they are coded from an interview, they are related to actual parenting behavior in our laboratory.

QUALITATIVE EXAMPLES

Two prototypes from our study may help bring to life the relationship between our meta-emotion variables and our parenting variables. When we first began collecting our data in 1986, after looking at our tapes over and over again, we began to see a great deal of unity in the behavior of families. We selected two families that particularly illustrated this unity, and we brought the videotape of these two families to a conference at Vanderbilt University on emotion regulation in children organized by K. Dodge and J. Garber. We were struck by the fact that these two familes were dramatically different, and they became our prototypes for trying to describe and understand the variation we were seeing in our sample. In teaching their children the Atari game in our laboratory, as the child played the game, one family called attention only to mistakes their child made, and was entirely critical in giving their child feedback. The other family was quite the opposite, acting like a cheerleading section, giving their child feedback only when it was positive. We were surprised to see that their marital conflict discussions paralleled these parent–child interactions. The positive family discussed the problem of the husband's failed search for a job with humor and affection, and they viewed the problem as if they were both confronting an outside enemy together. The other family discussed religion: the wife wanted the children to be religious and the husband questioned this. The discussion involved the husband confronting his wife, playing devil's advocate, putting her on the defensive, and then being critical of her responses to his challenges. There was almost no positive affect in their discussion. In the meta-emotion interview, as you might suspect, the critical family was primarily emotion-dismissing whereas the positive family expressed an emotion-coaching philosophy.

PART III

PARENTING, META-EMOTIONS, AND CHILD OUTCOMES

9

Parenting, Parental Meta-Emotions, and Children's Peer Relations

In this chapter we explore the predictive validity of the meta-emotion and parenting variables, taken when the child was 4–5 years old in predicting the child's peer relations at age 8.

This chapter presents evidence that the meta-emotion variables were related to the quality of children's interaction with other children.

DEVELOPMENTAL STABILITY OF THE MACRO SCALES FOR CODING CHILDREN'S SOCIAL INTERACTION

For purposes of data reduction, we adopted a conservative strategy in examining the child's peer play. We correlated the MACRO scales of the children at age 5 and at age 8 to assess their stability. Only five codes were stable, and they were summed into two summary codes. The first summary code was called *Play Quality*, and it was the sum of Connected Interaction, $r = .30, p < .05$, and Non-Stereotyped Fantasy Play, $r = .45, p < .001$. The second summary code was called *Observed Negative Affect*, and it was the sum of Negative Parallel Play, $r = .49, p < .001$, Noncompliant, $r = .36, p < .01$, and Crying, $r = .32, p < .01$. The developmental stability correlations were 0.49, $p < .001$, for Play Quality, and 0.51, $p < .001$, for Negative Affect.

TABLE 9.1
Meta-Emotion Variables and the Two Stable Scales of Peer
Interaction at Age 5

	Teacher Ratings Negative Peer	Observed Negative Peer	Play Quality
Father sadness			
Awareness own	.04	.08	−.04
Awareness child	.13	−.10	−.08
Coaching	.13	.14	.04
Mother sadness			
Awareness own	.18	−.23	.01
Awareness child	.15	−.19	−.02
Coaching	.27*	−.02	.02
Father anger			
Awareness own	.03	−.25*	−.10
Awareness child	.13	−.10	−.08
Coaching	.13	−.10	−.08
Mother anger			
Awareness own	.07	−.15	.06
Awareness child	.15	−.23*	.22
Coaching	.03	−.10	−.18

*$p < .05$.

META-EMOTION CORRELATES OF PEER INTERACTION WITH A BEST FRIEND AT 8

Table 9.1 is a summary of the correlations of the meta-emotion codes with these two scales when the child was 8 years old. None of the meta-emotion variables were related to the child's play quality at age 8. The father's awareness of his own anger was predicted lower levels of observed negative affect when with a best friend at age 8. The mother's awareness of the child's anger predicted lower levels of observed negative affect when with a best friend at age 8. The mother's coaching of the child's sadness predicted better ratings of the child's peer relations by the teacher at age 8.

PARENTAL INTERACTION AS PREDICTORS OF THE CHILD'S PEER RELATIONS AT AGE 8

Table 9.2 summarizes the predictions for our three dimensions of parenting and the three outcome variables at age 8. The dimension of Derogation was signifi-

TABLE 9.2
The Three Parenting Dimensions and Peer Relations at Age 8

	Teacher Ratings Negative Peer	Observed Negative Peer	Play Quality
Derogation	.38**	.47**	.01
Warmth	.11	.07	−.02
Scaffolding/Praising	−.24	−.17	.01

**$p < .01$.

cantly predictive of worse ratings by the teacher of the child's peer relations at age 8, and more observed negative affect when the child was playing with a best friend at age 8.

10

Parenting, Parental Meta-Emotions, and the Physical Health and Negative Affectivity of Children

In this chapter we explore the predictive validity of the meta-emotion and parenting variables, taken when the child was 4 to 5 years old in predicting the child's physical health and negative affectivity at age 8.

META-EMOTION, CHILD NEGATIVE AFFECTIVITY, AND CHILD PHYSICAL ILLNESS AT AGE 8

Table 10.1 is a summary of the relationships between the parents' meta-emotions when the child is 5 years old, and the child's negative affectivity (sum of teacher and mother[1] ratings) and physical illness when the child was 8 years old. The meta-emotion variables, particularly the mother's, seem to be strongly related to lower levels of the child's physical illness. The meta-emotion variables are

---

[1]Contrary to the view that the mother's child behavior checklist scores may not be a valid index of how her child is really functioning in the world, but more of an index of her own unrelated biases, distortions, or personal dissatisfactions, we found that the mother's child behavior checklist score had quite a bit of significant connection with other outcome variables in the study. To mention a few of these correlations, it correlated 0.40, $p < .01$, with teacher total child behavior checklist score, 0.53, $p < .001$, with teacher externalizing score, but only 0.11 with teacher internalizing score. It correlated 0.49, $p < .001$, with the amount of child anger in the parent–child interaction, 0.67, $p < .001$, with the amount of maternal whining in the parent–child interaction, 0.64, $p < .001$, with the amount of negative parallel play in the child–peer interaction, $-.32$, $p < .05$, with the child's mathematics score, $-.27$, $p < .05$), with the child's reading comprehension score, and $-.29$, $p < .05$, with the child's Stroop scores.

TABLE 10.1
Relationship Between the Meta-Emotion Variables and the Child's
Negative Affectivity (Mother's and Teacher's Ratings) and the Child's
Physical Illness at Age 8

	Child Negative Affectivity	*Child Physical Illness*
Father sadness		
Awareness own	.15	−.16
Awareness child	.31*	−.23
Coaching	.24	−.21
Mother sadness		
Awareness own	.05	−.25*
Awareness child	.26	−.53***
Coaching	.22	−.44***
Father anger		
Awareness own	.15	−.33*
Awareness child	.22	−.25*
Coaching	.07	−.23
Mother anger		
Awareness own	.26	−.21
Awareness child	.18	−.35**
Coaching	.00	−.51***

*$p < .05$. **$p < .01$. ***$p < .001$.

weakly related to the child's negative affectivity, with only the father's awareness
of the child's sadness a significant predictor.

PARENTING AND CHILD NEGATIVE
AFFECTIVITY, AND CHILD PHYSICAL
ILLNESS AT AGE 8

Table 10.2 is a summary of the correlations between our three parenting dimensions when the child was 5 years old, the teacher and the child's negative

TABLE 10.2
Relationship Between the Three Parenting Dimensions and the
Child's Negative Affectivity (Mother's and Teacher's Ratings) and the
Child's Physical Illness at Age 8

	Child Negative Affectivity	*Child Physical Illness*
Derogation	.37*	.22
Warmth	−.01	.02
Scaffolding/Praising	−.34*	−.04

*$p < .05$.

affectivity, and physical illness when the child was 8 years old. As can be seen from this table, the two parenting dimensions Derogation and Scaffolding/Praising were significant predictors of child negative affectivity, but not of child physical illness.

CHILD NEGATIVE AFFECTIVITY AS MEASURED BY SPONTANEOUSLY ELICITED FACIAL EXPRESSIONS WHILE VIEWING EMOTION-ELICITING FILMS

Table 10.3 summarizes the correlations between the number and type of facial expressions shown during the viewing of the emotion-eliciting films. This task is a good measure of the amount of positive or negative affectivity that children display spontaneously while viewing films designed to elicit emotion. As can be seen from this table, Derogation was related to increased facial expressiveness, particularly of anger, disgust, and sadness. It was also related to more happy facial expressions. Scaffolding/Praising parenting was related to fewer disgust and sadness facial expressions. Warmth was unrelated to facial expressiveness on this task. Because this developmental period is concerned with the down regulation of emotional expressiveness (see Maccoby, 1980), these results suggest that children whose parents are more negative and less positive are somewhat delayed in mastering this skill of inhibition.

TABLE 10.3
Correlations Between the Child's Facial Expressiveness During the
Emotion-Eliciting Films and the Parents' Meta-Emotion Dimensions

	Happy N = 45	Angry N = 40	Disgust N = 28	Fear N = 20	Sadness N = 20
Derogation	.29*	.39***	.37**	.03	.49***
Warmth	−.03	−.05	−.11	.17	.01
Scaffolding/Praising	−.07	−.04	−.24*	−.16	−.28*

$*p < .05.$ $**p < .01.$ $***p < .001.$

Parenting, Parental Meta-Emotions, and Children's Academic Achievement at Age 8

In this chapter we explore the predictive validity of the meta-emotion and parenting variables, taken when the child was 4–5 years old in predicting the child's tested academic achievement and attentional abilities at age 8.

META-EMOTION AND ACADEMIC ACHIEVEMENT AND ATTENTION AT AGE 8

Table 11.1 is a summary of the relationships between the meta-emotion variables and academic achievement in mathematics and reading comprehension and the Stroop Interference Test. The child's mathematics scores were significantly predicted by the mother's awareness of her own sadness. The child's reading comprehension scores were predicted by the father's coaching of the child's anger. The mother's awareness of her own sadness was related to good scores on the Stroop Interference test, widely used as a measure of attention deficit disorder and impulsivity (e.g., DeHaas & Young, 1984).

THE META-EMOTION PREDICTORS OF CHILD ACADEMIC ACHIEVEMENT AT TIME-2, CONTROLLING FOR TIME-1 CHILD INTELLIGENCE

If, as we hypothesize, the meta-emotion variables affect school achievement through emotion regulation, we should expect that the relationships between the

TABLE 11.1
Meta-Emotion Variables, the Child's Academic Achievement at Age
8, and Ability to Focus Attention (Stroop Interference Test)

	Mathematics	Reading Comprehension	Stroop
Father sadness			
Awareness own	.08	.06	−.05
Awareness child	−.14	−.13	−.10
Coaching	−.06	.02	.05
Mother sadness			
Awareness own	.40**	.20	.28*
Awareness child	.16	.19	.23*
Coaching	.07	.18	.10
Father anger			
Awareness own	.06	−.03	.08
Awareness child	−.01	.06	.05
Coaching	.17	.43**	.07
Mother anger			
Awareness own	.20	.09	.08
Awareness child	.18	.13	.13
Coaching	.01	.02	.09

$*p < .05.$ $**p < .001.$

meta-emotion variables and the child's achievement at age 8 will hold even, controlling the child's time-1 IQ at age 5. To test this hypothesis, we performed a regression analysis forcing in the three IQ scales (WPPSII Block Design, Picture Completion, and Information Scaled Scores) before entering the mother's awareness of her own sadness in predicting the child's math scores, and in a second analysis before entering the father's coaching of the child's anger. The F-ratio for change were computed, as well as the partial correlations. For the prediction of the child's mathematics scores from the mother's awareness of her own sadness, the F-ratio for change was $F(4, 48) = 6.12, p < .05$ (partial correlation = 0.34). For the prediction of the child's reading comprehension scores from the father's coaching of the child's anger, the F-ratio for change was $F(4, 44) = 9.41, p < .01$ (partial correlation = 0.37). For the prediction of the child's total score from both the mother's awareness of her own sadness and the father's coaching of the child's anger, the two variables were summed for the analysis; the F-ratio for change was $F(4, 45) = 4.13, p < .05$ (partial correlation = 0.29).[1]

---

[1]We performed a regression analysis forcing in the three IQ scales (WPPSII Block Design, Picture Completion, and Information Scaled Scores) before entering the mother's awareness of the child's sadness in predicting the child's Stroop scores. The F-ratio for change was $F(4, 47) = 2.15$, ns, (partial correlation = 0.21).

PARENTING AND ACADEMIC ACHIEVEMENT

In this section we explore the relationship between our parenting codes and academic achievement.

Parental Intrusiveness, Criticism, and Mockery

The relationships between the KEACS codes and the child's academic achievement at age 8 is summarized in Table 11.2. The father's criticism of the child at age 5 predicted lower attentional abilities at age 8, but, surprisingly, the father's mockery of his child at age 5 predicted higher attentional abilities at age 8. The mother's criticism of the child at age 5 predicted lower attentional abilities at age 8. The father's intrusiveness at age 5 predicted lower reading and mathematics achievement at age 8 and lower attentional abilities. The mother's intrusiveness at age 5 predicted lower attentional abilities at age 8.

Parental Warmth and Coldness

The relationships between the warmth and coldness Cowan Coding System of the parent–child interaction when the child was 5 years old and the child's achievement and attentional skills when the child was 8 years old are presented in Table 11.3. This table shows that the mother's warmth to the child, and the warmth between father and mother were significantly predictive of the child's reading comprehension scores.

Scaffolding/Praising Parenting

Table 11.3 also presents the summary of the Scaffolding/Praising parenting variable and the child academic achievement variables. Scaffolding/Praising

TABLE 11.2
KEACS Variables, the Child's Academic Achievement at Age 8,
and Ability to Focus Attention (Stroop Interference Test)

	Mathematics	Reading Comprehension	Stroop
Father			
Intrusiveness	−.25*	−.40**	−.24*
Mockery	−.12	.19	.40**
Criticism	−.11	−.09	−.24*
Mother			
Intrusiveness	.00	−.23	−.26*
Mockery	−.18	−.21	−.03
Criticism	−.12	−.14	−.26*

$^*p < .05.$ $^{**}p < .01.$

TABLE 11.3
Cowan Coding System Warmth Variables, Scaffolding/Praising
Construct and the Child's Academic Achievement at Age 8, and
Ability to Focus Attention (Stroop Interference Test)

	Mathematics	Reading Comprehension	Stroop
Cowans' Coding System			
Father warm	−.01	.17	−.06
Father cold	.19	−.06	.07
Mother warm	.12	.32*	.08
Mother cold	.—	.—	.—
Co-warm	.03	.26*	.08
Co-cold	.18	.01	−.01
Kahen Coding System			
Scaffolding/Praising	.31*	.43**	.02

—: Could not be computed; *$p < .05$. **$p < .001$.

parenting is positively correlated with both mathematics and reading comprehension scores.

COMBINING PARENTING AND
META-EMOTION IN PREDICTING
ACADEMIC ACHIEVEMENT

Regressions were performed to assess the ability of the parenting and meta-emotion variables, taken together, to predict academic achievement and attentional abilities. For mathematics scores, when the meta-emotion variable (mother's own sadness awareness) was first stepped in to the regression, $F(1, 50) = 9.44$, $p < .01$, and when the parenting variables were added, the F-ratio for change was not significant, $F(3, 48) = 0.86$. For reading comprehension scores, when the meta-emotion variable (father's coaching of the child's anger) was first stepped in to the regression, $F(1, 39) = 4.95$, $p < .05$, and when the parenting variables were added, the F-ratio for change was significant, $F(4, 36) = 4.45$, $p < .01$. For the Stroop scores, when the meta-emotion variable (mother own sadness awareness) was first stepped into the regression, $F(1, 49) = 4.57$, $p < .05$, and when the parenting variables were added, the F-ratio for change was significant, $F(2, 48) = 4.14$, $p < .05$. The multiple R's were 0.44 for mathematics, 0.59 for reading comprehension, and 0.40 for the Stroop scores. These analyses suggest that some portion of the variance in academic achievement and attentional abilities was predicted by parenting and meta-emotion variables, and that the meta-emotion variables, although related to these parenting dimensions, are also providing separate new information in the prediction of mathematics achievement.

DISCUSSION

Ginott said that when parents are intrusive, or mock and criticize their child when they are teaching the child something new, they are establishing in the child the idea that the child is inadequate. Furthermore, Ginott predicted that the child will try hard to live up to their negative image. Our data seem to bear this out. The derison parenting variable was related to lower scores on mathematics, reading comprehension, and the Stroop attentional abilities scores. The amount of warmth during a teaching–learning transaction by mothers was predictive of higher reading comprehension scores. Thus, maternal warmth has some, albeit weak, relationship to later achievement by the child. Also the Scaffolding/Praising parenting variable was significantly related to both mathematics and reading comprehension scores. Ginott would not be surprised that the meta-emotion codes were also related to later achievement, and, taken together, that parenting and meta-emotion codes account for chunks of the variance in later academic achievement and attentional abilities.

We intend these analyses of parenting to suggest that meta-emotion codes (e.g., coaching the child's anger) work within a context of parenting to have their effects. Significant stepwise regressions do not suggest anything different, because a natural covariation between meta-emotion and parenting exists.

We have found that our three parenting constructs influence a child's academic progress: Intrusiveness, mockery and derision hurt the child's progress. The mother's warmth and the parents' Scaffolding/Praising parenting facilitate it.

The positive relationship between the father's mockery of his child and the child's attentional abilities is puzzling. Perhaps the child has learned the adaptation of tuning out the father and focusing attention is a coping mechanism to avoid the pain of derision by the father.

PART IV ————————————

MECHANISMS, PROCESS MODELS, AND THE PARENTS' MARRIAGE

12

How Might Meta-Emotions Have Their Effects: Preliminary Tests of Our Theory

Now that we know that meta-emotion and parenting variables taken at age 4 or 5 are predictive of child outcomes at age 8, how might these effects work? We return to the theory we developed in chapter 5, operationalize the theory, and test some path models that were derived from the theory.

In this chapter, we discuss building path-analytic models that provide the best information available with correlational data about the theory we proposed in chapter 5, and provide some ideas about how things may work. We are aware of the intrinsic inferential restrictions one must suffer with longitudinal correlational data. Hence, we offer the usual caveats, and we do not consider the analyses we present in this chapter to be in the realm of theory testing. However, we do believe that we can receive encouragement or discouragement from these analyses about our theory construction. We can also get ideas for what variables may be suitable for experiments (see chapter 18).

DEVELOPMENTAL OUTCOME
VARIABLES REVISISTED

For our research, we also selected as both an outcome and a process measure the child's emotion regulation abilities, as measured with our down regulation scale, which was filled out by parents when the child was 8 years old. We selected the following outcome variables at age 8: (a) the child's academic achievement, which is the sum of mathematics and reading comprehension scores, (CACHIEV), (b) the child's Down Regulation score on the Katz–Gottman Emotion Regulation Scale, (CREGUL), (c) the child's negative affect, which is the sum of the mother's CBCL total score, the teachers CABI total score, and the mother's ratings of her child's negative daily moods on the Differential Emotions Scale, (CAFFECT), (d) the sum of the teacher's rating of negative peer interaction on the CABI, the teacher's rating of antisocial behavior on the CABI, and the teacher's ratings of aggression on the Dodge scales, (CPEER), (e) the scale we called *Observed Negative Affect,* which was the sum of Negative Parallel Play, Noncompliant, and Crying, (NEGAFF8), and (f) the Child Illness Questionnaire at age 8 (CMI88).

RATIONALE OF THE MODEL BUILDING

Why are we building these models at all? The reason is to build theory about meta-emotion and how it might have its effects. Hence, we built a family psycho-physiology laboratory, and we wrote our theory chapter based on the idea that the child's physiological responses would underly emotion regulation abilities or deficits. We hypothesized that meta-emotion, operating in part through parenting, would significantly affect these physiological variables. That is, we fundamentally believe that these physiological variables are not engraved in stone, even if they are biological, but, instead, we believe that they are malleable, that, in part, parents shape these dimensions of a child's biological responses through their emotional interactions with the child, beginning in infancy. Ultimately, we believe that these processes do affect child outcome.

Developmental Outcomes in the Modeling

Recall that there are a small set of developmental outcomes of interest to us, in decreasing order of importance:

1. The first and most important developmental outcome was the child's peer relations during middle childhood. The child's peer relations was calculated from the sum of three teacher rating scales, the Cowan Adaptive Behavior Inventory (CABI) negative peer scale, the CABI antisocial scale, and the Dodge Peer Aggression scale; this variable is called NEGATIVE PEER in our diagrams. We also measure the child's peer relations using coding of the child's interaction with a best friend at home at age 8; this latter assessment provides an optimal picture of the child's peer social performance.

2. Second, we selected the child's negative affectivity, which was combined with the development of behavior problems. Child negative affectivity in our study was the sum of three scales, the mother's child behavior checklist total score, the total teacher score for the CABI, and the mother's

report on the Differential Emotions Scale, summing all negative moods for the child, at age 8, is called CHILD NEGATIVE AFFECT in our diagrams.

3. Third, we selected the child's physical health. Child Illness was our usual health measure at age 8.

4. Fourth, we selected the child's ability to regulate emotion. To assess the child's emotion regulation abilities, we used the Down-Regulation scale of the Katz–Gottman Emotional Regulation Questionnaire, assessed when the children were 8 years old. This variable is called DOWN REGULATION in our diagrams. This variable assesses the extent to which the parents have to exert external control the child to reduce the child's level of activity, negative emotion, inappropriate behavior, and misconduct. Although it is technically an outcome variable and not a process variable, because it was measured when the children were 8 years old, the emotion regulation variable appears in every model.

5. Fifth, we selected the child's academic achievement. Child achievement was the sum of the mathematics and reading comprehension scores and it is called CHILD ACHIEVEMENT in our diagrams.

The Process Variables

Testing the statistical significance of these specific pathways is the goal of the modeling. In Fig. 12.1, we see the major constructs in the models we plan to construct. We are quite limited by our sample size to select very few variables for the modeling, but we also wish to be limited by considerations of parsimony as well.

We begin with the task of selecting the process variables for the modeling. We want to select two meta-emotion variables to characterize the family, one based on awareness of the child's emotions, and one based on coaching of the child's emotions. We seek to characterize both mother and father with these two variables. This involves some loss of information. We seek one variable to characterize the most potent aspects of the parent–child interaction, one variable that assess the child's emotion regulation abilities, and two variables that characterize the child's basal vagal tone and the child's ability to modulate vagal tone in response to challenges presented by events that require organizing one's self for coordinated action that requires the focusing or redeployment of attention.

The basic template for this modeling is provided by Fig. 12.1.

Walking Through the Model: What We Predict

We have numbered eight conceptual pathways in Fig. 12.1 that we expect will be significant pathways in our model. We predict that there will be lines (statistically significant path coefficients) from the meta-emotion variables to the par-

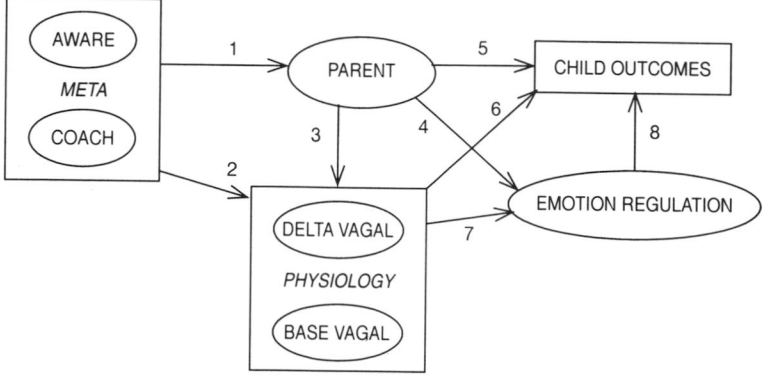

FIG. 12.1.   Outline of the general expected structure of a path model that fits our theory.

enting variable, from meta-emotion to the physiological variables, and from parenting to the physiological variables. We also predict that there will be lines connecting the child physiology variables to the child outcome variables. We predict that all these latter path coefficients will be statistically significant, which would suggest that parents do have an effect on relevant child physiology, both through meta-emotion and through parenting, and that child physiology at age 5 predicts child outcome at age 8. We also predict the physiological variables will predict the emotion regulation variable, and that the regulation and the parenting variables will relate to child outcome. We predict that parenting will have a direct effect on child regulation. There may be direct effects between the meta-emotion variables and the child outcome variables, but, to the extent that this is true, we have not completely succeeded in our theory, because we will not have a mechanism to explain these effects.

How to Understand the Results and How to Read the Figures

We used the Bentler computer program EQS for all analyses. For a model to fit, we are searching for a set of equations linking variables that produces a chi-square that is not statistically significant. This may come as a surprise for people not familiar with the technique. A significant chi-square would mean that the model did not fit the empirically obtained covariance structure between the variables. We also looked for a Bentler–Bonnett Normed statistic (BBN) that is close to one. Once the model fits, we next examine the path coefficients. In our figures we adopt a convention of drawing the path coefficients near the lines, and the z-scores for these path coefficients in parentheses. If a z-score is greater than 1.96, it is statistically significant at $p < .05$.

SELECTION AND VALIDATION OF THE PROCESS VARIABLES FOR MODELING

In this section, we discuss the selection and validation of a parsimonious reduced set of variables that are theory-driven. We discuss testing the validity of these variables before modeling. There are five categories of variables: (a) Meta-emotion; (b) Parenting; (c) Child Physiology reflective of emotional regulation; (d) Emotional Regulation; and (e) Child Outcomes.

Meta-Emotion

In the interest of parsimony, we need to cut down the choice of variables for the modeling, and it is thus necessary to limit the number of meta-emotion variables. We started with 12 variables (awareness of own emotion, awareness of the child's emotion, and coaching, for father and mother, and for sadness and anger). We decided to construct 2 variables from this set of 12, one of which is: (a) the sum of parental awareness of the parents' *own emotions* and the sum of the parents' awareness of *the child's emotions,* and the other (b) the sum of the parental coaching of the child's emotions. Table 12.1 is a summary of the correlations of these two variables with the meta-emotion variables. These correlations show that the two variables we constructed are related to all the awareness and coaching variables we have been discussing.

Parenting

For negative parenting we selected our Derogatory parenting variable, which is the sum of the following KEACS codes: the mother and father's criticism, mockery, and intrusiveness. The composite variable was labeled NEGPAR. The negative parenting variable was significantly correlated with the following parenting variables: mother mockery (0.55, $p < .0001$), mother criticism, $r = .27$, $p < .05$, mother intrusiveness, $r = .63$, $p < .001$, father intrusiveness, $r = .88$, $p < .001$, and mother sadness and whining, $r = .59, p < .001$. We were guided in selecting these negative parenting variables by testing the hypothesis that meta-emotion has some of its effects on parenting by inhibiting negative parenting behavior, not only by facilitating positive parenting behavior.

For positive parenting variables, the sum of the following were selected from the Kahen Engagement and Affect Coding Systems, a variable we have called Scaffolding/Praising. For each parent, the three positive engagement codes con-

TABLE 12.1
Validity of the Two Awareness and Coaching Variables
Selected for Model Building to Represent the Entire
Parental Meta-Emotion System

	Aware	Coach
Father sadness		
Awareness own	.80***	.55***
Awareness child	.68***	.37**
Coaching	.26*	.63***
Father anger		
Awareness own	.75***	.33**
Awareness child	.69***	.49***
Coaching	.44***	.74***
Mother sadness		
Awareness own	.56***	.32**
Awareness child	.66***	.63***
Coaching	.48***	.72***
Mother anger		
Awareness own	.57***	.29*
Awareness child	.64***	.36**
Coaching	.37**	.66***

$*p < .05.$ $**p < .01.$ $***p < .001.$

sisted of: (a) Engaged, which consisted of parental attention toward the child, (b) Responds to Child's Needs, in which parents responded to a child's question or complaint, and (c) Positive Directiveness, in which parents issued a directive in a positive fashion. For each parent, the two positive affect codes consisted of: (a) Affection, which consisted of praise or physical affection, and (b) Enthusiasm, which was coded as cheering and excitement at the child's performance. We omitted the father's enthusiasm code from this sum, because for the father alone, enthusiasm was significantly correlated with his criticism.

Child Regulatory Physiology

We recently reported (Hooven, Gottman, & Katz, 1995) that the child's physiology was related to the meta-emotion variables. We found that the father's awareness of his own sadness was related to the child (at age 5) having significantly lower levels of urinary catecholamines, $r = -.36$, $p < .05$, and cortisol, $r = -.34$, $p < .05$. The mother's awareness of sadness was related to her child's higher changes in heart rate variability (an index of being able to modulate vagal tone), $r = .31$, $p < .05$. The mother's coaching of the child's anger was related to the child's higher vagal tone during hearing a story, $r = .43$, $p < .001$, to lower baseline heart rate, $r = -.30$, $p < .05$, to higher baseline heart rate variability, $r = .31$, $p < .05$, and to lower baseline skin conductance level, $r = -.37$, $p <$

TABLE 12.2
Validity of the Two Child Physiology Variables
Selected for Model Building

Variable	DELVAGAL	BASEVAGAL
Mean heart rate		
Parent–child interaction	−.40**	−.26*
Mean heart rate		
First time in the laboratory	−.33**	−.28*
Heart rate reactivity in parent–child interaction (B1)	−.30*	−.24*
Heart rate variability (Baseline SXB1)	.39**	.25*
Skin conductance level after adaptation to laboratory (MX16)	−.22[a]	−.37**

[a]$p < .10$; *$p < .05$. **$p < .01$.

.01. We have previously reported that the child's physiology was related to parental marital quality. In particular, children whose mothers were unhappily married had higher levels of catecholamines in their urine (Gottman & Katz, 1989), had higher heart rate reactivity when directed to make a facial expression of emotion (Shortt, Bush, McCabe, Gottman, & Katz, 1994), and have slower heart rate recovery following a spontaneous facial expression of anger when watching emotion-eliciting films (Walker, Wilson, Katz, & Gottman, in preparation).[1] Thus, there is a clear link between meta-emotion variables and the child's physiological reactions in our laboratory, and there is a clear link between the parents' marriage and the child's physiological reactions. Our variables are defined in chapter 5. The variable we call BASE VAGAL in the model is an estimate of the child's baseline vagal tone. The variable we call DELTA-VAGAL, sometimes abbreviated as DELTA or as DEL, is an estimate of the ability of the child to regulate vagal tone in response to environmental demands for changing attentional focus or regulating emotion.[2] As Table 12.2 shows, the vagal tone variables we selected for modeling were related to the child's lower heart rate during the parent–child interaction, to the child's lower resting heart rate during the first visit to the laboratory (which is a mildly stressful and novel situation), to lower baseline skin conductance during the second visit to the laboratory (after

---

[1] We did not include the sympathetic portion of the child's physiology in our modeling. However, we did find that the child's concentration of adrenaline in the 24-hour urine sample at age 5 correlated 0.39 ($p < .001$) with the child's illness at age 8.

[2] We computed I6SPCS-I4SPCS, using variables derived by Beverly Wilson. These variables are the child's vagal tone computed by taking the area under the curve of the spectral density function only during the respiratory range for children aged 4 to 5. The SPEC program from the Gottman-Williams programs (Williams & Gottman, 1981) was used for the computations, sutibaly modified to compute area under the curve in any frequency range by Catherine Swanson. The program is available from the Gottman laboratory. See Appendix A.

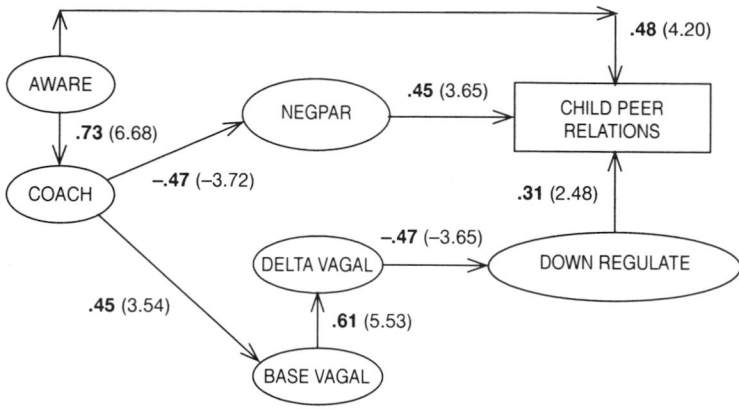

FIG. 12.2. Path model for child peer relations (teacher ratings) with NEGPAR = Derogation.

the initial adaptation), to higher baseline heart rate variability, and to lower heart rate reactivity in the parent–child interaction.[3]

RESULTS OF THE MODELING
WITH DEROGATORY PARENTING

The Child's Peer Relations

The results of our modeling are presented in Fig. 12.2. The model fit the data, with $\chi^2(13) = 17.95$, $p = .159$, $BBN = .986$; $R = .62$. Recall that the figures present the path coefficients, with z-scores for each coefficient in parentheses. As can be seen from these figures, the model building using our theory was generally successful. We were able to find linkages for the major pathways we proposed, between meta-emotion and parenting, between meta-emotion and the physiological variables, between parenting and the physiological variables for child peer relations, between physiology and emotion regulation, between emotion regulation and the child's peer relations, and between parenting and the child's peer relations.

---

[3]We correlated our two vagal tone variables with the baseline vagal tone when children were watching a neutral and fairly boring film (about fly fishing). Our Base Vagal Tone variable correlated 0.62 ($p < .001$) with this variable and the Delta vagal Tone variable correlated 0.24 ($p < .05$) with this variable.

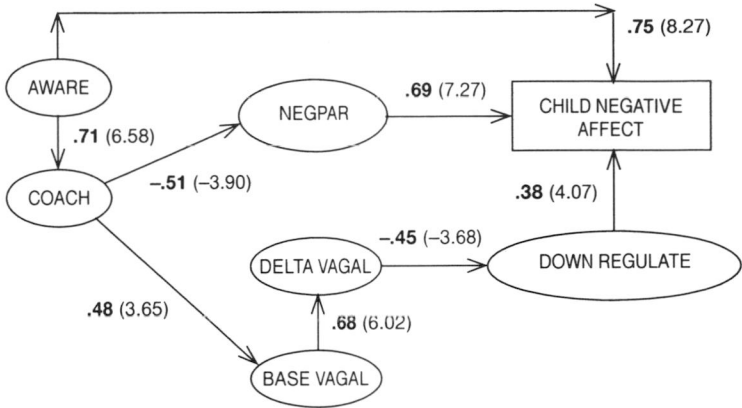

FIG. 12.3.   Path model for child negative affectivity (mother and teacher ratings) with NEGPAR = Derogation.

Child Negative Affectivity

Figure 12.3 shows that for child negative affectivity, the model again fit the data, with $\chi^2(13) = 20.53$, $p = .083$, $BBN = .993$, $R = .84$.

Child Physical Illness

For child illness, we had no hypotheses about what the linkages would be, and it turned out that the only significant paths to child illness were parental awareness of emotions and basal vagal tone and (negatively) the child's ability to regulate vagal tone. This finding with basal vagal tone is consistent with previous literature, and to be expected for a normal sample, although in at-risk samples (e.g., premature infants) we would also expect that basal vagal tone would be a predictor of good health. Figure 12.4 shows that for child physical illness, the model also fit the data, with $\chi^2(12) = 14.97$, $p = .243$, $BBN = .985$, $R = .55$.

Child Emotion Regulation Ability

It was interesting that in all models the child's ability to suppress vagal tone at age 5 was a significant predictor of the child's emotion regulation at age 8. The greater the child's ability to suppress vagal tone at age 5, the less the parents had to down-regulate the child's negative affects, inappropriate behavior, and overexcitement at age 8. In a moment we explore why this might be the case.

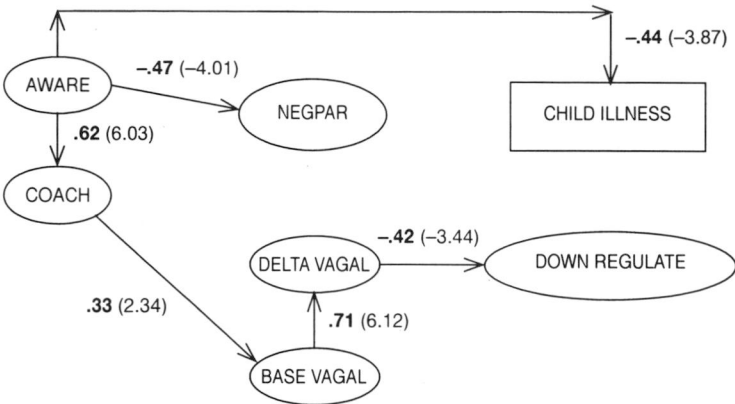

FIG. 12.4.   Path model for child illness with NEGPAR = Derogation.

Child Academic Achievement

Figure 12.5 shows that for the academic achievement outcome variable, $\chi^2(14)$ = 13.68, p = .474, BBN = .981, R = .41.

One encouraging aspect of the model was that, although parenting was not significantly related to the vagal tone variables, coaching was significantly related to basal vagal tone. This suggests the hypothesis that coaching may directly improve the child's regulatory physiology. In all models, coaching the child's emotions was negatively related to the negative parenting variable, suggesting

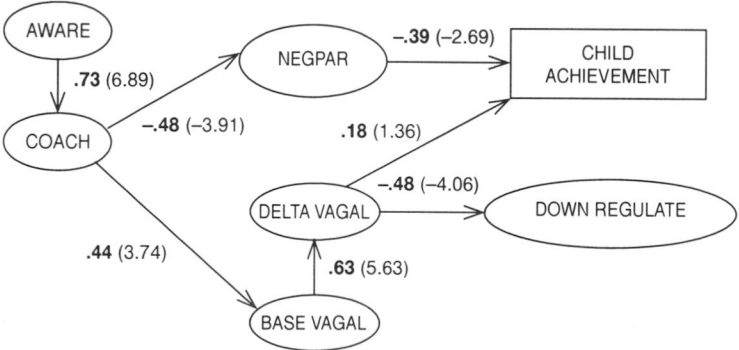

FIG. 12.5.   Path model for child academic achievement with NEGPAR = Derogation.

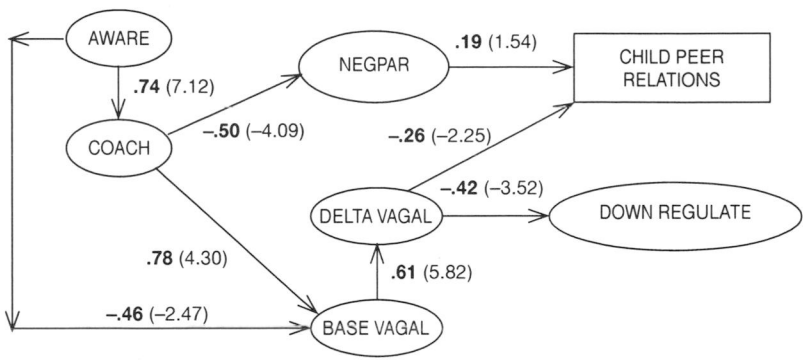

FIG. 12.6. Path model for negative child peer relations (observational data) with NEGPAR = Derogation.

the hypothesis that either coaching or awareness is an inhibitor of parental Derogation of the child.

For one outcome variable we were able to test whether the model for negative peer interaction was a function of method of measurement only. We fit a path model with the same variables, replacing the teacher negative peer variable with the observational data at age 8. This model fit the data well, with $\chi^2(12) = 15.99$, $p = .192$, $BBN = .987$; for negative peer interaction as coded by observers, $R = 0.41$. The data are presented as Fig. 12.6. The main point of this analysis is that the two models, with different measurement operations for assessing child negative peer relations, are essentially the same. There are a few interesting changes. The path from awareness to the outcome variable is significant only for the ratings of child negative affect. Furthermore, the path from meta-emotion to basal vagal tone is from coaching for the peer relations rating outcome, whereas it is from awareness to basal vagal tone for the observed child negative affect variable. The parenting path coefficient to the outcome is significant in both models. The pathway from emotion regulation to the outcome is significant only for the ratings of child peer relations model. The multiple R for negative peer decreased from 0.62 in the previous model to 0.41 in this model.

Directional of Effects Between Emotion Coaching and Child Regulatory Physiology: Testing the Temperament Hypothesis

Although our path models present data supporting the notion that emotion coaching can affect a child's vagal tone, it is possible that the direction of effects may be reversed. That is, it is quite possible that either child physiology could be a part of child temperament and that parents may select parenting style to be consistent with individual differences in child behavior, or that emotion coaching changes a child's vagal tone. Perhaps parents are more likely to do emotion coaching with a child higher in vagal tone, or perhaps emotion coaching can affect a child's basal vagal tone. Although we cannot answer causal questions in our path modeling, we conduct additional analyses that are either consistent with or disconfirm the temperament hypothesis.

The hypothesis that child vagal tone might affect emotion-coaching was tested by reversing the arrow between these two variables. The models fit just as well with the direction of effects reversed. First, consider the models derogatory parenting. For the child outcome of negative peer relations, $\chi^2(13) = 19.32, p = .113$, $BBN = .985$, and the path coefficient from basal vagal tone to emotion coaching was .37, $z = 3.62$. For the child outcome of child achievement, $\chi^2(14) = 11.28, p = .664, BBN = .989$, and the path coefficient from basal vagal tone to emotion coaching was .35, $z = 3.74$. For the child outcome of child illness, $\chi^2(12) = 13.36, p = .344, BBN = .986$, and path coefficient from basal vagal tone to emotion coaching was .33, $z = 3.05$. Next consider the models with scaffolding/praising. For the child outcome of academic achievement, $\chi^2(14) = 12.77, p = .545, BBN = .986$, and the path coefficient from basal vagal tone to emotion coaching was .34, $z = 3.35$. For the child outcome of negative peer relations, $\chi^2(15) = 19.82, p = .179, BBN = .982$, and the path coefficient from basal vagal tone to emotion coaching was 40, $z = 3.69$. For the child outcome of child illness, $\chi^2(14) = 19.77, p = .138, BBN = .982$, and the path coefficient from basal vagal tone to emotion coaching was .37, $z = 3.64$. Thus, our modeling cannot rule out one direction for effects, nor the possibility that the effects are bidirectional.

Given recent theorizing that vagal tone is a temperament dimension (Porges, Doussard-Roosevelt, Portales, & Suers, 1994), one concern with these results involves the direction of effects; the quesetion is whether parents are coaching their children differentially as a function of their temperament. To further test this hypothesis, we correlated coaching with our temperament measures from the Different Emotions Scale. Coaching was uncorrelated with the amount of child negative affect ($r = .02$, ns), the amount of child positive affect ($r = .20$, ns), and the amount of child total affect ($r = .16$, ns). We were also concerned that the direct effects of coaching on child outcomes might be qualified as a function of the child's basal vagal tone. Coaching was significantly directly correlated with only one of the three outcomes, the child's Time-2 physical illness ($r = -.55$, $p < .001$); the child's basal vagal tone was also significantly correlated with this outcome ($r = .30, p < .05$); however, the partial correlation between coaching and the child's physical illness, controlling basal vagal tone remained significant, $r = -.56, p < .001$. Hence it appears that the direct benefits of coaching are unaffected by the child's basal vagal tone.

RESULTS OF THE MODELING WITH SCAFFOLDING/PRAISING PARENTING

We tested whether the same equations we had used for negative parenting would fit when the parental Derogation variable was replaced with the Scaffolding/Praising parenting variable; of course, we expected that some of the path coefficients would change, but we first tested whether or not a similar model would fit the data. For the peer relations outcome variable (Fig. 12.7), $\chi^2(15) = 24.14, p = .063, BBN = .978$; for child negative affectivity (Fig. 12.8), $\chi^2(13) = 15.21, p = .295, BBN = .988$; for child illness (Fig. 12.9), $\chi^2(15) = 18.82, p = .222, BBN = .981$; and for the academic achievement outcome variable (Fig. 12.10), a very similar model fit the data, with $\chi^2(14) = 13.12, p = .517, BBN = .986$. For the observational measure of child negative affect with a peer (Fig. 12.11), $\chi^2(14) = 18.78, p = .173, BBN = .982$. These results are presented in Figs. 12.7 through Fig. 12.11.

Was positive parenting related to the variables of the model? For teacher ratings of peer interaction, the positive parenting variable was not directly related to the outcome, but it was significantly related to coaching. For child negative affect, the positive parenting variable was directly related to the outcome, and to coaching. For child illness, the positive parenting variable was unrelated to the outcome, but significantly related to coaching. For child academic achievement, the positive parenting variable was significantly related to the outcome and to coaching. In the model for observed negative affect with a peer, the positive parenting variable was significantly related only to coaching.

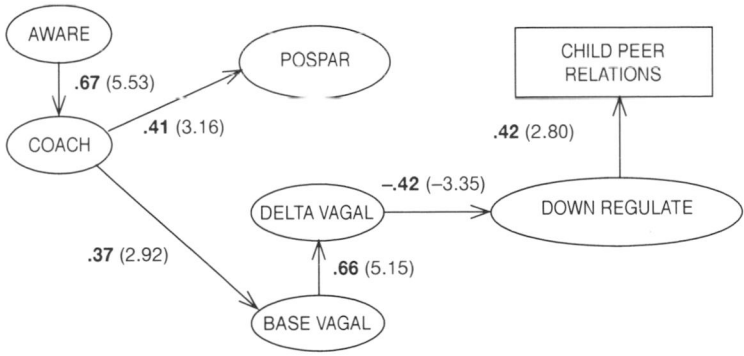

FIG. 12.7. Path model for child peer relations (teacher ratings) with positive parenting in the model. POSPAR = POSITIVE PARENTING.

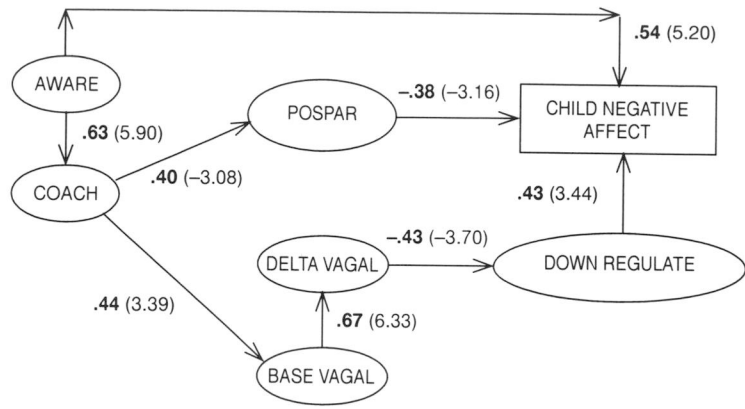

FIG. 12.8. Path model for child negative affectivity (mother and teacher ratings) with with positive parenting in the model. POSPAR = POSITIVE PARENTING.

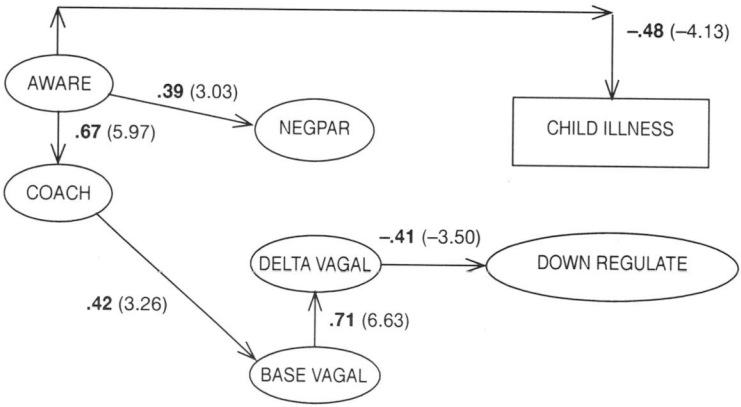

FIG. 12.9. Path model for child illness with positive parenting in the model. POSPAR = POSITIVE PARENTING.

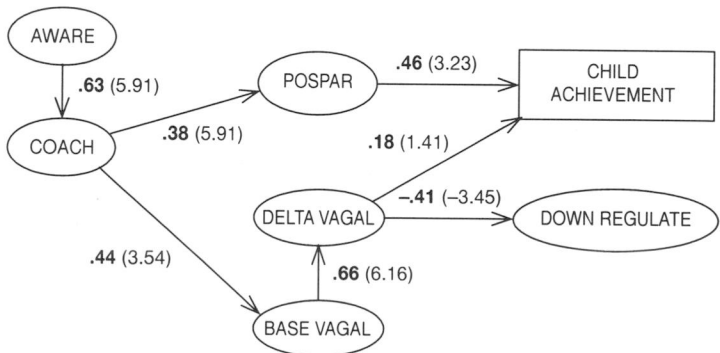

FIG. 12.10. Path model for child academic achievement with positive parenting in the model. POSPAR = POSITIVE PARENTING.

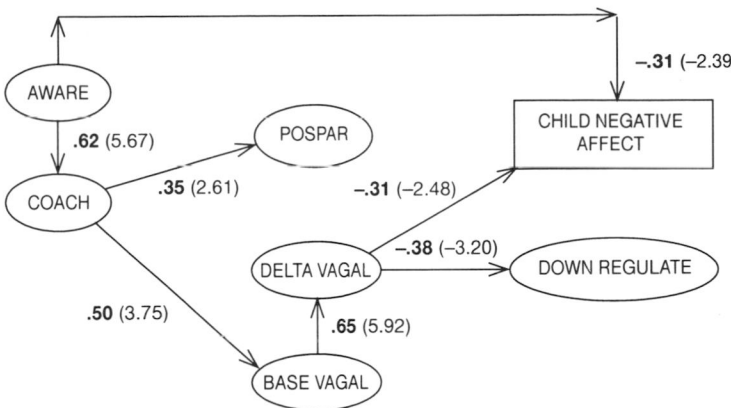

FIG. 12.11. Path model for negative child peer relations (observational data) with positive parenting in the model. POSPAR = POSITIVE PARENTING.

SUMMARY AND DISCUSSION

The major challenges we had set for ourselves when we undertook this research was in building linkages between the family's emotional world during the preschool years to the child's peer relations, negative affectivity, and behavior problems in middle childhood. Recall that we noted in chapter 5 that the theoretical challenge is in predicting peer social relations across these two major developmental periods, from preschool to middle childhood. Major changes occur in peer relations in middle childhood. Children become aware of a much wider social network than the dyad. In preschool, children are rarely capable of sustaining play with more than one other child (see for example, Corsaro, 1979). However, in middle childhood, children become aware of peer norms for social acceptance, and teasing and avoiding embarrassment suddenly emerge (see Gottman & Parker, 1986). Children become aware of clique structures, and of influence patterns as well as social acceptance. The correlates of peer acceptance and rejection change dramatically, particularly with respect to the expression of emotion. One of the most interesting changes is that the socially competent response to a number of salient social situations such as peer entry and teasing is to be a good observer, somewhat wary, cool and emotionally unflappable (see Gottman & Parker, 1986). Thus, the basic elements and skills a child learns through emotion coaching (labeling, expressing one's feelings, and talking about one's feelings) become liabilities in the peer social world in middle childhood. Therefore, the basic model linking emotion coaching in preschool to peer relations in middle childhood can not be a simple isomorphic transfer of social skills. Instead, it becomes necessary to identify a mechanism that makes it possible for the child to learn something in the preschool period that underlies the development of appropriate social skills across this major developmental shift in what constitutes social competence with peers.

Thus, the social skills related to peer social competence in middle childhood are not the same as the skills that emotion coaching parents are building in their children. For example, it has been well established that calling attention to one's self and one's feelings are precisely the opposite of what socially competent children do in a variety of critical peer situations in middle childhood. For example, in attempting to enter a group of one's peers, these behaviors that an emotion coached child learns are guaranteed to increase the chances of getting rejected (Asher & Gottman, 1981; Putallaz & Gottman, 1981). Another example is how socially competent children in middle childhood response to teasing (Asher & Coie, 1990; Gottman & Parker, 1986): They do not express their emotions. On the contrary, they act cool and unruffled. Teasing is a critical event in children's peer relations in middle childhood (e.g., see Fine, 1987, and Gottman & Parker, 1986). The point here is that children whose parents were emotion coaches at age 5 are acting in a way that teachers describes socially competent at age 8. Hence, they are skillful enough to know what to do to be competent with peers at age 8, and these social skills are not at all the same as what they learned from their parents at age 5. Apparently, emotion-coached children have learned to be savvy about peer social situations, and they can do what is called for. They may have a heightened sense of awareness of their own emotions, and better ability to self-regulate their own upset, and greater ability to attend to the salient aspects of any challenging peer situation. This sense of heightened awareness may lead them to be more likely to know what is called for, and to do it. This interpretation of our results suggests that what children learn from emotion coaching is not merely modeling of specific social skills. It is more likely that what they have acquired are the tools to learn how to learn in emotionally challenging situations.

Our path models suggest how this linkage between preschool and middle childhood occurs. Let us summarize the results of our modeling with respect to the eight conceptual paths numbered in Fig. 12.1.

- *Path 1: The Pathway From Meta-Emotion to Parenting.* It appears that meta-emotion is related to both the inhibition of parental Derogation of the child, and related to the facilitation of Scaffolding/Praising parenting.
- *Path 2: The Pathway From Meta-Emotion to Child Physiology.* For models including the child Derogation parenting variable, coaching was directly and significantly related in all the models (achievement, child negative affect, ratings of child peer relations, observed negative affect with a peer, and child health) to the child's physiology. This linkage was also evident in some of the models that included the Scaffolding/Praising parenting vari-

able (ratings of child negative affect, ratings of child peer relations, observed negative affect with a peer, child achievement, and child health). This suggests the intriguing hypothesis that parents can influence a child's physiology by emotion-coaching. However, we cannot rule out the opposite direction for effects without an experiment. The child's physiology, as we posited was significantly related to emotion regulation ability, which, in turn was related to child outcomes in many models (for negative parenting for the ratings of child negative affect, and ratings of negative child peer relations; for positive parenting, for the ratings of negative child affect, and teacher ratings of the child's negative peer relations). There were direct links between child physiology and child outcome. In the negative parenting models, for child health, basal vagal tone at age 5 was a predictor of *less* child illness at age 8, whereas, surprisingly, the ability to suppress vagal tone at age 5 was a predictor of *greater* child illness at age 8. This differential prediction of illness from the two vagal tone variables is interesting, particularly because the ability to suppress vagal tone may index a pattern of the child's active engagement with cognitively or affectively stressful events. The child who can suppress vagal tone may seek out challenges that imply a more stressful daily life, which has the cost of suppressing the child's production of T-cells (the vagus nerve innervates the thymus gland, which is involved in the production and maturation of T-cells). In the positive parenting models, there was a significant pathway between the child's ability to suppress vagal tone at age 5 and less observed negative affect with a peer at age 8.

- *Path 3: The Pathway From Parenting to Child Physiology.* This hypothesized pathway was not supported by any of the models.
- *Path 4: The Pathway From Parenting to Emotional Down-Regulation.* This pathway was not supported by any of the models.
- *Path 5: The Pathway From Parenting to Child Outcome.* This pathway was supported in 5 of the 10 models. For three of five models in the negative parenting models it was supported, and it was supported for two of five models for positive parenting. In all cases when this pathway was significant, the nature of the pathway was straightforward and easily interpreted.
- *Path 6: The Pathway From Child Physiology to Child Outcomes.* The pathway from child physiology to child outcome was statistically significant, but in only two models. The first model was when the outcome was negative peer relations using observational data, with a path coefficient of $-.26$ ($z = -2.25$), from the child's ability to suppress vagal tone. The second model for positive parenting revealed a similar result. When Scaffolding/Praising parenting was in the model, there was a significant path-

way (path coefficient $= -.31$, $z = -2.48$) from the child's ability to suppress vagal tone and the child's negative affect.

- *Path 7: The Pathway From Child Physiology to later Emotional Down-Regulation.* This pathway, which was from the 5-year-old suppression of vagal tone variable to the 8-year-old emotional down-regulation variable, was supported in all of the models.
- *Path 8: The Pathway From Emotional Down-Regulation (at age 8) to Child Outcome.* This linkage was supported in 4 of the 10 models, for both negative and positive parenting, and they were the same models, namely, teacher–peer interaction ratings, and teacher and maternal ratings of negative affect.

Unexpected Direct Pathway

In three models for negative parenting (ratings of child affect, teacher ratings of peer relations, and child illness) and for four models for positive parenting (ratings of child negative affect, and child illness, and observed negative affect with a peer), there was a direct pathway from awareness of the child's emotions and the negative child outcome. For the negative parenting models (child affect and child peer relations), more awareness predicted more negative ratings, opposite to what we might have predicted, whereas for child illness more awareness of the child's emotions was related to less child illness, which we might have predicted. For the positive parenting models, the same pattern held for *ratings* of child negative affect and child negative peer relations, but a significant negative path coefficient was obtained for *observed negative affect with a peer.*

There are two possible explanations of this unexpected linkage. One is that the parental awareness variable is not a good thing for children. Perhaps being attuned to a child's negative emotion fosters its expression, and even teachers pick up on this when the child is 8 years old, and rate it negatively. as part of this explanation, perhaps the arrow of causation should be reversed, meaning that parents have heightened awareness of their child's negative emotions *because* the child is highly expressive of them. With this possibility in mind, we attempted to fit path models with the arrow reversed (between awareness and child outcome) for the three models for which awareness was positively related to a negative child outcome. The results of these analyses were as follows. For the negative parenting models: (a) for the child negative affect outcome the new model did not fit the data, with $\chi^2(13) = 62.16$, $p < .001$; (b) for the child peer relations outcome, the new model did not fit the data, with $\chi^2(13) = 48.60$, $p < .001$. For the positive parenting model: (c) for the child negative affect outcome the new model also did not fit the data, with $\chi^2(13) = 28.02$, $p = .009$. Hence, this hypothesis is not consistent with our data.

A second possible hypothesis is that the pathway from awareness to child outcomes with coaching in the model represents the families we described in chapter 4, who have parental awareness (and even acceptance) of the child's emotion without coaching, and this may not be good for children. That is, maybe these are families who are accepting of emotion but do not coach children's emotion, so perhaps these children do not learn regulatory strategies and therefore have more negative outcomes. We found some evidence to support this hypothesis.[4]

On the other hand, perhaps the linkage exists because parental awareness of the child's negative emotions predicts adults' *ratings* of child negativity via predominately samples of child–adult interaction rather than child–child interaction. Perhaps children whose parents attend to their negative emotions are more prone to express these emotions to adults as they develop (parents and teachers), but less prone to express these negative emotions to peers. We tend to favor this explanation because the linkage between awareness and *observed* child negative affect with a peer at age 8 is negative (in the model that includes positive parenting), but our ideas at speculative at this point.

Overall Summary

The revised figure (Fig. 12.12) places the Time-1 meta-emotion variables as the exogenous or driving variables in the model, having their supposed causal effects on parenting, which predicts an 8-year-old child's outcome, and on child physiology, which has its major effects on outcome through the child's emotion regulation abilities at age 8. These results are generally quite consistent with the theory we proposed.

---

[4]The post-hoc exploratory evidence we found that supports this hypothesis is as follows. We split the families who were above the median in awareness into two groups, Group2: those above the median (N = 18) and Group1: those below the median (N = 8) in coaching. Thus, Group1 represented eight families high in awareness but low in coaching, while Group2 represented eighteen families high in both awareness and coaching. Group1 had children whose play quality at age 5 was significantly lower than Group2 $F(1, 24) - 4.29, p < .05$, Group1 = 14.13, Group2 = 16.00. There were also marginal effects at age 5 in the observed negative peer interaction with a best friend, in noncompliance $F(1, 24) = 3.05, p = .093$, Group1 = 2.75, Group2 = .83, and in crying $F(1, 24) = 3.74, p = .065$, Group1 = .63, Group2 = .00. Also, when the children were 8 years old, although we have not discussed this in this book, teachers also used the Dodge Rating Scale and rated the children on three scales of peer relations. The teachers rated the children in Group1 significantly lower in the Dodge social skills scale $F(1, 25) = 7.51, p < .05$, Group1 = −3.80, Group2 = −21, higher in the Dodge aggression scale $F(1, 25) = 4.56, p < .05$, Group1 = −3.29, Group2 = −.40, and lower in the Dodge scale of overall peer relations $(F(1, 21) = 5.83, p < .05$, Group1 = −2.21, Group2 = .21) than Group2. These post-hoc results support the hypothesis that the negative linkage between awareness and negative child outcomes may be due, in part, to those families who are aware of their child's emotion, and perhaps even accepting of it, but do not emotion coach their children.

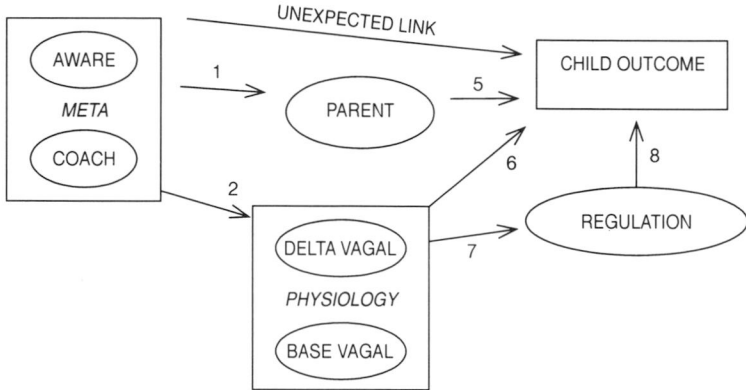

FIG. 12.12.   Revision of the path model derived from our theory.

OUR NEGATIVE PARENTING VARIABLE
IS NOT ANGER

In developmental psychology today there is a general equation of anger and negativity (see Cummings & Davies, 1994), which we consider unfortunate. In fact, in marital interaction, anger is not predictive of marital dissolution, whereas contempt is (Gottman, 1993, 1994; Gottman & Krokoff, 1989; Gottman & Levenson, 1992). Ginott distinguished anger from emotional interactions with the child that communicated contempt for the child, global versus specific criticism, criticism with blaming, or communications suggesting that the child was incompetent. He suggested that anger is not harmful to a child, whereas contempt is. In fact, Ginott suggested that a parent's expression of anger can be healthy within an overall context of emotional communication.

Most of Cummings' research is directed at the question of the effects of interadult anger that the child observes, whereas Ginott was talking about the effects of anger that a parent expresses toward a child. Clearly Cummings' experimental work suggests that unexpected anger between adults can be upsetting to children and have behavioral as well as physiological consequences, depending on whether the event has a clear and understandable resolution that the child understands.

To deal with a tendency to overgeneralize and conclude that parental anger toward children is harmful for children, the parental negativity codes we selected from the Kahen Coding Systems were designed to measure Ginott's cluster of negative parenting, and they are not the same as anger parents express toward children. In fact, the Kahen code of parental anger was uncorrelated with our measure of parental negativity (for father anger, $r = -.11$, for mother anger, $r =$

$-.06$), uncorrelated with the meta-emotion codes, and uncorrelated with negative child outcomes.

OUR POSITIVE PARENTING VARIABLE IS NOT WARMTH

We think it is important to show that the positive Scaffolding/Praising parenting code is not merely a dimension of global positivity, such as is tapped by the parental warmth and coldness variables. Our positive parenting codes were selected to tap a mixture of positive structuring, responsiveness, engagement, and maternal (but not paternal) affection/excitement. They are not redundant with the dimension of warmth, either toward the child or between parents when with the child (co-warmth). Of the warmth codes (Cowans' system), only maternal warmth was related to our Authoritative/Responsive parenting code, $r = .32$, $p < .05$, but not paternal warmth, or maternal and paternal coldness, nor co-warmth.

FURTHER EXPLORATIONS USING CHILD PHYSIOLOGY

How Might the Vagal Tone Variables Work to Predict Emotion Regulation at Age 8?: The Relational Database

As we reviewed in chapter 5, the research literature suggests that individual differences in basal vagal tone and in the ability to suppress vagal tone are related to enhanced attentional abilities and the ability to self-soothe. Porges (1991b) also speculated that vagal tone should relate to emotion regulation abilities in the developing child.

But how is this emotion regulation accomplished? How does the child with higher vagal tone and greater ability to suppress vagal tone manage to regulate emotions? To find a mechanism that might provide an answer to this question, we constructed a relational database that time-locked the parent's most negative and potentially stressful behaviors (intrusiveness, mockery, and criticism) to the child's physiology during the parent–child interaction in our laboratory. We then correlated the child's cardiac interbeat interval during these specific moments with our emotion regulation variable and with our two vagal tone variables, the child's basal vagal tone, and the child's the ability to suppress vagal tone.

Our reasoning was as follows. If a child has higher vagal tone and greater ability to suppress vagal tone, then, this child should be able to maintain a lower heart rate during these stressful negative parenting behaviors; a child with lower vagal tone should not. The child with higher vagal tone should also be able to regulate emotion at age 8. This would suggest that to the extent that the child's

TABLE 12.3
Relationship Between the Child's Cardiac Interbeat Interval and Basal
Vagal Tone, the Suppression of Vagal Tone at Age 5, and Emotion
Regulation Ability at Age 8

Variable IBI During	Basal Vagal Tone	Suppression of Vagal Tone	Need to Down-Regulate Child at age 8
Father mockery	.46[a]	.70**	−.49*
Mother mockery	.05	−.02	−.69*
Father criticism	.31*	.37*	−.31*
Mother criticism	.18	.10	−.19
Father intrusiveness	.23	.35[a]	−.59**
Mother intrusiveness	.43[a]	.47[a]	−.40

[a]$p < .10$. *$p < .05$. **$p < .01$.

vagal tone was being used to keep heart rate low during stressful parent–child moments at age 5, the child would be higher in emotion regulation ability at age 8.

Table 12.3 shows that this hypothesis was supported for negative behaviors by the father. For example, for father mockery, those children higher in basal vagal tone and higher in the ability to suppress vagal tone were able to keep their heart rates low (positive correlation with interbeat intervals, IBIs). The children lower in heart rate during moments of father mockery also required less down regulation at age 8. The child who maintained a lower heart rate during moments of mockery by the mother also required less down regulation at age 8; however, judging by the pattern of correlations, this latter effect was not mediated by the vagal tone variables.

A stronger statement of this hypothesis is: If a child has higher vagal tone and greater ability to suppress vagal tone, then, to the extent that this child can maintain a lower heart rate during these stressful negative parenting behaviors, the child should be able to regulate emotion at age 8. This statement of the hypothesis suggests that it is precisely by being able to lower heart rate during stressful moments that a high vagal tone child is able to regulate negative affect. If this hypothesis were supported it would suggest an explanation for the link obtained in our models between vagal tone at age 5 and greater emotion regulation at age 8.

To test this strong form of the hypothesis, we took the father's mockery, which seemed to best fit the weak form of the hypothesis in terms of its pattern of correlations, and we fit a path analytic model, attempting to place the child's interbeat interval during the father's mockery between DELTA VAGAL and DOWN REGULATION in our model. The reader will recall the old model as being part of our full theoretical model. The new model fit the data well (with $\chi^2(3) = 4.15$, $p = .246$, $BBN = .993$), and the path coefficients significant

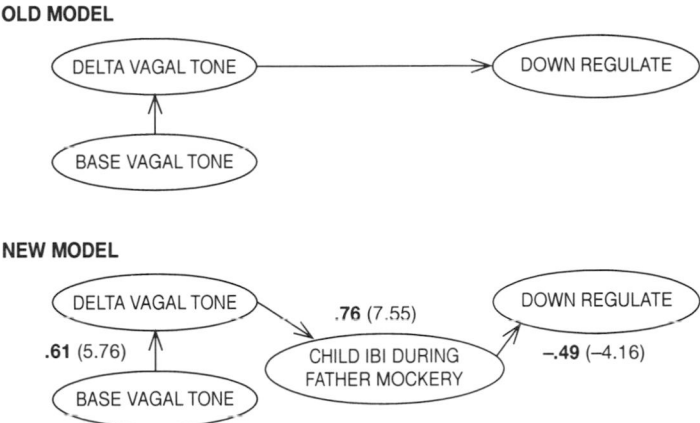

FIG. 12.13. A mediating variable between vagal tone at age 5 and down regulation at age 8.

between the DELTA VAGAL and the child's interbeat (IBI) when the father used mockery, and between the child's IBI when the father used mockery and DOWN REGULATION. Hence, the old path between DELTA VAGAL and DOWN REGULATION has been successfully replaced with an intervening variable, making the direct pathway an indirect pathway through our theoretical variable.

We also attempted to fit identical models as in Fig. 12.13 (new model) for father criticism[5] and father intrusiveness. For father criticism, the model did not fit, with $\chi^2(3) = 10.06$, $p = .018$, $BBN = .974$. However, the path coefficient from the child's interbeat interval (IBI) when the father used criticism to DOWN REGULATION was $-.32$, $z = -2.46$, $p < .05$, and the path coefficient from DEL VAGAL to the child's IBI when the father used criticism was .54, $z = 3.21$, $p < .01$. For father intrusiveness, the model also did not fit, with $\chi^2(3) = 8.07$, $p = .045$, $BBN = .983$. However, the path coefficient from the child's IBI when the father used criticism to DOWN REGULATION was $-.59$, $z = -5.41$, $p < .001$, and the path coefficient from DEL VAGAL to the child's IBI when the father used criticism was .47, $z = 2.88$, p $< .05$. Hence, in these two cases, although the overall model did not fit the data, the relevant paths for judging whether the variable of the child being able to keep his or her heart rate down

---

[5]If one asks only what was the general effect of criticism on the child's heart rate (regardless of increase or decrease), there is a significant coaching effect, $F(1, 255) = 9.79$, $p = .002$ (high coach group IBI decreased 22.23 msec, and the low coach group increased 4.08 msec). There was no effect for basal vagal tone. We would like to note here that the films we selected were not found to be consistent in the emotional reactions they elicited, so in many of our analyses we tend to use the child's facial expressions of emotion as our marker of emotion.

mediated significantly between DEL VAGAL and DOWN REGULATION in both instances.

Physiological Arousal and Recovery Using Interrupted Time-Series Analyses

We used interrupted time-series analysis to study the immediate effects on the child's heart rate of parental mockery, criticism, or intrusiveness, as well as the amount of the child's recovery from heart rate increases within a 5-second window. For our analyses we used the Crosbie (1993) interrupted time-series analysis computer program (see also Crosbie & Sharpley, 1989).

In this analysis, straight lines (each with an intercept and a slope) are fitted to the premoment an postmoment IBI data (the moments are parental mockery, intrusiveness, or criticism), after controlling for autocorrelation. To study physiological recovery, we selected all moments in which the child's IBI intercept decreased (i.e., the level of the child's heart rate increased) after the parental behavior, and then computed the change in slope from premoment to postmoment. We first split the sample at the median into those children high and those children low in coaching, so that we could compute and analysis of variance on the effects of parental coaching. For parental mockery and intrusiveness there were no significant differences between groups, $F(1, 21) = 0.86$, and $F(1, 32) = 1.25$, respectively, but there was a significant effect for criticism $F(1, 140) = 7.33$, $p < .01$ (low coached group slope change $= 6.97$, high coached group slope change $= 14.79$). There were many more moments of criticism than either mockery or intrusiveness. The coaching effect on the child's heart rate for criticism did not vary whether the mother or father did the criticizing (for mother, $F(1, 75) = 3.49$, $p = .065$; for father, $F(1, 63) = 3.81$, $p = .056$).

We also compared the extent of the child's heart rate increase in response to parental criticism as a function of whether the children were high or low in coaching. For mother, $F(1, 75) = 3.10$, $p = .083$, the low coached group IBI decreased 41.16 msec and the high coached group IBI decreased 66.69 msec. For father, $F(1, 63) = 6.58$, $p < .05$, the low coached group IBI decreased 31.43 msec and the high coached group IBI decreased 59.06 msec. Thus, children high in coaching whose heart rate increased in response to parental criticism had a greater heart rate increase in response to parental criticism and a faster recovery than children low in coaching. This is an unusual pattern in psychophysiology: Usually, a greater response is correlated with a *slower recovery* (Martin & Venables, 1980). The correlation for the model variables of awareness and coaching across all subjects with heart rate recovery following a heart rate increase to parental criticism was .28, $p < .05$, and .32, $p < .05$, respectively.

We also split the children at the median on their baseline vagal tone and recomputed the time-series analyses. Again, for mockery and intrusiveness there

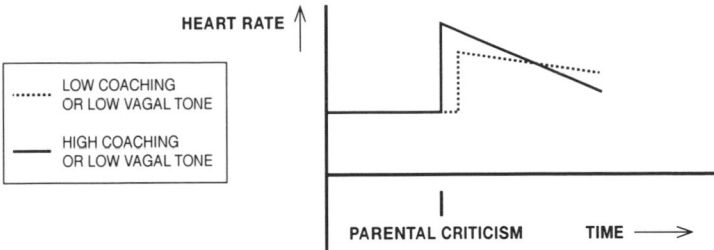

FIG. 12.14. Interrupted time-series analyses effects of parental criticism on children's heart rate as a function of whether the children were high or low on being coached by their parents, or high or low on basal vagal tone, showing a greater response and a greater recovery of children high in coaching or high in basal vagal tone.

were no significant differences between groups $F(1, 23) = 0.04$, and $F(1, 35) = 1.25$, respectively, but for criticism there was a significant effect, $F(1, 155) = 8.58$, $p < .01$ (low vagal tone group slope change $= 8.45$, high vagal tone group slope change $= 15.94$). There were many more moments of criticism than either mockery or intrusiveness. The basal vagal effect for criticism did vary depending on whether the mother or father did the criticizing for mother, $F(1, 85) = 5.88$, $p = .017$; for father, $F(1, 68) = 2.69$, ns. Again, comparing the extent of the child's heart rate increase in response to parental criticism as a function of whether the children were high or low in basal vagal tone. For mother, $F(1, 85) = 6.25$, $p = .014$, the low vagal tone group decreased 42.43 msec and the high basal vagal tone group decreased 73.35 msec. For father, $F(1, 68) = 0.20$, ns, the low basal vagal tone group decreased 46.63 msec and the high basal vagal tone group decreased 51.24 msec. Children high in basal vagal tone whose heart rate increased in response to parental criticism had a greater heart rate increase in response to maternal criticism increase and a faster recovery than children low in coaching. Splitting children on the suppression of vagal tone variable yielded no significant effects. Thus, children high in basal vagal tone have a greater heart rate increase in response to maternal criticism and a faster recovery than children low in basal vagal tone. These results are illustrated by Fig. 12.14.

The Relationship Between the Urinary Endocrine Variables and the Parasympathetic Variables

We wondered what the relationship might be between our sympathetically mediated catecholamine variables and the pituitary-adrenocortical cortisol variable and our heart rate variability and other parasympathetic measures such as our vagal tone measures. The urinary endocrine variables at age 5 were significantly related to only one outcome variable, child physical illness at age 8, with the child's epinephrine (adrenaline) concentration correlating 0.39, $p < .01$) with

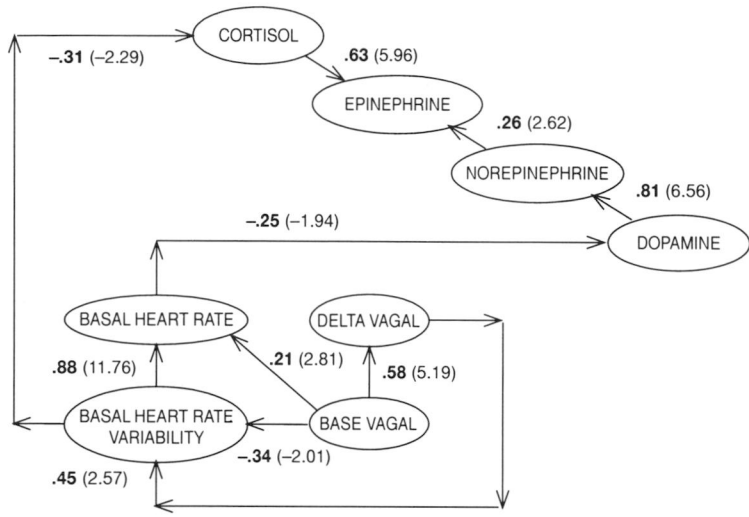

FIG. 12.15.   Relationships between stress-related endocrine variables and parasympathetic variables. (Basal = Condition 16)

child illness. The child's base vagal tone at age 5 correlated -0.27 with child illness at age 8. Vagal tone and child epinephrine were uncorrelated $r = 0.19$, ns. A simple path model (Fig. 12.15) fit this relationship, with $\chi^2(1) = 1.92$, $p = .166$, $BBN = .990$. The multiple R for these independent effects was 0.55. It was curious that the parasympathetic variables were independent of the urinary stress-related hormonal variables. To further examine the relationship between the parasympathetic variables and the stress-related hormonal variables, we fit the path model in Fig. 12.16 with $\chi^2(18) = 21.34$, $p = .263$, $BBN = .993$. In this path model we assumed that the catecholamines would be related as they are in their production in the adrenal medulla (the production is from dopamine to norepinephrine to epinephrine) This complex model showed no direct relationships between the heart rate and parasympathetic variables and the child's epi-

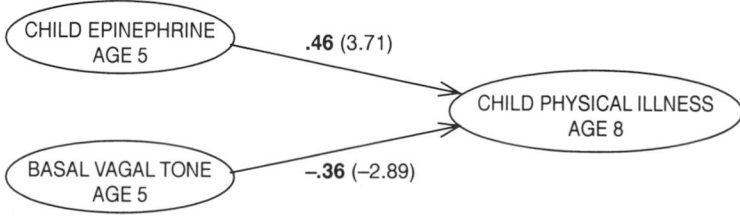

FIG. 12.16.   Epinephrine and basal vagal tone at age 5 predicting child illness at age 8.

nephrine concentration. However, there were significant pathways between baseline heart rate variability and baseline heart rate and the child's cortisol concentration, which was strongly related to the child's epinephrine concentration, and there was a marginally significant negative path coefficient between the child's baseline heart rate and urinary dopamine concentration. There is a relationship between cortisol production and the production of the catecholamines (e.g., see Axelrod & Reisine, 1984). Thus, we can see that there is indeed some linkage, albeit indirect, between the stress-related urinary hormones and our parasympathetic variables.

13

Parenting, Meta-Emotion, and the Parents' Marriage

This chapter explores the boundaries of the meta-emotion variables, assessing whether meta-emotion is also related to marital as well as parent-child relationships.

Today we have no idea of the enormous gaps between husband and wife that were created in the past by the lack of emotional connection that existed between them. The situation is dramatized beautifully in Galsworthy's (1951) *The Man of Property,* which portrays a British marriage in the 19th century. Soames desperately loves and admires his wife, Irene, and yet is unable to make a compassionate connection that would arise naturally from that love. Instead what passes between them becomes twisted into issues of propriety, appearance, and obedience. We can see dramatically how the shackles of personality mixed with social norms of propriety about being male and being female move their marriage from love to contempt. In one conversation we see the tragedy of this emotional distance:

> James: Soames is very fond of you—he won't have anything said against you; why don't you show him more affection?
> Irene flushed, and said in a low voice: "I can't show him what I haven't got."
> (p. 223)

In this chapter, we propose the hypothesis that meta-emotion is not merely a reflection of parenting related to the children's development, but that it is the very fabric of the emotional life of the family, and that meta-emotion constitutes the basic emotional life of the marriage itself.

We are witnessing the incredibly rapid and exponential increase in separation and divorce rates in the USA (see Cherlin, 1981), is mirrored, to a somewhat lesser extent, throughout the world. Sociologists have found that the cross-national divorce rate can be accounted for largely by measures of women's economic dependence. We briefly examine this work.

Why should women's increasing economic and psychological power explain the increase in the divorce rate? We suggest that we are in the midst of a worldwide revolution in women's rights, one that has been going on for several centuries, and hopefully will continue until it is done, but which has definitely accelerated in the 20th century. It is likely that across time only a small percentage of marriages were ever truly mutually satisfying, and even today we would speculate that the percentage of such marriages in the population is relatively small, perhaps only about 25% to 30%. If this estimate is anywhere near correct, it suggests that the rise in divorce may be a reflection of women's reasonable unwillingness to put up with miserable marriages, and the fact that economically, they no longer have to.

If economics is no longer the basis of most marriages, then what should their basis be? The key toward answering this question may lie with the exploration of meta-emotion.

RECENT RESEARCH ON
MARITAL DISSOLUTION

The observational research on marriages, which began in earnest in the early 1970s, was inspired by Gerald Patterson's research with families that have anti-social children. The research team (including Hyman Hops, Marion Forgatch, and Robert Weiss) found that these families were divorcing at a high rate and that made their family therapy very difficult (personal communication, 1980–1995). They decided, in the early 1970s, in a stroke of incredible optimism, to take a brief break from their work, and design a program to fix the marriages so they could go on with their family therapy research. In their groundbreaking early work on marital therapy, they started a wave of clinical psychologists who became interested in marriages, and this led to the realization that studying the quality of the marriage as well as the quality of parenting is essential in being able to understand what happens to children in families.

Fauber, Forehand, Thomas, and Wierson (1990) found that most of the relation between marital conflict and child adjustment could be explained by perturbations in parenting; they found a direct effect of marital conflict only for externalizing problems of children. In subsequent chapters we ask questions about the effects of marital conflict on children, and explore potential ways children can be buffered from the negative effects of marital conflict. However, in this chapter we are interested in examining the relationship between meta-emotion and the parents' marriage.

Sociological Studies of Divorce and Separation Rates

As an example of these studies, we review Trent and South (1989), who used data from 1983 on 66 countries and attempted to account for variance in the crude divorce rate, which is the number of divorces per population of 1,000. These authors admit that the crude divorce rate is only a rough estimate of actual divorce rates, because it is influenced by such factors as the age and the marital composition of the population. Trent and South used the following indices to account for variation in the divorce rate: (a) an index of socioeconomic development (a factor made up of the log of gross national product per capita, the infant mortality rate, life expectancy at birth, and the percentage of the population that is urban), as well as the square of this index, (b) the female average age at marriage, (c) the gender ratio (number of males per 100 females at ages 15–49), (d) the female labor force participation (percentage of adult women defined as economically active) and the square of this variable, (e) the percentage who were Catholic, and (f) whether the country was predominately Muslim. The explored 3 equations, and the second of these accounted for 43.9% of the variance in divorce rates. Based on beta weights, the divorce rate increased with development, decreased with female age at marriage, decreased with gender ratio, and decreased with female labor force participation, decreased with percent who were Catholic, and increased with whether the country was Muslim. They also found both a linear and a curvilinear relationship between the divorce rate and the development index, and found a curvilinear interaction between the divorce rate and female labor force participation rate. When the economic development index is low, women's participation in the labor force has a buffering effect on the divorce rate (i.e., it lowers it), whereas when countries are more developed, the reverse is true, women's labor force participation increases the divorce rate. They offer no explanation for this curvilinear interaction effect. However, many hypotheses can be proposed for their results. For example, it is likely that when societies are at a low level of development, women's entry into the labor force reflects some liberalization of attitudes toward women, but the jobs women obtain are likely to be fairly routine, low-status jobs. At higher levels of development, on the other hand, women may have access to jobs that are more interesting and professional; these jobs may provide both significantly more income and self-esteem. These more prestigious jobs may give women the freedom to leave a failing marriage that they do not have in countries at a lower level of development.

The Trent and South study illustrates advantages and disadvantages of a traditional sociological approach to the study of divorce. First, it is remarkable that so much of the variance is accounted for in the cross-national statistics by these variables. Second, it is clear that the regression models do not explain the phenomenon, nor do they come anywhere close to suggesting theory that might account for variation in divorce rates across countries. This is quite unfortunate.

A similar model had been developed by Brinton-Lee's (1980) cross-national analysis of 15 highly developed countries. Brinton-Lee also examined variation within Japan, a nation that has a relatively low divorce rate (this was, however, not always true—the divorce rate in Japan in the years 1884–1888 was 36.7%, see Burgess & Locke, 1945). Furthermore, Brinton-Lee examined variation within Japanese prefectures found consistency with cross-national models. She wrote, "Japanese prefectures with high rates of female employment, especially in wage-earning positions as opposed to positions in family enterprises, tend to have higher divorce rates than prefectures in which women participate less in the market economy." (p. 55)

Would these models indexing development and female labor participation also hold in a country that had a high divorce rate such as the United States? A study by Yang and Lester (1991) attempted to account for the statewide variation in the crude divorce rate and separation rate within the US (using 1980 Census data). They used a Principal Components analysis with a varimax rotation of 36 variables designed to measure "social instability," obtaining 7 non-orthogonal factors. Factor III correlated very highly with the separation rate, $r = 0.71$, whereas factor IV correlated very highly with the divorce rate, $r = -0.82$). Correlated with separation rate were the variables that loaded highly on factor III, which were: percentage in poverty, latitude (negative loading), percentage Black, homicide rate, southerness, percentage Roman Catholic (negative loading), and infant mortality. Correlated with the divorce rate were the variables that loaded highly on Factor IV (recall the negative correlation of this factor with the divorce rate), which were: suicide rate (negative loading), interstate migration (negative loading), church attendance (positive loading), alcohol consumption (negative loading), longitude (negative loading), the reciprocal of the gender ratio (positive loading), the percentage born in state (positive loading), and the strictness of the gun control laws (positive loading). Individual variables also were highly correlated with the divorce rate; for example, the correlation with suicide rate was 0.78, the correlation with the rate of interstate migration was 0.74, the correlation with church attendance was -0.49, and the correlation with alcohol consumption was 0.40. This pattern of results portrays quite a different picture from the cross-national results of Trent and South.

Variations Across Samples and Age at Marriage

It is important to realize that a clear and replicable pattern of factors at a macro-level associated with divorce may be difficult to obtain from any one study or group of studies. For example, an interesting retrospective study of divorce by Thornes and Collard (1979) obtained a random sample of people divorcing in England, in the West Midlands, and a sample of intact marriages from the same geographic region. On the basis of interviews and questionnaires, these investigators found that the couples who divorced differed from the intact marriages in some very dramatic ways. In particular, the divorcing couples had married quite young; in 44% the bride was younger than 20 years old, compared to a 28% figure for the intact marriages, that 32% of the brides from the divorcing group were pregnant at the time of marriage, compared to 19 % of the intact marriages, and that of the divorcing women, 51% reported that their parents were opposed to the marriage at its outset, compared to 13% of the intact marriages. This sample reveals one dramatic sample of failed marriages: those couples who married very young were likely to be pregnant and married despite parental disapproval. Despite the fact that this study highlights one set of risk variables for marital instability, the high-risk pattern they identified is probably a very general pattern across countries, in the sense that there may be some generality in the fact that an early age at marriage can be a risk factor for dissolution; for example, a similar finding was reported by Wong and Kuo (1983) for divorce among Muslims in Singapore (see also Broel-Plateris, 1961 for the United States). This factor of age at marriage and unplanned premarital pregnancy has been identified as a consistent high risk factor for marital dissolution. It can be found quite pervasively in the countries in Europe described in the book *Divorce in Europe*, edited by Chester and Kooy (1977). In fact, the factors that accompany marrying at a young age may underly another consistently observed relationship between lower socioeconomic status (SES) and divorce. The pattern was well described by Rubin (1976): One common way for a teenage girl to get out of a difficult conflict-ridden lower SES family is to marry. Teenage pregnancy may be more of a high risk factor for Whites in the US, and not for African Americans, due to a different culture surrounding extended intergenerational families among African Americans.

Psychological Studies of Divorce and Separation

Traditional sociological studies, although they provide the important knowledge of how macro-variables may have an impact on families, are unsatisfying for building theory about which processes may be operating in a marriage that predict (or cause) divorce.

A number of researchers have been working on models of relationship stability and dissolution. Recently, Rusbult has constructed a theory pertaining to the stability and dissolution of dating, marital, and homosexual relationships. She (Rusbult, Zembrodt, & Gunn, 1982) identified four responses to relationship dissatisfaction in close relationships: Exit (actively destroying the relationship), Voice (actively and constructively attempting to solve problems), Loyalty (passively but optimistically waiting for conditions to improve), and Neglect (passively allowing conditions to deteriorate). She then identified individual dispositions and features of relationships that make these responses more or less probable. For example, greater prior satisfaction and investment in the relationship was related to stronger tendencies to react constructively with Voice and Loyalty and lesser tendencies to react with Exit and Neglect (Rusbult, Johnson,

& Morrow, 1986). Johnson and Rusbult (1989) found that people who are more committed to their relationships devalue alternative partners as a means of maintaining commitment.

Kurdek has been studying the utility of alternative models in predicting stability and dissolution in both marital and homosexual relationships. Kurdek (1991) formulated two models for predicting relationship satisfaction and stability among gay and lesbian relationships. The two models were the contextual model (personality traits reflecting interpersonal competence) and the interdependence model (rewards and costs of the relationship, alternatives to and investments in the relationship). Demographic variables and both models discriminated between partners whose relationships dissolved and those whose relationships remained intact over 4 years. Kurdek (1993) also conducted a 5-year prospective study of marital dissolution. Couples who would dissolve their marriages declined more in interdependence scores and had greater increases in discrepancies on interdependence than stable couples. Similar models predicted relationship dissolution in both marital and gay and lesbian relationships.

In research based more on observational methods (Buehlman, Gottman, & Katz, 1992; Gottman, 1993a, 1993b, 1994; Gottman & Levenson, 1992), our laboratory has identified interactive processes that longitudinally predict which couples will separate and divorce. It turns out that of all the studies of divorce (several thousand), only a handful have been longitudinal, prospective studies attempting to predict which couples will separate and divorce. These studies are reviewed elsewhere (Gottman 1993a, 1994). Briefly, these studies have not done very well in prediction, nor have they been able to lead the way toward the development of a theory of marital dissolution.

Our laboratory has approached the problem as follows. First, recognizing both the need for and the limitations of short-term longitudinal research, we were able to identify an *outcome cascade* of events that form a Guttman-like scale of precursor events that lead to separation and divorce. It is important to be able to identify such a cascade because in our laboratory in any short term study only 2.5% to 5% of the sample divorces each year. Hence, divorce, a common event within the lifetime of a set of marriages, is a relatively rare event in any particular year of a longitudinal study. A similar problem faces any high risk research, such as the study of heart attacks. Heart attacks are rare in any particular sample in a short time period, and it would be helpful to be able to *predict a cascade of events*, with precursor events such as chest pain, which are more frequent. Such an outcome cascade exists for marriage. Second, we searched for *process cascades* that described the processes of marital interaction and change over time. We discovered these cascades in three domains: (a) *Behavior,* interactive marital behavior and sequences of interaction in various types of conversations (events of the day, conflict resolution, positive conversations), (b) *Thought,* self-report, thoughts about the interaction, attributions about the partner and the marriage, and (c) *Physiology,* particularly indices of autonomic arousal. These predictor cascades were organized into a theory about the mechanism of marital dissolution.

Probably the clearest prediction is the presence of four processes, which Gottman called "The Four Horsemen of the Apocalypse": Criticism, Contempt, Defensiveness, and Stonewalling. The best single predictor of dissolution across studies tends to be contempt, particularly the wife's contempt. Contempt is the single clearest index of the disintegration of affectionate and empathetic emotional connection in the marriage, and there is ample evidence that the antidote for contempt is admiration. The behavior of defensiveness is an essential element in this process cascade, and it fuels the process of emotionally distancing the couple. There is ample evidence across several laboratories that the antidote for defensiveness is validation (see Notarius & Markman, 1994).

We wish to note that anger in marital interaction is not predictive of marital dissolution. The damaging variables tap the dimensions of criticism, contempt, defensiveness, and withdrawal. Unfortunately, in many recent writings about marriage, there has been an equation of anger with hostility, and even violence (Cummings & Davies, 1994). There is no evidence that anger, if unblended with criticism, defensiveness, contempt, or stonewalling is harmful to a marriage. No one likes to have a loved one angry with them. However, it may be a necessary part of living together and making the continual adjustments necessary to keep a marriage close and intimate. We think, in fact, that anger is a natural part of the "irritability system" (Wilson & Gottman, 1995), which is balanced with the "affectional system" to create a set point for each couple. Gottman and Krokoff (1989) reached a similar conclusion in predicting longitudinal changes in marital satisfaction. We think that it is important for process researchers to be precise about which factors are harmful and which are protective to a marriage. It is important to know which factors are harmful and protective to marriages because of the implications of destructive processes in marriages for negative child outcomes. Grych and Fincham's provocative integrative model is quite helpful in this regard. However, although we agree that both destructive marital conflict and violence are harmful to children, we think it was unfortunate that Grych and Fincham (1990) lumped domestic violence with marital conflict to review effects on children. The effects on children of these two variables are likely to be quite different.

There were no consistent gender differences in Defensiveness and Contempt across studies, although when there was a difference, men were found to be more defensive than women, but this difference declined dramatically with the length of marriage (Carstensen, Gottman, & Levenson, 1995). Criticism and Stonewalling show consistent gender differences, with women consistently higher than men in criticism and men consistently higher than women in stonewalling. A related marital interaction pattern, called the "demand–withdraw" pattern, has been identified by Christensen and his associates (Christensen & Heavey, 1990; Christensen & Shenk, 1991; Heavey, Layne, & Christensen, 1993). Gottman and

Levenson (1988) reviewed research literature and speculated about the possible biological roots of gender differences, and Gottman (1994) reviewed research literature and speculated about the possible developmental roots of these gender differences. The Gottman–Levenson hypothesis about the biological roots of these gender differences is that men have a lower threshold of negative affect for physiological reactivity than women, and that men's physiological recovery is slower. This hypothesis was recently modified (Levenson, Carstensen, & Gottman, 1994) with results that suggest that men are somewhat more aware of their own states of physiological arousal than are women, so that when negative affect increases in a marital interaction, men are tuned into their bodies and respond to their physiological arousal with social withdrawal, whereas women, who are less aware of their own states of physiological arousal, respond to the negative affect in the marital interaction by becoming more engaged, responding to the social cues. The developmental hypothesis is that women have been socialized to code and decode emotion and have developed an expertise in emotion within relationships that is far greater than that of men. Maccoby (1990) proposed the idea that the cross-culturally universal sex-segregation effect in children's play is due primarily to the fact that girls will accept influence in play from both sexes, whereas boys will accept influence only from other boys. It is quite likely that women have also been socialized to take responsibility for keeping marriages in good repair, whereas men have been socialized not to accept influence from women. There is no evidence that this differential influence effect changes with increasing age to adulthood, although it may change in the elderly (Carstensen, Gottman, & Levenson, in press). In a marriage, the fact that most of the "business" of a marriage is emotional communication, the fact that women hold the greater expertise in the expression, decoding, and management of emotion in relationships, and the fact that men are socialized to not accept influence from women makes for a particularly volatile set of initial conditions for any marriage. There is a great deal of evidence to suggest that women are relentless in their pursuit of emotional intimacy and respect in marriages, and that they take the role of emotional managers in families (see Gottman, 1994, for a review). Thus, the critical dimension in understanding whether a marriage will work or not, becomes the extent to which the male can accept the influence of the woman he loves and become socialized in emotional communication.

Thus, the dimensions of meta-emotion that we have been discussing may have critical implications for the marriage itself, as well as for the child.

META-EMOTION AND THE MARRIAGE

We are interested in two aspects of the parents' marriage. First, we want to see if the meta-emotion variables are related only to parenting, or whether they can be used theoretically to represent a level of social skills applied to the marriage as well as to parenting. In approaching this question, we examine two things, marital interaction during conflict resolution and the longitudinal stability and happiness of the marriage. Second, we wish to assess whether the meta-emotion variables are related to the couple's overall philosophy of the marriage, particularly about the resolution of conflict, as assessed by our Oral History Interview. In this regard, Gottman (1994) identified a type of stable marriage in which people agree to avoid conflict, to let their differences lie without resolution, to agree to disagree. These couples were as likely as conflict engaging couples to have stable marriages. However, they were very low in affective expression, and had a philosophy of minimizing the expression negative affect, and of believing that just the passage of time alone would make things better. They avoided attempting to influence one another in a marital discussion of an area of continuing disagreement. These marriages tended to be traditional and nonequalitarian in their gender role divisions. The Buehlman Oral History coding system has a variable that assesses this conflict-avoiding philosophy of marriage.

THE META-EMOTION VARIABLES ARE RELATED TO HOW THE PARENTS' RESOLVE THEIR MARITAL CONFLICTS

Tables 13.1a and 13.1b are a summary of the relationships between the meta-emotion codes and the Specific Affect Coding System (SPAFF) variables derived from coding the marital conflict interaction, which are predictive of marital stability or dissolution.

First, consider the father's sadness meta-emotions. Fathers who are aware of their own sadness are more affectionate in the marital interaction, and their wives are significantly less contemptuous and belligerent. Fathers who accept their own sadness are less likely to stonewall. Fathers who coach their children's sadness are less disgusted, less defensive, and more affectionate; their wives are also less defensive and more affectionate.

Next consider the father's anger meta-emotions. Fathers who coach their children's anger are more affectionate and their wives are less contemptuous, less belligerent, less defensive, and more affectionate. However, fathers who are aware of their own anger and aware of their child's anger were more defensive, so the father's awareness of his own anger may not be such a positive quality, viewed from the standpoint of the marital interaction. These results may be partly responsible for the unexpected pathway in the model discussed in chapter 12 between parental awareness of child emotion and child outcomes. Perhaps the father's awareness is carrying the bulk of the variance in this relationship.

Consider the mother's sadness meta-emotions. Mothers who are aware of their own sadness have husbands who are less belligerent and they themselves are less contemptuous and belligerent. Mothers who are aware of their children's sadness

TABLE 13.1a
Correlation of the Meta-Emotion Variables and the SPAFF Coding of the Marital Interaction: Father's Behavior

	Father's Marital Interaction Behavior						
	Disgust	Contempt	Belligerence	Stonewalling	Defensiveness	Validation	Affection
Father sadness							
Awareness own	−.14	−.15	−.21	−.10	.14	.00	.31*
Awareness child	−.02	.06	−.04	−.12	.12	−.01	.18
Coaching	−.23*	−.02	.01	.03	−.34**	.11	.25*
Mother sadness							
Awareness own	.08	−.11	−.35**	.17	.01	.20	.14
Awareness child	−.69***	.07	−.21	.04	.08	.12	.16
Coaching	−.37**	.00	−.25*	−.10	.22	.17	.19
Father anger							
Awareness own	−.03	−.06	−.18	−.18	.26*	.00	.12
Awareness child	−.03	−.06	−.18	−.18	.26*	.00	.12
Coaching	−.14	−.14	−.20	−.02	−.22	.17	.28*
Mother anger							
Awareness own	.07	.09	−.03	.18	.06	.12	.05
Awareness child	.07	.09	−.04	.18	.06	.12	.05
Coaching	−.24*	.12	−.13	.09	.13	−.18	.22

*p < .05. **p < .01. ***p < .001.

TABLE 13.1b
Correlation of the Meta-Emotion Variables and the SPAFF Coding of the Marital Interaction: Mother's Behavior

	Disgust	Contempt	Belligerence	Stonewalling	Defensiveness	Validation	Affection
Father sadness							
Awareness own	−.08	−.33*	−.25*	.06	−.06	.16	.21
Awareness child	.08	−.06	.04	.10	.00	.06	.10
Coaching	−.17	−.02	.01	.11	−.25*	.07	.39**
Mother sadness							
Awareness own	.03	−.35**	−.35**	−.20	−.07	.11	.13
Awareness child	−.45***	−.26*	−.09	.00	−.15	.03	.03
Coaching	−.30*	−.13	−.24*	.09	−.09	.02	.08
Father anger							
Awareness own	.07	−.21	.03	.03	.06	.14	.15
Awareness child	.11	−.19	−.15	.10	.04	.13	.11
Coaching	−.05	−.41***	−.24*	−.01	−.33**	.10	.30*
Mother anger							
Awareness own	.08	−.12	.09	−.14	.08	.01	.05
Awareness child	−.07	−.36**	−.18	.14	.15	.01	−.23*
Coaching	−.21	−.16	−.17	.10	.04	−.11	.20

*p < .05. **p < .01. ***p < .001.

have husbands who are less disgusted and they themselves are less disgusted and less contemptuous. Mothers who coach their children's sadness have husbands who are less disgusted and less belligerent and they themselves are less disgusted and less belligerent.

Now consider the mother's anger meta-emotions. Mothers who are aware of their children's anger are both less contemptuous and less affectionate toward their husbands. This latter result is strange, and perhaps it is related to the unexpected pathway between awareness of child emotion and negative child outcomes; it may be worth exploring removing awareness of child anger from the awareness variable and explore whether awareness would no longer relate to negative child outcomes in the model. Mothers who coach their children's anger have husbands who are less disgusted.

Hence, for the father, awareness of his and his child's anger do not bode well for marital interaction. All the other dimensions of meta-emotion just mentioned above have positive implications for the quality of the marital interaction.

THE META-EMOTION VARIABLES ARE RELATED TO MARITAL SATISFACTION AND MARITAL STABILITY

As we mentioned earlier, Gottman and Levenson (1992), Gottman (1993a), and Gottman (1994, in the book *What Predicts Divorce?*) described a cascade toward marital dissolution. The cascade consists of precursor variables that predict divorce. Essentially, the cascade describes two trajectories couples take in their marriages, a happy and stable trajectory, and another headed toward dissolution. The structural equation model for this cascade links research on the correlates of marital dissatisfaction with research on divorce, showing that there is a Guttman scale of precursor variables in divorce prediction. Couples headed for divorce have been unhappily married for some time, seriously consider separation and divorce, and then actually do separate and divorce. Booth and White (1980) also found that thoughts about divorce were a good predictor of actual divorce. The Gottman and Levenson Cascade structural equation model has replicated in one study upon 4-year and 8-year longitudinal followup, and in the present study as well (Gottman, 1994). Here we ask the question, do the meta-emotion variables predict this cascade?

Tables 13.2a, 13.2b, 13.2c, and 13.2d are a summary of these correlations. These results show that the meta-emotion codes are uniformly related to higher marital satisfaction at Time-1 and at Time-2, fewer serious considerations of separation and divorce, less actual separation, and, if separation did occur, shorter separations and less likelihood of divorce. Hence an emotion coaching meta-emotion structure is related to greater marital stability and to greater marital satisfaction.

TABLE 13.2a
Correlation of the Meta-Emotion Variables and the Cascade Toward Marital Dissolution, Father Variables

| | Father Variables | | | | | | |
	MarSat1	MarSat2	CnSep	CnDiv	Sep	MoSep	Divorce
Father sadness							
Awareness own	.07	−.03	−.21	.10	.02	−.21	−.06
Awareness child	−.05	−.07	−.02	.20	.05	−.14	.05
Coaching	.03	.27*	.01	.21	−.07	−.03	−.08
Mother sadness							
Awareness own	.06	.13	−.14	−.06	−.12	−.37**	−.06
Awareness child	.13	.05	.06	.15	−.06	−.48***	−.14
Coaching	.05	.00	.04	−.08	.00	−.38**	−.06
Father anger							
Awareness own	−.01	−.02	−.11	.17	−.12	−.30*	−.10
Awareness child	.11	.06	−.18	.09	−.06	−.45***	−.17
Coaching	.35**	.34**	−.35**	−.06	−.16	−.26*	−.25*
Mother anger							
Awareness own	.05	.13	.06	.16	.06	−.16	.05
Awareness child	.10	−.10	−.05	.15	.06	−.31*	.03
Coaching	−.07	.00	.10	.05	.18	−.25*	.04

Note. MarSat1 = Marital Satisfaction Time 1; MoSep = Months Separated; MarSat2 = Marital Satisfaction Time 2; Divorce = Divorced or Not; CnSep = Serious Considerations of Separation; Sep = Separated or Not; CnDiv = Serious Considerations of Divorce
*p < .05. **p < .01. ***p < .001.

TABLE 13.2b
Correlation of the Meta-Emotion Variables and the Cascade Toward Marital Dissolution, Mother Variables

	MarSat1	MarSat2	CnSep	CnDiv	Sep	MoSep	Divorce
				Mother Variables			
Father sadness							
Awareness own	.25*	−.06	−.09	−.01	.02	−.21	−.06
Awareness child	.19	−.03	−.05	.10	.05	−.14	.05
Coaching	−.03	.22	−.07	.04	−.07	−.03	−.08
Mother sadness							
Awareness own	.31**	.14	−.13	−.22	−.12	−.37**	−.06
Awareness child	.33**	.04	−.05	−.09	−.05	−.48***	−.14
Coaching	.24*	.01	.04	.07	.00	−.38**	−.06
Father anger							
Awareness own	.20	.06	−.14	−.06	−.12	−.30*	−.10
Awareness child	.30*	.11	−.12	.00	−.06	−.45***	−.17
Coaching	.30*	.28*	−.32*	−.23	−.16	−.26*	−.25*
Mother anger							
Awareness own	.28*	−.11	.00	−.04	.06	−.16	.05
Awareness child	.24*	−.06	.01	−.01	.06	−.31*	.04
Coaching	.23*	−.11	.16	.18	.18	−.25*	.04

Note. MarSat1 = Marital Satisfaction Time 1; MoSep = Months Separated; MarSat2 = Marital Satisfaction Time 2; Divorce = Divorced or Not; CnSep = Serious Considerations of Separation; Sep = Separated or Not; CnDiv = Serious Considerations of Divorce
*p < .05. **p < .01. ***p < .001.

TABLE 13.2c
Correlation of the Meta-Emotion Variables and Parental
Health (Cornell Medical Index).

	Father Health	Mother Health
Father sadness		
Awareness own	.02	−.19
Awareness child	.01	−.17
Coaching	−.01	.21
Mother sadness		
Awareness own	−.25*	−.43***
Awareness child	−.04	−.24*
Coaching	−.03	−.32**
Father anger		
Awareness own	.01	−.30*
Awareness child	−.06	−.32*
Coaching	−.05	−.01
Mother anger		
Awareness own	−.02	−.29*
Awareness child	−.10	−.40***
Coaching	.09	−.11

Note. Higher Cornell scores represent greater illness.
*$p < .05$. **$p < .01$. ***$p < .001$.

TABLE 13.2d
Correlation of the Meta-Emotion Variables and Parental Health,
Using the Krokoff Index, Which Controls for Reporting Biases

	Father Health (Reported by Mother)	Mother Health (Reported by Father)
Father sadness		
Awareness own	.33*	.12
Awareness child	.24*	.07
Coaching	.11	−.05
Mother sadness		
Awareness own	.29*	.38**
Awareness child	.18	.17
Coaching	.30*	.10
Father anger		
Awareness own	.20	.16
Awareness child	.33*	.25*
Coaching	.34**	.27*
Mother anger		
Awareness own	.23	.15
Awareness child	.25*	.21
Coaching	.11	.12

Note. Higher Krokoff scores represent greater health.
*$p < .05$. **$p < .01$.

This is particularly true of the father's meta-emotions about anger and the mother's meta-emotions about sadness.

THE META-EMOTION VARIABLES ARE RELATED TO THE PHYSICAL HEALTH OF THE PARENTS

It is well-known that marital distress and disruption are related to increased physical illness and mortality. We now know that separation and divorce have strong negative consequences for the mental and physical health of both spouses. These negative effects include increased risk for psychopathology, increased rates of automobile accidents including fatalities, increased incidence of physical illness, suicide, violence, homicide, and mortality from diseases (for a review see Bloom, Asher, & White, 1978; Burman & Margolin, 1992). Marital disruption may not merely be related to these negative life events, it may actually be among the most powerful predictors of them. In the Holmes and Rahe (1967) scale of stressful life events, marital disruption weighs heavily among the major stresses in discriminating those who become ill from those who do not. There is even evidence from one large sample 9-year epidemiological prospective study on the predictors of dying or staying alive that the stability of marriage was the best predictor, even controlling factors such as initial health and health habits (Berkman & Breslow, 1983; Berkman & Syme, 1979). In this study, 4,725 people in Alameda County, California were studied at two time points separated by 9 years. The presence or absence of four types of social ties (marriage, friendship, church membership, and informal groups) were associated with the likelihood of a person staying alive in the 9-year period. Marriage and friendship were the stronger predictors of staying alive; marriage had the strongest buffering effect for men whereas friendship had the strongest buffering effect for women. The effect was stronger as people aged, and the differences were significant when statistically controlled for self-reports of health at Time-1, socioeconomic status, health practices (e.g., smoking, drinking, obesity, exercise) and the use of preventive health services.

A recent analysis of longevity data from the Terman study of intellectually gifted children found that one's own marital disruption had a significant effect in reducing longevity for both men and women (Friedman et al., 1995).

We now have some ideas about what the mechanism may be for these powerful health effects of marital disruption (for a review, see Gottman, 1994). Recent evidence has suggested that the quality of the marital relationship is correlated with in vitro measures of immune functioning. Kiecolt-Glaser et al. (1987, 1988) found that lower marital quality was related to a suppressed immune system. Poorer marital quality was related to poorer cellular immunity. Using dose-response curves with two mitogens, PHA and ConA, there was a significant

difference in blastogenic response between low and high marital quality sub-
groups for all mitogen concentrations of PHA and for the higher mitogen concentrations of ConA. There was also reduced immune response assessed with Eps-
tein-Barr virus antibody titers.

The dissolution of marital relationships is also known to be a more powerful
stressor than marital unhappiness and it is also related to greater suppression in
immune functioning. In the Kiecolt-Glaser et al. study, recently separated or
divorced women were compared to married women. The separated or divorced
women had reduced immune response. This reduced response was assessed as
significantly higher EBV VCA titers, significantly lower percentages of natural
killer (NK) cells, and lower percentages of T-lymphocytes than the married
women. There were also differences in the blastogenesis data between the two
groups for PHA and the higher doses of ConA. Furthermore, although the two
groups differed on self-report psychological variables, they did not differ markedly on other variables assessing sleeplessness, nutrition, or weight loss. Relationships undergoing separation that differed in the emotional conflict surrounding the separation could also be discriminated using the in vitro immune
measures. Separated or divorced women who were still high in attachment to
their husbands had lower lymphocyte proliferation to ConA and PHA than similar women who were less attached. Attachment was assessed by self reports of
preoccupation and disbelief about the separation or divorce.

Table 13.2c is a summary of the correlations of the meta-emotion variables
with parental physical health as measured by the Cornell Medical Index. A
negative correlation indicates better health, or fewer symptoms. The father's
health was related to his awareness of his own sadness. The mother's health was
related to her awareness of her sadness, her coaching of her child's sadness, her
husband's awareness of his anger, and to her awareness of her own anger. To
control for reporting biases (men tend to under-report illness), we also used the
Krokoff (1984) health index, which asks each spouse to report on their partner's
health. Table 13.2d summarizes these correlations. Once again, the meta-emotion
variables were predictive of reports of greater physical health.

THE META-EMOTION VARIABLES
ARE RELATED TO THE PARENTS'
PHILOSOPHY OF MARRIAGE

Tables 13.3a and 13.3b are a summary of the meta-emotion variables to the variables we derived from the Oral History Coding System. These results show that the
meta-emotion variables are not isolated and limited to only the parent–child family
subsystem, but are also related to the couple's philosophy of marriage.

In marriages in which the father was aware of his sadness, during the oral

TABLE 13.3a
Correlation of the Meta-Emotion Variables and Oral History Coding
Variables for the Father

	Father Variables					
	Fondness[a]	We-ness[b]	DiscEmo[c]	Glory[d]	Chaos[e]	Neg[f]
Father sadness						
Awareness own	.36**	.42***	.39**	.42***	−.27*	−.16
Awareness child	.19	.07	−.17	.00	−.19	.05
Coaching	.25*	.22	.20	.22	−.18	−.17
Mother sadness						
Awareness own	.17	.17	.18	.17	−.27*	−.18
Awareness child	.33**	.35**	−.12	.15	−.12	−.24*
Coaching	.33**	.29*	.18	.19	−.14	−.19
Father anger						
Awareness own	.27*	.36**	.09	.20	−.23	−.07
Awareness child	.44***	.32*	−.33*	.15	−.18	−.22
Coaching	.43***	.55***	.31*	.40**	−.39**	−.37**
Mother anger						
Awareness own	.24	.05	.30*	.06	−.13	−.04
Awareness child	.17	.19	.01	.13	−.10	−.25*
Coaching	.25*	.17	.07	.07	.01	−.04

[a]Fondness = fondness toward spouse expressed in interview
[b]We-ness = amount of we-ness expressed in interview
[c]DiscEmo = How much they discuss emotional issues (named "VOLT" on output)
[d]Glory = Belief that it is worth it to struggle to communicate in the marriage
[e]Chaos = Feeling that they have no control over their lives.
[f]Neg = Amount of negativity expressed about their marriage
*$p < .05$. **$p < .01$. ***$p < .001$.

history interview, the father was more likely to spontaneously express fondness for his wife, to talk about the importance of we-ness or a companionate philosophy of marriage, and the couple was more likely to say that it is important to discuss emotional issues, to believe that marital conflict is worth the struggle, and to feel less chaotic and out of control of their lives. The father's awareness of his sadness was correlated with more expressions of we-ness for the wife as well.

The mother's awareness of her sadness was related to the couple's feeling less chaotic and out of control of their lives. The mother's awareness of the child's sadness was related to greater fondness toward the wife, greater we-ness expressed by the husband, and greater we-ness expressed by her in the interview. The mother's coaching of the child's sadness was related to the father's expressions of fondness and we-ness, and the mother's expressions of we-ness.

The father's awareness of his anger was related to his expressions of fondness for his wife, his expressions of we-ness, and his wife's expressions of we-ness in

TABLE 13.3b
Correlation of the Meta-Emotion Variables and Oral History Coding
Variables for the Mother

	Mother Variables					
	Fondness[a]	We-ness[b]	DiscEmo[c]	Glory[d]	Chaos[e]	Negativity[f]
Father sadness						
Awareness own	.21	.35**	.39**	.42***	−.27*	−.02
Awareness child	.08	.06	.07	.00	−.19	.05
Coaching	.08	.21	.20	.22	−.18	−.07
Mother sadness						
Awareness own	.21	.16	.18	.17	−.27*	−.10
Awareness child	.17	.27*	−.22	.15	−.12	−.04
Coaching	.16	.24*	.18	.19	−.14	−.10
Father anger						
Awareness own	.08	.25*	.09	.20	−.23	−.04
Awareness child	.13	.28*	−.10	.15	−.18	−.06
Coaching	.28*	.15	.31*	.40**	−.39**	−.27*
Mother anger						
Awareness own	.25*	.01	.30*	.06	−.13	.03
Awareness child	−.18	.11	−.25*	.13	−.10	−.23
Coaching	.15	.14	.07	.07	.01	−.13

[a]Fondness = fondness toward spouse expressed in interview
[b]We-ness = amount of we-ness expressed in interview
[c]DiscEmo = How much they discuss emotional issues (named "VOLT" on output)
[d]Glory = Belief that it is worth it to struggle to communicate in the marriage
[e]Chaos = Feeling that they have no control over their lives.
[f]Neg = Negativity
*$p < .05.$ **$p < .01.$ ***$p < .001.$

the interview. The father's awareness of his child's anger was related to greater fondness expressed by the father toward his wife, greater we-ness expressed by the father and mother, and less of a conflict-avoiding philosophy of marriage expressed by the father. So here, the father's awareness of the child's anger has positive relations with marriage. This was unexpected, given the observational data.

The father's coaching of his child's anger was related to his expressions of fondness toward his wife, his and his wife's expressions of we-ness, the couple being more likely to say that it is important to (a) discuss emotional issues, (b) believe that marital conflict is worth the struggle, and (c) feel less chaotic and out of control of their lives.

The mother's awareness of her own anger was related to her expressions of fondness for her husband. The mother's awareness of her child's anger was related to less negativity about the marriage expressed by the father and less of a conflict-avoiding philosophy of marriage expressed by the mother. The mother's coaching of her child's anger was related to the father's expressions of fondness toward her. The father's coaching of the child's anger was negatively correlated with the amount of negativity they each expressed about the marriage in the oral history interview.

META-EMOTION DISCREPANCY

We noted in examining the transcripts of couples' meta-emotion interviews that a discrepancy between husband and wife in meta-emotion structure appeared to be strongly related to problems in the marriage. We computed two variables to index this discrepancy, the squares of the differences between spouses in coaching anger (a variable we called x), and coaching sadness (a variable we called y), respectively. These two variables alone were able to predict divorce or marital stability in a discriminant function analysis with 80% accuracy (Wilks' Lamba for $x = 4.85$, $p < .05$, Wilks' Lamba for $y = 5.25$, $p < .05$). The F-ratio for the multiple regression for divorce was $F(2, 47) = 4.16$, $p < .05$, $R = .39$.

The implications of a meta-emotion discrepancy on coaching sadness was that to the extent that there is a discrepancy, *the father* is less likely to coach the child's sadness, $r = -.31$, $p < .05$, and the child's anger, $r = -.46$, $p < .001$; the equivalent correlations for the mother's coaching of sadness and anger were not significant, $r = .13$ and $-.08$, respectively. The implications of a meta-emotion discrepancy on coaching anger was that to the extent that there is a discrepancy, *the father* is less likely to coach the child's sadness, $r = -.57$, $p < .001$, and the child's anger, $r = -.59$, $p < .001$; the equivalent correlations for the mother's coaching of sadness and anger were not significant, $r = -.21$ and $-.10$, respectively.

These effects were unrelated to social class variables (nonsignificant correlations with occupational status, education, and income). They were also not mediated through marital interaction (i.e., they were uncorrelated with the marital interaction codes). They were not mediated through the husband's considering separation or divorce, but they were correlated with the wife's considerations of separation and divorce.

Discrepancies between husband and wife in how they should deal with emotion seem to be fundamental to the character of the marriage. This is an area that warrants further exploration. Using a mathematical model of marital interaction, we discovered (Cook et al., 1995) that a discrepancy in influence functions between husband and wife predicted divorce. It also appears that influence pattern discrepancies are related to meta-emotion discrepancies (for details, see Gottman, 1994).

SUMMARY AND DISCUSSION

In this chapter we can see the frustration of having only correlational data at our disposal. What comes first, a particular orientation toward one's own and others' emotions and then the quality of the marriage, or is the converse true? At this juncture, without true experiments, we can only speculate. Our hypothesis is that meta-emotion precedes marital quality, for the reasons we gave in our earlier review of the processes predictive of marital stability and the gender differences we have observed.

At this point in our work, we can only conclude that not only do the meta-emotion variables have validity in terms of the quality of the parent–child interaction, but, amazingly, they are related to the quality of the marital interaction, marital satisfaction, and marital stability as well. The oral history variables provide some insight into these relationships. The meta-emotion variables are related to the couple's entire philosophy of emotional communication. Couples who have an emotion coaching meta-emotion structure are also more validating and affectionate during marital conflict, they are less disgusted, belligerent, and contemptuous during marital conflict, and the husbands are less likely to stonewall. They express a philosophy of marriage that emphasizes companionship, we-ness, and they express fondness and admiration for one another. They say spontaneously that they believe in expressing their negative feelings about the marriage and discussing them rather than avoiding them, they believe the pain and struggle of working on the marriage is worth it, and they feel less chaotic and out of control in their lives together.

Is it possible that the meta-emotion variables tap a fundamental quality about emotional connection in the marriage as well as in the parent–child system? Could it be the case that many fundamental incompatibilities in marriage come from having divergent views about emotion, (i.e., disparate meta-emotion structures)? We think that this is a real possibility, and wish to elevate these findings into an hypothesis about marital stability: *Spouses who have different meta-emotion structures will have unstable marriages and their interaction will be characterized by disappointment, negativity, criticism, contempt, defensiveness, and by eventual emotional withdrawal.* We suggest that this "meta-emotion compatibilty" is the fundamental dynamic that operates to either to make marriages work, or not.

The following excerpt is from a conversation of a married couple who have a newly blended family. It took place recently in our laboratory, as part of a series of experiments to change marital interaction. It illustrates the point that many problems couples have is in the domain of differences about meta-emotions, that is differences in how they feel about emotions, or meta-emotions structure, which would also include their thoughts and philosophy about emotions. It begins with the husband saying that he tries to avoid being emotional because there is already so much emotion.

210

H: There's so much emotion goin' on already that to me it works better to react with *less* emotion, to sort of tone it down.

W: But what emotions, what emotions are you feeling?

H: (quiet)

W: You mean you're feeling so many emotions yourself that you'd like to show them less?

H: Well yes, I'm feeling emotions but maybe it's a strategy I'm using, natural strategy to not show so much, to not react or over react, or react so emotionally, umm. I guess I'm afraid that an emotional reaction to an emotional situation will bring up more emotion.

W: And?

H: And then (pause) I don't know that's where I feel uncomfortable, I don't even know where it's going to lead. It doesn't have any direction or purpose.

Here we see a difference between them in how much they value the expression of emotion. The wife thinks it is fine, but the husband feels somewhat overwhelmed by it, and wants to "tone it down," and feels it is aimless and without purpose.

W: But you're saying, well, how do you know? If it gets that far, it's pretty hard to say, isn't it? But you are saying you purposely over this last year, you didn't have, you tried, that it would work better you tried to honor your style because it seemed to work better because there was already so much emotion, so like when I'm having a lot of emotion cause it will add too much emotion, the whole thing could go sky high.

H: Yeah, that's pretty accurate.

The wife has hit on a metaphor she thinks underlies the husband's worries, and it is a metaphor of playing with fire near explosive materials, that if he adds more emotion to the emotional situation, the whole thing will explode like a powder keg.

W: Yeah, it's I was thinking here too in listening to to that I feel like I've kind of done what I've done growin' up too is tailor my emotions so that I don't have 'em as often. I mean it's caused me a lot of anxiety to kind of repress my feelings and try to be more logical and rational and go off and have 'em by myself and not get I don't know it's been nice, it'd be nice for me to have more reaction from you. Just like the littlest things like lately you reacting more to Jason. I mean your face changes, you show more emotion, because this is a challenge to you that I can't do, and I can't solve the problem, and I don't have to deal with it. It's just, it feels good, not only does it feel relief, but it feels like you're participating more in *life*. Sometimes I feel like I'm left alone doing it. I feel better in the last few weeks because you're coming in my direction for whatever reasons for whatever feeling you've got. But see, *they're coming from a feeling*. An emotion you had and that feels really good, feels like you're more vulnerable, and maybe there's something you need from me, not just the other way around, like I've been in distress and I have these feelings, to feel that *loneliness*.

H: (has been nodding his head repeatedly in agreement as his wife has been talking) Yeah, well that's a good example. I feel more free to express my emotions because the rest of life is more stable.

The husband needs her to understand that he only feels comfortable being emotional when all around him is not in chaos, that he needs that context to be emotional. His wife, on the other hand, wants him to understand how good it feels for him to be emotional. She is worried that his involvement is only tentative.

W: You mean the minute the kids react I'm not gonna get anything because you're gonna hold down the fort, keeping down everything stuffed inside? I mean, I don't react sometimes so you, I don't rock the boat so you won't withdraw love from me. And that doesn't really work because underneath it I do I feel like it's too big of a price to pay for me for too much stuffing. I mean what's gonna happen if you have to feel more and express more? And come out more? What's gonna happen?
(pause)
Obviously I think something bad too.

H: Well part of what's going on is you're so better at expressing your emotions. I think you are. Can verbalize it better. And I feel a disadvantage to you, so into a competition.

W: Oh.

H: If you're expressing emotion and I have to match you, I can't do it, so it's like I don't even want to try. Whereas when things are more neutral and I express emotion with that setting the tone then you can easily match that or even exceed it, I don't have to feel so bad, but when you're the one expressing intense emotion . . .

W: You feel competitive like you can't so you don't.

H: Yeah, I can't, I mean, does she want me to react at the same level of intensity as she. I can't do it.

W: Well, who says I want that?

H: I don't know.

W: I can see what you're saying. I've learned that. But it puts me at an unfair advantage. 'Cause I have to change my behavior or you won't come out.

In this discussion we see a fairly typical marriage scenario revealed in the context of expressing emotion, valuing the expression of emotion, competitiveness between the genders, fear or trust in where the whole process of expressing and exploring emotions will eventually lead. We suspect that it is the resolution of these issues that is critical for a family to have a coaching meta-emotion structure, and for that structure to have a positive effect on the parents' marriage itself.

14

The Effects of Marital Conflict
and Buffering Children
from Marital Conflict

In this chapter, we explore one of the major reasons we began this research, to determine how marriages affect the development of emotion regulation in children. We explore the effects of marriages on children, our ability to predict the longitudinal course of marriages from dysfunctional marital interaction, and whether there are any variables that can serve as buffers for children from the harmful and powerful effects of both dysfunctional marital conflict and marital dissolution.

HOW AILING MARRIAGES
AFFECT CHILDREN

There is now convincing evidence to suggest that marital distress and conflict are associated with a wide range of deleterious child outcomes, including depression, withdrawal, poor social competence, health problems, poor academic performance, and a variety of conduct-related difficulties (Cowan & Cowan, 1987; Easterbrooks, 1987; Emery & O'Leary, 1982; Forehand, Brody, Long, Slotkin, & Fauber, 1986; Gottman & Katz, 1989; Hetherington, Cox, & Cox, 1982; Peterson & Zill, 1986; Porter & O'Leary, 1980; Rutter, 1971; Whitehead, 1979).

There is evidence that children of unhappily married parents are chronically aroused physiologically, and have slower recovery from emotional arousal. Gottman and Katz (1989) found that children of unhappily married parents have higher levels of stress-related urinary catecholamines. In the same study, Shortt et al. (1994) found that when directed to move their faces into a facial expression of emotion, children from unhappily married parents showed greater heart rate reactivity. Walker, Wilson, Katz, and Gottman (in preparation) found that when making facial spontaneous expressions of anger during emotion-eliciting films, children whose parents were unhappily married took longer to recover from a heart rate increase following the facial expression.

Although this literature is suggestive of a link between the parents' marriage and child outcomes, the direct relationship between marital quality and child outcomes has rarely been examined in a prospective longitudinal study (e.g., Cowan & Cowan, 1990; Easterbrooks, 1987; Howes & Markman, 1989). One issue in this research is that marital quality has been almost uniformly conceptualized in terms of relationship satisfaction. Although this approach has generated important new findings, the simple, unidimensional focus on marital satisfaction has failed to identify the specific dimensions of marital quality that are correlated with or predictive of child functioning. As a result, although there is evidence that distressed marriages are correlated with negative child outcomes, it is unclear exactly what it is about those marriages that are most caustic to children's well-being.

At the conceptual level, there is a need to question the information that is obtained from the finding of a relationship between self-report of marital distress and child outcomes. It is well-known that people who are stressed in other areas of their life also report being unhappily married. For example, marital satisfaction has been found to covary with a diverse range of negative life stressors and states, such as the quality of life, job stress, a variety of dysfunctional personality characteristics, and depression (e.g., see Barton & Dreger, 1986; Beach, Arias, & O'Leary, 1986; Burgess, Locke, & Thomes, 1971; Krokoff, 1984; Lewak, Wakefield, & Briggs, 1985; Smolen, Spiegel, & Martin, 1986; Yogev, 1986). Thus, self-report measures of marital satisfaction may, in part, reflect a general stress dimension rather than something specific about the marriage. An assessment of marital quality that is independent of the couple's own ratings would add precision to understanding the relationship between functioning in the marital and child systems. Such an assessment is possible using the quantitative observation of marital interaction (e.g., Gottman, 1979; Weiss & Summers, 1983). Observing couples discussing issues important to their relationship is now an established approach for specifying dimensions of marital quality (e.g., see Markman & Notarius, 1987).

Research on marriage has consistently demonstrated that the way in which couples resolve conflict is an important context in which to examine differences between happily and unhappily married couples (e.g. Gottman, 1979; Olson, Spengle, & Russell, 1979; Raush, Barry, Hertel, & Swain, 1974; Revenstorf, Vogel, Wegener, Hahlweg, & Schindler, 1980; Vincent, Weiss, & Birchler, 1975).

Happily married couples have been found to display higher ratios of agreement to disagreement (Gottman, 1979), and exhibit more positive nonverbal cues (Birchler, 1977; Haynes, Follingstad, & Sullivan, 1979), more agreement and approval (Vincent & Friedman, 1979), and less coercive and attacking behaviors (Billings, 1979) than unhappily married couples.

One of the most consistent discriminators between happily and unhappily married couples has been the degree of negative affect expressed during conflict-resolution. Unhappily married couples have been found to show more negative affect and negative affect reciprocity than happily married couples (e.g., Gottman, 1979; Revenstorf et al., 1980, 1984). Affective differences that are independent of marital satisfaction have also been noted. For example, Margolin (1988) proposed that couples differ in the way in which emotions are expressed during conflict-resolution, with some couples expressing their negativity very openly and directly, and others keeping the conflict silent and hidden. The consequences of these different affective patterns of marital conflict-resolution for children's socioemotional development have been largely unexplored. There is some preliminary data to support the hypothesis that the different ways that adults resolve conflict have negative consequences for children. In a series of investigations, Cummings and his colleagues have demonstrated that exposure to interadult anger is associated with distressed, angry, and physically aggressive reactions in children, with concomitant physiological arousal (Cummings, 1987; Cummings & Davies, 1987; Cummings, Iannotti, & Zahn-Waxler, 1985; Cummings, Zahn-Waxler, & Radke-Yarrow, 1981). Based on clinician's ratings of interviews with individual spouses, Rutter and his colleagues (Rutter, Yule, Quinton, Rowlands, Yule, & Berger, 1974) found a stronger relation with child behavior problems in unhappy marriages characterized by interviewers as "quarrelsome" than those characterized by interviewers as "apathetic." Thus, both these studies support the hypothesis that the particular way couples engage in conflict may be associated with negative or dysfunctional behavior patterns in children.

We examined negative marital interaction patterns that have been found to predict marital dissolution. Gottman and Levenson (1992) and Gottman (1994) reported that marriages headed toward dissolution are characterized by disgust, contempt, and belligerence, particularly by the wife. When spouses are contemptuous toward each other, they communicate a sense of superiority and moralistic disapproval through insults, mockery, or attributions of the partner's incompetence. Contemptuous statements are often accompanied by belligerent demands in which the spouse contests their partner's statements by trying to provoke a response or get a rise out of the partner. Given the substantial body of research identifying the numerous negative consequences of divorce for children (Hetherington, Cox, & Cox, 1978; 1982; Shaw & Emery, 1987; Wallerstein & Kelly, 1975, 1980), we also examined the direct effects of the marriage heading for dissolution.

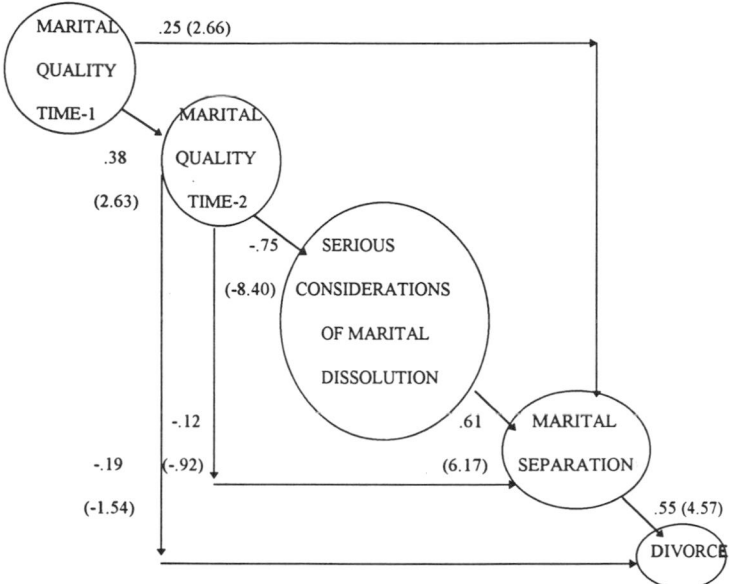

FIG. 14.1. Cascade toward marital dissolution.

THE CASCADE TOWARD MARITAL DISSOLUTION

Figure 14.1 summarizes the cascade toward marital dissolution. This model fit the data, with $\chi^2(3) = 4.63$, $p = .20$, $BBN = .998$. As can be seen, there is a strong correlation among these variables, compatible with the idea that serious considerations of dissolution are precursors of actual separation, and that separation is a precursor of divorce. These results are consistent with other research (Bloom & White, 1980; Gottman, 1994). Other variables could have been included in this cascade, as Table 14.1 illustrates.

TABLE 14.1
Other Variables in the Cascade Toward Marital Dissolution

Variable	Husb Cons Diss	Wife Con Diss	Separation	Months Sep	Divorce
Husb Cons Diss	1.00				
Wife Cons Diss	.66**	1.00			
Separation	.81**	.74**	1.00		
Months Sep	.57**	.44*	.61**	1.00	
Divorce	.59**	.60**	.81**	.67**	1.00

Note. Hus Cons Diss = Husband Considers Dissolution; Wife Cons Diss = Wife Considers Dissolution; Months Sep = Months Separated.
*$p < .01$. **$p < .001$

TABLE 14.2
Correlation of the Marital Interaction Variables Known
to be Predictive of Marital Dissolution and Parenting
and Child Outcome Variables

	Husband			Wife		
Variable	Disgust	Contempt	Belligerence	Disgust	Contempt	Belligerence
Parent	−.04	−.08	.25*	−.11	.58***	.07
Play Comp	.00	−.02	.00	−.43***	.07	.01
Neg Affect Obs	.00	−.02	.00	−.06	.52***	−.03
Negat Affect Rat	−.12	.02	.05	−.07	.46**	.26
Neg Peer	−.06	.13	.08	−.11	.41**	.23
Child Illness	.41**	−.04	.16	.52***	.15	.17
Child Achiev	.01	−.01	−.22	−.15	−.38**	−.21

Note. Play Comp = Play Competence; Neg Affect Obs = Negative Affect Observed; Neg Affect Rat = Negative Affect Rated; Neg Power = Negative Power; Child Achiev = Child Achievement.
*$p < .05$. **$p < .01$. ***$p < .001$.

THE EFFECTS ON CHILDREN AND PARENTS OF MARITAL DISSOLUTION AND OF MARITAL INTERACTION PROCESSES THAT PREDICT DISSOLUTION

The Effects of Processes that Predict Marital Dissolution

Table 14.2 summarizes the correlations of the parenting and child outcome variables with a small set of specific affect marital interaction behaviors that are known to be predictive of marital dissolution (Gottman, 1994), namely, disgust, contempt, and belligerence. Play competence was unrelated to the wife's contempt; however, aside from the prediction of the child's illness from the husband's disgust toward his wife in the marital interaction three years earlier, the overwhelming conclusion one draws from this table is the power of the wife's affect, particularly her contempt toward her husband to predict child outcomes three years later.

The Effects of Marital Dissolution

Table 14.3 summarizes the correlations of the parenting and child outcome variables with variables indexing actual marital dissolution. Considerations of dissolution are the sum of serious considerations of separation and serious considerations of divorce. Both actual dissolution and the processes that predict dissolution have a significant relationship with the parenting variable. Play com-

TABLE 14.3
Correlation of the Marital Dissolution and Parenting and Child
Outcome Variables

Variable	Husb Consid Dissol	Wife Consid Dissol	Months Separated
Parent	−.21	.15	.54***
Play Comp	.00	.05	.00
Neg Affect (Obs)	.28*	.25*	.10
Neg Affect (Rat)	.04	.21	.28*
Neg Peer	−.06	.13	.00
Child Illness	−.14	−.04	.23
Child Achiev	−.21	−.25*	−.30*

Note. Husb Consid Dissol = Husband Considers Dissolution; Wife Cons Diss = Wife Considers Dissolution; Play Comp = Play Competence; Neg Affect (Obs) = Negative Affect Observed; Neg Affect (Rat) = Negative Affect Rated; Neg Peer = Negative Peer; Child Achiev = Child Achievement.
$*p < .05. ***p < .001.$

petence was not related to separation or to considerations of dissolution. Observed negative affect with a peer was related to serious considerations of dissolution and actual dissolution. Negative child affect as rated by mother and teacher was related to actual dissolution. Negative peer ratings by the teacher was unrelated only to the dissolution variables. Child physical illness was unrelated to the dissolution variables, but child academic achievement was related to wife's serious considerations of dissolution, and to actual dissolution.

We must conclude from these tables that the parents' marital relationship, and the cascade toward marital dissolution have an enormous impact on the child, as well as on parenting.

CAN CHILDREN BE BUFFERED FROM AILING MARRIAGES, AND HOW BUFFERED ARE THESE CHILDREN?

As the marital variable we took the combined effects (sum) of months separated and the wife's contempt plus the wife's disgust. For child outcomes we considered the child's negative affect, both observed and rated, the child's peer relations, the child's physical illness and the child's academic achievement. Play competence was not considered because it was unrelated to both wife contempt and marital separation. To answer these questions about buffering, we performed a series of regression analyses in which we asked the question, what would happen if we first stepped our buffers into a regression attempting to predict child outcomes and then stepped in the marital process and dissolution variables? Table 14.4 presents the results of the analyses of first stepping in the buffer

TABLE 14.4
Is There Any Evidence of Children Being Buffered From the
Deleterious Effects of Marital Conflict and Marital Dissolution? If So,
How Complete Are the Effects of Buffering?

Dependent Variable	Buffers	F-change for Marital Variable
Parenting variables as buffers		
CACHIEV	Scaffolding/Praising, low Derogation	$F(3, 45) = .58$ *ns*
CREGUL	Scaffolding/Praising, low Derogation	$F(3, 47) = .85$, *ns*
CAFFECT	Scaffolding/Praising, low Derogation	$F(3, 33) = 9.04^{**}$
CPEER	Scaffolding/Praising, low Derogation	$F(3, 40) = 2.18$, *ns*
NEGAFF8	Scaffolding/Praising, low Derogation	$F(3, 45) = 6.44^{*}$
CMI88	Scaffolding/Praising, low Derogation	$F(3, 47) = 3.56$, *ns*
Meta-emotion variables as buffers		
CACHIEV	Awareness and Coaching	$F(3, 42) = 5.40^{*}$
CREGUL	Awareness and Coaching	$F(3, 47) = 1.79$, *ns*
CAFFECT	Awareness and Coaching	$F(3, 31) = 8.29^{**}$
CPEER	Awareness and Coaching	$F(3, 37) = 3.02$, *ns*
NEGAFF8	Awareness and Coaching	$F(3, 42) = .49$, *ns*
CMI88	Awareness and Coaching	$F(3, 39) = .06$, *ns*
Vagal tone variables as buffers		
CACHIEV	Basal Vagal Tone, Suppression Vagal Tone	$F(3, 44) = 7.15^{*}$
CREGUL	Basal Vagal Tone, Suppression Vagal Tone	$F(3, 46) = 1.51$, *ns*
CAFFECT	Basal Vagal Tone, Suppression Vagal Tone	$F(3, 33) = 8.34^{**}$
CPEER	Basal Vagal Tone, Suppression Vagal Tone	$F(3, 39) = 5.62^{*}$
NEGAFF8	Basal Vagal Tone, Suppression Vagal Tone	$F(3, 44) = 7.26^{*}$
CMI88	Basal Vagal Tone, Suppression Vagal Tone	$F(3, 41) = 3.26$, *ns*

Note. F-ratios for change stepping in the marital variable after stepping in the buffering variables.

Marital variable = wife contempt plus wife disgust plus months separated.

CACHIEV = Child Achievement; CREGUL = Emotional Down Regulation; CAFFECT = Negative Affect of Child Rated; NEGAFF8 = Negative Peer Interaction Observed; CMI88 = Child Physical Illness.

$^{*}p < .05.$ $^{**}p < .01.$

variables into a regression and then stepping in the marital variable that is the sum of negative marital interaction predictive of divorce (wife contempt) and a variable indexing actual marital dissolution (months separated in 3 years); we present the F-ratios for change in the second step of the regression. These F-ratios tell us how much variance is left that can be accounted for by the marital variable, and, thus how complete a buffer the buffering variables were. Our buffering analyses in Table 14.4 present an extremely optimistic picture that there are variables that can buffer the child completely against many of the harmful effects of marital conflict. The two parenting variables, low Derogation and Scaffolding/Praising parenting can be said to provide a complete buffer for the harmful effects of marital conflict on achievement, Emotional Dysregulation, teacher ratings of negative peer relations, and child physical illness at age 8. Meta-emotion variables provide complete buffers for Emotional Dysregulation, teacher ratings of negative peer relations, and observed negative affect with a peer at age 8. The vagal tone variables provide complete buffers against the negative effects of marital conflict and dissolution on Emotional Dysregulation and child physical illness at age 8. The only unbuffered variable is child negative affect; the marital variable still exerts harmful effects on child negative affect as rated by mother and teacher. It appears that only the child's negative moods persist in the face of marital conflict and marital dissolution, even when parenting, meta-emotion, and vagal tone are buffers. However, we have not considered what sort of buffer all the buffers taken together would form for this affective variable. When this analysis was done, with all the buffers stepped into the equation first, the effect of the marital variable on the child's affect was no longer significant, $F(7,25) = 3.64$, ns, $p = .068$. However, we must be cautious about this result because the p value is marginally significant, and the regression has relatively low power. Hence, to be cautious, we must conclude that the one child outcome that will not be buffered from the negative effects of marital conflict and dissolution by the buffering variables we have considered is the child's negative affectivity.

OTHER APPROACHES TO THE BUFFERING QUESTIONS

Are there other ways to know that a variable is a buffer against marital conflict and dissolution?

In this section, we explore two other methodological approaches toward the buffering issue. We begin by asking the question, by what criteria will we know that a variable in our model is a buffer against the effects of marital conflict and marital dissolution?

One approach we explore, is from Rutter (1979, 1990). He addressed this question. He suggested that the most important answer to this question lay in finding a protective mechanism, rather than a protective variable. A protective mechanism suggests how, theoretically, the buffering may take place. Rutter suggested that buffering needs to take place in the presence of the risk factor, and it must be shown that reduced risk is not the result of less exposure to the risk factor.

Let's assume that we have three variables, a marital variable, M, a child outcome variable, O, and a potential buffer variable, B. We suggest two types of criteria and analyses. The first is to view a buffer, B, as a switch. If a variable is to be a buffer, then, when it is off or low there should be a significant correlation between M and O. When it is on, or high, the correlation should be substantially reduced. Furthermore, if M and B are correlated, we must demonstrate that there is no significant difference in exposure to the risk factor, M, once we split the sample on high versus low B; this can be tested with a t-test. Thus, to test whether B is a buffer, we divide our sample of families at the median on B, then compute two correlations between M and O, and do a Fisher's z-test between the correlations; this is followed by a t-test on M.

There is a second approach. We divide that sample on M, and then compute the correlation between B and O; if it is significant and in the right direction, then B is a buffer with respect to O in the presence of the risk variable, high M. It does not matter if the buffer B operates in a similar way when no risk is present, so long as it does not operate the opposite way (i.e., more of the buffer means a worse outcome if there is no or reduced risk present). That would be a strange buffer indeed.

IS THERE ANY EVIDENCE FROM THESE TWO ALTERNATIVE METHODS THAT PARENTING, META-EMOTION, OR VAGAL TONE CAN BE PARTIAL OR COMPLETE BUFFERS?

The First Approach: Rutter's Buffer-as-a-Switch Analyses—Split on potential buffers and assess the extent to which the marital variable correlates with child outcomes with buffer high or low.

Recall that as the marital variable we took the combined effects (sum) of months separated and the wife's contempt plus the wife's disgust, and that for child outcomes we considered the child's negative affect, both observed and rated, the child's peer relations, the child's physical illness, and the child's academic achievement. Play competence was not considered because it was unrelated to both wife contempt and marital separation. Table 14.5 summarizes the correlations and Fisher's z-scores we computed with the Rutter buffer-as-a-switch analysis.

First, a set of preliminary t-tests of the marital variable confirmed that none were significant; this means that children high or low on the buffer do not differ on their exposure to the risk variable (the marital variable). The t-tests were nonsignificant for parenting, for awareness, for basal vagal tone, for change in vagal tone, and for negative parenting.

The results showed that parenting was a buffer against the harmful effects of the marital variable on the child's negative affect, for the harmful effects of the marital variable on the child's physical illness (marginally), and the harmful effects of the marital variable on the child's academic achievement. Basal vagal

TABLE 14.5
Rutter's Buffer-As-A-Switch Analyses, Presenting Correlatons
With the Marital Variable and Fisher's z-Tests.

Variable	Negative Affect (OBS)	Negative Affect (RAT)	Negative Peer	Child Illness	Child Achievement
Parenting					
Not negative	−.06	.61**	.25	−.20	−.07
Negative	.58***	.63**	.51**	.39*	−.52**
z	2.06	ns	ns	1.92	2.11
Awareness					
Low	.27	.53*	.55*	.25	.60**
High	−.21	.45*	.08	−.11	.00
z	2.06	ns	ns	ns	2.17
Coaching					
Low	.53**	.56**	.48*	.27	−.57**
High	−.28	.48*	.25	−.15	.13
z	2.79	ns	ns	1.30	2.49
Basal Vagal Tone					
Low	.59***	.75***	.44*	.39*	−.62***
High	−.17	.30	.33	−.17	−.20
z	2.78	1.82	ns	1.84	1.71
Suppression of Vagal Tone					
Low	.51**	.73***	.45*	.38*	−.61***
High	−.06	.16	.31	−.03	−.18
z	2.04	2.17	ns	ns	1.79

Note. Method: Split on potential buffers and assess the extent to which the marital variable correlates with child outcomes with buffer high or low.

Negative affect (OBS) = Negative Affect Observed; Negative Affect (RAT) = Negative Affect Rating.

*$p < .05.$ **$p < .01.$ ***$p < .001.$

tone was a buffer against the harmful effects of the marital variable on the child's negative affect (observed). The suppression of vagal tone was a buffer for the harmful effects of the marital variable on the child's negative affect, both observed and rated. The parent's awareness of the child's emotions was a buffer against the harmful effects of the marital variable on the child's academic achievement. Coaching the child's emotions was a buffer against the harmful effects of the marital variable on the child's negative affect (observed), the harmful effects of the marital variable on the child's physical illness, and the child's academic achievement. Using this analysis, no variable in the model was a significant buffer against the harmful effects of the marital variable on the child's rated peer relations, and on the harmful effects of the marital variable on the child's physical illness (although parenting was marginally).

The Second Approach: Split on marital risk variable and assess the extent to which the potential buffer variable correlates with child outcomes. Here we look for significant correlations of the potential with child outcome at high levels of the risk variable.

Table 14.6 summarizes the correlations splitting on the marital risk variable, for each potential buffer. Low levels of negative parenting when the marital variable is high was a buffer for observed negative affect, for ratings of the child's negative affect, and for the child's achievement. The child's basal vagal tone was a buffer for play competence, observed negative affect, and health. The ability to suppress vagal tone was a buffer for observed negative affect and ratings of negative affect. It apparently operated to *reduce* play competence in the presence of the buffer. This result seems strange at first, but play competence involves playing at a high level of play, and Gottman and Katz (1989) reported that children of unhappily married parents tend to play with their best friend at a relatively low level, one that is likely to minimize both conflict and excitement. Awareness of the child's emotions was a buffer for observed negative affect and

TABLE 14.6
Buffer-As-A-Switch Analyses, Splitting on the Marital Variable

Variable	Negative Affect (OBS)	Negative Affect (RAT)	Negative Peer	Child Illness	Child Achievement
Negative parenting					
Marital low	−.18	.19	.29	−.02	−.27
Marital high	.53***	.41*	.40*	.34*	−.45*
Awareness					
Low marital	.03	.58*	.15	−.22	−.23
High marital	−.51**	.32	.14	−.75***	.28
Coaching					
Low marital	.27	.31	.26	−.22	−.12
High marital	−.18	.11	.16	−.77***	.48*
Basal vagal tone					
Low marital	−.08	.16	.26	−.40*	.01
High marital	−.45**	−.17	.05	−.34*	.17
Suppression of vagal tone					
Low marital	−.27	.01	.10	−.11	−.12
High marital	−.50**	−.39*	−.12	−.22	.24
Positive parenting					
Low marital	.30	.17	−.10	.02	.22
High marital	−.23	−.45*	−.23	−.09	.61***

Note. Method: Split on marital risk variable and assess the extent to which the child outcomes correlate with each of the potential buffers for the condition in which the risk variable is high.

Negative affect (OBS) = Negative Affect Observed; Negative Affect (RAT) = Negative Affect Rating.

*$p < .05$. **$p < .01$. ***$p < .001$.

child illness. Coaching was a buffer for child illness and for poor child academic achievement.

Splitting on the Marital Risk Variable: Positive Parenting as a Potential Buffer

Table 14.6 also summarizes the analyses for Scaffolding/Praising parenting, splitting on the marital risk variable. The positive parenting variable is seen to be a buffer for child negative affect and for poor academic achievement.

Summary

In this summary, we combine our results across the two methods of analysis and summarize these results separately for each of the five child outcomes. These results show that, across the two analyses there is not an outcome variable for which the child is not buffered using these six potential buffers.

Child Negative Affectivity (Observed).   Using the Rutter analysis, for observed child negative affectivity, the inhibition of negative parenting, parental awareness of the child's emotion, emotion coaching, basal vagal tone, and the suppression of vagal tone were all buffers. In the second type of analysis, the buffers were the inhibition of negative parenting, parental awareness of the child's emotion, basal vagal tone, and the suppression of vagal tone.

Child Negative Affectivity (Rated).   Using the Rutter analysis, for rated child negative affectivity, only the suppression of vagal tone was a buffer. In the second type of analysis, the buffers were the inhibition of negative parenting, and positive parenting.

Child Negative Peer Relations.   Using the Rutter analysis, for observed child negative peer relations, none of the potential buffers qualified. In the second type of analysis, the buffer that emerged was the inhibition of negative parenting.

Child Physical Illness.   Using the Rutter analysis, for child physical illness, none of the potential buffers qualified, although the inhibition of negative parenting and basal vagal tone were marginally significant. In the second type of analysis, the buffers were the inhibition of negative parenting, parental awareness of the child's emotion, and emotion coaching. Basal vagal tone appeared to be a buffer regardless of the level of the marital variable.

Child Achievement.   Using the Rutter analysis, for child achievement, the inhibition of negative parenting, parental awareness of the child's emotion, and emotion coaching were all buffers. In the second type of analysis, the buffers were the inhibition of negative parenting, emotion coaching, and positive parenting.

SUMMARY AND CONCLUSIONS

It is clear that marital dissolution as well as the marital interaction processes predictive of marital dissolution have a powerful negative effect on children. However, our three buffering analyses present an optimistic picture that there are variables in the model that can buffer the child against the harmful effects of marital conflict. We have identified parenting factors that moderate the negative impact of those marital interaction processes predictive of marital dissolution. Our analyses indicate that when parents are more aware of their children's emotions despite high levels of marital conflict, children are buffered against the harmful effects of marital conflict on the child's academic achievement. Coaching the child's emotions was a buffer against the deleterious effects of marital conflict on the child's negative affect, physical illness, and academic achievement. Furthermore, positive parenting and the inhibition of negative parental affect buffered against the effects of marital conflict on the child's negative affect and academic achievement. The child's regulatory physiology was also a buffer against the harmful effects of marital conflict on child negative affect (rated and observed). Furthermore, for all child outcomes we studied, except perhaps for ratings child negative affect, these buffers were complete; that is, stepping in the marital variable accounted for no additional variance in child outcome once the buffers had first been stepped into the regression equation. This suggests that we have yet to find a complete buffer from an ailing marriage for children's daily negative moods of dysphoria and anxiety.

Given the ubiquity of marital conflict and dissolution in the US today, and the known deleterious effects of these events on the developing child, these data offer hope for the many families experiencing marital conflict and distress. They also provide specific direction for the development of intervention strategies that can help children in families experiencing marital discord and marital dissolution. Interventions focused on increasing parental awareness, gaining ability to coach their children's emotions, and helping to promote positive and decrease negative parent–child interactions can help reduce the adjustment problems in children whose parents' marriages are ailing.

It is interesting that none of the parenting variables buffered children against the harmful effects of the marital variable on the child's rated negative affect. Perhaps living in a dissolving family where adults resolve conflict in a destructive fashion is a powerful negative stimulus that is hard to get over even if the quality of one's relationships with parents remains high.

PART V

EXTENSIONS

15

Meta-Emotion and Gender

In this chapter we explore differences between boys and girls in our variables, and also ask questions about the effects of fathers versus mothers.

In chapter 12, we built a model of how parenting may impact a child's developing emotion regulation ability, and through that impact many facets of a child's functioning. We also found that a parent's awareness and coaching of emotion had indirect and direct influences on a variety of child outcomes such as school achievement, peer success, emotion regulation, and physical health. In that chapter, we focused on parenting as a sum of parent practices a child experiences from both parents. That helped us understand the pathways by which parenting influence worked, but did not distinguish which parent was doing more influencing; nor did it distinguish which gender was being more influenced. In this chapter, we again look at variables from our family process model, but with particular interest in the effects of the genders of the participants.

MOTHERS AND FATHERS, SONS AND DAUGHTERS: BRIEF REVIEW OF LITERATURE ON GENDER VARIABLES

In general, mothers tend to be more verbal and directing, whereas fathers are more physical and arousing (see Parke, 1981, for a review). In the emotion area mothers also appear to exert their influence via direct instruction, whereas fathers appear to teach more successfully through play. There is substantial research evidence that parenting practices also differ based on a child's gender (e.g.,

MacDonald & Parke, 1984), and that this distinction begins at an early age, continuing in varying forms throughout childhood. In the emotion arena, Fivush (1991) found mothers making gender distinctions in the emotion arena: When they talked to their 3-year-old sons and daughters about anger and sadness they talked more to their daughters about sadness, and more to their sons about anger. Furthermore, a number of studies have found that it is fathers more than mothers who treat their children differently based on their gender, particularly in the areas of discipline and physical involvement (Fisher & Fagot, 1993; Maccoby & Martin, 1983; Mulhern & Passman, 1981; Starrels, 1994). Kerig, Cowan and Cowan (1993) also found that it was fathers, not mothers, who distinguished between sons and daughters in a laboratory teaching task, particularly when faced with marital conflict and disagreement regarding parenting style. Distressed fathers of daughters were more authoritarian (more cold, angry, and disengaged) than distressed fathers of sons, and these differences were exacerbated by the level of marital conflict. However, mothers did not show these differences. Kerig, Cowan and Cowan (1993) found that maritally dissatisfied parents of girls were more negative than dissatisfied parents of boys, and dissatisfied fathers were more critical than dissatisfied mothers; the most negative parent was the father of a daughter. The mothers tended to be critical of daughters only when they asserted themselves (see also Pratt, Kerig, Cowan, & Cowan, 1992).

In addition, parenting practices show different child outcomes based on whether the child is a boy or a girl, as well as whether the parent is a mother or father (Cassidy, Parke, Butkovsky, & Braungart, 1992; MacDonald & Parke, 1984). MacDonald and Parke (1984) found that father's playfulness predicted popularity particularly for girls, whereas for mothers it was directiveness that predicted popularity for her children. Both mother's directiveness and father's play predicted daughter's expression of positive affect, whereas father's directiveness had negative outcomes for his children.

In our research we have relatively low power to test many of these hypotheses. What we predict is that fathers differ from mothers with respect to anger and sadness. In particular, we expect fathers to be more aware of anger and to coach a child's anger more than their sadness, particularly for boys. Mothers, on the other hand are more aware of sadness than fathers and coach their children's sadness more than their anger, particularly for girls.

Gender Differences

A series of analyses of variance comparing boys with girls on the child outcome variables revealed no significant differences on any outcome variable for achievement, $F(1, 30) = .02$, for negative affectivity, $F(1, 30) = .02$, for teacher ratings of negative peer relations, $F(1, 30) = .09$, for child illness, $F(1,30) = 1.92$, ns, for observed negative affect with a peer, $F(1, 30) = 1.12$, *ns*. A series of analyses of variance comparing boys with girls on the process variables revealed that boys and girls differed significantly in basal vagal tone, $F(1, 51) = 5.80, p <$ .05 (boy mean $= 16.10$, girl mean $= 15.03$), but not on the suppression of vagal tone $F(1, 51) = 2.15$, ns or on Down Regulation $F(1, 52) = 1.12$, ns.

Gender Effects

We conducted two $2 \times 2 \times 2$ repeated measures multivariate analyses of variance, one for awareness and one for coaching, each with two levels of child gender as the between subjects factor, and two within subjects factors, parent (father/mother) and emotion (sadness/anger). For awareness, the only significant effects were parent $F(1, 49) = 38.42, p < .001$, with mothers more aware of emotion than fathers: father mean $= 34.37$, mother mean $= 34.94$, and the interaction between parent and emotion $F(1, 49) = 6.88, p < .05$; fathers were less aware of sadness than mothers $F(1, 49) = 6.11, p < .05$, father mean $= 33.68$, mother mean$= 34.66$, whereas there was no significant difference for the awareness of anger $F(1, 49) = .15$, ns. For coaching, there was only a significant spouse effect $F(1, 50) = 21.80, p < .001$, with mothers coaching more than fathers (mother mean $= 22.10$, father mean $= 21.51$).

A series of repeated measures multivariate analyses of variance with two levels of gender (boys and girls) as a between subjects factor and father/mother as a within subjects factor revealed that there was a significant spouse main effect for the awareness of sadness (father mean $= 33.68$, mother mean $= 34.66$) but no gender effect or gender by parent interaction. There were no significant main or interaction effects for the awareness of anger, or for coaching anger or sadness. For parental Derogation there were no significant main or interaction effects. However, for Scaffolding/Praising parenting, there was a significant mother/father effect, with $F(1, 53) = 5.39, p < .05$ (father mean $= 580.95$, mother mean $= 600.67$). For both Derogation and Scaffolding/Praising parenting, there were significant inhomogeneities of variance for fathers compared to mothers, with fathers having much larger variance than mothers; for Derogation $\chi^2(3) = 28.52, p < .001$; for Scaffolding/Praising parenting, $\chi^2(3) = 14.19, p < .01$.

We would like to be able to statistically compare models for fathers and mothers separately for boys and girls, but we lack the power to be able to perform these comparisons. There is not enough power with these Ns (with 24 males and 27 females for most analyses) to adequately test for differences between boys and girls. Using a Fisher-z test, at this N, the z-scores based on the correlations would need to be different by at least 0.586 to reach statistical significance at the 0.05 level!

However, we would like to present one table for hypothesis generating purposes. Table 15.1 breaks the parenting variables down by parent. Imagine trying to construct separate path models for other and father from this table. The pattern of correlations in Table 15.1 suggests that one would be successful constructing father models but unsuccessful constructing mother models for both negative and positive parenting. Generally, it appears that the major effects of the parenting

TABLE 15.1
Correlations Between Parenting Variables Separated
by Fathers and Mothers

	Correlations					
	PARENT	NEGDAD	NEGMOM	POSPAR	POSDAD	POSMOM
CACHIEV	−.37	−.38	−.16	.43	.38	.27
	p = .00	p = .00	p = .13	p = .00	p = .00	p = .03
CAFFECT	.37	.33	.32	−.34	−.36	−.19
	p = .01	p = .02	p = .03	p = .02	p = .01	p = .13
CPEER	.38	.34	.20	−.24	−.31	−.10
	p = .00	p = .01	p = .10	p = .05	p = .02	p = .26
CREGUL	.30	.38	.00	−.37	−.36	−.21
	p = .02	p = .00	p = .49	p = .00	p = .00	p = .07
CMI88	.22	.24	.08	−.04	−.10	.04
	p = .06	p = .05	p = .29	p = .40	p = .25	p = .41
NEGAFF8	.47	.60	.01	−.17	−.37	.09
	p = .00	p = .00	p = .46	p = .12	p = .00	p = .27
AWARE	−.45	−.42	−.41	.26	.35	.08
	p = .00	p = .00	p = .00	p = .03	p = .01	p = .29
COACH	−.39	−.37	−.34	.28	.36	.07
	p = .00	p = .00	p = .01	p = .03	p = .01	p = .30
BASVAGAL	−.28	−.27	−.14	.15	.14	.09
	p = .02	p = .02	p = .15	p = .14	p = .16	p = .26
DELVAGAL	−.24	−.32	.01	.24	.29	.09
	p = .04	p = .01	p = .46	p = .04	p = .02	p = .26

Note. PARENT = Negative Parent; NEGDAD = Negative Dad; NEGMOM = Negative Mom; POSPAR = Positive Parent; POSDAD = Positive Dad; POSMOM = Positive Mom.

CACHIEV = achievement, CREGUL = down regulation, CAFFECT = negative affect (ratings), CPEER = negative peer relations (teacher ratings), NEGAFF8 = negative peer affect observed, CMI88 = child illness, all at age 8; AWARE = awareness variable, COACH = Coaching variable; BASVAGAL = Basal Vagal Tone; DELVAGAL = Suppression of Vagal Tone.

variables are father effects. If we scan down the father Derogation column there are eight significant correlations whereas there are only three significant for the mother column; for Scaffolding/Praising Parenting again eight correlations are significant for father and only three for mother. Although we will not present these data, this pattern held for both boys and girls.[1]

---

[1]For girls the Derogation parenting variable was significantly related to two of the seven outcomes. However, three father variables were significant whereas only one of the mother variable was significant. For positive parenting, for boys the Scaffolding/Praising parenting variable was significantly related to two of the seven outcomes. Of the two, two father variables were significant whereas no mother variable were significant. For girls the Scaffolding/Praising parenting variable was significantly related to three of the seven outcomes. However, three father variables were significant whereas only one of the mother variable was significant. Clearly this pattern suggests that the father, compared to the mother, is having a much more pervasive effect on outcomes for both boys and girls.

MARITAL DISCORD AFFECTS FATHER AND MOTHERS DIFFERENTLY, AND LEADS TO DIFFERENT CHILD OUTCOMES

Katz and Gottman (1993) discussed the effects of their construct of "hostile marital interaction," which consists of the wife's contempt and the husband's belligerence, as coded by our Specific Affect Coding System (SPAFF). Hostile marital interaction predicts divorce and it also predicts the development of externalizing problems in children. Recently Katz and Gottman (1995) reported that hostile marital interaction affects fathers and mothers differently. The "father rejecting" construct in the following figures is measured by paternal intrusiveness during the laboratory teaching task. Recall that parental intrusiveness involves the parent taking over the game, and we believe that it is a communication to the child that the parent thinks the child is incompetent. The father rejecting construct predicts aggressive peer play as observed when the children are 8 years old and coded with our MACRO coding system (it is the sum of negative parallel play, negative teasing, fighting, crying, and noncompliance). The teacher ratings of aggressive peer play are taken from the Cowan Adaptive Behavior Inventory. These children were seen by their teachers as uncooperative with peers, stubborn, and attention seeking. Figures 15.1 and 15.2 is a summary of their findings with respect to fathers. Father's rejecting parenting during parent–child interaction mediated the pathway between marital hostility and both teacher ratings and the observation of aggressive peer play. They also examined a similar model using mother's rejecting parenting to see if it would fit the data, and it did not.

They next asked how do these effects occur? They used the child's heart rate during parent–child interaction, arguing that children with higher heart rate are poorer at regulating emotion during the parent–child interaction. We saw in chapter 12 that there is evidence to support this contention. They also coded the

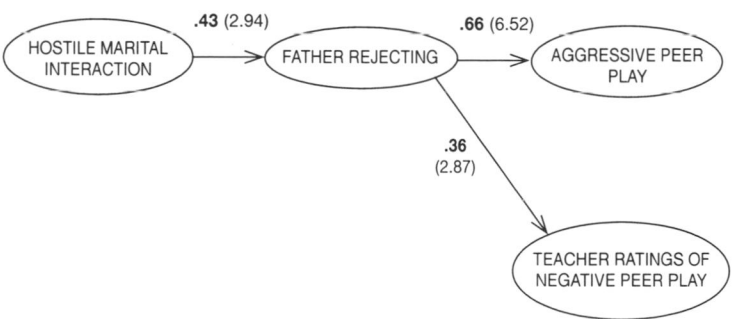

FIG. 15.1. Father's rejecting parenting mediates between marital hostility and aggressive peer play (from Katz & Gottman, 1995).

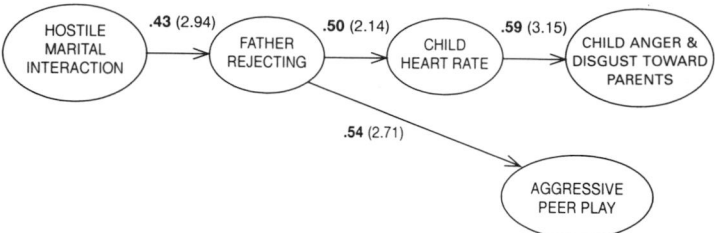

FIG. 15.2. Father's rejecting parenting is related to increased child heart rate and to child's anger and disgust toward parents (from Katz & Gottman, 1995).

child's expressions of anger and disgust with the SPAFF coding system during parent-child interaction. Figure 15.2 summarizes their findings. Father's rejecting parenting was related to higher heart rate in their children, and that the children with higher heart rates expressed more anger and disgust toward their parents. As before, the father's rejecting parenting was also predictive of aggressive peer play when the children were 8 years old.

Katz and Gottman (1993) reported that internalizing behavior in the children at age 8 was predicted by a different pattern of marital conflict resolution indexed by the husband's withdrawal as a listener. Christensen and his associates (Christensen, 1991; Christensen & Heavey, 1990; Heavey, Layne, & Christensen, 1993) have suggested that this demand–withdraw pattern is dysfunctional. They next examined whether mother's rejecting parenting was related to this pattern of marital interaction, and then related to the children's internalizing behavior problems at age 8. Figure 15.3 demonstrates that his was indeed the case.

To summarize, Katz and Gottman (1995) found that when the child was 5, hostile marital conflict was related to the father's rejecting parenting, and this, in turn predicted observed children's aggressive peer play at age 8 and teacher ratings of negative peer play at age 8. The child's heart rate during the parent–child also mediated between the father's rejecting parenting and the amount of anger and disgust the child displayed toward the parents during the parent–child interaction. For mothers, however, a different pattern of marital conflict, the

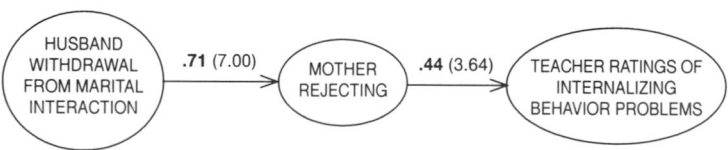

FIG. 15.3. Mother's rejecting behavior mediates between husband withdrawal from marital interaction and teacher ratings of internalizing behavior (from Katz & Gottman, 1995).

demand–withdraw pattern was related to mother's rejecting parenting, and this, in turn predicted the child's internalizing behavior problems at age 8. These results are consistent with Cohn, Cowan, Cowan, and Pearson (1992), who reported that children's externalizing behavior is mediated through the father whereas children's internalizing behavior is mediated through the mother.

16

When Parents Feel Emotionally Out of Control

Part of the meta-emotion coding system assessed the extent to which parents report having personal problems with either anger or sadness. In this chapter, we explore the correlates of feeling out of control with either anger or sadness.

In this chapter, we review two areas related to emotional experience and expression by men and women. The first area we review concerns the expression and experience of emotion, and gender differences in emotion. This is a large and disparate area, and one that is difficult to review briefly. The second area concerns a particlular class of feelings about sadness and anger, that is a particular class of meta-emotions, namely feeling out of control. This is an extremely small literature, one that is relatively easy to review briefly.

THE EXPERIENCE AND EXPRESSION OF EMOTION

Anger

Overall Findings about Anger. Averill (1982) conducted an extensive series of questionnaire studies on the experience, expression, and aftermath of everyday anger. Averill asked about the anger experienced, the duration and intensity of the anger, and he attempted to discriminate annoyance from anger. He found that people tend to get angry about 1 to 2 times a week, and that the anger lasts either 5 to 10 minutes or about 1 hour (the distribution of durations was bimodal). He found a correlation between the intensity of the anger experienced and the feeling of losing control, that the more inhibited the expression, the longer the internal experience of anger lasted and the more likely the person was to still become angry when thinking about the incident. More than 50% of the angry incidents were directed to a person in a close affectional relationship (love relationship or friendship), and an additional 26% toward acquaintances. With a loved one, subjects said that the goal of the anger was overwhelmingly either to strengthen the relationship or to gain revenge for a past incident.

Averill (1982) actually tried to get subjects to rate how they felt about their own anger, that is, their meta-emotions about anger, "however, most subjects simply described their ongoing feelings following the initial response" (pp. 204–205). Most subjects reported continuing feelings of dysphoria (they felt either irritable, depressed, anxious, or ashamed); only 30% felt relieved. Hence, negative feelings about one's own everyday anger are quite common.

In early research on marital conflict, before specific emotions were studied, anger was depicted as something to be controlled or eliminated, a potentially destructive state. Anger management programs have been developed, and applied for the treatment of battering husbands, assuming that marital violence has anger as its roots. Jacobson et al. (1994) actually found that it was not anger, but contempt and belligerence that discriminated violent from distressed but nonviolent marriages. In marriages, the longitudinal effects of anger do not seem to be negative.

Gottman and Krokoff (1989) reported that, in observations of marital conflict discussions, compliance by the wife was related to contemporaneously higher levels of marital satisfaction (particularly the husband's), but was related to declines in marital satisfaction over time, whereas a pattern of wife disagreement and anger was related to increases in marital satisfaction over time. Gottman and Levenson (1992), and Gottman (1993a, 1993b, 1994) reported that the pattern of marital interaction that predicted the cascade toward divorce was not anger but what he called "The Four Horsemen of the Apocalypse," namely, Criticism, Contempt, Defensiveness, and Stonewalling (listener emotional withdrawal).

Gender Differences.   In the words of Bardwick (1979), "Women are not entitled to anger. Anger, except in some girlish tantrum, is unfeminine. Direct, bold, eyeball-to-eyeball, confronting, dominating, resisting, insisting anger has been traditionally forbidden to women" (p. 48). What does the research literature say about gender differences in the expression and experience of anger?

Averill found that males were more often the target of anger, but this was only true when the relationship was not with a loved one; males were viewed as more provocative than females, but not in love relationships. Women rated anger as more intense than men did, women were more likely than men to want to talk the incident over with the instigator, they were more likely than men to cry and to respond to another's anger with hurt feelings than were men. Women were also more likely than men to believe that their anger was greater than the incident called for.

Frodi, Macaulay, and Thome (1977) reviewed 72 studies of adult anger and aggression. In studies of unprovoked aggression, men were more aggressive than women. Men were also more likely than women to engage in physical aggression when they were not angry, and to displace their aggression to some other person. They found no evidence of gender differences in the frequency of verbal or physical displays of aggression. This is also true in violent marriages; in incidents when violence occurs, the data actually suggest that women initiate the first violent act approximately 70% of the time (for a review, see Dutton, 1988); however, men inflict greater physical damage. In her own research, Frodi and her colleagues found that women were more angered by condescending treatment whereas men were more angered at verbal or physical aggression. When she conducted a study in which men and women were each provoked by the type of incident that supposedly makes them the most angry, she found that men and women became equally angry, showed the same increases in physiological arousal, and showed similar amounts of aggression. However, when she studied the stream of consciousness thoughts of the subjects, she found evidence that the men were preoccupied with thoughts of anger, keeping themselves stirred up, whereas the women tended to preoccupy themselves with nonaggressive thoughts. Similar findings have been reported in the marital literature, with men more likely to rehearse distress-maintaining thoughts than women after a marital argument (Holtzworth-Munroe & Jacobson, 1985).

As Tavris (1982) noted, the public–private difference in anger between genders is critical. Women behave very differently in public than they do in their families, in private. In research on conflictual marital interaction, there is, in fact, consistent evidence that women are *more* angry, confronting, and critical than men, whereas men are more withdrawing, reconciling, compromising, and avoidant of conflict (Gottman, 1979, 1994; Rausch, Barry, Hertel, & Swain, 1974; Schaap, 1982). Christensen and his colleagues have called this pattern the "demand–withdraw" pattern. In this pattern, the demander, usually the wife, pressures by complaining, criticizing, making emotional requests, and the person who withdraws, usually the husband, retreats through defensiveness and passive interaction. Christensen and Heavey (1990) had couples discuss two issues, one raised by the husband and one raised by the wife. No evidence of one spouse being the demander and the other being the distancer was found for the husband's issue, but when the wife raised the issue, the most common pattern was the wife-demand/husband-distance pattern. Previous research has shown that most marital conflict discussions begin with the wife raising the issue (Gottman, 1994). In fact, Christensen (1991) studied three groups of couples, one distressed, one divorcing, and one nondistressed. The wife-demand/husband-withdraw was characteristic of all three groups, so the pattern is not just characteristic of distressed couples. Heavey and Christensen (1993) replicated and extended these results, showing that the standard pattern predicted declines in the wife's marital satisfaction over 1 year, whereas the reverse pattern (husband-demand/wife-withdraw) predicted increases in the wife's marital satisfaction.

Gender Differences in Physiological Responses.   There is evidence that, during marital conflict, men tend to withdraw emotionally when they are physiologically aroused, whereas women become engaged (Gottman, 1994; Gottman & Levenson, 1988). Levenson, Carstensen, and Gottman (1994) suggested that this effect may be due to the fact that men's ratings of how negative the interaction was significantly related to their physiological arousal, but this was not the case for women in their study. They suggested that because previous research has found that men are more accurate at perceiving their own physiological responses than women, perhaps men tune more into their bodies when they are physiologically aroused to decide what to do, whereas women are more likely to look toward social cues, which keep them in a conflictual interaction regardless of what is going on in their bodies.

Zillmann (1979) summarized his own and others' research on laboratory studies of anger provocation. In one study in which he asked men and women to wait and to try to relax after being provoked by a rude confederate, he found that men were more likely to rehearse thoughts that maintained the anger and to maintain a high blood pressure, whereas women's thoughts distracted themselves (e.g., they thought about what they were going to do this afternoon, after they left the experiment) and they calmed down physiologically. When given an opportunity to retaliate, men's physiology returned to baseline, whereas, in the retaliation condition women's stayed elevated, particularly when they were required to complain about the experimenter's apparently rude behavior to the supervisor.

Brown and Smith (1992) had married couples interact in two tasks, one a marital discussion and one in which they each tried to persuade and influence one another. Husbands in the condition in which they were attempting to influence their wives showed larger increases in systolic blood pressure (SBP) before and during the interaction. These increases in SBP were accompanied by increases in anger and what they described as a "more hostile and coldly assertive style." Wives engaged in the influence condition showed a similar pattern of behavior, but no physiological effects. Smith and Brown (1991) examined the relationship of the Cook–Medley MMPI scale, which purportedly measures cynical hostility to the variables in this study. They found that cynical hostility was related to heart rate reactivity in husbands in both interaction conditions and to increases in SBP in the persuasion condition. However, for wives cynical hostility was unrelated to their own or to their husband's reactivity.

Health Consequences of Anger.   Appel, Holroyd, and Gorkin (1983) reviewed research on the effects of anger on the etiology and progression of physical illness. They compared the effects of the suppression of anger with its expression. They reviewed evidence for the hypothesis that it is *suppressed hostility* that is a significant factor in the etiology of essential hypertension. Esler et al. (1977) found that high renin (a part of the body's blood pressure control renin-angiotensin system) hypertensives were more likely to be described as "guilt-prone, submissive persons with a high level of unexpressed anger" (p. 409). There was support for this finding in other studies Appel, Holyrod and Gorkin reviewed. One study of physiological responses of hypertensives found heightened physiological responses after seeing an anger-eliciting film, but they denied feeling any anger. There is also evidence that high blood pressure males yield more often during arguments, when paired with low blood pressure males (Harburg et al., 1964). Other research has supported the hypothesis that the inhibition of anger expression and cardiovascular reactivity are important factors in cardiovascular disease (e.g., Holroyd & Gorkin, 1983). In general, there is now evidence that shows that the suppression of facial expressions during emotional arousal leads to heightened physiological responses (Gross & Levenson, 1993).

For coronary heart disease (CHD), it is now well-known that Type A men had twice the incidence of CHD as Type B men, even controlling for the standard risk factors associated with CHD. The evidence supports the hypothesis that Type A men are more hostile, particularly when provoked. They also tend to endorse MMPI items that suggest they view other people suspiciously (Williams et al., 1980). As we mentioned previously, a series of studies by T. Smith found that Type A personality and heightened cardiovascular reactivity are related to a heightened overt expression of hostility during a laboratory conflictual marital interaction (Brown & Smith, 1992; Smith & Brown, 1991). A similar result has been reported by K. Matthews in a series of studies on Type A patterns in fathers and children. The effect holds for women (MacDougall, Dembroski, & Krantz, 1981). The general results suggest that some negative health consequences may be associated with both styles that are characteristically hostile and suspicious of others, and styles in which subjects are either unaware of their hostility or characteristically suppress it. Clearly, more work is needed to clarify these phenomena and how they work to create ill health.

Gender Differences in Health and Physiological Responses to Stress. What about gender differences in physiological response and health? Polefrone and Manuck (1987) reviewed evidence on gender differences in cardiovascular and neuroendocrine responses to stressors. The evidence suggests that females show a smaller elevation in urinary epinephrine than males, and smaller blood pressure reactions, but that there are no differences in heart rate reactions. Cleary (1987) reviewed gender differences in physical health and concluded that in the U.S., women live about 7 years longer than men, have lower death rates for most causes of death, and lower rates of infectious illness, although this figure declines after menopause. However, women experience greater morbidity from acute and nonfatal chronic conditions.

However, there is also evidence that women suffer more physical illness when they are in an ailing marriage than is the case for men (Gottman & Levenson, 1992). The evidence on immunosuppression in unhappy marriages is clearer for unhappily married women than it is for unhappily married men (Kiecolt-Glaser et al., 1987, 1988). Gottman (1994) found that it was possible to predict husband illness from marital conflict four years before, but that the effect was mediated, for men only, by loneliness. Those husbands in conflicted marriages who were also lonely in the marriage were most likely to become physically ill. He discussed these differences in terms of well-known gender differences in social support systems; in an ailing marriages, particularly, the male's already smaller social support system shrinks whereas the female's does not. Still, not all males become lonely in this situation.

Sadness

Balswick and Avertt (1977) conducted a diary study to assess how often people experience various emotions. They found that women reported being more expressive of love, happiness, and sadness more than men. There is much less research just on sadness, although there are literatures on grief following bereavement and on depression. Van Dyke and Kaufman (1993) reviewed research on the psychobiology of bereavement. There is evidence that conjugal bereavement is associated with increased mortality (Jacobs & Ostfeld, 1977); in one study, in 1 year after conjugal death in a community in Wales, there was a sevenfold increase in death compared to the control population. The risk was greatest for males; men were far more likely to die after their wives died than conversely. Women are now believed to be at greater risk for depression, but the mechanisms are not well-understood (e.g., Wetzel, 1994).

Women's depression has been studied in the context of marriage. The results show that in happy marriages with a depressed mother, both the father and the children are providing high levels of social support. Also, a woman's sadness in this context of marital conflict has been found to lessen the probability of immediately subsequent hostile behavior by the husband, so it is a behavior that is functional for her (Biglan, Rothlind, & Hops, 1989; Hops, Biglan, Sherman, & Arthur, 1987). Blier and Blier-Wilson (1989) asked subjects how much confidence they felt expressing various emotions to people as a function of their gender. Males reported feeling less confident in expressing anger to women than to men. Women reported less confidence expressing anger to women but more confident expressing anger to men. Women reported greater confidence expressing fear and sadness regardless of the target's gender than did men.

Summary

In the area of marriage, anger, taken alone, appears not to have clear negative consequences. The most common pattern of wife-demand/husband-withdraw,

although characteristic of marriages, is not characteristic of distressed or divorcing couples. Instead, contempt, defensiveness, criticism, and stonewalling have
been found to be more characteristic of unstable marriages. These patterns of
interaction seem consistent with the patterns induced in the laboratory by Smith
and Brown and their colleagues, in which the husband's physiological reactivity
is heightened and the wife's is not. However, on the basis of other research, in an
ailing marriage characterized by these patterns of interaction, one would also
expect the wife's health to become compromised.

There seems to be no consistent conclusion one can make from these literatures about the expression of anger or sadness or its suppression. What conditions
put people at health risk? Are the conditions the same for men as for women? At
this time these remain open questions. One possibility is that it is not the expression or the inhibition of anger or sadness that are potentially problematic, but
one's meta-emotions about anger or sadness. We explore this possibility later in
this chapter.

FEELING EMOTIONALLY OUT OF CONTROL

Ekman (1984) introduced the concept of *flooding,* by which he meant that
through emotional conditioning a wide range of stimuli eventually become capable of eliciting blends of anger, fear, and sadness. Gottman (1994) suggested
adding to the term "flooding" the idea that the emotional state becomes disre-
gulating in the sense that a person can attend to or do little else when flooded. In
this manner, flooding may be highly disruptive of organized behavior. Second,
Gottman suggested that people in relationships that chronically generate negative
affect blends that leads to flooding may become hypervigilant to potentially
threatening and escalating interactions. They may become likely to misattribute
threat potential to relatively neutral or positive acts. All of these processes have
implications for the course of a conflictual marital interaction.

Flooding is clearly an emotional recation to negative emotions, and, hence it is
a meta-emotion about negative affects. In Gottman (1994), flooding was part of a
set of five self-report processes that were predictive of divorce. Flooding was
related to increasing distance and isolation, the couple leading parallel lives (less
interconnected) and to eventual loneliness.

In this chapter, we explore a similar process in which people discussed feeling
out of control with respect to either sadness or anger in the meta-emotion interview.

Our Data

One scale of the meta-emotion coding system was designed to measure the extent
to which parents feeling out of control, either with sadness or anger. The items on

this scales are for both sadness and anger: the person has difficulty regulating the intensity of the emotion, the emotion occurs often, the emotion is difficult to get over, the emotion has been a problem or a concern, the person thinks this emotion can be dangerous, and the person has needed help with this emotion. Some of our subjects said that they avoided the emotions of either anger or sadness and structured their lives to do so, but this was too small a percentage of subjects to study, and the dimension does not seem to be the same as suppression.

Qualitative Analysis of Our Data

When Parents Have Problems With Anger.   When a parent has trouble with the emotion of anger, this is reflected in her approach to anger with her child (141, mom). The following mother has trouble with her anger.

M: Um, for me personally, anger tends to cloud my judgment and I do things that I regret.

I: Um-hmm.

M: And I don't like being angry. I don't like the way it makes me feel and I don't like the things that it makes me do. Ah, of course I'm responsible for my own actions and I have nobody to blame but myself and I think that anger is normal. Human beings become angry. I mean things do not go your way and it's not abnormal to explode sometimes when you're feeling angry. But I also think sometimes it comes from, ah, the more negative parts of life that would be selfish or, for me it's just that I'm being selfish or I'm being, you know, just irritable, sleepy, often when I'm very tired or I'm very hungry, those are the two worst times for me, those are the times when I'm usually angered and, you know, it reminds me of those killer bees, (laughs), you know, and I just think, you know, I'm not accomplishing anything here and if I'd really just eaten a little snack, I probably would have handled this a little bit differently.

I: Right.

M: So I, I wouldn't want to judge anybody. I'm not saying, you know, you're a bad person if you get angry. I would never say that. Ah, I do think that it clouds one's judgment, I don't think it's necessarily a positive force.

I: O.k. You talked about how anger makes you do some things. What is it that anger makes you do?

M: Well, there will be times when my kids, they won't misbehave, maybe I have a legitimate complaint, but instead of handling it smoothly and with equanimity, the way I would if I weren't say hungry or tired or irritable for whatever reason, I yell. Ah, I, I just, you know, I yell. I raise my voice to a loud (laughs) extreme and all that really happens is that I probably make them disgusted with me or maybe they chew me out. I don't think I'm dealing with them as effectively.

I: It's not solving anything.

M: No, it really doesn't. It's just me blowing off steam, looking bad in their eyes. It's kind of the way I see it whereas if they were doing something that I didn't like and I was not in that kind of a bad mood or, you know, not having any of those problems that would cause me to be angry, I might deal with it in a completely different way in which they would respect me and respect the way I deal with it and that's what I mean.

In the following excerpt, the father talks quite candidly about his own problems with anger (Father, 128).

F: I changed my, I used to be destructive when I was younger. My anger would result, uh, I killed a cat one time I got mad. I just took a cat and smacked it dead and threw it away. I just, I was that impulsive. Or put my hands through walls. I broke my hands twice doing it. But then I stopped. What happened was, it's just that I never went to high school, I went to high school but we played, we played around with drugs a lot when we were in Chicago. So we never really, we never really cared about school, and I got job at Ford Motor Company when I turned sixteen, and then I worked from there until economics, you know, it got us all laid off.

I: Um-hmm. Yeah.

F: Ahhh, when that period happened, when I got out of high school and started working, I related to the older people, the more responsible and I'd seen how they act, and I stopped my wildness. I stopped reverting away from being a jerk to half-jerk to being somebody sensible and not doing stupid things. It took like a year, but after that period, I didn't pull any more stupid stunts, my anger, when I got mad I didn't do stupid things like go out and put my hand through a car windshield or punch things or anything like that. I stopped.

I: Uh-huh. Uh-huh. So you had that real tendency in you, but you managed to stop it.

F: Yeah. It wasn't a frequent occurrence, but I would blow up. That's where I had like I had an assault and battery charge. It wasn't against some guy in a bar, it was against a state cop I, I knocked out. And it all, it all started coming to me that this, that I'm not, I was never a dumb person. Ah, I didn't go to school because I didn't want to go to school. I knew they were wastin my time but I wasn't dumb. I took my GED and passed the first time. After I was out of high school, I was eligible without studying up, but I passed and now I passed all my tests.

I: Um-hmm.

F: It's just that I learned that that's not the right way to do it. If I'm going to make it to twenty-one years old, I'm going to have to stop being a jerk.

I'm going to have to quit smoking cigarettes. I'm going to have to stop dropping pills, and revert back and be a normal person.

I: How did you do that? How did you get yourself to do that? That's pretty amazing.

F: I'm just stubborn.

I: You just put your mind to it?

F: Yeah. It's like with cigarettes, I, I start, it's like with pot too, ah, I smoked a lot of pot before I came into the service. Once I entered the service, that was it. There was, there was, I smoked it up to the day I left and never have touched it since then. There's no, there's been opportunities, you know. I've gone back to friend's house, you know, and they'd be passing stuff around, but I would say, "No, thank you." Cigarettes would be the same way too. I started smoking cigarettes and then I smoked off and on for like ten years, and it finally came to the point where just about three years ago, I had a pack of cigarettes and I just didn't want to smoke anymore. I said, "I've just gotten tired of it." Put 'em there, and that's just how it sits. The only thing is my weight, and that's what I'm working on now.

I: Um-hmm.

F: But ah I just, with the anger I mean, I just learned to control it. And now I don't explode anymore.

I: So what do you do with it?

F: Hmmm?

I: How do you control it?

F: I scheme. Get even.

I: Mmmmm. How do you get even?

F: I think of things, that's all.

I: (Laughs.)

F: Yeah, if somebody really twerps me off or, ah, ah, I just think of ways I get even with these guys real easy. Or, you know, I'll just wait. They'll screw up someday, and I'll get them. But I won't wa, I won't waste my time with it now.

I: So what do you think about being angry? Do you think it's a good thing, or it's a bad thing?

F: It's a good thing. It's a release. I think it'd be, you know, you have to let yourself out, I guess, 'cause if you build it up in you too long you start getting like, you start getting like that . . .

I: Yeah. So you let it out by . . .

F: Talking.

I: Oh. To the person that you're mad at?

F: Yeah.

I: O.k. But you said you scheme. You, you, so you're not destructive . . .

F: I'm not destructive, but I'll scheme like, ahh, I accidentally got mad at IGA (grocery store) a time back. And, um, I scheme against them so here's what I thought about IGA, and I'll do this in three minutes flat, I thought of this, I said, O.k. how do you get back at a store without hurting them? A food store? You spread a rumor one of the food handler's got AIDS. You type, you write up on a piece of paper, you get a photostated a hundred of times, put a few in the post office, put a few in the mailbox, where the people get their newspapers at. You call maybe a radio station in town or a newspaper and say, "I've been hearing this rumor, is it true?" You start this like little rumor. And it's gonna, it's just gonna bother them. They're gonna get a lot of phone calls, and a lot of people are gonna ask, and it's gonna create a headache for them for a couple of days and that's it. You get even.

I: Um-hmmm.

F: Just a little. I read a book on it one time that probably stuck in the back of my head. It's called, ahhh, Don't Get Mad, Get Even. And it's a guide, it's a master of practical, a master of dirty tricks. He was the guy that said, if you don't like somebody, or he did something nasty to you, pull your car in front of him, let him tailgate you, then hit your brakes. 'Cause, the guy in fault, always hits you from behind is at fault in accidents. Then you sue him. But that's, that's a different subject.

I: Um-hmmm. What about, ummm, would I know that you're mad if I saw you? Do you hold it back?

F: (Shakes head no.)

. . . .

In the segment in the interview when the he is asked about which emotions are still hard for him, he says more about his daily struggle with anger.

I: What emotions are still hard for you?

F: Anger, I would say anger 'cause I can still have a violent moment. And I can, you know, go out and do something. That's probably my worst. If I've ever get to that point, if I, I'll rubber bank and stamp on my head if anger finally got me I was so mad at something I'd go out and probably would hurt somebody. I wouldn't hurt Susan. I'd go out at the source, find out who it was. Disgust, nah. Sadness, nah. Contempt, nah.

I: O.k. How do you make sure that you don't feel angry that often if it's something you don't like to feel? How do you keep it out of your life?

F: Ah, that's a hidden secret in my head. Um (pause) I really don't know. I'm just sayin that the intelligent half of my head talks to it. It says, "all right, asshole, don't screw up." Talk, you know, "You're gonna go out, and you're gonna do something dumb, you're gonna get in all kinds of trouble, embarrass your family, and slow down and stop." I never, I guess I never let my mind get angry anymore. That's all. It's just that they do something dumb or they or I do something dumb, most of the time if I do get angry, it's because of me. I'll do something stupid. But, um, I usually just think it over, think it out. Talk, you know, start, start bringin it out and see, and then finally after, after, I have a very fast relief valve. If I do get angry now which is seldom it Sssss quickly. I'm back. I'm out of it then. And that's probably what it is. I just don't let it, I just don't keep it in me very long.

Notice how this father dismisses his child's anger.

F: (Laughs.) Jackie being mad? Ahh, when's the last time . . . I laugh.
I: You think it's cute?
F: I think, yeah, it is.
I: Uh-huh.
F: She, she, she'll, "Gosh Darn It." And she'll walk away like a little midget human. It's so funny.
I: (Laughs.) Well how does she react to when she watches you laugh?
F: Huh?
I: What does she, what do you think she thinks when she watches you laugh?
F: She gets embarrassed. Yeah, she'll go, she's got a shy streak in her about a mile thick. She'll go, "Daddy!" And then that's it.

In the following excerpt (Mother, 124), this mother has no idea what to do with her own anger, so she can't effectively deal with her son's anger. First she talks about her own experience with anger:

I: If, if you were angry with someone not in your family, somebody, ummm, ahhh, a friend, at work or something, how would you handle that?
M: (Sigh.) I would probably just have to shut it up inside, and, if it was a close friend, I would probably raise my voice, you know, if I wasn't in a public place. If I were in a public place, I would probably deal with it later, just sort of, you know, try and calm myself down and then, you know, certainly talk about it later. Probably, you know, talk about it in a heated manner. Go home and talk to John, just sort of, you know, maybe, you know, stomp around the room and, you know, get angry like that.
I: And that, then you feel that, that gets it out of your system? And it's pretty much done then?
M: Yeah. Yeah, I think so.

About her son's anger:

I: O.k., let's talk about Max again. How, ahh, how do you respond to him and how does it make you feel when you see him angry?

M: I think it depends if, I think it's different from the crying, I think sometimes I get mad at him, and I'm not quite as free with support, I don't think. That, 'cause his anger can make me very mad sometimes depending on, you know, the reason for it. I don't know, maybe I do, I don't let him get rid of it. You know, I can't, if I could think of a specific instance, maybe I could think of how I deal with it. I can't think of anything right now. I can't think of how I've dealt with his anger.

I: Does he throw a tantrum?

M: Usually he still just cries. Ummm . . .

I: What kind of things make him mad?

M: Ummm, mostly his little brother stealing his toys, or biting him, for good reason. But they, they like to quarrel a lot and most of the time, since it's Max who would go up to his room and stay there, you know, if they're mad at each other, I'll just separate them, you know, or if Max has done something, or if Rudy had done something to make Max angry, you know, I, I don't know, I think I let him deal with it. You know when I'll send him to his room, I'll hear toys being thrown, (laughs) screaming, yelling, and threats. (Laughs.)

I: And so it's like, it's O.k. if he does it there then . . .

M: I think I let him deal with it by himself because I, you know when he gets angry sometimes it make me mad and it seems to set us both off really badly, so . . .

I: So, ummm, what do you think you're trying to teach him about anger and feeling angry.

M: That's a good question. I don't know. I've never really thought about it before.

I: Some of these questions are pretty hard.

M: Yeah.

I: They are not things that . . .

M: Yeah, I'm just sort of realizing that maybe there is some kind of a double standard between letting him cry, that's O.k., but anger, maybe, you know, "Don't have it," you know, "Go upstairs, get rid of it and then come down and be pleasant," you know. I can deal with the crying, you know, I can say, "Poor Max," and stroke his head, but when he's mad I don't say, "Poor Max," and stroke his head, I say, "Take it somewhere else. I don't want to hear it." I don't know. It's kind of interesting.

I: Do you have an idea of what you'd like to teach him about it that may be different from what you actually do?

M: I don't think I've ever really thought about it. Maybe if you ask me in a week, I would have thought about it more, but, I just, I don't think I ever realized that I, I did different ways of, because they are similar emotions in some ways, you know. And I'm doing completely different things.

Quantitative Analysis of Our Data

In this chapter, we explore the correlates of people feeling dysregulated, or out of control with respect to the emotions of anger and sadness, and how this may differ for men and women. It is clear that, according to stereotypes about emotion socialization, anger is an emotion that we typically think of as more appropriate for males and that sadness is more appropriate for females. Actually, Averill's (1982) classic study of the experience and circumstances of anger for men and women changed many of these stereotypes for normal everyday experiences of anger. The equivalent study has not been done for sadness. We have seen that in our data awareness of sadness is significantly more likely for women than for men, and that men who are more aware of and accepting of sadness are very different in families, both in their marital interaction and in their interaction with their children.

As far as independence, feeling out of control with anger and sadness were uncorrelated for the father, $r = .22$, *ns,* and for the mother, $r = .16$, *ns.*

We wish to know to what extent the dimensions of a parent's control of anger or sadness are different than the dimensions for this parent of Awareness of one's own or of one's child's emotions, or Coaching, and whether the dimensions of feeling out of control with anger and feeling out of control with sadness are independent. For the father, the results of these analyses are summarized in Table 16.1a. For the father, feeling out of control with either sadness or anger was

TABLE 16.1a
Correlations Between the Father Feeling Out
of Control With Sadness and Anger and the
Meta-Emotion Dimensions.

	Father	
	Sadness	*Anger*
Father sadness		
Awareness own	−.16	.01
Awareness child	−.12	.15
Coaching	−.01	−.01
Father anger		
Awareness own	−.14	.21
Awareness child	−.14	.02
Coaching	−.19	−.19

TABLE 16.1b
Correlations Between the Mother Feeling Out
of Control With Sadness and Anger and the
Meta-Emotion Dimensions.

| | Mother | |
	Sadness	Anger
Mother sadness		
Awareness own	.19	−.25*
Awareness child	−.25*	.02
Coaching	.34**	.00
Mother anger		
Awareness own	.34**	−.10
Awareness child	−.29*	−.15
Coaching	.26*	−.05

*$p < .05$. **$p < .01$.

unrelated to his meta-emotion variables. However, for the mother (Table 16.1b), her feeling out of control with sadness was related positively to her coaching the child's anger and sadness, and with awareness of her own anger. We can suggest the hypothesis that, for the mother, feeling out of control with sadness is related to her greater involvement with coaching her child's emotions; no such relationship exists for her feeling out of control with anger, and no such relationships exist for the father.

There were no significant gender differences in the expression of anger or sadness in the marital interaction, for anger, $t(55) = −.06$, ns, for sadness, $t(55) = −.86$, ns, nor in the parent-child interaction, for anger, $t(54) = −.08$, ns, for sadness, $t(54) = −.57$, ns. For feelings of being out of control, there were no gender differences for anger, $t(52) = 1.20$, ns, but there were for sadness, $t(52) = −3.30, p < .01$, with women feeling more out of control with sadness than men, female mean = 13.68, male mean = 12.53.

Feeling Out of Control Emotionally and Marital Interaction

One advantage that we have in this study over studies like Averill's that deal exclusively with self-report data is that we can link self-report data with actual behavior. Tables 16.2a, 16.2b, 16.2c, and 16.2d summarize our analyses of the feeling out of control meta-emotion codes with negative marital interaction as coded by the SPAFF and the RCISS. These results show that the father is correlated with marital interaction behaviors that were predictive of the cascade toward marital dissolution, namely, belligerence, contempt, and stonewallling. However, for the mother, only her feeling out of control with anger was related to

TABLE 16.2a
Correlations of the SPAFF Codes of Marital
Interaction and the Father's Feeling Out
of Control With Sadness or Anger

| | Feeling out of control | |
| | Father | |
SPAFF Code	Sadness	Anger
Husband Marital Code		
Disgust	−.04	−.16
Contempt	.21	.15
Belligerence	.25*	.19
Anger	−.04	.11
Sadness	.14	−.02
Defensiveness	−.09	.02
Stonewalling	−.09	−.14

*$p < .05.$

her marital interaction, and these codes were anger and sadness, not codes that predict marital dissolution.

Feeling Out of Control Emotionally, the Cascade Toward Marital Dissolution, and Parental Health

Tables 16.3a and 16.3b are a summary of the father's and mother's feeling out of control with respect to sadness and anger and the cascade variables and physical

TABLE 16.2b
Correlations of the SPAFF Codes of Marital
Interaction and the Mother's Feeling Out
of Control With Sadness or Anger

| | Feeling out of control | |
| | Mother | |
SPAFF Code	Sadness	Anger
Wife Marital Code		
Disgust	−.10	−.09
Contempt	.12	.22
Belligerence	.03	.00
Anger	.06	.36**
Sadness	−.07	.32**
Defensiveness	.09	−.17
Stonewalling	−.13	.12

**$p < .01.$

TABLE 16.2c
Correlation of Father's Feelings of Being Out of Control
with the Four Horsemen of the Apocalypse RCISS
Codes of the Marital Interaction.

| | Feeling Out of Control | |
| | Father | |
RCISS Code	Sadness	Anger
Husband Marital Code		
Criticism	.21	.07
Defensiveness	.06	.03
Contempt	.46***	.33**
Stonewalling	.24*	.02

$^*p < .05.$ $^{**}p < .01.$ $^{***}p < .001.$

illness at Time-2. For the husband being out of control with sadness predicted the number of months the couple would be separated in the next 3 years. For the mother feeling out of control with anger was a significant predictor of her marital unhappiness at Time-1 and at Time-2, of the number of months the couple will be separated in the next 3 years, and her physical illness at Time-2.

Feeling Out of Control Emotionally and the Oral History Variables

Tables 16.4a and 16.4b summarize the relationship between the father or mother feeling out of control and the oral history interview codes. These tables show no

TABLE 16.2d
Correlation of Mother's Feelings of Being Out of Control
With the Four Horsemen of the Apocalypse RCISS
Codes of the Marital Interaction.

| | Feeling Out of Control | |
| | Mother | |
RCISS Code	Sadness	Anger
Wife Marital Code		
Criticism	.10	−.01
Defensiveness	.17	.13
Contempt	−.02	.09
Stonewalling	.02	−.06

TABLE 16.3a
Correlation of Father's Feelings of Being Out of Control
With Sadness or Anger, the Marital Cascade Variables,
and Father's Health

| | Feeling Out of Control | |
| | Father | |
	Sadness	Anger
Husband Marital		
Time-1 marital satisfaction	−.01	−.04
Time-2 marital satisfaction	.00	−.21
Considers separation	.05	−.21
Considers divorce	−.11	.20
Couple Variable		
Separation	.04	.21
Months separated	.30*	.19
Divorce	.11	.16
Husband illness	.02	−.10

*$p < .05$.

relationship for the father. However, when the mother feels out of control with sadness and anger, she is more negative about the marriage in the interview, and her feeling out of control with sadness is correlated with her saying that it is not worth it to work on marital conflict. Both variables were predictive of divorce (Buehlman, Gottman, & Katz, 1992).

TABLE 16.3b
Correlation of Mother's Feelings of Being Out of Control
With Sadness or Anger, the Marital Cascade Variables,
and Mother's Health

| | Feeling Out of Control | |
| | Mother | |
	Sadness	Anger
Wife Marital		
Time-1 Marital Satisfaction	.07	−.31**
Time-2 Marital Satisfaction	−.19	−.23*
Considers Separation	.13	.12
Considers Divorce	.08	.15
Couple Variable		
Separation	.05	.12
Months Separated	−.05	.24*
Divorce	.09	.05
Wife Illness	−.02	.35**

*$p < .05$. **$p < .01$.

TABLE 16.4a
Correlation of Father's Feelings of Being Out
of Control With Sadness or Anger and the Father's
Oral History Variables.

| | Feeling Out of Control | |
| | Father | |
Oral History Variables	Sadness	Anger
Husband		
Fondness	−.07	−.07
We-ness	−.17	−.16
Negativity	.19	.17
Couple Variable		
Discuss emotions	−.11	−.07
Glory	−.05	−.20
Chaos	.03	.17

Summary of Relationships Between Marital and Out of Control Variables

It seems that when the husband feels out of control with sadness or anger he behaves in the interaction so as to undermine the marriage, using contempt, belligerence, and stonewalling, but the wife does not. However, the husband's marital satisfaction and his views of the marriage are not affected by his feeling

TABLE 16.4b
Correlation of Mother's Feelings of Being Out
of Control With Sadness or Anger and the Mother's
Oral History Variables.

| | Feeling Out of Control | |
| | Mother | |
Oral History Variables	Sadness	Anger
Wife		
Fondness	−.09	.05
We-ness	−.09	−.17
Negativity	.24*	.30*
Couple Variable		
Discuss emotions	.05	.12
Glory	−.27*	.02
Chaos	−.03	.13

*$p < .05$.

TABLE 16.5a
Correlation of Father's Feelings of Being Out of Control
With His Parenting Behavior

| | Feeling Out of Control | |
| | Father | |
	Sadness	Anger
Warm	−.15	.14
Derogation	.26*	.07
Scaffolding/Praising	−.02	−.18

*$p < .05$.

out of control with sadness or anger. For the wife this picture is reversed. Although she may not be acting in the marital conflict discussion to undermine the marriage, she is unhappy with the marriage, she is seriously thinking of leaving, and she is giving up hope on the marriage.

Correlates of Feeling Out of Control with Parent-Child Interaction

Tables 16.5a and 16.5b show that if the father feels out of control with his sadness, he is significantly more likely to be high on Derogatory parenting; on the other hand, if the mother feels out of control with her anger, she is significantly more likely to be high on Derogatory parenting.

TABLE 16.5b
Correlation of Mother's Feelings of Being Out of Control
With Mother's Parenting Behavior

| | Feeling Out of Control | |
| | Mother | |
	Sadness	Anger
Warm	.15	.11
Derogation	−.16	.27*
Scaffolding/Praising	.20	−.14

*$p < .05$.

TABLE 16.6
Correlation of Parental Feelings of Being Out of Control
With Child Outcomes

| | Feeling Out of Control | | | |
| | Father | | Mother | |
Child Outcomes	Sadness	Anger	Sadness	Anger
Academic Achievement				
Achievement	−.13	.00	.23	−.13
Stroop	−.08	.04	.30*	−.02*
Peer Interaction—Observation				
Play Competence 8 years	.01	.06	.11	.12
Negative Affect 8 years	−.06	−.03	−.08	.44***
Negative Peer Rating	−.12	−.03	.10	.01
Child Negative Affect Ratings at age 8	−.09	−.04	.15	.25
Child Illness	.21	.19	−.02	−.06

*$p < .05$. **$p < .01$.

Feeling Out of Control Correlates with Child Outcomes

Child–Peer Relationships. The only significant result in Table 16.6 for the observed peer interaction variables shows that when the mother feels out of control with anger, it predicts that her child will be observed as affectively negative with a best friend at age 8. The out of control variables were unrelated to the teacher's ratings of negative peer relations.

Child Negative Affect. The out of control variables were unrelated to the ratings of child negative affectivity.

Child Illness. The out of control variables were unrelated to child illness at age 8.

Child Achievement. Table 17.6 shows that of the four out of control variables were not significantly associated with child achievement at age 8. The mother's feeling out of control with sadness was related *positively* to the child's ability to focus attention. This result may be related to the mother's greater coaching of the child's emotions when she feels out of control with sadness.

Summary. In fact, the child outcome variables that were predicted by the parents' feeling out of control with their emotions were the child's being observed as high in negative affect with a best friend, and positively predictive of higher Stroop scores.

To explore the relationship between the mother's feeling out of control with her own anger and the child's negative affect with a peer at age 8, we explored variables related to both and created a construct of the mother's perception that the child was a difficult child. This was the sum of two variables, the mother's Child Behavior Checklist score of the child as hyperactive, and the mother's score on the Katz–Gottman emotional down-regulation scale, both at age 8. The father's intrusiveness was related to these variables, and we constructed a successful path model that was able to tell one possible story about the relationship between the mother's feeling out of control with her own anger and the child's negative affect with a peer at age 8. Figure 16.1 summarizes these relationships. The model fit the data, with $\chi^2(1) - 2.80$, $p - .094$, $BBN = .967$.

This model suggests that the mother's feeling out of control with her own anger affects the father who in turn is more intrusive with the child, and that the father's intrusiveness with the child affects her perception of their child as difficult, and, in turn, the father's intrusiveness and the mother's feeling out of control with her anger affect the child's negative affect with a peer. For the variable of the child's negative affect with a peer at age 8, the multiple R for this path model was 0.66, which is a reasonable correlation. The model is also interesting because the only mother parent–child interaction variables related to her feeling out of control with her anger is her neutral affect, $r = 0.27, p < .05$, and her positive direction of the play, $r = 0.32, p < .01$. Hence, the model suggests the hypothesis that the mother's feeling out of control with her anger somehow gets a triadic interaction to work, which, despite her neutral affect and positive structuring, somehow recruits the father's intrusiveness.

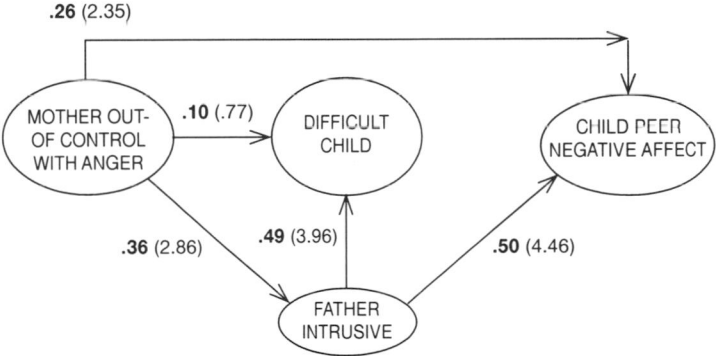

FIG. 16.1. Path model suggesting one hypothesis for the link between maternal feelings of being out of control with her anger and child negative affect with peer.

SUMMARY

There is evidence that, to some degree, feeling out of control with either anger or sadness is not associated with positive events in the family. We can summarize the correlations as follows. When the father feels out of control with anger and sadness, this relates to his acting belligerent, contemptuous, and stonewalling in the marital interaction, to his being high in limit setting and critical with his child, to the child being coded high on anger during the parent–child interaction, to the teacher rating the child as socially withdrawn, and to the mother rating the child as having behavior problems and low on positive daily moods. When the mother feels out of control with her sadness, this is related to her coaching her child more on both sad and angry emotions. It is likely that this a mother who is compensating for an ailing marriage by being a good mother to her children and buffering her children from marital conflict. However, in contrast, the mother who is out of control with her anger is actually more sad and angry in the marital interaction, she is more unhappily married, more negative about the marriage, more negative about the benefits of trying to resolve marital issues, and thinking more of leaving the marriage. She is more physically ill. There is some evidence to suggest the hypothesis that although she is not negative affectively with her child, her child is sad and whines more, that she sees the child as difficult temperamentally, and that the family operates to influence the child's negative affect with a peer.

These data support the results we previously obtained (Gottman & Levenson, 1992) that the negative physical health effects of an ailing marriage can be seen in the wife and not the husband. However, these results suggest that when the husband feels out of control emotionally, the husband is acting behaviorally to put the couple on the cascade toward marital dissolution, even if his own thinking is not toward dissolution. However his wife's thinking is toward dissolution when she feels out of control with her anger, even if her behavior is not.

Hence, the feeling parents expressed in the meta-emotion interview that some emotions were very difficult for them had echoes in the marriage, in the parent–child interaction, and in affecting some child outcomes, particularly those having to do with the child's emotional life.

17
Meta-Emotion, Emotional Expressiveness, and Parental Social Class

This chapter explores some of the potential limits of the emotion coaching concept. Is emotion coaching limited to emotionally expressive people, or is it limited to one particular social class?

Based on the coaching meta-emotion results, we recommend that parents need to be emotionally aware and more emotionally responsive to their children. However, the immediate image that this recommendation conveys is that *parents need to be more emotionally expressive*. This suggests that there is only one style of emotionality and emotional expressiveness that is functional for children. However, this would only be the case if greater emotional awareness meant greater emotional expressiveness. If this were true, it would suggest that cultural variation might have differential outcomes for children. We believe that this is not the case, and that parents can be aware of emotion in themselves and in their children regardless of individual and cultural differences in emotional expressiveness.

The construct of how emotionally expressive a family is has been shown to have considerable value (e.g., Halberstadt, 1991). It is also clear that cultures vary a great deal in the extent to which they value emotional expressiveness versus inhibition and control (Briggs, 1970; Dixon, Tronick, Keefer, & Brazelton, 1981), even for specific emotions such as anger (Lambert, Hamers, & Frasure-Smith, 1979). Family expressiveness has also been found to vary with social class, with working class families generally more restrictive and less expressive (Bugental, Love, & Gianetto, 1971; Halberstadt, 1985; Lambert et al., 1979).

Halberstadt (1991) reviewed literature suggesting that children from expressive families should be better senders of emotional messages, whereas children from less expressive families should be better receivers. The hypothesis has received limited support in research with children, although it has been supported in research with college students. Children from expressive homes appear to be better at sending and receiving emotional messages. However, Halberstadt, Fox, and Jones (1993) found that children of low-expressive mothers were more positively expressive than children of high-expressive mothers, whereas children of high-expressive mothers were more negatively expressive than children of low-expressive mothers. Cassidy, Parke, Butkovsky, and Braungart (1992) found that parental expressiveness, particularly the expressiveness of the same-sex parent was related to the children's popularity, and the expressiveness of parents and children were positively correlated.

We need to explore what the relationship is of a coaching meta-emotion structure to emotional expressiveness. We are very interested in this question, in part because we think that the construct of expressiveness, although very interesting, is limited in its ability to describe a family's patterns of emotional communication. Is it possible that people can live in a family that expresses a high level of anger, for example, and yet the parents can be dismissing of emotion? We think that this is quite possible. If expressiveness and meta-emotion were unrelated, then people's level of emotional understanding could vary a great deal, even if people were matched on emotional expressiveness.

META-EMOTION AND THE PARENTS' FACIAL EXPRESSIVENESS DURING MARITAL AND PARENT-CHILD INTERACTION

Tables 17.1a and 17.1b are a summary of the correlations with the total number of facial action units coded with Ekman and Friesen's (1978) Emotion Facial Action Coding System (EMFACS) during marital interaction. With the EMFACS we are able to examine specific emotional expressions as well as nonemotional expressions that serve to control facial expression (e.g., chin boss contractions).

These results suggest that facial expressiveness and the meta-emotion variables are generally unrelated and that when they are related, there are negative correlations: between the father's control and sadness facial expressions during the marital interaction and his awareness of his own and his child's anger, respectively, and between the father's awareness of his own anger and his sadness and anger facial expressions, and the father's awareness of his child's anger and the father's sadness facial expressions. For the mother, her awareness of her own anger is negatively correlated with control facial expressions, whereas her awareness of her child's anger is negatively correlated with her own anger facial expressions. The total number of the facial action units was uncorrelated with the meta-emotion variables for both mother and father. There is, however, evidence of fewer control facial expressions, which are visible attempts to control or mask

TABLE 17.1a
Correlations Between the Father's Facial Expressiveness During
Marital Interaction With Sadness and Anger
and the Meta-Emotion Dimensions.

	Father			
	Sadness	Anger	Overall Expressiveness	Control
Father sadness				
Awareness own	−.17	−.17	−.22	−.25*
Awareness child	−.25*	−.02	−.09	.03
Coaching	−.08	−.07	−.14	.14
Father anger				
Awareness own	−.28*	−.31*	−.21	−.10
Awareness child	−.30*	.09	−.03	−.06
Coaching	−.23	−.11	−.12	.03

*$p < .05$.

facial expressiveness. For the father this was related to awareness of his own sadness, and for the mother it was related to awareness of her own anger.

However, facial expressiveness is a limited way of measuring emotional expressiveness. In Table 17.2, we examined the SPAFF codes of neutral affect as indices of being non-emotionally expressive in the marital and the parent–child interaction. The SPAFF measures affect in the marital interaction in all channels, face, voice, body position and movement, words, and context. For the parent–child interaction, we used the neutral codes of the Kahen affect system. As Table

TABLE 17.1b
Correlations Between the Mother's Facial Expressiveness During
Marital Interaction With Sadness and Anger
and the Meta-Emotion Dimensions.

	Mother			
	Sadness	Anger	Overall Expressiveness	Control
Mother sadness				
Awareness own	−.03	−.09	−.05	.02
Awareness child	.07	−.18	−.01	.07
Coaching	−.03	−.16	.00	.20
Mother anger				
Awareness own	.06	−.02	−.16	−.25*
Awareness child	.06	−.24*	−.08	−.10
Coaching	−.04	.04	.04	.07

*$p < .05$.

TABLE 17.2
Correlations Between the Neutral SPAFF Affect During Marital
Interaction and KAHEN Neutral During Parent–Child Interactions
With the Same Parent's Meta-Emotion Dimensions

	Father		Mother	
	Marital	*Parent–child*	*Marital*	*Parent–child*
Sadness				
Awareness own	−.14	−.22	.13	−.18
Awareness child	−.14	−.11	.20	−.30*
Coaching	.04	−.08	.15	−.19
Anger				
Awareness own	−.20	−.11	.08	−.17
Awareness child	−.12	−.22	.10	−.07
Coaching	−.04	−.05	.05	−.16

*$p < .05$.

17.2 shows, except for a negative correlation between neutral affect and the mother's neutral affect and the mother's awareness of the child's sadness, there was generally no relationship between the amount of emotionality, as measured by the SPAFF or the Kahen in the two contexts, and the meta-emotion codes. The only significant correlation was that mothers who were aware of their own sadness were less neutral (i.e., more affectively expressive) in the parent–child interaction.

META-EMOTION AND THE CHILD'S FACIAL EXPRESSIVENESS

Directed Facial Action Task

Table 17.3 is a summary of the number of facial expression children made during the Ekman and Friesen's (1978) Directed Facial Action Task (DFA) and their parents' meta-emotion variables. Not all the children could make all the expressions, particularly fear and sadness, so the N's are lower for those columns. In general, these results suggest that, except for fear, the parents' meta-emotion variables are related to less facial expressiveness of the children on the DFA task. We have no idea why there would be a positive correlation between fear facial expressions and the father's awareness of his own anger.

Spontaneous Facial Expression Elicited During the Films

Table 17.4 summarizes the correlations between the number of angry, contemptuous, disgusted, frightened, happy, and sad facial expressions displayed by the

TABLE 17.3
Correlations Between the Child's Facial Expressiveness During
the Directed Facial Action Task and the Parents'
Meta-Emotion Dimensions

	Happy $N = 45$	Angry $N = 40$	Disgust $N = 28$	Fear $N = 20$	Sadness $N = 20$
Father sadness					
Awareness own	−.11	−.03	−.07	.07	−.39*
Awareness child	−.07	.03	.01	−.04	−.07
Coaching	−.15	.18	−.11	.28	−.49*
Father anger					
Awareness own	−.05	.09	−.08	.35*	−.25
Awareness child	−.15	−.34**	−.22	.01	−.39**
Coaching	−.05	.21	.06	.07	−.32
Mother sadness					
Awareness own	−.25*	−.11	.07	−.08	−.13
Awareness child	−.22	−.14	−.20	−.18	−.35**
Coaching	−.22	−.16	−.02	.01	−.03
Mother anger					
Awareness own	−.22	−.17	.06	−.11	.11
Awareness child	−.12	−.10	−.15	−.05	−.30*
Coaching	−.39**	.11	−.11	.16	−.19

*$p < .05$. **$p < .01$.

TABLE 17.4
Correlations Between the Child's Facial Expressiveness During the
Emotion-Eliciting Films and the Parents' Meta-Emotion Dimensions

	Happy $N = 45$	Angry $N = 40$	Disgust $N = 28$	Fear $N = 20$	Sadness $N = 20$
Father sadness					
Awareness own	−.05	.02	−.03	.06	−.09
Awarenesss child	−.07	.03	.01	−.04	−.07
Coaching	−.10	.04	−.05	.05	−.02
Father Anger					
Awareness own	.01	−.17	−.04	−.08	−.28*
Awareness child	−.15	−.34**	−.22	.01	−.39**
Coaching	−.08	−.05	−.06	.14	−.18
Mother sadness					
Awareness own	−.11	−.12	−.18	.01	−.23
Awareness child	−.22	−.14	−.20	−.18	−.35**
Coaching	−.42***	−.07	−.22	−.13	−.30*
Mother anger					
Awareness own	−.10	.02	−.19	−.12	−.09
Awareness child	−.12	−.10	−.15	−.05	−.30*
Coaching	−.27*	−.09	−.17	−.20	−.15

*$p < .05$. **$p < .01$. ***$p < .001$.

children as they watched the emotion-eliciting film clips. We summarized the number of expressions a child displayed across all films because some children found the disgust film or the fear film amusing whereas others were scared by the anger film, and so on. The table suggests that if anything, the meta-emotion variables are related to less spontaneous facial expressiveness in the children.

META-EMOTION AND THE GOTTMAN (1994) TYPOLOGY OF STABLE MARRIAGE

We have already found that an emotion coaching meta-emotion structure is related to higher marital satisfaction and greater marital stability. However, Gottman (1994) found that there were three types of stable marriages, Volatile, Validating, and Conflict Avoiding. The three types of stable marriage differed in how emotionally expressive they were during a conflict discussion, with Volatile being the most expressive, Validating the next most expressive, and Conflict Avoiding the least expressive. However, all three types of couples were somewhat emotionally expressive. All three types of marriages had a 5.0 positive-to-negative ratio of an observational coding system (the RCISS behaviors), whereas unstable marriages had a ratio of 0.8. The three types of stable marriages differed most dramatically from one another in the amount and timing of persuasion attempts during the conflict discussion. Volatile couples began attempts at persuasion immediately in the first 5 minutes of the conversation, Validating couples were lowest in persuasion attempts in the first and last five minutes and highest in the middle five minutes; they listened during the first five minutes. Conflict Avoiding couples were very low in persuasion attempts throughout the 15-minute conversation.

All the couples were classified using the criteria of Gottman (1994), which involves computing the slopes of the cumulated speaker and listener point graphs (the number of positive minus negative RCISS codes for a turn at speech is cumulated over turns at speech), and the total emotionality (i.e., non-neutral codes) on the SPAFF coding system. In our typology, Volatile and Validating couples had positive husband and wife speaker slopes, and listener slopes greater than 0.30. Conflict Avoiding couples had positive husband and wife speaker slopes, and listener slopes less than 0.30. Volatile and Validating couples differed from one another in that Volatile couples were above the median of total husband plus wife non-neutral episodes on the SPAFF (median = 393.0), with Volatile above the median and Validating below the median. There were 4 Conflict Avoiding couples, 26 Validator couples, and 12 Volatile couples in the sample.

Analyses of variance resulted in no significant differences between these groups on any meta-emotion variable. We expected that Conflict Avoiding couples might do less emotion coaching, but that was not the case. For the coaching of anger, for example, the F-ratio for the father was $F(2, 37) = 0.78$, ns

(Avoiders mean 22.00, Validators mean 21.40, Volatile mean 20.33), and the F-ratio for the mother was $F(2, 37) = 0.12$, *ns* (Avoiders mean 22.33, Validators mean 22.04, Volatile mean 21.73). For sadness coaching, the F-ratio for the father was $F(2, 37) = 1.13$, *ns* (Avoiders mean 22.67, Validators mean 22.28, Volatile mean 21.33), and the F-ratio for the mother was $F(2, 37) = 1.23$, *ns* (Avoiders mean 24.33, Validators mean 22.58, Volatile mean 22.45). We should mention that we had very little power to detect differences between Avoiders and other types of marriage in this study. However, the means do not suggest even a trend that Conflict Avoiders are less likely to be their children's emotion coaches, for either sadness or anger.

In hindsight, it is important to note that Conflict Avoiding couples differ from the other types of couples primarily on the amount and timing of persuasion attempts. Contrary to Raush et al.'s (1974) speculations about Conflict Avoiders, they are somewhat emotionally expressive. These results suggest that they are as likely as the other types of stable marriage to coach their children.

SUMMARY

One would have to conclude from these data that meta-emotion structure and emotional expressiveness are unrelated or negatively related, except for the possibility that people who have a coaching meta-emotion structure are less likely to be controlling their faces during marital interaction. However, they are not more facially expressive, nor are they more emotionally expressive when other channels of emotional communication are considered using the SPAFF during both marital and parent–child interaction.

We are pleased with these results because we hope that a family can be oriented toward coaching a child's emotions regardless of their own cultural group membership, and regardless of the type of marriage they choose to have. People in less expressive cultures may have a different style of talking to children about their feelings, but these styles might be equal in the amount of emotion coaching they do. Also, it is of interest that the direct consequences of being in a family that coaches a child's emotions is not a child or parents who are necessarily highly expressive emotionally. They *can be*, but that is not a corollary of a coaching meta-emotion structure.

PARENTAL INCOME, EDUCATION, AND OCCUPATIONAL STATUS AND PARENTAL META-EMOTION VARIABLES

Table 17.5 summarizes the relationships between a person's meta-emotion structure and the demographic variables that have been used to index social class. One

TABLE 17.5
Correlations Between the Parental Demographic Variables
Measuring Social Class and the Parents' Meta-Emotion Dimensions.

	Income	Occupational Status	Father's Education	Mother's Education
Father sadness				
Awareness own	.07	−.06	.07	.15
Awareness child	−.08	−.14	.05	.12
Coaching	−.20	.10	.09	.07
Father anger				
Awareness own	−.09	−.08	.13	.10
Awareness child	−.09	.12	.32**	.23*
Coaching	−.12	−.07	.24*	.23
Mother sadness				
Awareness own	.15	−.01	.17	.21
Awareness child	.05	.01	.07	.03
Coaching	−.04	.10	.06	.12
Mother anger				
Awareness own	.03	−.10	.03	.06
Awareness child	.11	.08	.16	.22
Coaching	−.16	−.20	.03	−.01

$^*p < .05.$ $^{**}p < .01.$

can conclude from this table that some key variables among the meta-emotion variables are related to social class. In particular, the father's coaching of the child's anger, and his awareness of the child's anger was positively related to his education, and his awareness of the child's anger was also related to his wife's educational level. No other social class variable was related to the meta-emotion variables. It is not surprising that parental education would be related to a coaching meta-emotion structure. We reviewed research earlier relating a stricter and more authoritarian parenting style with working class rather than middle class families. Also, these child-emotion ideas have been available primarily to a very specialized reading public, parents who read books about parenting are somewhat more likely to have been exposed to Ginott's ideas.

CONCLUSIONS

It is interesting to us that the meta-emotion variables are unrelated or negatively related to emotional expressiveness. If anything, they are related to the control of the expression of emotion in emotion-eliciting laboratory situations. This does not mean that these families would not score as expressive on a questionnaire designed to measure expressiveness, such as Halberstadt's FEQ. The oral history interview revealed that parents who have a coaching meta-emotion structure claim to be nonconflict-avoiding, which might be one dimension of emotional expressiveness.

An equally plausible interpretation of these data is that meta-emotion structure may be orthogonal to emotional expressiveness. Perhaps one can be aware of emotion, and positively responsive to it, and still be either personally fairly reserved or expressive. We would like to think that a coaching meta-emotion structure could be independent of individual personality characteristics or group cultural norms. This may suggest that the reserved Norwegian father is as likely to have a coaching meta-emotion structure as the more expressive Italian father.

The fact that education is important, particularly for fathers is encouraging, because it suggests to us that paternal meta-emotion structures may be influenced by education. Perhaps more specific parent training in a coaching meta-emotion structure may make a difference for fathers, as the work of Levant and Kelly (1991) suggests.

Appendix 17.1
Vagal Tone and the Inhibition of Expressiveness

We speculated in chapter 5 that, contrary to the case for infants, basal vagal tone for the preschool age range would be related to the *inhibition* of emotional expressiveness. This is probably the case because it is the inhibition of emotional expression and its control that is emphasized during the preschool years (Block, Block, & Keyes, 1988; Maccoby, 1980). We report these results here. The correlation between baseline vagal tone and the child's total expressiveness during the Directed Facial Action Task was -0.26, $p < .05$, and the correlation between the suppression of vagal tone and the child's total expressiveness during the Directed Facial Action Task was 0.11 (*ns*). We next correlated basal vagal tone and change in vagal tone with the child's SPAFF codes during the parent–child interaction. These correlations are summarized in Table 17.6. These correlations suggest that, at this age range, vagal tone is either unrelated to emotional expressiveness, or negatively related to it.

In the spontaneous expression of facial affect during the emotion-eliciting films, the only correlation that was significant was a correlation of $-.29$ ($p < .05$) between basal vagal tone and the number of happy facial expressions.

TABLE 17.6
Correlations Between Basal Vagal Tone and Suppression of Vagal
Tone and the Child's Emotional Expeessiveness During
the Parent–Child Interaction

Variable	Basal Vagal Tone	Delta Vagal Tone
Neutral	−.09	−.03
Humor	−.08	−.02
Affection	−.26*	.08
Interest	.09	.01
Excitement	−.13	−.07
Anger	−.09	.09
Disgust	−.06	.14
Whining	−.07	.07
Sadness	−.22	−.06
Anxiety	−.15	.13
Humor/excitement blend	−.26*	.08
Whining/anxiety blend	−.35**	.12

$*p < .05; **p < .01.$

Appendix 17.2
Child Temperament

When the child was 4–5 years old, both parents filled out a scale of child temperament. This scale was our own combination of the Buss-Plomin (Buss & Plomin, 1984) and Rothbart (see Rothbart & Derryberry, 1981) scales; we combined the father and mother ratings, and the temperament scale yielded five dimensions: Emotionality, Activity, Shyness, Calm, and Persistence.

Validity of the Child Temperament Scales. Table 17.7 is a summary of these scales with our Age-8 outcome variables. As this table shows, the child temperament scales were significant predictors of child outcome. Emotionality was significantly related to more observed negative affect with a best friend at age 8. Activity was significantly related to teacher ratings of more negative peer relationships at age 8. Shyness was significantly related to lower teacher ratings of negative peer relations, and to lower teacher ratings of negative affect at age 8. Calmness was related to teacher ratings of more negative peer relationships at age 8. Persistence was significantly related to more child illness at age 8, to higher academic achievement at age 8, to less need for parents to have to down regulate the child at age 8, and to lower teacher ratings of negative affect at age 8.

Interaction of Child Temperament With Emotion Coaching? Next, we conducted a series of regression analyses to assess whether there was any interaction of the child temperament with the model's emotion coaching variable. In these analyses, for each child outcome variable we asked the following question: If the child temperament variable was significantly related to a child outcome variable, did emotion coaching interact with the relationship between the child temperament variable and the child outcome variable?

TABLE 17.7
Child Temperament as a Predictor of Child Outcomes

Temperament Variable	Illness	Achievement	Child Outcome			
			Down Regulation	Neg Peer	Neg Affect Rating	Neg Affect Observed
Emotion	−.08	−.11	.11	.17	.19	.25*
Activity	.13	−.04	.14	.39**	.16	−.09
Shyness	−.05	.08	.00	−.36**	−.27*	−.20
Calm	.02	.13	.04	.27*	.10	.03
Persistence	.36**	.37**	−.32*	−.16	−.30*	−.17

Note. Neg Peer = Negative Peer; Neg Affect Rating = Negative Affect Rating; Neg Affect Observed = Negative Affect Observed.
*$p < .05$. **$p < .01$.

To answer this question, first the child temperament variable was stepped into the analysis and then the coaching variable was stepped into the analysis. Finally, the interaction was assessed by stepping into the regression the product of emotion coaching with the child temperament variable.

Only one such interaction was statistically significant, for the child physical illness outcome, and for the child temperament variable of persistence. For this analysis, the first result was that persistent children, although they have higher levels of academic achievement and fewer problems with negative affect, have higher levels of physical illness. However, when these children are emotion coached, this physical illness effect is significantly less likely to be the case, with partial correlation equal to −.31, $F(3, 39) = 4.25$, $p < .05$.

18

Discussion and a Research Agenda

This chapter is a discussion of our findings, their potential implications, the limitations of the findings, and an agenda for future research on meta-emotion in families.

Our species is only about 250,000 years old (Leakey, 1994). One of the great changes that occurred in the evolutionary history of our species was the change in our brain's size; the average brain size of *Homo Sapiens* is 1350 cubic centimeters (ccs). The brains of newborn apes are 200 ccs, about half of adult size. However, the brains of human newborns are one third of adult size and triple in size in early, rapid development. In evolution toward our species, the pelvic opening increased to accommodate the larger brain size of newborns. However, there were limits imposed by the need for bipedal locomotion, and this limit was reached when the newborn's brain size was 385 ccs.

The evolutionary invention that our hominid ancestors represented accommodated this larger brain size with a newly extended period in which our offspring were physically helpless while their already larger brain continued to grow. Thus, part of our evolutionary heritage was offspring who are helpless and need our care and nurturance for years longer than our nonhuman primate ancestors. This is followed later by a period of rapid adolescent growth. Growing children are significantly different in size from adults for a long time, which fosters what Leakey has called a student–teacher relationship (Leakey, 1994, p. 45).

For these reasons parenting became a central part of who we are as a species. We know little about parenting before the dawn of recorded history. Nonetheless we do know that since the beginning of recorded history, which is only a few thousand years old, childhood and parenting have undergone a slow set of changes. The early history of parenting was marked by infanticide, later by abandonment, then by discipline and cruelty, and, only in the 18th century by ideas of kindness and empathy toward children.

We have only to look back a short time to see how markedly different is our own approach to children. Susanna Wesley was only expressing a view common to her culture when, in 1732, she wrote her son, John Wesley, the founder of Methodism, a letter about how to raise children. She began her letter: "When turned a year old (and some before) they were taught to fear the rod and to cry softly, by which means they escaped abundance of correction which they might otherwise have had: and that most odious noise of the crying of children was rarely heard in the house, but the family usually lived in as much quietness as if there had not been a child among them" (Greven, Jr., 1973, pp. 46–47).

She wrote about the great discipline that was imposed at mealtime, so that the children at their table might not disturb the adults at their table, and then she proceeded to the more important issue of the education of the children, expressing a commonly held view that before children could be educated and civilized, *their will had to be broken*:

> In order to form the minds of children, the first thing to be done is to conquer their will and bring them to an obedient temper . . . by neglecting timely correction they will contract a stubbornness and obstinacy which are hardly ever after conquered . . . When a child is corrected it must be conquered, and this will be no hard matter to do, if it be not grown headstrong by too much indulgence. And when the will of a child is totally subdued, and it is brought to revere and stand in awe of the parents, then a great many childish follies and inadvertencies may be passed by. (Greven, Jr., 1973, pp. 47–48)

According to deMausse, our time will be characterized as one that attempts to help and assist the development of our offspring. But we lack a clear blueprint for accomplishing this objective. Perhaps scientific investigations can help develop this blueprint. The scientific study of human psychology and the development of children is relatively new. In the 19th century, Charles Darwin published a book on his son's daily development, which facilitated great interest in his contemporaries in knowing more about children. But it is only relatively recently that we have begun to learn about the amazing cognitive, perceptual, and social-emotional capabilities of infants. Also, in studying social behavior, after nearly 50 years of attempting to discover order in the individual human personality, we are just beginning to discover that there is great order and predictability in the development of children if we observe family interaction patterns. Most of this research on family interaction patterns has emerged only in the last 25 years, and most of these results demonstrate the power of studying emotional communication in families.

Our prospective longitudinal research has put the spotlight on meta-emotion structure as a set of dimensions that organize other processes such as negative and positive parenting in the family's emotional communication. Our findings were summarized in a parsimonious model that relates parenting to the child's regulatory physiology at age 5, to emotion regulation abilities at age 8, and to a set of child outcomes that are related to the child's social-emotional development. We found, as have many other researchers, that the quality and stability of the parents' marriage is very important to children's welfare. Our results were quite optimistic in suggesting some buffers from the harmful effects on the child of marital conflict and marital dissolution in our variables of meta-emotion, parenting, and the child's regulatory physiology. Our results also suggest that today, in the U.S., among two-person families, the father's role is central to the development of his children. The father can do great harm as well as great good.

Our findings are really quite simple. Emotion coaching is the centerpiece of our work. Families who coach are very different from families who dismiss or disapprove of the child's sadness or anger. They are more likely to view their child's sadness as an opportunity for intimacy and teaching. They are also more likely to view their child's anger as natural and as another opportunity for intimacy and teaching. They also problem solve with their children about the situations that engender these emotions. For these coaching families, the parent's feelings about their own feelings is also radically different. They are aware of emotions in themselves, and they value the world of emotional experience in their own lives.

This awareness of their own emotions has profound implications for the marriages of emotion-coaching parents. In their marriages, they express the view that conflict is a part of life and is worth exploring, and that constructive things emerge from facing emotional conflicts. When they attempt to resolve these conflicts in their marriages they do so in an entirely different way than parents who are dismissing or disapproving of emotion. Indeed, the marriages of emotion-coaching parents are both more satisfying and more stable over time. Thus, meta-emotion has implications for family relations in general, and not just for parent–child relationships.

We think that we have hit on a central aspect of the family's emotional life, an aspect that appears to have profound implications for the child's later development. How do we think this process works? The processes through which these effects between meta-emotion and child outcome are created do not seem to be very hard to understand. Many of these processes were proposed by Ginott 38 years ago. In short, we would propose the notion that the process of making an emotional connection is central to these families.

Haim Ginott would say that when it comes to emotion, process is everything. Ginott would say that children cannot be taught to have respect for the emotions of others simply with a family rule. He would say that children can not be taught empathy only by having their parents repeating the Golden Rule, nor only by referring to God's commandments. They do not learn to know and trust their own feelings by parental admonitions to do so. They learn these things by example, by witnessing a particular style of marital interaction and by participating in a particular style of parent–child interaction.

As we have discovered, it is a style that shuns intrusiveness, derogation, criticism, and mockery of the child. Instead it communicates respect for the child's emotions, a valuing of intimacy, and problem solving about emotion. It facilitates an authoritative and responsive form of parenting and uses scaffolding and praising in teachings.

We think we have presented some evidence that suggests the causal hypothesis that emotion coaching may directly affect a preschool child's regulatory physiology. Through emotion coaching, they may develop higher basal vagal tone and greater ability to suppress vagal tone. They are less stressed autonomically. They have lower resting heart rates, and their autonomic nervous systems respond less to negative parental acts in our laboratory. They secrete lower levels of stress-related hormones. They are physically healthier. Although there is some evidence to suggest that these physiological variables are, in part, temperamental, based on our path models we think that these aspects of a child's regulatory physiology may be, to a significant extent, controlled by the way the parents relate to the child's emotions.

These children are better able to regulate their own emotions, to self-soothe and to focus attention when they need to. The mechanism for this relationship between the child's regulatory physiology at age 5 and their ability to self regulate at age 8 was to be found by the relationship between regulatory physiology and the child's ability to maintain a lowered heart rate when their fathers were mocking them, being critical, or intrusive at age 5.

Children whose parents coach emotion do better in school. Their peer relationships are better. They are more socially skillful. They have fewer behavior problems. They have less negative and more positive affect. They are physically more healthy.

The story we have told is relatively simple, but quite limited. It represents only a beginning of research on meta-emotion. In this chapter we discuss our findings and explore the limitations of our study so that we can suggest a research agenda that will begin the next step in the process of exploring these findings. We now begin by exploring the implications of our results, assuming that they are completely true.

TOWARD A RESEARCH AGENDA ON META-EMOTION

Figure 18.1 is the familiar schematic diagram of our theoretical model. In it there are the usual 5 boxes, labeled Meta (previously broken down into Awareness and Coaching), Parenting, Child Regulatory Physiology (previously broken down

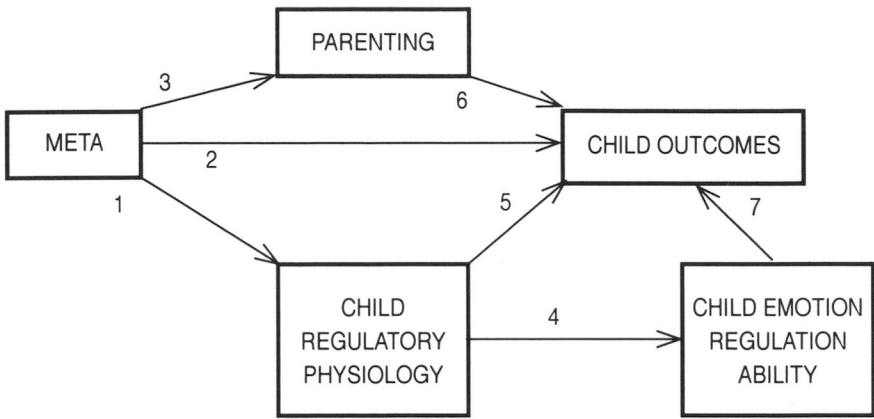

FIG. 18.1.   Schematic representation of our theoretical model, with indicated lines of research (the numbers) to further explore empirically obtained linkages.

into basal vagal tone and the suppression of vagal tone), Child Emotion Regulation Ability (previously labeled DOWN REGULATION), and, Child Outcomes. In Fig. 18.1, the seven lines going between boxes represent linkages we wish to discuss and explore. Later we show that each of these lines actually represents a line of research studies or part of a research study that can be proposed to further investigate the linkages in the theoretical model.

In the following sections of this chapter we discuss the seven linkages in the figure.

THE LINKAGE BETWEEN EMOTION COACHING AND CHILD REGULATORY PHYSIOLOGY (#1)

In this section we ask a fundamental question about why Emotion Coaching should affect the child's regulatory physiology, namely, Why should talking about feelings to a child while the child is having the feelings entail a different regulatory physiology?

In a programmatic series of studies with adults and children, both Davidson and his associates and Fox and his associates have developed a theory of frontal brain activation and emotion. We briefly review some of their findings here and refer the interested reader to primary sources for additional reading.

The methodology of much of the Davidson and Fox research is quite straightforward. Electronencephalograpic (EEG) recordings are made from a variety of scalp sites, usually including frontal, parietal, and temporal regions. In addition to these measures, ocular activity and heart rate data are usually collected to eliminate artifacts. The continuous EEG data is then subjected to spectral time-series analysis (see Gottman, 1981, for an introduction to these methods), using the fact that the amount of power in bands near the 8 to 13 Hz alpha frequency region of the EEG (a slightly different region is used for children) is *inversely* related to brain activation. Davidson (1994) recently summarized his major findings. The major findings were summarized as follows:

> On the basis of an extensive body of literature, we have proposed that the left frontal region subserves a major approach system in the brain, whereas the homologous right frontal region is implicated in a withdrawal system. Emotions that are predominantly associated with relative left-sided frontal action should therefore be associated with relative left-sided frontal activation, whereas those accompanied by withdrawal-related action should be associated with relative right-sided frontal activation (see Davidson, 1984; Davidson & Tomarken, 1989; and Davidson, 1992a, for reviews). (p.522)

The terms approach and withdrawal emotions are used in this summary of the research primarily because anger is lateralized on the left side rather than on the right side. Davidson considers anger as an affect unlike the other negative affects such as disgust, sadness and fear (lateralized on the right), arguing that it is "an approach affect," because it engages people with one another and the world whereas disgust, sadness, and fear disengage people with the world and one another, and are therefore are "withdrawal emotions."

In collaborative studies by N. Fox with infants, 10-month-old infants showed greater left-frontal activation in response to the positive part of a videotape showing an actress displaying laughter versus distress (Davidson & Fox, 1982). Using positive or negative taste stimuli with neonates, they found that greater right-frontal activation was present for tastes producing facial expressions of disgust than for tastes producing more positive facial expressions (Fox & Davidson, 1986).

In the Davidson (1994) review, he cited a recent study conducted in collaboration with P. Ekman, in which subjects were shown film clips designed to elicit either disgust or happiness/amusement. Their facial expressions were videotaped unobtrusively during the viewing. Subjects did indeed show relatively more left frontal activation during the periods they displayed happy facial expressions, and relatively more right frontal activation when they displayed disgust expressions. Also, during the film designed to elicit disgust compared to the film designed to elicit happiness, all subjects showed relatively more right than left frontal activation.

Davidson has made a distinction between baseline frontal EEG asymmetry, and reactivity. He has suggested that the baseline differences tap traits or temperamental differences, whereas the reactive effects are common to all subjects. In a recent study using the Kagan procedure for identifying inhibited and uninhibited children (e.g., Kagan, Reznick, & Snidman, 1988), in which Davidson added a middle group to the two extreme groups used in Kagan's studies, he found that inhibited children can be characterized as different from uninhibited children in a relatively unstressful baseline condition as having "underactivation in a frontal approach system, rather than hyperactivation in a frontal withdrawal system" (p. 532).

Talking about Emotion while Having the Emotion and Frontal EEG Reactivity

On the basis of this work, we propose the following hypothesis about frontal EEG asymmetry in reactivity and emotion: *Talking* about emotion *while also genuinely displaying the emotion* puts the left hemisphere in control of both hemispheres. This effect should be apparent when the data are compared to a control conditions in which the child is either encouraged to be dismissive of the emotion by the parent's trying to introduce a positive affect to replace the negative one, or a control condition in which the parent is dismissive by using distraction (e.g., refocusing the child's attention on a non-emotional aspect of an emotion-eliciting film). We propose that the use of emotion language as part of the experience of emotion does two things: (a) It controls the emotion, and (b) it blends positive affects with the negative. Thus, teaching children to be able to talk about feelings changes the brain pathways and changes the brain activation in response to emotion.

Talking about Emotion while Having the Emotion and Autonomic Reactivity

Another part of our hypothesis is that: *Talking* about emotion *while also genuinely displaying the emotion* changes the peripheral autonomic control of the cardiovascular response to emotional expressions from a relatively more sympathetic to a relatively more parasympathetic control. In particular, vagal tone should increase (over a baseline), and sympathetic drive to the heart should decrease.

In our research agenda we propose that sympathetic drive to the heart be measured, in part, by lower frequency spectral analysis of the heart period spectrum (Akselrod et al., 1982). Other measures are also possible (see Cacioppo & Tassinary, 1990).

As part of our research agenda we propose that these two hypotheses be tested. This test requires the construction of a laboratory that collects simultaneous electroencephalographic (EEG) data and autonomic data from children. The paradigm we suggest is to compare children's synchronized behavioral (primarily facial), autonomic, and EEG data under several conditions. These experiments involve a systematic dismantling of the parent–child coaching interaction in this new laboratory. Major problems have to be solved in designing this research to deal with the influence that the processing of language will have on the left hemisphere, but the underlying paradigm is straightforward. In all conditions a father or mother would watch a videotape with their child that is designed to elicit emotion. Under one condition the child would just experience the emotion in the presence of the parent. In the other set of conditions the parent will call either the child's attention to nonemotional events in the film, emulating a dismissing parent to greater and greater degrees across conditions, or directly attempt to induce a more positive different emotion in the child. In another set of conditions the parent will emulate the processing of emotion and emotion coaching. Sections of the EEG would have to be selected for analysis that are free of artifacts due only to the processing of language.

What do we expect would be learned from such experiments? We expect that, to the extent that parents succeed in getting children to talk about their feelings and do the components of emotion coaching, the child's frontal EEG will be left rather than right dominant, and that their autonomic variables (particularly heart rate and vagal tone) will show calming rather than arousal.

Why do we expect such results? There is evidence of direct connections between the frontal lobes and the limbic system. The limbic system is, to some extent, the gatekeeper of connections between emotional and autonomic events, in part through its interaction with the brain stem, and in part through its hormonal activity (hypothalamic-pituitary connections).

THE LINK BETWEEN EMOTION COACHING AND PARENTING (#3)

Talking About Emotions While Having Them

The events of talking about emotions while having them are common to many clinical interventions. For example, a good deal of psychotherapy includes the client learning how to talk about emotions, first making the emotions available to consciousness, understanding the origin of these emotions, and learning to talk about alternatives in a problem-solving mode. This is not a natural way of dealing with emotions in normal everyday interaction, but it does resemble, in part, what happens in Emotion Coaching.

Also, in the most commonly used exercise in marital therapy, often called the listener–speaker exercise, couples are taught to listen to one another in a nonjudgmental and nondefensive manner, to accept the emotions of the partner (even if it involves criticism), and then to reverse roles of listener and speaker. Another large part of marital therapy interventions involve teaching couples about problem solving, combining both the processing of emotions about an issue with deliberate attempts to change one another's actions. This talk about feelings modality has become more common in popular psychology, self-help books, and talk show media events with the increasing popularization of psychology. Although it is often criticized as psycho-babble, perhaps at its best it can be thought of as bringing into the vernacular these relatively technical terms about emotions and self-examination that previously only psychologists were trained to use. Perhaps we can look forward to the day when that specialization of knowledge about emotions will no longer exist.

We suspect that direct talk about emotions is not the only way that children can learn to regulate their own emotions, but rather that direct talk about emotions is very efficient compared to other ways of dealing with feelings that are more experiential and more purely right brained. In this section we explore possible connections between Emotion Coaching and Parenting, asking what are the basic principles of Emotion Coaching.

What Do We Think Are the Principles of Emotion Coaching? A New Form of Parent Training Called "Meta-Emotion Training"?

In chapter 4, we noted that emotion coaching parents are doing the following five things.

- The parent is aware of the child's emotion.
- The parent sees the child's emotion as an opportunity for intimacy or teaching.
- The parent helps the child to verbally label the emotions the child is having.
- The parent empathizes with or validates the child's emotion.
- The parent helps the child to problem solve.

In this section we speculate about the potential ingredients of an intervention program with parents that applies the findings of meta-emotion reported in this book.

Parent Training in Emotion Coaching.   Gottman and his wife Julie have been developing a group educational parent training program based only on these five steps of emotion coaching. The group runs for six sessions, each 1 ½ hours in length. The first session was devoted to exploring the parents' own childhood with respect to emotion, their emotional connections to their own parents, and their own meta-emotion structure with respect to anger, sadness, and fear. Thereafter, parents were given microcasette recorders and asked to record one conversation they had with their child that week in which their child was emotional. We began with sadness and then moved on to anger and fear. Each week index cards were handed out and each parent would write down the setting conditions for an incident that happened recently with their child. They would then exchange cards so that each parent had someone else's card. We would then go around the room role playing each incident twice, first as a dismissing parent might handle it, and then as an emotion coaching parent would handle it. These exercises were designed to teach the five components of emotion coaching. We also would note when it was inappropriate to attempt to emotion coach, for example, when setting limits following misbehavior, when there was no time to talk about feelings (e.g., when rushing to get a young child to school), and the expression of parental anger. The five components of emotion coaching were embedded within Ginott's principles.

The Parent's Own Emotions are Central to Meta-Emotion Training.   In chapter 7, we noted that there is a strong relationship between awareness of one's own emotions and awareness of the child's emotions. Assuming for the moment that this is true, and ignoring the problems of common method variance, we note that previous parent training programs have been based on shoulds. Parents are admonished to change the way they parent their children because it is the right thing to do. Of course, this is true. However, our results may suggest that we can think of intervening with parents by using more narcissistic motivations that people have, an interest in and concern with themselves. There is clearly a strong relationship between the parent being aware of emotion in his or her own life and the parent's awareness of emotion in the child. Similarly, all the dimensions of the meta-emotion interview we have coded suggest that the place to start is with the parent's own emotional world. Levant (1992) proposed using the clinical term of *alexythymia* in his Fatherhood Project. By this term he meant a restriction of feelings and feeling vocabulary he has observed among the fathers in his groups, in which feelings of stress and anger predominate before the groups. After the groups the fathers are discussing what Levant calls the more *vulnerable* emotions (e.g., sadness, empathy, and fear).

Making Emotional Connections at Low Levels of Emotional Intensity Is Central to Meta-Emotion Training.   If we could boil down the basic principle of a coaching meta-emotion approach, it would be that emotion-coaching families see the child's negative emotion as an opportunity for making an emotional connection in which the tasks are first intimacy and then teaching.

To some extent, we suspect that making emotional connections in families is critical to marriage as well as to parenting, although teaching is not a task in marital interaction. Let's begin by talking about marriage. For example, if one's partner comes into the bathroom in the morning and says "I just had a disturbing dream," the response that sets up an emotional connection is "what did you dream?" This emotional connection is in contrast to not responding at all or saying, "I really don't have time for this right now." This example is one from positive interaction, but more important are emotional connections that are made around negative affect, particularly in which you are the target of your partner's negativity. If your partner says, "One thing that's annoying me is that you don't help me fold the laundry when we sit at night and watch TV. You see me sitting with a huge laundry basket and doing it, and you just watch the TV program. Why don't you help?" Research with couples suggests that an appropriate and functional emotional connection here requires listening and a nondefensive response and also changing one's behavior, such as, "You're right, I have been avoiding it. I hate doing it as much as you do. OK, hand over a pile." The emotional connection is often brief, it happens often and at low levels of emotional intensity. It feels good. When these emotional connection do not happen, and this becomes a pattern, then people escalate the intensity of their negativity or adapt to a new norm of emotional distance, which is a kind of unnoticed active avoidance of one another we have called *Parallel Lives,* that starts a cascade of increasing distance and isolation (see Gottman, 1994).

With children the emotional connection also needs to happen often. Sometimes it is harder to make because young children do not always speak as clearly as adults. Preschool children often speak in the context of fantasy and pretend play, and their ideas are a nexus of thoughts, not very organized. For example, you may have noticed that your preschool child does not want you and your partner to leave these days, suddenly has a good deal of trouble separating at day care, and one day she might say, "This is the bridge of age. You are walking through it and you might die. Go under here. See, the dolly is getting gray hair too. Is the dolly's mommy going to die soon?" It isn't easy to hear this as her concern about the her parents' dying and her being left all alone. But this stream of play talk is her invitation to talk about her fear and her thoughts about it, just as if she had said, "Dad, I'm worried about what's going to happen to me when you and mom die. Can we talk about my fears about this vital subject?"

Ginott also pointed out that children are different in that they are likely to take your disapproval of them very seriously and to internalize it, eventually making it a self-fulfilling prophecy. When parental admonitions to the child to improve include negative trait labels for the child ("You are so lazy. can't you help your brother rake the yard?"), the child will accept your characterization and try to live up to it ("I'm lazy. What do lazy people do? I will do those things.").

We would suggest that when people fail to make an emotional connection at a lower level of negative emotional intensity, they will escalate their attempts to make an emotional connection, and the affect will become more negative. In the case of anger, this can lead to a cycle of increased demanding and to the subsequent withdrawal of the partner as the negative affect becomes more aversive. However, it can also happen if marital partners are consistently not making positive emotional connections. We have described the eventual effect of the lack of emotional connection and its subsequent escalation cycle as flooding followed by increased distance and isolation. Christensen and colleagues (Christensen, 1987, 1988, 1990; Christensen & Shenk, 1991; Heavey, Layne, & Christensen,

1993; Sullaway & Christensen, 1993) have described a similar pattern as the demand–withdraw cycle.

Developmental Considerations.   One guideline that can be suggested is that there are a set of fears that are very common among children at different ages. In preschool children these are: (a) fears of being abandoned by their parents, or their parents' dying; (b) fear of the dark; (c) fear of being excluded from the action (a part of not wanting to go to bed); (d) fear of growing up and having to take care of one's self and no longer get taken care of; (e) fear of not growing up, part of which is a fear of being powerless and staying little (hence there is an ambivalence about growing up); (f) fear of monsters. This latter type of fear represents a kind of love affair that young children have with fear itself. They are trying to master their fears, so they need to find things to be afraid of so they can deal with their fears. In middle childhood, children's fears involve primarily rejection, mockery, or lack of acceptance by the peer group. In adolescence, children's fears center around peers as well as family and involve a dialectic between two things a loss of self (not understanding or accepting one's self), and a loss of connection and community; the struggle often plays itself out with issues of autonomy and independence and issues of emotional closeness with others (see Gottman & Parker, 1986).

These issues play themselves out in different ways at different developmental periods. Because the issues have different "arenas," it is important for parents to learn that young children have different strengths and limitations that make it hard to listen to their feelings. These ideas stem from a theory advanced by Gottman (1986), which emerged from empirical studies of children's friendship in the book *Conversations of Friends* (Gottman & Parker, 1986). We have already discussed the fact that preschool children are likely to use more symbolic ways of expressing their emotions than older children. The most common form of this is projection, in which, for example, the child may say "This dolly is tired," or "This dolly is scared of her mommy," rather than saying "I am tired," or "I am scared of you mommy." In middle childhood, children are likely to talk a great deal in terms of rigid rules that are fair and logical (they are prone toward seeing things rigidly in blacks and whites), to talk about avoiding embarrassment, and use mockery as part of social rejection. They are working on being emotionally cool, partly as the best response to teasing by peers, and they tend to shun all emotional displays. They overemphasize logic. In adolescence we see a merging of emotion and logic, as adolescents deal with their own sexual attractions, often being attracted to aspects of a person and repulsed by other aspects of the same person (and this is true of themselves as well). The lens they see everything through is self-exploration and self-understanding, and this language of self-exploration and exploration through relationships is the one through which they express their emotions.

Parents Being Comfortable with Strong Emotions
Without Trying to Make Them Go Away Is Central
to Meta-Emotion Training

We have discovered that some parents hear their child's negative emotions such as sadness as a demand that they make it all better. They tend to see these emotional displays as manipulative and very aversive. They see in it an expectation that they play God and fix everything, know everything, be in complete control, and be perfect. A stressed parent who views a child's emotional displays this way will resent these displays and want to see less emotion, and maybe want to flee the scene entirely. A similar pattern exists in many marriages, and usually it is the husband who, on hearing a complaint of his wife, feels that the task is for him to fix everything. So husbands begin proposing solutions to their wives' complaints instead of listening empathetically. They cannot believe that if that "all" they do in this situation is listen, it will work, and they are often amazed at the power of listening empathetically. Just being able to be there when your partner or child is having a strong feeling, that is, to be really with the person emotionally is a very powerful thing. Instead of this view, many families take a dismissing view of negative emotion and try to make the emotion go away and to comfort and reassure the person that it will all work out, that it is not so bad, that a different attitude would be best, that the passage of time takes care of all things, not to worry, and so on. Strong emotions are disturbing because they seem to carry with them this demand that we do something, anything. But the task is just to listen, empathize, and understand. It is a task of intimacy, not of trying to change anything.

Parenting May Have to Be Considered As Well
as Emotion Coaching

We believe that our data suggest the hypothesis that any parenting intervention also has to teach parents to avoid Derogation, and to employ Scaffolding/Praising parenting as well as using emotion coaching. Although these parenting behaviors are strongly correlated with emotion coaching, it may not be the case that the relationship is necessarily causal. This suggests an experiment in which one group receives only training in emotion coaching and another group receives training in emotion coaching plus training in avoiding Derogating and employing Scaffolding/Praising parenting.

The Marriage May Have to Be Repaired.   Ginott's work did not consider the marriage and its impact on children. Our data suggest that there is a relationship between an emotion coaching meta-emotion structure and the quality and stability of the parents' marriage. However, we cannot determine the direction of causation. We suggest that a study be conducted in which there are four groups, two that vary the order of marital intervention and training in emotion coaching, and two that use each alone. M. Forgatch (personal communication, 1995) designed a study similar to this one in a recent grant application, which has now been funded.

The Child's Peer Relationships May Have to Be Directly Worked On.   Although we would expect that parental emotion coaching would eventually have an impact on the child's relationships with other children, in an actual intervention program, we may have to target this area of the child's life directly.

Five-Stage Parent Training Program.   On the basis of our speculations, we further propose that parents who come from a background that is not very oriented toward using emotion language are at a distinct disadvantage. Thus, we suggest that parent training should be oriented toward greater emotion coaching. Thus, we would recommend that parent training consist of the following five components: (a) increasing the parent's awareness of his and her own emotions and the labeling of these emotions with appropriate words, (b) increasing the parents' awareness of the child's emotions and of what we might call the child's developmental "emotion vocabulary" [for example, in preschool this involves projection and pretend play; in infancy it might involve Stern's notions of affective attunement (intersubjectivity across modalities), or Tronick's notions of communicative repair], (c) using empathy rather than dismissing, punishing or Derogating the child's negative emotions (and attributions of negative traits to the child), (d) helping the child to label his or her feelings, and (e) problem solving about emotions and appropriate actions (this includes communicating the parents' values, discussing limit setting, and discussing the child's goals and strategies—Asher, 1983; Renshaw & Asher, 1985).

There may be initial resistance to parents acquiring the strategies associated with these five stages, particularly by fathers, and particularly when the marriage is ailing. This resistance should be measured and its prediction should be one of the goals of intervention research. We have designed this intervention program and it is available as a book (Gottman & deClaire, 1997) and a training videotape (Gottman & Schulman, 1997).

THE LINK BETWEEN EMOTION COACHING, PARENTING AND THE CHILD OUTCOME OF AGGRESSION (#2, #6)

Violence By Children

Probably the biggest problem we have in the U.S. today is the escalating violence perpetrated by children. On December 3rd, 1994, *The New York Times* reported an incident of Thomas Reilly, a truck driver who was robbed by some children at gunpoint. He had just delivered some meats and $175 had been torn out of his pocket. The *Times* wrote:

> As the three teen-age bandits prepared to bolt from the truck's side door, the 41-year-old Mr. Reilly found himself staring into the stony face of a 15-year-old pointing an automatic weapon at him. He saw no panic in the boy's eyes, no fear, and neither he nor the teenager spoke. Then came the gunshot. It hit Mr. Reilly above the heart, penetrated his spinal column and left the lower half of his body paralyzed. (p. 1)

The frightening thing about this story is that the shooting was not done out of any emotion that was out of control in the child, that it was completely unnecessary for the robbery, and that Mr. Reilly was looking into the eyes of a cold and hardened killer who was only 15 years old. What makes children this way? Why would a child have such total disregard for the life of another person and such disregard for the pain and suffering he was to create in a complete stranger who had never hurt him?

We now know that the major result of the epidemic of ailing and dissolving marriages on children is the increase of aggression and violence in the children. This effect is mediated but not entirely mediated by less effective parenting that results from an ailing marriage. It is also mediated by the father's emotional withdrawal from his children when a marriage is ailing or ends in dissolution.

We now are also beginning to know a fair amount about these kinds of children, as well as other aggressive and antisocial, violent children. We suspect that it is the case that a small percentage of these violent children are not shaped by their families or society to be violent, but rather appear to be born with a set of predispositions or are shaped very early in their (perhaps fetal[1]) development toward violence with the right environmental conditions (e.g., see Raine, Venables, & Williams, 1990). A wide variety of such conditions have already been identified, such as marital conflict and dissolution violence, neglect, and psychological or physical abuse (see Cummings & Davies, 1994).

We read the evidence to suggest that the majority of violent children and their subsequent graduation to the status of adjudicated criminals appears to be associated with the family stresses associated with poverty, ineffective parenting, where relevant, an ailing or dissolving marital system, and possibly by an emo-

---

[1]The reason we mentioned fetal development is as follows. Large scale adoption research studies on criminality conducted in the Scandanavian countries suggest that the probability of becoming a criminal is partly a function of who adopts an infant and who the infant's biological parents are (father criminal or not). These biological parent effects are usually attributed to genetics in these studies. However, this may not be the case. If part of the biological father's criminality (or some of the subjects) involves spouse abuse, this violence is enhanced during the female's pregnancy (Dutton, 1988). Often these females live in a climate of fear during their pregnancy. Denneneberg & Rosenberg (1967) have shown that there are cross-generational effects of greater excitability, fear, and poorer emotion-regulation ability on rat offspring of inducing fear in a pregnant rat. In fact, these effects are transmitted to the next generation of offspring without any intervention. These cross-generational effects exist without any genetic changes.

tionally or physically absent father. Systematic research has discovered that the family dynamics of creating a violent child are actually quite mundane. The patterns of parental rejection, inept parenting and the lack of parental monitoring of the child's whereabouts, a coercive family interaction pattern, and contemptuous marital conflict have been identified and replicated by several research groups (for example, the Patterson and associates OSLC group; the Forehand and associates group; the Conger-Simons and associates group; the Olweus-Roland and associates group). Both correlational studies and intervention studies have been conducted that suggest that the pattern of variables active in longitudinal prediction may be causal. A similar pattern of results has been reported in the creation of both male and female bullies at school, and to some extent in the victims of bullies (for a review see Besag, 1993). These associations have been generally replicated across studies and sites, and these relationships are not weak. A large proportion of the variance in child aggression and subsequent criminality can be accounted for by these factors.

Our own data suggest that the most powerful linkages in the theoretical model are for child outcomes most closely related to child negative affectivity, including antisocial behavior and negative child–peer relationships. These child outcomes form a familiar cluster of child aggression and child failure in school. Katz and Gottman (1993) reported that the child outcome predicted by marital interaction patterns that are in turn predictive of marital dissolution is the child's antisocial behavior as rated by the teacher on the Cowans' CABI.

THE LINKS BETWEEN THE CHILD'S REGULATORY PHYSIOLOGY, EMOTION REGULATION ABILITY, AND CHILD OUTCOMES (#4, #5, #7)

These three linkages are central to the theory we proposed in chapter 5. The child's inability to down regulate negative affect, Child Emotion Regulation Ability, was central to our theorizing, as well as the theorizing of other developmental psychologists (e.g., see Fox, 1994; Garber & Dodge, 1991). We expect it to be related to child outcomes through a constellation of variables that involve the child's inability to focus attention (a central skill needed for success at school as well as in peer relations), and the increased likelihood that a child who cannot down regulate negative affect will encounter many daily situations that require external intervention by adults, including disruption of school activities, increased aggression with peers, and a drift toward a deviant peer group.

We discussed one possible linkage between the child's regulatory physiology and the child's ability to down regulate negative affect in chapter 12, when we showed that one mediator of this linkage was the child's with higher vagal tone's ability to keep a lowered heart rate in the face of parental Derogation, and this child's ability to recover more quickly from physiological arousal.

In this section we also explore possible physiological pathways that may mediate this linkage.

Review of Frontal-Limbic and Limbic-Brainstem-Autonomic Connections

Frontal-Limbic-Brainstem Linkages and the Vagus Nerves.   In general, the connections between the frontal lobes and the limbic system are involved with the processing of emotional experience and the coordination of emotion with the brainstem and the autonomic nervous system. Benes (1994) reviewed the phylogenesis, ontogenesis, and development of the corticolimbic system, outlining the connections and physiology between the prefrontal cortex (motivation), frontal eyefield 8, and the inferior parietal area (logical reasoning) with the cingulate cortex and the entorhinal cortex, the hippocampus, and limbic and other structures (amygdala, septal nuclei, lateral hypothalamus, habenula, interpeduncular nucleus, and reticular formation). He noted that the phylogenetic evolution of these connections were probably involved with the greater mammalian emphasis on nurturing the young:

> Accordingly, the evolutionary trend toward developing more elaborate behaviors to nuture the young and presumably to perpetuate the species probably involved a corresponding increase in both the amount and complexity of cortical ties with limbic structures. With the spectrum of mammalian forms, there has been a striking increase in the relative proportion of neocortex. (p. 180)

Porges, Doussard-Roosevelt, and Maita (1994) recently proposed a theory that suggests that there are two brain-stem nuclei of the X-th cranial nerve, which is commonly known as the vagus, and that these two nuclei have different functions. The two nuclei are the Dorsal Motor Nucleus (DMN) and the Nucleus Ambiguus (NA). Porges (1994) suggested that the DMN is the older (reptilian) system, and that the newer NA is the more flexible, mammalian adaptive vagal system that makes adaptive interaction with the environment possible.

Porges, Doussard-Roosevelt, and Maita start by noting that the peripheral organs innervated by the vagus are asymmetrical: The heart is on the left side of the body, the stomach is tilted, one lung is larger than the other, and one kidney is higher than the other. They suggest that the central wiring of the vagus is lateralized. The vagus is bilateral, with a left and a right branch. Fibers originate from either the DMN or the NA. They wrote:

> Pathways from the left and right DMN have different functions of regulation: The left dorsal motor nucleus innervates the cardiac and body portions of the stomach that promote primarily secretion of gastric fluids . . . The right dorsal

motor nucleus innervates the lower portion of the stomach that controls pyloric sphincter regulation and the emptying of the duodenum . . . The right nucleus ambiguus provides the primary vagal input to the sino-atrial node to regulate atrial rate and determine heart rate, the left nucleus ambiguus provides the primary vagal input to the atrio-ventricular (AV) node to regulate ventricular rate. (p. 170)

They suggest that the DMN is involved with the more vegetative aspects of regulation, whereas the NA is involved more with the processes associated with motion, emotion, and communication.

They also suggested that the right hemisphere of the brain plays a regulatory role in peripheral autonomic activity. They wrote:

> Because the neural control of the vagus is ipsilateral (e.g., the left vagus originates in the left side of the brain stem), the right hemisphere—including the right cortical and subcortical structures—would promote the efficient regulation of autonomic function via the source nuclei in the brain stem. For example, neuroanatomical and electro-physiological studies demonstrate the important regulatory function of the right central nucleus of the amygdala in regulating the right nucleus ambiguus. (p. 175)

Limbic-Autonomic Connections

The direct linkages between the child's regulatory physiology and child outcomes are probably mediated through psychological processes that are disrupted by decreased vagal tone, decreased ability to suppress vagal tone, and increased diffuse physiological arousal. These process were reviewed in chapter 5, and they include attentional processes. Furthermore, Gottman (1990) reviewed evidence that suggests that diffuse physiological arousal is likely to have the effect that people do not process new information very well, do not have as much access to recently acquired behaviors and thoughts, and rely instead on reflexive (e.g., fight or flight) or on overlearned behavior and thought patterns. Thus, diffuse physiological arousal is likely to lead to decreased flexibility in solving everyday problems and in coping with everyday stresses.

The linkage between emotion and autonomic physiology is central to this linkage (#5 in Fig 18.1). The limbic system has been called the Reptilian brain by MacLean (1949, 1970). Through the amygdala and the hypothalamus, the limbic system regulates the autonomic nervous system in response to various efferents. These include efferents from stretch receptors in arteries such as the carotid artery that give information about blood pressure and form part of the baroreceptor mechanism, information about blood volume (e.g., in response to hemorrhage) that regulates the vasopressin system, information about body temperature, information apparently related to a sadness/distress dimension involving the pituitary-adrenocortical axis, and information related to fight or flight responses. The limbic system serves as the gatekeeper between these many efferents and specific autonomic responses.

The work of Field and her associates demonstrates the general power of parental depression on the developing infant. Field, Healy, and LeBlanc (1989) studied the behavior and heart rate spectra of mothers and infants of depressed and nondepressed infants and reported that depressed mothers and babies were more likely to be in the same negative affective states. However, the heart rates of the mothers and babies were more likely to be coherent for nondepressed mothers and babies. Field, Fox, Pickens, and Nawrocki (1995) studied the vagal tone of 3 and 6-month old infants and found that the vagal tone of 6-month-old babies of depressed mothers was significantly lower than those of nondepressed mothers. Three month olds did not differ in vagal tone. This led the authors to conclude that the developmental increase in vagal tone that occurred from 3 to 6 month for infants of nondepressed mothers did not occur for infants of depressed mothers. The higher vagal tone for the 6-month-old babies was related both to their increased expressiveness (vocalizations) and to their higher neurological scores. This result is consistent with an earlier finding reported by Pickens and Field (1993) that the babies of depressed mothers differed markedly in facial expressiveness from the babies of nondepressed mothers. Babies of depressed mothers displayed significantly more facial sadness and anger and less interest expressions than babies of nondepressed mothers. Field et al. (1995) concluded that this pattern of results suggest greater overall neurological development for the babies of nondepressed mothers than for the babies of depressed mothers. Field (1995) also reported that the infants of depressed mothers eventually can develop a mood style that generalizes to other nondepressed adults. She also suggested that if the mother's depression continues for 1 year, her infant will begin to show growth and developmental delays. She wrote: "If the mother remains chronically depressed over the first few years, the children show behavior problems at preschool age." Field et al. (1995) also reported a pattern of greater right frontal EEG asymmetry in both mothers and infants. However, there may be hope for a reversal of these patterns in infants. Pelaez et al. (1994) reported that the interaction patterns of infants of depressed mothers showed considerable improvement when they interacted with familiar nursery school teachers. They wrote that the "Infants' low activity levels and negative affect were specific to their interactions with their depressed mothers." In fact, Hossain et al. (1994) reported that nondepressed husbands of depressed mothers can act as a buffer to protect the infants. Pickens and Field (1993) go even further. They suggested a game involving attention getting and imitating the baby that appear to have beneficial effects. They wrote, "Data suggest that the attention-getting condition was the most effective "intervention" for eliciting positive behavior in the depressed mother–infant dyads."

Summary of Right-Left-frontal to Limbic to Autonomic Connections

Fig. 18.2 is a crude summary of some of the connections we have been discussing. They suggest that the left-frontal lobe is capable of modulating right frontal

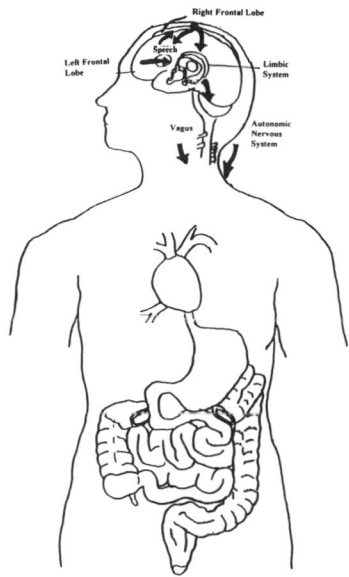

FIG. 18.2.   Schematic diagram of Frontal-Limbic-Brainstem-Autonomic connections with respect to emotion (within the central nervous system and between the central nervous system and the autonomic nervous system).

activity (the reverse is also true), that the right frontal lobe then has the primary connections to limbic and brain stem nuclei that affect the autonomic nervous system. From this hypothetical functional map, we propose another hypothesis, namely, that: when emotion coaching parents talk to children about negative withdrawal emotions while the children are having these emotions, the increased left-frontal brain activation will lead to the children's increased ability to regulate autonomic activity, assessed by faster recovery from autonomic arousal.

WHY WOULD THE FATHER'S VARIABLES
BE SO IMPORTANT IN OUR DATA?

The Changing Family in the U.S.

The structure of the family in the U.S. has changed dramatically over the last 30 years. The Census Bureau noted that the traditional nuclear family defines only about half of families today (56% of Caucasian children live in a nuclear family, 26% of African-American children, and 38% of Hispanic children). However, when the definition of nuclear family is expanded to include two-parent families (blended and adoptive families), 71% of children live in two-parent families

(Center for the Study of Social Policy, 1992). In 1960, the figure was 88% of children living in two-parent families. Among African Americans, 42% of children live in two-parent families today.

Part of these changes is due to the rising incidence of pregnancies outside of marriage. In 1950, only 4% of all births was to unmarried women. In 1980 the figure was 18.4%, in 1986 the figure was 23%, and in 1991 the figure was 29.5% (National Center for Health Statistics, 1993). The statistics for Anglo mothers were 11% in 1980 and 21.8% in 1991. In comparison, African-American mothers had 55.2% of their babies out of marriage in 1980, and 67.9% in 1991. In 1991, Hispanic mothers had 39% of their babies outside of marriage.

Although most of these women eventually marry, in 1989, 28% of all households were headed by women, up from 21% in 1970. Among African Americans the figure today is 40%, and for Hispanic families the figure today is 23% (Chadwick & Heston, 1992). About 50% of children who live in mother-only households are poor whereas about 24% of children who live in father-only households are poor (Census of Population and Housing, 1990). This is true despite the fact that 70% of these single-parent households have the parent working.

These demographic changes are a combination of rising divorce rates (two-thirds of recent marriages are likely to experience a disruption according to Castro, Martin, and Bumpass, 1989), and the rising incidence of teenage pregnancy and an increase of births by unmarried women at every socioeconomic level.

The family has also changed dramatically as a function of the increasing proportion of women who work. In 1960, 36% of women worked, whereas the comparable figure in 1988 was 56%. If we consider women with young children. in 1950 12% of mothers worked, whereas today the figure is 57% (Chadwick & Heston, 1992). Many writers have commented on the fact that despite the high increase of two-earner households, the average family income has not increased very much since 1975 (IPA, 1992, p. 44).

The world today is a more dangerous place to raise children than it was 30 years ago. Today every 21 minutes there is a murder in the U.S., one violent crime every 17 seconds. Today one of every five high school children carries a gun (*The New York Times,* January 9th, 1995). The number of arrests of males under 18 for all reasons increased from 1,260,123 in 1989 to 1,355,638 in 1990; the equivalent figures for females under age 18 were 351,541 in 1989 and 398,904 in 1990. There is a high incidence of violent crimes against teenagers, and this figure has been increasing over time (Information Please Almanac, IPA, p. 824). Gang violence has become a national problem, with gang members armed with automatic assault weapons (IPA, p. 830), with its concomitant urban gang warfare, drive-by shootings, turf bullets, and killing of informers. In 1989, it was estimated that there were 1,500 youth gangs nationwide, with more than 120,500 members. The drug problem has become quite serious. The proportion of newborns exposed to drugs is between 11% and 18% in several surveys of hospitals conducted in 1988, and the proportion is increasing; the incidence and prevalence of drug abuse is also increasing (IPA, 1992, p. 444). Children are under increased risk from drugs; in 1990, high school students spent $651 million on all drugs. In 1990, students in grades 6 through 12 consumed an estimated 6,173 pounds of cocaine and 74,956 pounds of marijuana.

The Changing Father in the U.S.

There is converging evidence that the workplace does not support fathers in dual career marriages spending time after work hours with the family. A recent *New York Times* (1994, October 12) article summarized a number of these studies. Men in families whose wives stay home to take care of children earn 25% more than men whose wives work, and they are likely to get more promotions as well. One study, conducted by L. Stroh on 348 male managers at 20 Fortune 500 companies found that traditional fathers had 20% higher raises than the men with working wives. F. Reitman's study of 231 men who received MBA degrees in the late 1970s, found that men whose wives were at home with the children earned 25% more than men whose wives held jobs. Reitman's study found that men in more traditional marriages earned $24,140 more per year than men whose wives worked; salaries were 1993 salaries, adjusted for number of hours worked, number of years experience, field of employment, and career interruptions. The adjusted salary increases of traditional men from 1987 to 1993 was 64%, compared to 45% for men whose wives worked. Traditional men worked an average of 53.7 hours per week, compared to 51.9 for men whose wives worked (difference was not significant). One suggestion made in the article by Reitman was that bosses, who tend to be older and are more likely to be in more traditional marriages, and are more likely to give raises and promotions to men who are more similar to themselves. It is also possible that men whose wives work are less aggressive in their motivation because they know they have another income coming in; however, there was no evidence to support this hypothesis in any study. Rather, it is more likely that men who do things like playing golf on Sundays with the boss or with clients, or who go out for a drink with the boss after work instead of going home are rewarded with promotions and higher raises (Brett, Stroh, & Reilly, 1993; Schneer & Reitman, 1994). These differences in salary are quite striking, particularly if one thinks of them in the context of the fact that in the U.S. college graduates earn an average of only $12,000 more per year than high school graduates.

Where Have All the Fathers Gone?   It is a startling fact that after divorce only 17% of fathers see their children more than once a year (Doherty, 1995). A number of studies suggest that the quantity and quality of fathering (but not mothering) is mediated through the quality of the marriage. This means that when the marriage is ailing, fathers tend to withdraw from their children as well as their wives, whereas this is not true for women. Many writers and legislators (including the President of the U.S.) have suggested that there is a national crisis in child support payments after divorce.

It was not always considered tolerable that fathers would vanish after divorce. In fact, until the evolution of the tender years doctrine, the father traditionally got custody of the children after a divorce, and were considered morally responsible for their upbringing and education. Tibbits-Kleber, Howell, and Kleber (1987) wrote:

> In Roman society continuing through the Middle Ages, children were regarded as the father's property . . . However, as a result of the influences of the Industrial Revolution, in addition to the importance and emphasis placed upon childhood, awards began to favor the mother. . . . The 1889 court opinion . . . [led to the] "tender years doctrine," which was a presumption, not a law, [that] basically stated that "nature had given women a unique attachment to children and that the baby would thus receive better care from its mother." (p. 28)

The tender years were considered birth to age 7. The tender years doctrine was gradually replaced by the guiding principle that custody awards are to be made with the "best interests of the child" in mind.

Iron John and the Fathers of the Past.   The Hite report (Hite, 1987) asked men whether they had a close relationship with their fathers. The study, although not a representative sample, startlingly revealed that over 90% of men claimed that their relationships with their fathers were not close. This kind of result has been echoed in the cry of anguish in what Levant has called the *Mythopoetic Men's Movement,* represented, in part, by the writings of the poet Robert Bly. The phrase *father hunger,* initially introduced by James Herzog and used by many of the writers of this movement, undeniably represents an echo of the great pain caused by the emotional absence of fathers in the United States of the past. Levant (1992) wrote:

> It is important to acknowledge Bly's and his associates' contributions, in tilling the barren soil of men's groups for many years, in successfully engaging large numbers of men in a process of reexamining masculinity, and in Bly's modeling (through openness about his own work on his relationship with his alcoholic father) the grieving process that many men need to go through in order to come to terms with their relationships with their own fathers. (p. 382)

Later in his research, Levant described typical processes he has observed in his groups with fathers in his Fatherhood Project. He wrote:

> One man would start to speak, bottom lip quivering, struggling to maintain control: "You know, the reason why I am here is so that my little son Jimmy will not grow up to feel as bad about me as I feel about my own dad." This would open the flood

gates, and the men would pour out their stories and their grief about their own fathers: Never knowing their fathers; nor how their fathers felt as men; nor if their fathers ever really approved of them. This acutely painful feeling of father loss is very widespread and requires grief work to resolve. Bly's most significant accomplishment may have been to facilitate this process of grieving on a large scale. (p. 39)

However, Levant critiqued the mythopoetic men's movement. He described a weekend retreat he attended in 1991 led by Robert Bly. In this weekend Bly urged men to "reject the path of the 'soft male,' which he views as feminist-inspired" (p.383). Indeed, Bly (1992) wrote about marriage as follows:

A contemporary man often assumes that a woman knows more about a relationship than he does, allows a woman's moods to run the house, assumes that when she attacks him, she is doing it "for his own good." Many marriages are lost that way. (p. 64)

Bly thus confounds emotional communication with dominance or power struggles, suggesting that confrontations in marriage be viewed as attacks and that men guard against letting a woman's moods run the house. Levant has suggested that this movement is "not helpful, and potentially destructive" (p.383). One reason Levant offers this appraisal is that, "the essentialist thrust, which requires separation from women, is exactly the opposite of what is required. Men today . . . need a closer connection with women, not a more attenuated one" (p. 384).

The Issue Is Not Just Whether Fathers Are There but How They Are There. In one study we are conducting with N. Jacobson on marital violence, a mother reported a story to us about her husband. One evening the father and his 5-year-old son were rough-housing in the living room when the boy accidentally got his lip hurt and began to cry. The father took the crying child into the kitchen and took out a meat cleaver and said to the boy, "If you don't stop crying, I'm going to cut your lips off!" The child stopped crying. This child was so terrified of his father that whenever the father asked the boy to do anything the boy did it immediately. Such behavior is, of course, quite unusual in 5-year-olds, and it speaks to the great fear that this child had of his father.

As we have noted in this book, fathers, even when they are present can either do a great deal of harm to their children or a great deal of good. Even fathers who are not as abusive to their children as the father we just described can hurt their children's development with Derogatory parenting. They can also do a great deal of good. Our point is simple: It is not enough for fathers to be in their children's lives. They need to be there as emotionally engaged and sensitive fathers.

Sons Writing About Their Fathers. Keyes (1992) edited book on sons writing about their fathers provides many poignant examples of father hunger. Most of the contributors did not feel they knew their fathers very well, rarely expressed love toward them, and rarely received affection or understanding from them. For example, Cristopher Hallowell wrote that when he was 6 or 7 years old his father tried to teach him to build a wooden box, saying "If you can't build a box square, you can't build anything." When he built his first box it was far from perfect. It wobbled and rolled, but nonetheless he was proud of his work. But his father, on examining his work, scowled and told him he didn't get it square and that he would never be a good builder. He wrote: "each time I lifted the top . . . never far away was a picture of my father's disapproving look" (p. 17). Son after son in this collection of essays said they never really felt close to their father, that they felt uncomfortable with their fathers, that they hated their fathers, that there was a strong sense of competition between them, and that they saw their fathers as terrifying, angry, authoritarian people. Moments of closeness were often mysterious and mixed, often obtained during a hunting expedition, or a sporting event. Sons seemed to yearn for their fathers to express pride and respect toward them as well as love and acceptance.

The so-called emotionally absent father has apparently been absent for his daughters as well as his sons (see the edited book by Scull, 1992). The evidence seems fairly clear that for a large proportion of children today, their fathers have been distant emotionally, disrespectful, and derogatory, and often they have also been unkind and unaffectionate. Sometimes this has been a result of their attempts to toughen up and masculinize their boys and their discomfort with their girls.

However, Levant's (1988) review about education for fatherhood showed that the fathers of today are undergoing great changes. Levant cites support for a model of a reciprocal relationship between husband's participation in housework and wives' work over time. In the 1960s, time-budget studies showed that men's participation in housework was much less than their wives (1 to 1.6 hours per day, compared to 7.6 to 8 hours per day for wives). In this era, husbands increased their participation in housework only slightly if their wives worked (Robinson, 1977; Robinson & Hobson, 1978). However, by the mid-1970s, husbands' and wives' participation in housework showed evidence of having changed: Husbands were spending 3.3 hours per day if their wives did not work and 3.9 hours per day if their wives did work, whereas working wives spent 4 hours per day and nonworking wives spent 6.8 hours per day. Furthermore, and probably more important, the evidence suggests an increasing general trend in husbands' psychological involvement with their own families, placing the importance of their families toward their psychological well-being above that of work. Levant (1988) wrote, "This trend (that men experience their family role as more psychologically significant than their work role) is so far-reaching that its ramifying effects have yet to be fully appraised" (p. 254).

No doubt all these changes occurring simultaneously is part of the cause of the great variability of fathering in our data. This variability includes strong trends away from fathers being involved with their children's emotions. As the religious right gains strength in the U.S., there is also a movement of some fathers toward authoritarian parenting in child rearing patterns of discipline. In the U.S. the religious right has reacted to the child advocacy movement as if it were a movement of the government designed to take away what they claim are the "rights" of parents to use corporal punishment with their children, and especially to not have corporal punishment of children be viewed as child abuse. Thus, they are advocating corporal punishment of children as part of what they see as "strengthening" the family. An example is Christian ministry advocate Dennis Rainey, part of the *Family Life Today* series of books and other media presentations, who will do a week in his radio show on the positive aspects of spanking (personal communication, B. Coffin, 1995). This point of view is well-expressed in a recent manual from this school about spanking, which instructs parents in how to spank their children (see also Dobson, 1992). As part of this series of books there is a book by Chase (1982) titled, *Discipline Them, Love Them*. In the book, "Method 2" is spanking, which is justified by Biblical quotations that sparing the rod spoils the child. The book then goes on to suggest five "principles" and seven steps about spanking, such as "Do not spank in anger" (p. 27). The book continues:

A parent's conversation during these seven steps might sound like this: (Place the child on your lap). "Timmy, what did mommy say about throwing your ball in the house?" . . . "Yes, that's right, no ball playing in the house. But what did you do?" . . . "Yes, you disobeyed the rule. What happens when you disobey Mommy or Daddy?" . . . "That's right, we give you a spanking. We love you, Timmy, and want to help you learn how to obey and do what's right. A spanking now will help you to remember to do the right thing next time." (Lay the child over lap, and give a few brief, but painful swats on the buttocks *until Timmy stops his angry cry and cries softly*. Return child to your lap and hold him close. Be quiet a moment to allow for crying) . . . "Timmy, are you sorry you disobeyed Mommy and threw the ball in the house?" . . . "Good, I'm glad, and I forgive you. Now sweep up the broken glass from the picture that fell down when the ball hit it. I'll hold the dustpan." (p. 28, italics added)

This book appears to be part of parenting advice suggestive of the 18th-century idea that the child's will must be broken as part of discipline. The expected changes in the child's crying is quite reminiscent of this philosophy. It is not unlike the comments of a father in our study, who said:

(Father 118)
F: . . . you teach people to do right or wrong at least as they perceive it. And you teach them to react as they feel they should and not be ashamed for it. . . . And if they do something wrong to take the consequences for it.

Dawn picks her nose, I've told her many, many months ago, that every time I see her finger in her nose, that I'm going to slap her hand.

I: Um-hmm.

F: Slap the back of her hand. And I used to grab her hand and hold it and slap it, you know, and sometimes pretty hard even. Now I said, Dawn, "What did you just do?" She says, "Put my finger in my nose." (He imitates a scared child's voice.) And I said, "What do we do then?" She says, "Slap my hand." And I said, "Why don't you put it out there then," and she holds it out and I slap her hand.

Another force pushing men toward more authoritarian family patterns may be the Promise Keepers movement. This is a fundamentalist Christian movement of many hundreds of thousands of men. It was organized by former University of Colorado football coach Bill McCartney. A recent article on the movement by Waggenheim (1995) quoted from a manual that these men are issued in "instructing husbands how to reclaim their manhood" (Waggenheim, p. 80). The manual read:

> The first thing to do is to sit down with your wife and say something like this: "Honey, I've made a terrible mistake. I've given you my role. I gave up leading this family and I forced you to take my place. Now I must reclaim that role." Don't misunderstand what I'm saying here. I'm not suggesting that you *ask* for your role back. I'm urging you to *take it back*. If you simply ask for it, your wife is likely to say, "Look, for the last ten years, I've had to raise the kids, look after the house, and pay the bills. I've had to get a job and still keep up my duties in the home. I've had to do my job *and* yours. You think I'm just going to turn everything back over to you?' Your wife's concerns may be justified. Unfortunately, however, there can be no compromise here. If you're going to lead, you must lead. Listen. Be sensitive. Treat the lady gently and lovingly. But *lead*.

The forces pushing fathers toward authoritarian parenting are not limited to the religious right. For example, as Levant has noted, the Men's Movement has not advocated that men become more emotionally sensitive to their children. In fact the Men's Movement has suggested that men avoid becoming "feminized," by which they mean emotionally more expressive and responsive. This is related to a macho reaction we see in our sample against what is perceived as women's approach to emotion. For example, consider the following excerpt from a meta-emotion interview from the father we just quoted as having said "every time I see her finger in her nose, that I'm going to slap her hand."

(Father 118)

F: You'll find that I'm very cold in this whole thing, in this whole survey, you'll find that I don't react the way most people, especially my wife.

I: Hmm.

F: My wife is exceptionally emotional.

I: Hmm.

F: That's one of our real problems too. Of course you didn't ask any questions about that, but she is highly emotional and I'm very unemotional.

I: So you have different styles.

F: I cry at my grandmother's and grandfather's funerals and every once in a while a movie. (Laughs.)

I: Um-hmm.

F: But she cries over everything. You know, she can sit and watch a movie and blubber through the whole thing.

I: Um-hmm.

F: You know, she sees a dead animal beside the road, she's an animal lover, she wants cats, I'd just as soon shoot them, but, you know, that type of thing, she gets real, real affectionate over that. That goes back to our daughter too. You know the two of us have a harshness and a leniency.

I: Right.

No doubt misogyny plays a role in some of these forces that are attempting to influence men. As we have seen from the data presented in this book, to the extent that the advice of the mythopoetic movement leads to dismissing children's emotions and more derogatory parenting, it is potentially harmful to children.

On the other hand, in addition to Levant's reviews, Schwartz's (1994) book, *Peer Marriage,* has suggested that the opposite phenomenon is at work. Some men are moving toward a far less authoritarian and more emotionally involved stance toward their children. Many men are establishing equalitarian relationships with their wives in which they play an equal and active role in household work and child care. Schwartz suggested that these men pay a price for having this kind of marriage; their careers are not as well developed as the careers of traditional men. She also suggested that their sex lives may not be as satisfying as those of traditional men. However, she also suggested that there are great rewards that come from emotional connection with spouse and children for these men who have peer marriages.

No doubt some of these factors are responsible for the great variability in fathering (compared to mothering) in our data. In our analyses of variance the test for inhomogeneity of variance in parenting across parents was always statistically significant. In our data, for Derogation alone, fathers had three times the variance of mothers. The Greek Island Study of Roe (1980) suggests an analogous picture, but one in which the greater variability was in mothering, and mothers accounted for great variance in child outcome (a measure of child empathy). In the Greek Islands, the fathers are described uniformly as harsh, cold, and distant. Mothers, on the other hand, are described as quite variable, with some mothers compensating for the father's distance by having a close relationship with their children. In this case, we might expect that mothers have the potential to account for more of the variance in child outcome than fathers. Perhaps a similar process is occurring in the U.S. today, with the largest variance in fathers rather than mothers.

Indeed, when we examine the effects of mothers in modern Toronto when an extremely wide range of families is considered, the effects of variations in mothering is quite large. Pepler (1995) reported the results of a study of mothers who were either homeless, were recruited from battered women's shelters, or came from intact two-parent families. A significant proportion of the variance in the development of psychopathology in children was accounted for by variation in mothering.

Thus, converging lines of evidence suggest that fathers in the U.S. and Canada may be undergoing increasing polarization over time. The forces that mediate this change involve the increased stresses on families, the loss of a clear bread-winner role as a greater percentage of women pursue not just work but meaning-ful careers, the increased pressure on fathers from the workplace to avoid family life and become workaholic, the increased pressure fathers feel from within due to their own disappointments with their fathers and their own father hunger, and the increased value that today's fathers are placing on family life compared to work.

The changes in fathering occurring today have led some writers such as Levant (1992) to propose a new ethic for fathers, one that is both masculine and emotionally connected. Levant has called for a program that increases men's abilities to be empathic and emotionally expressive, increasing men's abilities to experience a wide range of emotions (Levant calls this dealing with men's relative "alexithymia," and says that for many men at first their main emotions are "stress" and "anger," but that after the group experience they report more of the "vulnerable" emotions of sadness and fear, personal communication, 1994), and men's greater expression of anger, rage and violence. These skills form the basis for Levant's program for creating involved and emotional fathers instead of distant and detached fathers (Levant & Kelly, 1989). Levant (1992) wrote:

> To help men overcome alexithymia, we first worked with them to develop a vocab-ulary for emotions, particularly the vulnerable ones, such as hurt, sadness, disap-pointment, rejection, abandonment, and fear, as well as the tender ones, such as warmth, affection, closeness, and appreciation. We then asked the men to keep an Emotional Response Log, noting when they experienced a feeling that they could identify, or a buzz that they became aware of, and what circumstances led up to that feeling or buzz. The logs were then discussed in the group, with emphasis on learning how to apply verbal labels to emotional states. *We also taught men to tune into their feelings through watching and discussing immediate play-backs of role-plays designed to engender feelings. By pointing out the nonverbal cues and asking such questions as "What were your feelings, Don, when you grimaced in that last*

segment?", fathers learned how to access the ongoing flow of emotions within. the
video play-back was so effective at times that we came to refer to it as the "mirror to
a man's soul." (p. 389, italics added)

In research with married couples, Gottman and Levenson (1985) reported that during a video playback session in which spouses watched a marital interaction individually and rated their own emotions, they tended to physiologically relive the emotions they experienced during the interactions in the sense that when they rated their tapes, they sweat more, and their hearts beat harder and faster at the same moments as during the actual marital interaction. Hence, we suggest that this video playback condition is likely to be a condition of talking about the emotion while re-experiencing it.

However, despite our conclusions about fathering becoming polarized today, the overwhelming trend is still for fathers to spend relatively little time with their children compared to mothers. A recent study (Rustia & Abbott, 1993) concluded that the "culture of fatherhood has changed more rapidly that the conduct of fatherhood," meaning that fathers' role performance lagged behind their rhetoric.

LIMITATIONS OF OUR RESEARCH
AND A RESEARCH AGENDA

There are some limitations of the research we have reported here. First, we need to extend our work to a wider range of family types. There are applied and theoretical reasons for doing so. Single-parent families of all varieties and step-families are not represented in our studies to date, and these constitute an increasing proportion of the families in the U.S. today. Racial and cultural variations have not been considered in our work. Cultural variations also provide an opportunity to test theory. For example, we can compare two cultures that differ primarily by their meta-emotion philosophy. Israeli couples, for example, do not link the expression of anger in the marriage with marital unhappiness the way Jewish couples in the U.S. do (Winkler & Doherty, 1983). Do parents in the two countries differ in meta-emotion? We can examine variation within each culture on this dimension as well as between cultures to assess the consistency of cross-cultural comparisons.

Second, we need to see what the variation is across parents, particularly emotion-coaching parents who are not very emotionally expressive. Third, it is clear to us that we need to study the emotional transactions between parents and children more naturalistically. We are currently collecting samples of everyday emotional moments between parents and children, in addition to our standard laboratory interactions. Fourth, we have not studied fear, such as list children's everyday fears and nightmares. Fifth, we need to develop child meta-emotion assessment procedures, probably starting with children at age 8. Sixth, we need to broaden our description of parental and child meta-emotion systems. One way we are pursuing this is by the study of emotion metaphors, following the ideas of George Lakoff (see chapter 19). Seventh, we need to study fathers more.

Eighth, we need to systematically dismantle the coaching interaction and understand its effects on the developing child. Ninth, emotion regulation probably begins much earlier that the preschool years. We need to understand what happens during infancy. We are currently studying this in a longitudinal transition toward parenthood study. Tenth, we are acutely aware of the fact that correlation does not imply causation. Thus, as we have suggested, every pathway in the model needs to be tested with an experiment.

The Inappropriateness of a Social Skills Metaphor for Understanding the Emotion Coaching Effect

We need to point out that the skills that children learn through parental emotion coaching are not isomorphic to the social skills that children need with peers. If a preschool child is assertive and tells a bossy preschooler how he or she feels, this may work and be an appropriate peer social skill. However, when attempting to enter a play peer group, even preschoolers are more likely to be rejected if they call the group's attention to themselves and their feelings (Putallaz, 1983; Putallaz & Gottman, 1981). The most appropriate entry strategy is to emulate the group's norms and follow their behaviors responsively. In middle childhood, teasing by peers becomes prominent and the most socially skillful response to teasing is for the child being teased to act cool, that is to act as if he or she is not at all upset. Revealing one's feelings of distress during teasing would be a big mistake. Thus, it is clear that a social skills metaphor for understanding what the child learns through parental emotion coaching is totally inappropriate. The emotion coached child does not learn a set of social skills that work in other situations (such as in the peer system). Instead, coached children learn to know what they feel and how to problem solve in emotion-arousing situations, while they are having the feeling; they learn to regulate their own emotions through enhanced regulatory physiology.

A Research Agenda on Meta-Emotion

Figure 18.1 (see p. 276) is a schematic diagram of our theoretical model. In this figure the seven lines going between boxes can also represent research studies designed to further investigate the linkages of the path models we derived. Each of these lines actually represents a line of research studies that can be proposed by us to further investigate the linkages in the theoretical model.

1. Line 1 can represent an intervention study in which we would randomly assign parents either to a meta-emotion skills group or to a control group,

and test whether their children change on regulatory physiology following the training and upon a series of followup assessments. We would study the children every two months for at least a year, assessing their regulatory physiology in a number of situations, including an attention task, our emotion films condition, and some tasks we have used in our laboratory such as entering a group of unfamiliar peers (Wilson, 1994).

J. Gottman and his wife, Julie have been conducting parent training groups to teach parents the five basic components of emotion coaching. These are (a) increased awareness of affective expressions of sadness, anger, and fear of low intensity; (b) viewing this event as an opportunity for intimacy or teaching; (c) validation of the emotion, perhaps accompanied by affection and soothing; (d) verbal labeling of the child's emotions; and (e) limit setting (on behavior), and problem solving. This training program is facilitated by a book for the general public (Gottman, in press) and an instructional film. The training group consists of eight group sessions with eight sets of parents, each lasting 1½ hours.

The format of the meetings is as follows: In the first session, the group discusses their own metaphors about anger, sadness, and fear (shame and guilt are also discussed) and their own experiences with these emotions growing up in their primary families and in their peer groups. The five components of emotion coaching are handed out to each group member, and a lecturette summarizes our research findings and describes each of the components. The group discusses how their metaphors about emotions might affect their own philosophy about their children's emotions. In the second group meeting, the idea of a parental "agenda," or set of developmental concerns for each child's development is a part of being a parent, but that it can get in the way of seeing the child's emotions. The group uses microcassette tape recorders to record weekly interactions with a child about an emotion *as the child is having the emotion*. In each subsequent group meeting, each of the participants writes on an index card an incident about a child emotion that occurred that week. The cards are then randomly shuffled and a different set of parents role plays the incident, once in an emotion-dismissing way, and then in an emotion-coaching way. The group also discussed the tape-recorded actual interactions of the parents with their children. Although marital problems are not dealt with in these parenting groups, about 30% of the participants talk of these problems as being central to their parenting difficulties. The limitations of emotion coaching are also discussed (see Gottman, in press, for further details and training materials).

This line also represents a series of autonomic/EEG studies that attempts to dismantle the Emotion Coaching interactions between parents and children compared to the Emotion Dismissing interactions between parents and children to determine what is regulatory about the child's talking about emotion while experiencing emotion in the way the children of Emotion Coaching parents do.

2. Line 2 represents the same outcome study just described, testing whether training parents in meta-emotion would eventually change the child outcomes we have been discussing. This work needs to include single parents.

3. Line 3 represents an empirical study (the same study as in Line 1) to determine whether parent training in just meta-emotion skills affects our parenting variables Warmth, Scaffolding/Praising, and Derogatory, and, if so, in which sequence these variables change. Again, the assessments would be relatively frequent so that we have a chance at mapping out these potential sequential changes over time in parenting as a function of meta-emotion training and potential changes in the child's regulatory physiology. The clinical trial represented by this study needs to be a 2×2 study in which parents are trained or not trained in emotion coaching or parenting.

4. Line 4 represents the same empirical longitudinal study with frequent assessments to map out the linkages between regulatory physiology and emotion regulation abilities. For example, we would examine those children who changed in regulatory physiology and assess the extent to which these changes were followed by or preceded by changes in the child's emotion regulation abilities.

5. Line 5 represents an empirical longitudinal study with frequent assessments to map out the linkages between emotion regulation abilities and the child outcomes we selected for study. Perhaps the most important child outcomes we are interested in at this point are, negative affectivity, antisocial behavior, and child–peer relations, which have the closest linkage with meta-emotion. We predict that increases in child regulatory physiology will first be followed by increases in attentional abilities, and that these changes will lead to increases in emotion regulation ability. This hypothesis requires us to construct a laboratory that assesses the child's ability to focus attention. We have recently constructed such a laboratory and used it in a dissertation by Wilson (1994) to study normally developing and developmentally delayed children's attention, vagal tone, and peer entry skills in six-person groups and a laboratory analogue of an entry situation.

6. Line 6 represents the evaluation of a the parent training main effect in our 2×2 parent training study combining On/Off conditions of parent training on all three parenting behaviors we have studied plus On/Off conditions of meta-emotion training.

7. Line 7 represents our anticipated link between the child's down regulation ability and child outcomes, which would be evaluated in the same study.

CONCLUSION

The overall message of our admittedly preliminary findings is quite optimistic. Hopefully, parental training in emotion coaching will provide a new way of helping families in need and of preventing problems from developing in other families. These constructs have also opened up new lines of research into the role of emotion in families and child development.

We are keenly aware of the limitations of our initial work. However, as we have tried to show in this chapter, the use of our theory and our model that includes the meta-emotion constructs raises interesting questions and suggests interesting new directions for research. We would respectfully submit that one can ask nothing more of a first study in a new area than that.

19
Emotion Metaphors

We end this book with this qualitative analysis of people's metaphors for emotion derived from the meta-emotion interview. We do this to give the reader a feeling for how rich and complex this area of meta-emotion is and how much we have yet to explore. We have only scratched the surface of this aspect of people's and families' emotional lives. Lakoff (1993) suggested that to understand how someone thinks about some aspect of their lives, study their metaphors about it. As we go through some of these metaphors for sadness and anger, we can imagine what the implications are of having these metaphors for dealing with one's child's sadness or anger.

POSITIVE SADNESS METAPHORS

Many people had positive metaphors for sadness. Some people said that sadness is productive, that it is there for a reason, to inform you about some aspect of your life, to make you slow down and reflect, that sadness is good because it means you can feel and empathize, that it sometimes is pleasant to feel sad in some movies, and that there is such a thing as a good cry. For example, one father said:

> Ahhh, I do think that, ahhh, sadness can hit ya and there could be a very positive reason for that happening when it does happen. Ummm, you could be going through very fast times and, ummm, sadness could be a reason to slow down and to think about what your doing or where you've been or what's happening to you. Yeah, I think it's positive for that 'cause it is running, ummm, rest of the, ummm, emotional well-being of yourself. I mean you can't be happy all the time, but when it does hit,

ummm, if you can recognize it for that, I think that, I think you can recognize that it is time to slow down, then I think that you're handling it positively, or at least I feel that I'm handling it positively.

The views of the wife of this man were similar to his. She said:

I think sadness is real important. I think that if you don't feel sadness at some point whether it's in your life or during the week or anything, I think your missing a big part of the importance of life. Ummm, Lindsey is a lot like me. We are both very sensitive, and ummm, you know, we can get sad watching "Highway to Heaven." Ummm, we watched it together the other night, and we both sat there crying. And, I think "Highway to Heaven" is a real good show for her to watch, and I think that it allows her to learn how to express those feelings of sadness, you know, because the kitty didn't get out of the house before it burned down. Ummm, I think that's real important that you go through that stage.

Other parents echoed this idea. For example, one father said:

A couple of occasions we've lost a couple of cats and [their child] he's been really upset about that and I think that, I think it's good that he, that he cares enough about something to feel sad about it.

Another mother talked about attending to sadness as a healing experience. She said:

I don't think you can ignore your feelings. Maybe I tend to overdo it, you know, but I, I just don't like to ignore them. You have to sort of, *it's kind of a cleansing thing.* You know, if you ignore your problems, they're just going to come back and bother you later, so, if you feel sad, deal with it, find out why you feel sad.

Although Gross & Levenson (1994) recently concluded that crying during sad films is physiologically arousing and found little evidence that it provided any physiological relief, some parents talked about the positive aspects of feeling sad and mentioned the "good cry."

I have a good cry or (laugh) at the drop of the hat. I mean I could watch a sad movie and cry. (Laughs.) Ummm, and just quiet and crying, quiet, you know, I don't always cry, but sort of thoughtful.

Another mother talked of being sad together during movies as an example of intimacy:

Ummm, I am a very soft-hearted, emotional person, and I don't think I've ever grown up in, in the sadness area. Ummm, I watch "Old Yeller" and I cry. . . . Ummm, so I think that her and I are a lot alike when it comes to be tender hearted, and, you know, when we see a cat run over in the street and we both sit there and cry.

SOMEWHAT BUT NOT ENTIRELY POSITIVE SADNESS METAPHORS

In contrast to these parents, many parents had metaphors for sadness that were not positive, but not negative either. One father viewed sadness as if it were a limited positive resource like the amount of money in a checking account. He was concerned that sadness not be "spent" on trivial matters. He said:

> Like losing a toy or tearing a page in the book or something like that is not something to waste your time being sad on. You save sadness for, you know, (laughs) one of the things we could be sad for is flat dogs, you know, the death of a pet or something like that.

We think that this father is likely to react to his daughter's sadness in a very complex manner, ignoring some expressions entirely and being very supportive during others. His responsiveness must convey to her some amount of judgment, that he does not approve of her being sad on this occasion because it is not important enough in his eyes. What will she learn from this philosophy of her father's about being sad?

Other parents' responses to sadness depended on other factors, such as how long the sadness lasted. One father said:

> **F:** Yeah, well, you know, when somebody has a death in their family or a major crisis in their family, yeah, you've got every right to sit around and get yourself together.
>
> **I:** Um-hmm.
>
> **F:** But I guess not, but, you know, for my own case, I wouldn't want that to be a prolonged period of time. I wouldn't, you know, sit in the corner in a sack cloth for six months or something.

This father went on to say that, contrary to the prevailing view, in his view being sad is okay for men and boys, as long as it is over quickly:

> I think that it's O.k. to be sad, you know, which I think is a lot of it, that's, maybe that's part of the thing, maybe that's something that, ah, especially for men in America it hasn't been O.k. for them to be for a long time. But then I think that maybe that's part of the way that I've been brought up. The fact that, you know, it's O.k. to be sad but it's not something to dwell on forever, it's something that you have to pull yourself out of eventually. You know, I don't know if I would tend to, you know, if I would tend to brush, rush into getting over sadness or not because of the way I've been brought up but I'd like Chase to know that it's O.k. to be sad but also to, you know, to try and work through it and get on your way eventually.

NEGATIVE SADNESS METAPHORS

Other parents were far less ambivalent in their negativity toward sadness. Some parents viewed sadness as toxic. An example of this was one father who feared that sadness was just the beginning of a major pathological condition. He said [I = interviewer; M = Mother; F = Father]:

I: Um-hmmm. So you shouldn't stay negative. Do you think that, what do you think would happen if you stay negative?
F: I don't know. I've never been there. Ahhh, I don't know. It would be poor judgment, I guess.
I: Do you ever see other people when they, when they get really sad?
F: Um-hmmm. We had a schizophrenic skitzo living with us or near us so we knew from what she was like, we could see that she was always, you know, didn't smile much.
I: Um-hmm, Um-hmm. So what do you think it did to her?
F: Almost killed her. (Pause.) It did. Almost killed her.
I: So it's a really bad thing.
F: Must be.

One father said that his only goal about his son's sadness was for him to have very little of it in his life:

I: So you would like for your son to be less sad.
F: Yeah.
I: To have less sadness in his life.
F: Right.

Some parents articulated the reason for this attitude, viewing sadness as appropriate only when death is present:

F: Um, when I thought of sadness, the first thing that came to me was death. Um, a loved one dying, you feel sad. Um, a kid may feel that way more toward an animal or a possession. Um, when I was a kid I remember my grandpa died and, um, it was really the first death in the family. Both my parents are still living so it's still really the first death, major death that had occurred. When I was in fifth grade. It was around when John Kennedy, same month as John Kennedy's death. Um, both of those things affected me in being sad then I looked at my parents and saw how they were handling it. It's part of life. Ah, going to the funeral, they thought, "Eric you're mature enough to go to the funeral." And I was really thankful that they felt that way toward me rather than keep me home with a baby-sitter. They let me go and it was my first experience. I felt sadness but then I felt very, not relieved, I felt a part of the family.

I: Um-hmm.

F: That I could go to the funeral and, ah, look at my grandpa lying there. And, ah, that was the first experience I ever had with it. Uh, I guess I'm relating deaths to sadness (laughs) but I don't really know of anything of late that I've been really sad about.

Many of these parents say that they suffer when they see their children being sad. For example, this father, who said:

F: You know, I, I don't know how other parents react, but when you see your child hurt, you, ah, the parents hurt more than they are actually.

These ideas were echoed by the following mother:

M: Oh, I hate to see her sad.

I: Why is that?

M: You know for someone so young to be sad about something . . .

I: Does it make you sad, does it make you angry?

M: Well it makes me sad to see her sad, you know, and I, I try to do what I can to alleviate whatever it is that's making her sad, you know. Sometimes it's possible, sometimes it's not.

Other parents don't see the sadness as so inappropriate, but they do see the child's sadness as unproductive, as a state to be altered and changed, equating sadness with other serious negative states, such as depression.

F: Oh, nothing good can ever come out of depression unless you come out of depression. A depressed mood to me is a useless time. It's when you're doing nothing constructive whatsoever. You're feeling sorry for yourself if nothing else.

These parents often feel it is best not to react at all when the child is sad. For example, one father said:

F: I, I classify myself as a realist in the scheme of life, you know, there's, I try to look at things and see them as at least as close as I can find to what they are. She's sad. What am I going to do? Am I going to go tickle her chin or cheer her up? I don't know if that's really what you need to do. I think a lot of times people need to work out their own problems.

I: Is that what you encourage her to do?

F: Well, like I said, I don't have much reaction to it at all.

I: Um-hmm.

Some parents viewed sadness in themselves as a time when they wanted to be alone and not talk to anyone about their feelings.

I: Hmm. Sadness is the kind of feeling that you just want to be alone with?
M: Um-hmm. Yeah.

A father echoed this philosophy:

F: Um-hmm. Ah, yeah, I, I'm, I don't, I don't usually share. I haven't done the, you know, the times that I've really been sad about things, I, ah, I, I've always kept it to myself. (Laughs.)

These metaphors that suggest that for some parents sadness is seen as toxic, that it ought to be cleansed from the child as quickly as possible, or that it is to be ignored, perhaps with the infected person being quarantined will greatly affect the way that parents respond to their child's sadness.

ANGER METAPHORS

Metaphors of anger as heat or pressure are quite common across cultures (Lakoff, 1993). In our study, there were many metaphors for anger that suggested that people viewed anger in terms of fire, heat, blowing off steam, and calming down as cooling. The following excerpts illustrate these metaphors. In the first a mother says:

Oh, what do I do, I'm trying to think? (Laughs.) Really I don't think there's really anything, it depends on where I'm at or the situation or, you know. Sometimes I'll spout off, you know, start yellin, you know, if it's with Steve I'll start yellin. If I'm angry with the kids, I'll set myself down and say, you know, "You can't yell at them, or you can't, you know," I'll set myself down and *cool off* before I talk with them. But if it's somethin in the family, I think I'm more or less say things I shouldn't say, more or less things like that.

Another mother also echoes this point of view:

You know, if you need that kind of thing, then that's the way you should do things, but, I don't seem to need to *blow off steam* like that so, you know, I don't very often.

In the following excerpt a father uses a similar metaphor:

No, definitely *heated up*. Somewhat a little embarrassed also, definitely mad. Point at which it was mostly a situation where it just wasn't one situation, it was probably building up. . . . No, definitely heated up. Somewhat a little embarrassed also, definitely mad. Point at which it was mostly a situation where it just wasn't one situation, it was probably building up. . . . So, that was encouraging, but I still was apologetic for this outburst.

This idea of anger as positive because it makes it possible to let go of some built up pressure was expressed in the following excerpt that viewed expressing anger is letting off steam:

> **F:** Well, you know, if you're working on something that doesn't go right, get real mad, and (pause) just, I think it *lets off some steam* and kind of clears your head once it's over with. And it kind of relaxes you once it's over with.

POSITIVE ANGER METAPHORS

Lakoff & Johnson (1980) analyzed anger using the metaphor "Argument is war." In our study many parental metaphors in the meta-emotion interview suggest that anger is viewed by some parents as energizing. One mother said that anger gave her the motivation to say things that need to be said.

> **I:** Um-hmm. O.k. So you sort of like anger because it helps you get things done. And what kind of things do you get done?
> **M:** Oh, probably nothing. (Laughs.)
> **I:** (Laughs.)
> **M:** Cause I feel anger just gets me, I get things said . . .
> **I:** O.k., right.
> **M:** that I've been wanting to say.

This sentiment was also reflected by another mother:

> **M:** (Sigh.) I think it's invigorating at first.
> **I:** Um-hmm.
> **M:** Because I'll find myself saying, well, to hell with it, I'm angry, let it all hang out. And (laughs) I'll go, I'll just go off and I'll say, you know, what I feel and then after a while I just don't feel really good about that I've done it, you know, that I've let go.

A commonly expressed view was that anger was productive for being assertive, that anger showed people they could not push the angry person around. The father in the following excerpt expressed this idea clearly:

> Well, it definitely made it, it wasn't that wrong because it made a point that I can't be pushed around so much.

The idea of anger being linked to fighting was expressed by the father in the following excerpt:

They're just, they've been put in a position where they might fight back or say something that they don't mean just because they feel like they have to say it faster to get back to being even or where they want to be in the conversation.

Parents also express assertiveness as a goal with their children's anger.

> **I:** what is it that you'd like Kevin to know about being angry? What is it that you'd like to teach him if you could?
> **F:** Um, I, to, ah, to, yeah, probably to, ah, you know, to stick up for himself.

At a minimum many parents expressed the idea that anger is positive because it requires one to have contact with people, that it entails communication, and was therefore positive. For example, one mother said:

> Um, (pause) I think if you're angry about something, then it calls for communication. You're angry so there's some, you need to communicate with somebody or some issue or something that's making you angry and to do it in such a way that it's going to help the situation and not make it worse.

SOMEWHAT BUT NOT ENTIRELY POSITIVE ANGER METAPHORS

Some parents expressed a somewhat positive, but more qualified view of anger. Some expressed the view that anger, *if controlled*, was acceptable and even positive. One mother said:

> I mean, it's right to have anger but kind of control it.

Another mother:

> [talking about anger] what really makes me happy is when he can say something to me that would normally set me off but I don't go off and I think . . . What's the circumstances and how he could be feeling and try to understand, . . . you know, that makes me happy.

This idea of control was well expressed by the following father:

> **I:** So you enjoy anger?
> **F:** Yeah, as long as I can control it and not let it get too out of hand.

This idea was also reinforced by the view expressed by a mother, who said that for her not expressing anger was to court disaster.

> And my sister was such that she was the sweetest thing. She still is. She's just as sweet as she can be. She takes and she takes and she takes and she takes. She takes

so much, I wouldn't take half of the stuff she takes on one given day, you know. Um, she has a real picky, picky husband now. She takes and she takes and boy you think, wow, why is she letting him get away with these things and then when you look at it and she decides to let loose, it is so, (laughs) embarrassing for you sitting there with him till you feel so badly for him when she finally does let loose. Well, that was fifteen years ago or so, fourteen years ago. She's always been that type of person.

This view was often expressed as a "hydraulic" metaphor, that, if unexpressed, the pressure of the anger would go somewhere and would have to come out somewhere else.

> **M:** Yeah, they see me get angry quite often with other things and I try not to, you know, I don't like arguing in front of them because I feel that that would make them more nervous or, but I try not to get angry in front of them. I try to calm down. But if I get angry I try to calm down, you know, before, but things will pop up, you know, (laughs) if I get angry with something else.

NEGATIVE ANGER METAPHORS

Some parents view anger in themselves and in their children as entirely toxic. In the following excerpt, a mother is talking about what she is like in her own marriage when she gets angry:

> **M:** I think I like anger. (Laughs.) I don't know why but I think, I get a lot of things out in the open, I'm not keeping them inside. Um, I'd say in a way I'm kind of a spiteful person, well, I wouldn't say kind of, he says I'm *spiteful* all the time. (Laughs.)
>
> **I:** Huh.
>
> **M:** But, um . . .
>
> **I:** What sort of things do you do that he says . . . ?
>
> **M:** Well, if somebody does something to me I'm out bound and determined I'm going *to get them back,* which is wrong, I know I shouldn't. But I, I don't know, it's inside me, I guess I was born that way or whatever. (Laughs.) I just figure well *if they're going to do it to me, then they're going to pay for it,* you know.

There is a strange mixture of pride and self-derision in her description of herself as spiteful when she is angry. The most common negative set of metaphors accompanying anger were *metaphors of fire and explosion,* metaphors that suggested that expressing anger was throwing a lighted match into a fuel dump, that things could "blow, " that anger like fire can consume you, and so on. For example, one mother said:

M: Somewhere in the middle. I don't get angry very easily. I mean, I have slow fuse, and, ahhh, I, at the kids, I get angry at the kids much more quickly than I would with somebody, you know, that something else would make me angry. The kids will make, *I have a shorter fuse* when it comes to them. And I will express it usually verbally. And I will usually say, "That makes me very angry." And most, sometimes, it's obvious by the tone of my voice, or that I'm yelling. . . . [talking about the child] Yeah. *He has a short fuse.*

I: I was going to ask you about that.

M: He has a very short fuse, and, ummm, I've tried to tell him that it's o.k. to be angry, but ummm, it's not o.k., sometimes he'll hurt Bubba and his sister which is not o.k., or throw something which is also not o.k. and ummm, that if he could say that, that really, that makes him angry and what makes him angry and not hit his sister or hurt his friend or do something like that which he's had a tendency to do.

The father in the following excerpt expressed the metaphor that anger can use you up like things are consumed in a fire:

Um, and I think that we're trying to do the best we can with, um, having him understand that fears are real and that we want to help him through them and that anger is there but don't let anger consume you. . . . It's o.k. to have those feelings and, um, not, I think we have to learn not to let the feelings rule us but that we understand the feelings so that we can go through them and cope with them and let them help us rather than just to be *consumed by them* and everything like that.

Think of how having these metaphors about anger would affect the way a parent responds to a child's anger. The metaphor of the explosion for anger expression was expressed in the following excerpt expressed by a father:

Well probably with the girls again. I was at work where I was trying to conduct classes and I wasn't getting the cooperation or respect or the attention that I was desiring and *I just blew up.* I'm usually a little bit more reserved than that. I just said, "Read it yourself. I don't have to put up with this."

and by the mother in the following excerpt:

I don't like it because I think of, "This is the only way that I can get something done," you know. I don't like it. (Laughs.) (Pause.) I *don't like blowing up.* (Laughs.) It makes me feel bad afterwards.

There are negative views of anger that suggest that some parents view the expression of anger as destructive:

M: She's learning with sadness, too, but anger is for a four year old just so much more exciting than it is to sit down and cry. Ummm, maybe because it shows them a lot more different things; it shows destruction

I: How do you feel when you see her angry?

M: (Pause.) Depends on what, it depends on what she's doing. If she's being destructive, I don't like it.

The following father explains that when he was younger anger did imply his being destructive:

F: I changed my, I used to be destructive when I was younger. My anger would result, uh, I killed a cat one time I got mad. I just took a cat and smacked it dead and threw it away. I just, I was that impulsive. Or put my hands through walls. I broke my hands twice doing it.

Metaphors in this vein describe anger as uncivilized. The following excerpt from a father's interview illustrates this idea:

It gets back to reasoning, you know, you ought to be able to reason and talk with people. You know, *civilized people should be about it reason things out without getting hostile toward each other*, you know, yeah.

Or, many parents express the view that anger is the same as aggression. Witness the father in the following excerpt:

Oh, anger is something that, ha, ha, anger I can get into, you know. It's not a good thing, don't get me wrong. You know, Sue says I need to have a punching bag sitting in the corner where when I get angry I can go in there and punch it. It really doesn't do any good.

When asked what this father wanted to teach his child about anger, he immediately connected it to teaching her to avoid becoming aggressive:

I just think, yeah, we're just trying to bring her up to be ready and to deal with things as they come up and she's starting school next year. She's gonna, you know, all little kids at times one time or another might have a problem with other little kids because they do things to hurt each other. We want her to realize that that could happen and for her to not automatically turn around and strike back and hurt them back. . . . Maybe if she has a problem to go to someone, an authority, you know, other than just taking matters into her own hands.

Many parents express the view that a child's anger should be punished, regardless if it involves misbehavior. This is illustrated by the father in the following excerpt:

I: Well, how is Dawn, is she more like her Daddy this way? Does she get angry more like you do?

F: Yeah, yeah. She has that emotion.

I: So you can really tell . . .

F: She flies off the handle a little bit more than she should probably.

I: So what do you do then? How does it make you feel?

F: Most of the time I react to that rather abruptly and harshly, you know, spank her bottom, sometimes slap her bottom. Sue says it's much too harsh, but of course any blow to the head I guess I shouldn't be doing. That's one of my shortcomings that I do have. I do smack her on top of the head occasionally. (Hits counter.) Like that, much harder, I'm sure, but, um, I'm sure I react much too harshly in that respect, but that's becoming tempered also.

I: Um-hmm.

F: I've always been of the opinion personally that you get treated the way you treat people and vice versa.

I: So when she gets mad, you get mad at her.

F: Basically.

I: But that wasn't the same with sadness though. When she gets sad, you didn't necessarily get sad.

F: But I'm a little cold, see.

The mother in the following excerpt suggests that this mother had some ambivalence about her own views of supporting the child's sadness but punishing his anger:

Yeah, I'm just sort of realizing that maybe there is some kind of a double standard between letting him cry, that's o.k., but anger, maybe, you know, "Don't have it," you know, "Go upstairs, get rid of it and then come down and be pleasant," you know. I can deal with the crying, you know, I can say, "Poor Max," and stoke his head, but when he's mad I don't say, "Poor Max," and stoke his head, I say, "Take it somewhere else. I don't want to hear it." I don't know. It's kind of interesting.

There were a fair number of very negative views of anger that had to do with extreme bodily functions. One parent had such a negative view of the expression of anger that he used the metaphor that *when people get angry they are relieving themselves on others*, another used mastication, chewing on others, another used vomiting on others, another used drowning. Some parents expressed the view that anger was best left unexpressed, or that anger and hurt always go together, or that people who were angry should be quarantined, or that it was shameful if people see you angry, or that if a person were healthy there would be no anger. It is clear that these negative concepts that accompany meta-emotions about anger affect the way a parent responds to the child's anger. Many of our parents used a variety of punishments soley for the child's expression of anger (not misbehavior), such as spanking and time out.

EMOTION METAPHORS CONNECTED TO THE PARENT'S OVERALL EMOTION PHILOSOPHY

A Pro-Expressing Philosophy

Parents had a fair number of emotion metaphors as they talked about their general philosophy of emotion. The positive expressive philosophy was that it was important to get anger or sadness "out of your system" (like clearing your throat). The following excerpts illustrate this idea:

1. **M:** When daughter is having a temper tantrum, she says to her, "This is the way it is and it's not going to change, so just *get it out of your system*, go do something else, you know."
2. **F:** Well, it's something that you feel. Ummm, I don't know, it depends. It could be (pause) . . . Sadness can be a violent thing. Ahh, that's not me though; I'm not violent, but, ummm, you could feel morose that, ummm, you want to tear paper or something or just run around; that it's starting to get into rage, yeah or anger I could see that. But, ummm, but to *just get that out of your system* so you could, ummm, feel clear about yourself and about the situations that are around you. That's what I think.

Some parents expressed the concept that emotions are always there; that they are a part of life. This is illustrated by the following excerpt from a mother's interview:

M: Upset. Angry upset, sad upset, all of them rolled into one. Well, you're always going to feel one of them. You know, one of them is always going to be there. You're either happy or you're sad or you're angry or you're afraid. Ummm, that's a real difficult question because I think that's what life is about. That's what life is. And, I don't, I want her to know how to deal with all of them, but like I said, I want it to be constructive patterns that she deals with them, I don't want it to be destructive, and I want, I want her to be sure of herself when she does deal with them. . . . I think sadness is real important. I think that if you don't feel sadness at some point whether it's in your life or during the week or anything, I think your missing a big part of the importance of life.

An Anti-Expressing Philosophy

Some parents expressed the philosophy that negative emotion must simply be endured, as illustrated by the following excerpts:

1. **F:** That you just got to keep on going on even though you are sad. There's other things that you have to do. You can't let an emotion like that get in your way. Cause I know that it affects me a lot. I try to, you know, I'm like him, not to be as the way I am about it, like wanting him to be able to overcome it whenever it comes about.

2. **I:** O.k. And what was it that you're trying to teach him about sadness by saying that?

   M: Just to teach him that there's better things, you know, or other things to come that will make him happy. That the sadness is not, you know, going to last forever. (Laughs.)

3. You see you've got to pull out of it if you are sad. If I, if I had a particular situation come up this week, lets say my wife dies this week, um, I'm going to be sad about that and my kids are going to be sad and we have to go into that period of mourning if it's just a few days, a few weeks, whatever and then realize, o.k. we've got to go on. We can't just stay home and lock up in our shells. We must go, maybe go slowly depending on the whole situation, go back to work eventually, and, uh, yes there's going to be periods of times after that where you're going to be sad again.

4. (He has explained that the primary cause of his sadness is financial). Ah, for one thing, basically what makes me sad sometimes is something financial or something happens and you have to put out an extra hundred dollars here or there. And we've been on a tight budget ever since we've been married and it's, it's loosening up now, it's starting to turn around the other way which we knew it would, we projected in kind of long term instead of, you know, we don't take every loss and gain as a total thing in itself, you know, it's just kind of an ends to make a means, you know, or vice versa whatever, a means to make an end. But, that's basically, *we just bite the bullet* on it and go from there, you know.

Some parents expressed the view that the passage of time alone will solve emotional problems; this idea is illustrated by the following excerpts:

1. **F:** And I, I, you know, I want to wait until tomorrow when I feel better.

2. **I:** O.k. What do you do to get over being angry?

   M: I just let time (pause) get it out of me. I mean, I'm sure there's been occasions where there's been something I could do to get rid of it, to solve the situation. I can't think of an example now, but, ah, usually like I said, is to suppress. And I have to find something else to do until it finally just seeps back into it's little, it's never gone, I guess, but it goes back into it's little cubby hole where it's not so important at the moment.

3. **M:** I keep telling myself it's another day, you know. I've got another day and it will be o.k., you know, and sometimes it just seems to go away by itself, you know, just don't concentrate, I find that if I just don't concentrate on him feeling then I'll be, it's o.k.

A BALANCE PHILOSOPHY

A common point of view in our data was that negative emotion must be balanced by positive emotion. One philosophy we heard was that to get over a negative emotion, just get on with life's routines. For example, one father said:

> I think that's part of *the healing process*. From a major, a major sadness, is getting back, trying to get back from a routine or making new routines. And, ah, going from there. . . . It's like we talked about before try to get back into your routines or establish some new routines and, ah, you know, just go on. You have to go on living and, ah, you know, that helps you in the process of getting over it I think is to try to get back into routines and get on with your life.

Another view was to accentuate the positive instead of harping on the negative. In the following excerpt, a mother has learned this from being a stepmother in her previous marriage:

M: Yeah, like with Judy I've kept a positive attitude on everything with her and try to be positive and everything. But like with Sara the one that gave me the most trouble it seems like I brought out the negative things instead of bringing out the positive things. Of course I've had studies and stuff that I'd taken before on child development. Like when she did bad in school, you know, I'd kind of harp on the bad things instead of trying to point out the good things to her. You know, to bring up her attitude about herself. You know, little things like that that I could have done with them. So little things like that that I didn't know that I know with Sara.

This woman's husband expressed a similar philosophy:

F: And I don't like worrying in advance about something that might not happen, you know, so . . .

I: Um-hmm.

F: That's the way I look at it. You know, I try to be on an upbeat, positive, you know.

This idea of positive emotion as an antidote to the toxicity of negative emotion is expressed in the following excerpts:

1. **F:** The same things that make you happy I guess will keep you from being sad. I suppose the same things that you do to be happy keeps you from being sad.

2. **M:** And then I get over it and think of something else and do something else to make me feel (laughs) happy.

3. **I:** Um-hmm. What would you like your child to know about upset feelings?

    M: That's hard to answer. I try, well, I'd say that I try to teach him not to take them out on other people for one thing. You know, take your fear, your anger out on other people like his brother. I teach him how to deal with them, that better things are to come than bad feelings, you know. And, ah, more or less, also to think about what he's angry about or what he's frustrated about. Just try harder the next time to make like you know, if he's frustrated with himself. And just more or less try to tell him to *look on the bright side.*

4. **F:** Ah, try to, ah, gear toward positive thoughts. Uh, not taking things too serious. Uh, which sometimes I do. Uh, using tools such as a funny movie to make me more humorous. Um, a good, clean story or a humorous joke would put me in that, ah, sphere of wanting to have the goal of being humorous.

5. **M:** You have to outweigh the good things in life, you know, let the good things in life outweigh the bad. (Pause.) Oh, I guess in the past I've had some bad, you know, experiences. When I was, you know, growing up in my teens, but I've just learned to put those bad things behind me and go for the good.

In addition to positive emotion is a philosophy that minimizes the importance of the upset that has led to the anger; this is illustrated by the following excerpt from a father's interview:

How do I overcome or get over frustration? (Pause.) Well, again back to focus. O.k. Lets say I've been frustrated. (Pause.) Uh, I try to focus, I'm trying to think of circumstances where I've done this. I try to focus on the positive, looking at, counting my blessings, counting the good things that I do have which are numerous and usually I always outweigh the frustrating side of it. And usually when I look at it, I really analyze why I was frustrated, it's so petty. It's so small.

A pragmatic, problem solving view was expressed, viewing the expression of emotion in cost-benefit terms. The following excerpt from a mother's interview illustrates this:

Or if I really analyze it and think that it's silly of me to be angry, it's not worth saying anything about it. Then I work it out with myself and just forget it kind of thing. Um, but, there is a lot of energy that's consumed in anger and I think, um, I think it's kind of important to analyze why you're angry. Is it 'cause you feel that your rights have been, you know, taken advantage of, that you've been stepped on? Is it your pride that got smushed in the whole thing or is there something really to be angry about legitimately? Um, is it a matter of just your own, um, you feel like somebody did you in or if there's something really valid to be angry about? I don't know if I'm saying this the right way.

The most common element of the balance philosophy is the idea of not losing control, and the idea that one can change one's feelings at will, even in dreams, well expressed by the following mother:

M: Ah, it bothers me and I hate for her to be sad but yet I want her to be able to express her feelings to me that she's upset about stuff. But then *I always get her to change fast too, you know, so she don't stay sad forever.* Try to bring things into her mind that make her feel better. Like when she had a nightmare, you know, that upset her the other night, I said, "Well, change the nightmare around so it wouldn't be a bad nightmare or a sad thing. It would be something better." So, she had a nightmare that the cat that she's going to get ate the goldfish that she just got. And so then she turned around and she said, "The goldfish ate the cat." So that changed it so she wasn't sad anymore.

CONCLUSION

This qualitative analysis in this chapter illustrates the richness of parents' metaphors about emotion. It also points out the fact that we have barely scratched the surface of this area of investigation in the lives of families. The concept of meta-emotion is clearly a very fertile and potentially interesting area of the family's life, one that is worthy of further study. We hope that other investigators agree and that we have company in continuing to study the role of meta-emotion in families.

Appendix A
Methodology for the Vagal Tone Computations

BRIEF HISTORY

The original concept of vagal tone began with the Porges (1972) observation that *heart rate variability* was related to performance (reaction time) following the onset of a warning signal during tasks demanding continuous attention. When a preparatory interval was used before a required response, heart rate variability was related to reaction time (higher variability was related to faster reaction times) only when the preparatory interval was not fixed. Porges, Arnold, and Forbes (1973) began suggesting that pretrial heart rate variability may be used as an index of a newborn's responsivity to its environment. These results were extended by Porges, Stamps, and Walter (1974) to the newborn's responses to changes in illumination. Only newborns with high pretrial heart period variability responded to changes in illumination. Porges (1974) then suggested that heart rate variability in newborns and in adults was an index of increased attention. Porges and Humphrey (1977) extended the results to retarded populations, examining the suppression of heart rate variability. They found that nonretarded children suppressed heart rate variability during tasks that demanded sustained attention, whereas the retarded subjects increased heart rate variability during these tasks. As we have previously reviewed in this book, Porges also began extending these findings to assessments of infants and children at risk.

Porges' original explorations using time series analysis were to refine the statistic of total heart rate variability by limiting this variability to only the respiratory component. There is a well-known respiratory rhythm in the heart period. The time between R-spikes of the electrocardiogram decreases when people inhale (faster heart rate) and increases when they exhale (slower heart rate). This creates a respiratory rhythm in the heart period time series. There are individual differences in this "respiratory sinus arrhythmia (RSA)."

In 1980, Porges, working with a mathematician at the University of Illinois, Robert Bohrer, published a paper in the *Psychological Bulletin* suggesting that heart period variability was indexing the respiratory-cardiac coupling that the vagus nerve created. They suggested a new time-series statistic for evaluating this coupling called *vagal tone,* and they called the new statistic *the weighted coherence,* also called *v-hat.* The unweighted coherence (similar to a correlation coefficient squared) assesses the relationship between two time series, computing the amount of rhythmic co-occurrence. The weighted coherence is like a beta-weight; it is weighted by the amount of the variance in one of the series. Porges et al. (1980) used the weighted coherence statistic. They showed that for hyperactive children there was a dose-response relationship between methylphenidate and teacher ratings of disruptive behavior and a parallel relationship with this statistic.

Porges later found that there were correlations in the high .90s between the v-hat statistic and computations of RSA using only a standard respiratory range for children of a particular age, instead of using the subject's individual respiratory rate. Lately this idea has been the subject of some debate. Grossman, Karemaker, and Wieling (1991) argued that it was important to control for respiratory parameters (rate and tidal volume) in computing RSA. They used propranolol to create a beta-adrenergic blockade of the heart in 6 healthy males, arguing that after beta blockade all variations in heart period would be mediated vagally. Respiratory parameters influenced RSA magnitude. Only when they statistically controlled respiratory variables did they find a relationship between heart rate and RSA amplitude. However, it is unclear why this would be the litmus test for including respiratory parameters in computing RSA.

COMPUTATIONS

There are essentially three methods for computing vagal tone using just the heart period time series. The first method is spectral analysis. The second method is filtering; this is an attempt to filter out or remove all the components of the heart period time series that are *not* respiratory. The third method is to work with the time series (called working in the time domain), to use peak-valley studies to determine cardiac oscillations associated with the respiratory range. Porges' programs use the filtering approach. In this book we have used a modification of the spectral analytic approach. Grossman, Van-Beek, and Wientjes (1990) compared the measures they derived from these three techniques and found them to be highly correlated.

In this appendix we review the spectral analytic approach, together with our modification of this approach.

Definition of and Computations of the Spectral Density Function

The following presentation is based on a more extended presentation in Gottman (1981). Consider any time series, x_t, $\{x_0, x_1, x_2, \ldots, x_{T-1}\}$, which is a set of T observations. To simplify matters, assume that the series has a mean of zero (or that the mean has been subtracted from each observation) and that the number of observations, T, is an odd number. If T is an even number a correction term must be added to the following formulas. Once we know how many observations there are, this number determines the frequencies available to us for best least squares estimation of the data using sine and cosine functions. These frequencies are called the "overtone series." The angular frequencies w_J are determined by the formulas:

$$w_J = (2\pi \, J)/T, \, J = 1, 2, 3, \ldots, (T-1)/2$$

These frequencies are in cycles/unit time, f_J:

$$f_J = J/T, \qquad J = 1, 2, 3, \ldots, (T-1)/2$$

Note that these correspond to cycles of period T, T/2, T/3, . . . , 2 time units in length. For example, if T = 31, w_J would go from $2\pi \, (1/31) = .202$ in multiples up to $2\pi \, (15/31) = 3.040$. This is the grid of frequencies we have to work with for our approximation. Note that we are talking of an *approximation,* albeit the best linear least squares approximation we can make with a set of orthogonal functions (the sines and cosines at the frequencies of the overtone series).

Now the problem is simply the estimation of a_J and b_J in the equation:

$$x_J = \Sigma(a_J \cos w_J t + b_J \sin w_J t) + e_t,$$

where e_t is normally distributed white noise, and where the summations extend from t = 0 to T-1. Then it can be shown that the least squares estimates of the coefficients are just the sample covariances:

$$a_J = (2/T) \sum_{t=0}^{T-1} x_t \cos w_J \, t$$

$$b_J = (2/T) \sum_{t=0}^{T-1} x_t \sin w_J \, t.$$

This is the *projection* of the time series on the orthogonal set of functions. The periodogram is a decomposition of the total variance or energy of the time series as a function of frequency. It is given by:

$$I(f) = \frac{1}{2\pi \, T} \, [(\Sigma \, x_t \cos 2 \, \pi \, f t)^2 + (\Sigma \, x_t \sin 2 \, \pi \, f t)^2],$$

where the summations extend again from t = 0 to T-1.

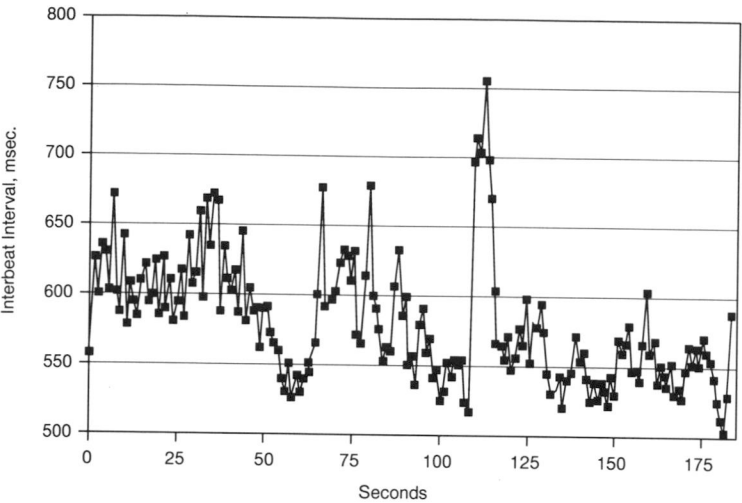

FIG. A.1a. Heart period data, Subject #181, 3 minutes, neutral film.

The periodogram is of limited usefulness because it only has degrees of freedom 2 for each frequencies, so a variety of "spectral windows" have been proposed. These windows average the periodogram to create the spectral density function, p(f), which has more degrees of freedom at each frequency.

Figures A.1a and A.1b illustrate 3 minutes of two children's heart period data while watching a neutral film about fly fishing. The interbeat interval data are

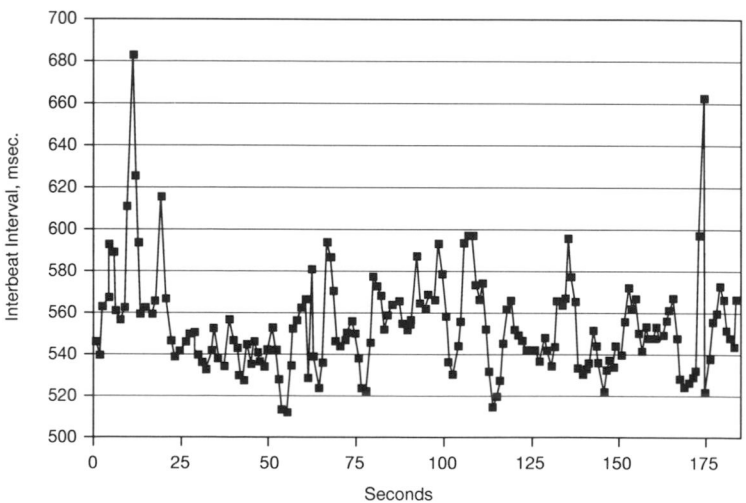

FIG. A.1b. Heart period data, Subject #181, 3 minutes, neutral film.

Spectral Density Function

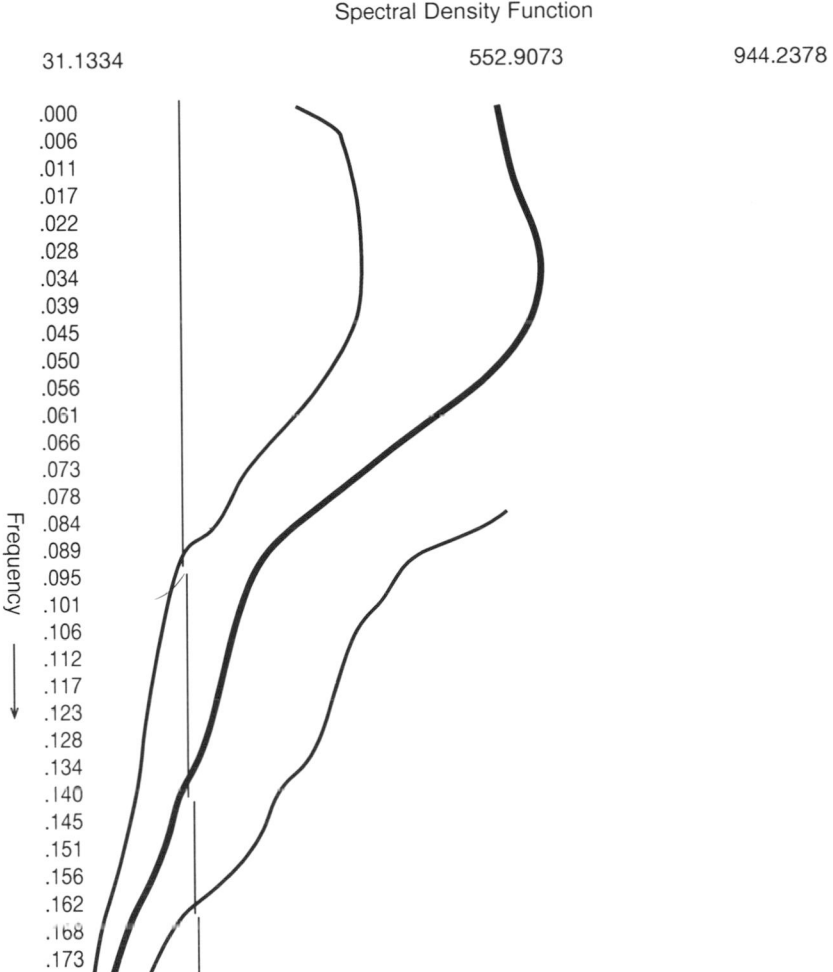

FIG. A.2a.   Subject #121, detrended, spectral density function.

presented here second-by-second, using a prorating procedure dues to Porges in which the subject's time between heartbeats are averaged into one-second bins. Figures A.2a and A.2b illustrate the spectral density functions for these data, computed with the spectral density function program called SPEC, developed by Gottman and Williams (see Williams & Gottman, 1981). In each case we computed the area under the curve in the child's respiratory range, using K. Swanson's Area-under-the-Curve program. The data are first detrended using the Gottman-Williams program called DETRND.

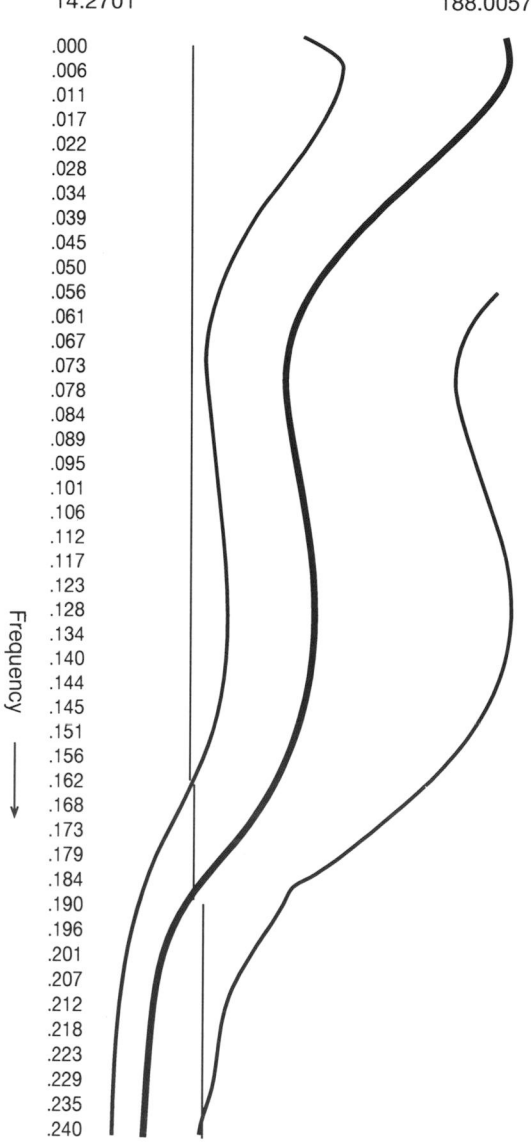

FIG. A.2b.   Subject #181, detrended, spectral density function.

In recent years Beverly Wilson serendipitously discovered a new algorithm for smoothing these data and reducing the variation across families. This new algorithm adds a zero point as the last data point. The data are then detrended. The vagal tone estimates for these two computations were highly correlated across our 56 families, $r = .807$, $p < .001$. For our suppression of vagal tone

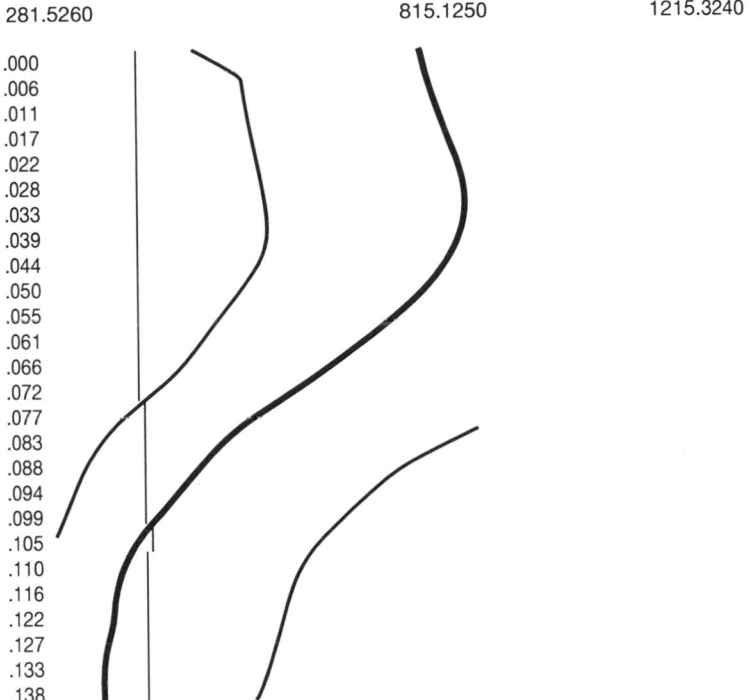

FIG. A.3a.   Subject #121, detrended, with zero point added, spectral density function.

variable, the two computations also were highly correlated across our sample, r = .813, p < .001. However, the new procedure appears to give us both smoother estimates and better definition of peak values. The spectral density functions for our two subjects are presented in Figures A.3a and A.3b.

As can be seen from these graphs, the general shapes of the spectral density functions are maintained under this new procedure, but the peaks are a now bit more sharply defined. With the new calculations, The basal vagal tone during three minutes of the neutral film for subject 121 was 17.13, whereas the basal vagal tone for subject 181 was 16.16.

Figure A.4 shows that these two families were not selected as extreme cases, but they were still very different in both the parent–child and marital interactions. In fact, these differences were so striking, given that these were not extreme families. Family 121 was an African- American family. On the parent–child interaction, Family 121 was quite calm and affectionate toward their daughter. They tended to comment on their daughter's performance on the video game they were teaching her primarily when she did something right, acting as a kind of

251.0440   393.2037   499.8234

FIG. A.3b.   Subject #181, detrended, with zero point added, spectral density function.

VAGAL TONE NEUTRAL FILM

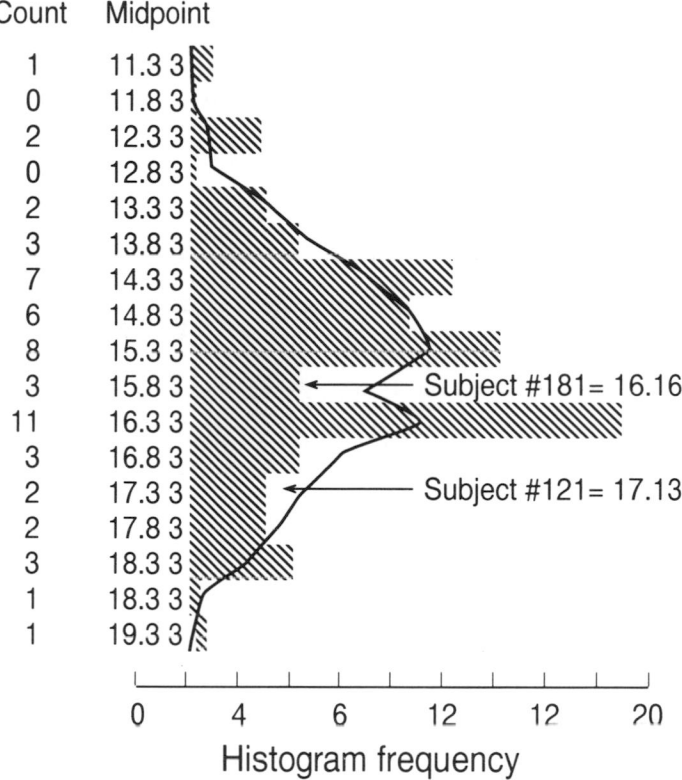

Count	Midpoint
1	11.3 3
0	11.8 3
2	12.3 3
0	12.8 3
2	13.3 3
3	13.8 3
7	14.3 3
6	14.8 3
8	15.3 3
3	15.8 3
11	16.3 3
3	16.8 3
2	17.3 3
2	17.8 3
3	18.3 3
1	18.3 3
1	19.3 3

Subject #181= 16.16

Subject #121= 17.13

Histogram frequency

0   4   6   12   12   20

FIG. A.4.   The two subjects are on either side of the mean, but not extreme.

cheering section. During the marital interaction, they discussed a very difficult issue, the husband's search for a job and their moving to another state. They discussed this issue with humor and affection, discussing their emotional reactions to each other as they went along. Family 181 was a marked contrast. They were a Caucasian family, who, unlike Family 121 commented on their son's performance primarily when he made a mistake, and then the expressed disappointment and criticism. Their marital interaction paralleled their parent–child interaction. The wife wanted the children to receive religious education, and the husband played devil's advocate, attempting to poke holes in her argument with criticism and mockery. She was on the defensive throughout the conversation, the affect was quite negative, and there was no communication about emotion throughout the discussion.

TABLE A.1
Correlations among Vagal Tone Computations across Films,
Using the Zero Point

	Correlations					
	RSA04X	*RSA05X*	*RSA06X*	*RSA07X*	*RSA08X*	*RSA09X*
RSA04X	1.00					
RSA05X	.36**	1.00				
RSA06X	.43***	.65***	1.00			
RSA07X	.45***	.48***	.46***	1.00		
RSA08X	.27*	.65***	.55***	.47***	1.00	
RSA09X	.44***	.50***	.57***	.53***	.56***	1.00

Key to films: 04: neutral; 05 = anger; 06 = fear; 07 = sadness; 08 = disgust; 09 = happy.

Neutral used for basal vagal tone. RSA06X - RSA04X used for suppression of vagal tone.

Correlation of RSA04X with basal vagal tone measure used in this book = .34, $p < .01$.

*$p < .05$. **$p < .01$. ***$p < .001$.

Vagal tone computations using the zero point method across the films were moderate to highly correlated across the films (see Table A.1).

REFERENCES

Achenbach, T. M., & Edelbrock, C. (1983). *Manual for the child behavior checklist and revised child behavior profile*. Burlington, VT: University of Vermont, Department of Psychiatry.

Achenbach, T. M., & Edelbrock, C. (1986). *Manual for the teacher's report form and teacher version of the child behavior profile*. Burlington, VT: University of Vermont, Department of Psychiatry.

Adler, A. (1970). *The education of children*. Chicago: Regnery.

Adorno, T. W., Frenkel-Brunswick, E., Levinson, D. J., & Sanford, R. N. (1950). *The authoritarian personality*. New York: W. W. Norton.

Ainsworth, M. D. S., Bell, S. M., & Stayton, D. J. (1971). Individual differences in the strange situation behavior of one-year-olds. In H. R. Schaffer (Ed.), *The origins of human social relations*. London: Academic Press.

Akselrod, S., Gordon, D., Ubel, F. A., Shannon, D. C., Berger, A. C., & Cohen, R. J. (1982). Power spectrum analysis of heart rate fluctuation: A quantitative probe of beat-to-beat cardiovascular control. *Science, 213*, 220–222.

Allen, B. A., & Armour, T. E. (1993). Construct validation of metacognition. *Journal of Psychology, 127*, 203–211.

Appel, M. A., Holroyd, K. A., & Gorkin, L. (1983). Anger and the etiology and progression of physical illness. In L. Temoshok, C. Van Dyke, & L. S. Zegans (Eds.), *Emotions in health and illness: Theoretical and research foundations* (pp. 73–87). New York: Grune & Stratton.

Arnold, J. E., Levine, A. G., & Patterson, G. R. (1975). Changes in sibling behavior following family intervention. *Journal of Consulting and Clinical Psychology, 43(5)*, 683–688.

Asher, S. R. (1983). Social competence and peer status: Recent advances and future directions. *Child Development, 54(6)*, 1427–1434.

Asher, S. R., & Coie, J. D. (Eds.). (1990). *Peer rejection in childhood*. New York: Cambridge University Press.

Asher, S. R., & Gottman, J. M. (Eds.). (1981). *The development of children's friendships*. New York: Cambridge University Press.

Averill, J. (1982). *Anger and aggression*. New York: Springer-Verlag.

Axelrod, J., & Reisine, T. D. (1984). Stress hormones: Their interaction and regulation. *Science, 224(4648)*, 452–459.

Bakal, D. A. (1992). *Psychology and health, 2nd edition.* New York: Springer-Verlag.

Barclay, D. R., & Houts, A. C. (1995). Parenting skills: A review and developmental analysis of training content. In W. O'Donohue & L. Krasner (Eds.), *Handbook of psychological skills training: Clinical techniques and applications* (pp. 195–228). Boston: Allyn and Bacon.

Bardwick, J. (1979). *In transition: How feminism, sexual liberation, and the search for self-fulfillment have altered America.* New York: Harcourt Brace.

Barnett, R. C., & Marshall, N. L. (1993). Men, family role quality, job role quality, and physical health. *Health Psychology, 12(1),* 48–55.

Barton, K., & Dreger, R. M. (1986). Prediction of marital roles from normal and pathological dimensions of psychology: 16PF and MMPI. *Psychological Reports, 59,* 459–468.

Bates, E. (1979). Intentions, conventions, and symbols. In E. Bates (Ed.), *The emergence of symbols: Cognition and communication in infancy.* New York: Academic Press.

Bates, J. E. (1980). The concept of difficult temperament. *Merrill-Palmer Quarterly, 26,* 299–319.

Baumrind, D. (1967). Child care practices anteceding 3 patterns of preschool behavior. *Genetic Psychology Monographs, 75,* 43–88.

Baumrind, D. (1971). Current patterns of parental authority. *Developmental Psychology Monograph, 1971, 4.*

Baumrind, D. (1987). A developmental perspective on adolescent risk-taking in contemporary America. In C. Irwin (Ed.), *New directions for child development* (Vol. 37, pp. 93–126). San Francisco: Jossey-Bass.

Baumrind, D., & Black, A. E. (1967). Socialization practices associated with dimensions of competence in preschool boys and girls. *Child Development, 38,* 291–327.

Beach, S. R. H., Arias, I., & O'Leary, K. D. (1986). The relationship of marital satisfaction and social support to depressive symptomatology. *Journal of Psychopathology and Behavioral Assessment, 8,* 305–316.

Becker, W. C. (1964). Consequences of different kinds of parental discipline. In M. L. Hoffman & L. W. Hoffman (Eds.), *Review of child development research* (Vol. 1). New York: Russell Sage.

Benes, F. M. (1994). Development of the corticolimbic system. In G. Dawson & K. W. Fischer (Eds.), *Human behavior and the developing brain* (pp. 176–206). New York: Guilford.

Berkman, L. F., & Breslow, L. (1983). *Health and the ways of living: The Alameda County study.* New York: Oxford University Press.

Berkman, L. F., & Syme, S. L. (1979). Social networks, host resistance, and mortality: A nine-year follow-up study of Alameda County residents. *American Journal of Epidemiology, 109,* 186–204.

Berne, R. M., & Levy, M. N. (1987). *Cardiovascular physiology* (4th ed.). St. Louis, MO: C. V. Mosby Company.

Berndt, T. J., & Ladd, G. W. (Eds.). (1989). *Peer relations in child development.* New York: Wiley.

Besag, V. E. (1993). *Bullies and victims in schools.* Philadelphia: Open University Press.

Bhavnagri, N. P., & Parke, R. D. (1991). Parents as direct facilitators of children's peer relationships: Effects of age of child and sex of parent. *Journal of Social and Personal Relationships, 8(3),* 423–440.

Biglan, A., Rothlind, J., & Hops, H. (1989). Impact of distressed and aggressive behavior. *Journal of Abnormal Psychology, 98(3),* 218–228.

Billings, A. (1979). Conflict resolution in distressed and nondistressed couples. *Journal of Consulting and Clinical Psychology, 47,* 368–376.

Birchler, G. (1977, April). *A multimethod analysis of distressed and nondistressed marital interaction: A social learning approach.* Paper presented at the meeting of the Western Psychological Association, Seattle, WA.

Blier, M. J., & Blier-Wilson, W. L. A. (1989). Gender differences in self-rated emotional expressiveness. *Sex Roles, 21,* 287–295.

Block, J. H. (1979). Another look at sex differentiation in the socialization behavior of mothers and fathers. In J. Sherman & F. L. Denmark (Eds.), *Psychology of women: Future directions of research.* New York: Psychological Dimensions.

Block, J., Block, J. H., & Keyes, S. (1988). Longitudinally foretelling drug usage in adolescents: Early childhood personality and environmental precursors. *Child Development, 59(2),* 336–355.

Bloom, B., Asher, S., & White, S. (1978). Marital disruption as a stressor: A review and analysis. *Psychological Bulletin, 85,* 867–894.

Bly, R. (1990). *Iron John: A book about men.* Reading, MA: Addison-Wesley.

Bly, R. (1992). The hunger for the king in a time with no father. In C. Scull (Ed.), *Fathers, sons, and daughters* (pp. 60–71). New York: Putnam.

Booth, C. L., Rose-Krasnor, L., & Rubin, K. H. (1991). Relating preschoolers' social competence and their mothers' parenting behaviors to early attachment security and high-risk status. *Journal of Social and Personal Relationships, 8(3),* 363–382.

Booth, A., & White, L. (1980). Thinking about divorce. *Journal of Marriage and the Family, 42,* 605–616.

Bracke, P. E. (1986). Parental child-rearing practices and the development of Type A behavior in children. *Dissertation Abstracts International, 46,* June, Vol (12-B-Pt 1), 4421.

Brazelton, T. B., Koslowski, B., & Main, M. (1974). The origins of reciprocity: The early mother–infant interaction. In M. Lewis & L. A. Rosenblum (Eds.), *The effect of the infant on its caregiver* (pp. 49–76). New York: Wiley.

Brett, D. (1988). *Annie stories.* New York: Workman Publishing Co.

Brett, J. M., Stroh, L. K., & Reilly, A. H. (1993). Pulling up roots in the 1990s: Who's willing to relocate? *Journal of Organizational Behavior, 14,* 49–60.

Briggs, J. L. (1970). *Never in anger.* Cambridge, MA: Harvard University Press.

Brinton-Lee, M. C. (1980). *The determinants of group dissolution: A study of divorce rates in contemporary Japan.* Masters thesis, University of Washington, Seattle, WA.

Brody, G. H., & Shaffer, D. R. (1982). Contributions of parents and peers to children's moral socialization. *Developmental Review, 2(1),* 31–75.

Broel-Plateris, A. (1961). *Marriage disruption of divorce law.* Chicago: University of Chicago Press.

Brooks, L. D., Spearn, R. C., Rice, M., & Crocco, D. (1988). Systematic training for effective parenting (STEP): And evaluative study with a Canadian population. *Canada's Mental Health, 36(4),* 2–5.

Brown, P. C., & Smith, T. W. (1992). Social influence, marriage and the heart: Cardiovascular consequences of interpersonal control in husbands and wives. *Health Psychology, 1(2),* 88–96.

Buckhult, J. A., Rutherford, R. B., & Goldberg, K. E. (1978). Verbal and nonverbal interaction of mothers with their Down syndrome and nonretarded infants. *American Journal of Mental Deficiency, 82,* 337–343.

Buehlman, K. (1996). The oral history coding system. In J. Gottman (Eds.), *What predicts divorce? The measures.* Mahwah, NJ: Lawrence Erlbaum Associates.

Buehlman, K., Gottman, J. M., & Katz, L. (1992). How a couple views their past predicts their future: Predicting divorce from an oral history interview. *Journal of Family Psychology, 5,* 295–318.

Bugental, D. E., Love, L. R., & Gianetto, R. M. (1971). Perfidious feminine faces. *Journal of Personality and Social Psychology, 23,* 314–318.

Bulloch, K., & Pomerantz, W. (1984). Autonomic nervous system innervation of thymic-related lymphoid tissue in wildtype and nude mice. *Journal of Comparative Neurology,* 228(1), 57–68.

Bulloch, K., & Moore, R. Y. (1981). Innervation of the thymus gland by brain stem and spinal cord in mouse and rat. *American Journal of Anatomy, 162(2),* 157–66.

Burgess, E. W., & Locke, H. J. (1945). *The family, from institution to companionship.* New York: American Book.

Burman, B., & Margolin, G. (1992). Analysis of the association between marital relationships and health problems. *Psychological Bulletin, 112,* 39–63.

Buss, A. H., & Plomin, R. (1984). *Temperament: Early developing personality traits.* Hillsdale, NJ: Lawrence Erlbaum Associates.

Bvinelli, D. J. (1993). Reconstructing the evolution of mind. *American Psychologist, 48,* 493–509.

Cacioppo, J. T., & Tassinary, L. G. (Eds.). (1990). *Principles of psychophysiology: Physical, social, and inferential elements.* New York: Cambridge University Press.

Campos, J. J., & Sternberg, C. R. (1981). Perception, appraisal, and emotion: The onset of social referencing. In M. E. Lamb & L. R. Sherrod (Eds.), *Infants social cognition: Empirical and social considerations.* Hillsdale, NJ: Lawrence Erlbaum Associates.

Cannon, W. B. (1914). The interrelations of emotions as suggested by recent physiological research. *American Journal of Psychology, 25,* 256–282.

Carstensen, L. L., Gottman, J. M., & Levenson, R. W. (1995). Emotional behavior in long-term marriage. *Psychology and Aging, 10,* 140–149.

Case, R., Haywood, S., Lewis, M., & Hurst, P. (1988). Toward a neo-Piagetian theory of cognitive and emotional development. *Developmental Review, 8(1),* 1–51.

Cassidy, J., Parke, R. D., Butkovsky, L., & Braungart, J. M. (1992). Family-peer connections: the role of emotional expressiveness within the family and children's understanding of emotion. *Child Development, 63,* 603–618.

Census of Population and Housing, 1990: Guide. (1990). New York: Diane Publishing Co.

Center for the Study of Social Policy. (1992). *The challenge of change: What the 1990 Census tells us about children.* Washington, DC: Author.

Chadwick, B. A., & Heston, T. (1992). *Statistical handbook on the American family.* New York: Oryx Press.

Chase, B. N. (1982). *Discipline them, love them.* Elgin, IL: David Cook Publishing Co.

Cherlin, A. (1981). *Marriage, divorce, remarriage.* Cambridge, MA: Harvard University Press.

Chester, R., & Kooy, G. A. (1977). *Divorce in Europe.* Leiden: Martinus Nijhoff Social Sciences Division.

Christensen, A. (1987). Detection of conflict patterns in couples. In K. Hahlweb & M. J. Goldstein (Eds.), *Understanding major mental disorder: The contribution of family interaction research* (pp. 250–265). New York: Family Process Press.

Christensen, A. (1988). Dysfunctional interaction patterns in couples. In P. Noller & M. A. Fitzpatrick (Eds.), *Perspectives on marital interaction* (pp. 31–52). Avon, England: Multilingual Matters.

Christensen, A. (1990). Gender and social structure in the demand/withdrawal pattern of marital conflict. *Journal of Personality and Social Psychology, 59,* 73–81.

Christensen, A. (1991). *The demand withdraw pattern in marital interaction.* Paper presented at the annual meeting of the Association for the Advancement of Behavior Therapy, New York.

Christensen, A., & Heavey, C. L. (1990). Gender and social structure in the demand/withdraw pattern. *Journal of Personality and Social Psychology, 59(1),* 73–81.

Christensen, A., & Shenk, J. L. (1991). Communication, conflict, and psychological distance in distressed, clinic, and divorcing couples. *Journal of Consulting and Clinical Psychology, 59(3),* 458–463.

Church, P., Forehand, R., Brown, C., & Holmes, T. (1990). Prevention of drug abuse: Examination of the effectiveness of a program with elementary school children. *Behavior Therapy, 21(3),* 339–347.

Cohn, D. A., Cowan, P. A., Cowan, C. P., & Pearson, J. (1992). Mothers' and fathers' working models of childhood attachment relationships, parenting styles, and child behavior. *Development and Psychopathology, 4,* 417–431.

Cohn, D. A., Cowan, P. A., Cowan, C. P., & Pearson, J. (1992). Mothers' and fathers' working models of childhood attachment relationships, parenting styles, and child behavior. *Development and Psychopathology, 4(3)*, 417–431.

Cohn, D. A., Patterson, C. J., & Christopoulos, C. (1991). The family and children's peer relationships. *Journal of Social and Personal Relationships, 8(3)*, 315–346.

Cohn, J. F., & Tronick, E. Z. (1983). Three-month-old infants' reaction to simulated maternal depression. *Child Development, 54*, 185–193.

Cohn, J. F., & Tronick, E. Z. (1989). Specificity of infants' response to mothers' affective behavior. *Journal of the American Academy of Child and Adolescent Psychiatry, 28(2)*, 242–248.

Cook, J., Tyson, R., White, J., Rushe, R., Gottman, J., & Murray, J. (1995). The mathematics of marital conflict. *Journal of Family Psychology, 9*, 110–130.

Corsaro, W. (1979). We're friends, right?: Children's use of access rituals in a nursery school. *Language in Society, 8*, 315–336.

Corsaro, W. (1981). Friendship in the nursery school: Social organization in the peer environment. In S. Asher & J. M. Gottman (Eds.), *The development of children's friendships.* New York: Cambridge University Press.

Costenbader, V. K., & Adams, J. W. (1991). A review of the psychometric and administrative features of the PIAT-R: Implications for the practitioner. *Journal of School Psychology, 29*, 219–228.

Cowan, P. A., & Cowan, C. P. (1982). *The parent–child interaction coding system.* Unpublished manuscript, University of California, Berkeley.

Cowan, P. A., & Cowan, C. P. (1987, April). *Couple's relationships, parenting styles and the child's development at three.* Paper presented at the Society for Research in Child Development, Baltimore, MD.

Cowan, P. A., & Cowan, C. P. (1990). Becoming a family: Research and intervention. In I. Sigel & A. Brody (Eds.), *Family research.* Hillsdale, NJ: Lawrence Erlbaum Associates.

Cowan, C. P., & Cowan, P. A. (1992). *When parents become partners.* New York: Basic Books.

Crosbie, J. (1993). Interrupted time-series analysis with brief single-subject data. *Journal of Consulting and Clinical Psychology, 61(6)*, 966–974.

Crosbie, J., & Sharpley, C. F. (1989). DMITSA: A simplified interrupted time-series program. *Behavior Research Methods, Instruments, and Computers, 21(6)*, 639–642.

Cummings, E. M. (1987). Coping with background anger in early childhood. *Child Development, 58*, 876–984.

Cummings, E. M., & Davies, P. (1994). *Children and marital conflict: The impact of family dispute revolution.* New York: Guilford.

Cummings, E. M., Iannotti, R. J., & Zahn-Waxler, C. (1985). Influence of conflict between adults on the emotions and aggression of young children. *Developmental Psychology, 21*, 495–507.

Cummings, E. M., Zahn-Waxler, C., & Radke-Yarrow, M. (1981). Young children's responses to expressions of anger and affection by others in the family. *Child Development, 52*, 1274–1282.

Damon, W. (1983). The nature of social-cognitive change in the developing child. In W. F. Overton (Ed.), *The relationship between social and cognitive development* (pp. 103–141). Hillsdale, NJ: Lawrence Erlbaum Associates.

Davidson, R. J. (1984). Affect, cognition, and hemispheric specialization. In C. E. Izard, J. Kagan, & R. Zajonc (Eds.), *Emotions, cognition, and behavior* (pp. 320–365). New York: Cambridge University Press.

Davidson, R. J. (1992). Anterior cerrebral asymmetry and the nature of emotion. *Brain and Cognition, 20*, 215–151.

Davidson, R. J. (1994a). Asymmetric brain function, affective style, and psychopathology: The role of early experience and plasticity. Special Issue: Neural plasticity, sensitive periods, and psychopathology. *Development and Psychopathology, 6*, 741–758.

Davidson, R. J. (1994b). Temperament, affective style, and frontal lobe asymmetry. In G. Dawson &

K. W. Fischer (Eds.), *Human behavior and the developing brain* (pp. 518–536). New York: Guilford.

Davidson, R. J., & Fox, N. A. (1982). Asymmetrical brain activity discriminates between positive versus negative affective stimuli in human infants. *Science, 218,* 1235–1237.

Davidson, R. J., & Tomarken, A. J. (1989). Laterality and emotion: An electrophysiological approach. In F. Boller & J. Grafman (Eds.), *Handbook of neuropsychology,* (Vol. 3, pp. 419–441). Amsterdam: Elsevier.

Day, D. E., & Roberts, M. W. (1983). An analysis of the physical punishment component of a parent training program. *Journal of Abnormal Child Psychology, 11(1),* 141–152.

de-Boeck, P. (1976). An alternative factor solution to the mother's form of the Parental Attitude Research Instrument and the relationship of PARI factors with social class. *Journal of Psychology, 94(1),* 79–86.

DeGangi, G. A., DiPietro, J. A., Greenspan, S. I., & Porges, S. W. (1991). Psychophysiological characteristics of the regulatory disordered infant. *Infant Behavior and Development, 14,* 37–50.

DeHaas, P. A., & Young, R. D. (1984). Attention styles of hyperactive and normal girls. *Journal of Abnormal Child Psychology, 12(4),* 531–545.

Deley, W. W. (1988). Physical punishment of children: Sweden and the U.S.A. *Journal of Comparative Family Studies, 19(3),* 419–431.

deMausse, L. (1974). The evolution of childhood. In L. deMausse (Ed.), *The history of childhood* (pp. 1–74). New York: Harper & Row.

Dennenberg, V. H., & Rosenberg, K. M. (1967). Nongenetic transmission of information. *Nature, 216,* 549–550.

Dickstein, S., & Parke, R. D. (1988). Social referencing in infancy: A glance at fathers and marriage. *Child Development, 59,* 506–511.

DiPietro, J. A., Larson, S. K., & Porges, S. W. (1987). Behavioral and heart rate pattern differences between breast-fed and bottle-fed neonates. *Developmental Psychology, 23,* 467–474.

DiPietro, J. A., & Porges, S. W. (1991). Relations between neonatal states and 8-month developmental outcome in preterm infants. *Infant Behavior and Development, 14,* 441–450.

DiPietro, J. A., Porges, S. W., & Uhly, B. (1992). Reactivity and developmental competence in preterm and full-term infants. *Developmental Psychology, 28,* 831–841.

Dinkmeyer, D., & McKay, G. (1976). *Systematic training for effective parenting.* Circle Pines, MN: American Guidance Service.

Dishion, T. J., Patterson, G. R., Stoolmiller, M., & Skinner, M. L. (1991). Family, school, and behavioral antecedents to early adolescent involvement with antisocial peers. *Developmental Psychology, 27(1),* 172–180.

Dixon, S., Tronick, E., Keefer, C., & Brazelton, T. B. (1981). Mother–infant interaction among the Gusii of Kenya. In T. M. Field, A. M. Sostek, P. Vietze, & P. H. Liederman (Eds.), *Culture and early interaction* (pp. 149–168). Hillsdale, NJ: Lawrence Erlbaum Associates

Dobson, H. (1992). *The new dare to discipline.* Wheaton, IL: Tyndale House.

Dodge, K. A., McClaskey, C. L., & Feldman, E. (1985). A situational approach to the assessment of social competence in children. *Journal of Consulting and Clinical Psychology, 53,* 334–353.

Dodge, K. A., Schlundt, D. G., Schocken, I., & Delugach, J. D. (1983). Social competence and children's social status: The role of peer group entry strategies. *Merrill-Palmer Quarterly, 29,* 309–336.

Doherty, W. J. (1995). The vanishing American father. In W. J. O'Neill, Jr. (Ed.), *Family: The first imperative* (pp. 77–86). Cleveland, OH: The William J. and Dorothy K. Oneill Foundation.

Downey, A. M., Cresanta, J. L., & Berenson, G. S. (1989). Cardiovascular health promotion in children: "Heart smart" and the changing role of physicians. *American Journal of Preventive Medicine, 5,* 279–295.

Dreikurs, R. (1964). *Children: The challenge.* New York: Plume.

Dunn, J. (1977). *Distress and comfort.* Cambridge, MA: Harvard University Press.

Dutton, D. (1988). *The domestic assault of women: Psychological and criminal justice perspectives.* New York: Allyn & Bacon.

Easterbrooks, M. A. (1987, April). *Early family development: Longitudinal impact of marital quality.* Paper presented at the Meeting of the Society for Research in Child Development, Baltimore, MD.

Eisenberg, N., & Strayer, J. (Eds.). (1987). *Empathy and its development.* New York: Cambridge University Press.

Ekman, P. (1984). Expression and the nature of emotion. In K. R. Scherer & P. Ekman (Eds.), *Approaches to emotion* (pp. 319–344). Hillsdale, NJ: Lawrence Erlbaum Associates.

Ekman, P., & Friesen, W. V. (1978). *Facial Action Coding System.* Palo Alto, CA: Consulting Psychologist Press.

Ekman, P., Friesen, W. V., & Simons, R. C. (1985). Is the startle reaction an emotion? *Journal of Personality and Social Psychology, 49(5),* 1416–1426.

Ekman, P., Levenson, R. W., & Friesen, W. V. (1983). Autonomic nervous system activity distinguishes among emotions. *Science, 221,* 1208–1210.

Emery, R. E., & O'Leary, K. D. (1982). Children's perceptions of marital discord and behavior problems of boys and girls. *Journal of Abnormal Child Psychology, 10,* 11–24.

Esler, M., Julius, S., Zweiffer, A., Randall, O., Harburg, E., Gardiner, H., & DeQuattro, V. (1977). Mild high-renin essential hypertension: Neurogenic human hypertension? *New England Journal of Medicine, 296,* 405–411.

Esters, P., & Levant, R. F. (1983). The effects of two parent counseling programs on rural low-achieving children. *The School Counselor, 31(2),* 159–166.

Eysenck, M. W. (1982). *Attention and arousal: Cognition and performance.* New York: Springer-Verlag.

Faber, A., & Mazlich, E. (1974). *Liberated parents, liberated children: Your guide to a happier family.* New York: Avon Books.

Faber, A., & Mazlich, E. (1980). *How to talk so kids will listen & listen so kids will talk.* New York: Avon Books.

Faber, A., & Mazlich, E. (1987). *Siblings without rivalry.* New York: Avon Books.

Fauber, R., Forehand, R., Thomas, A. M., & Wierson, M. (1990). A mediational model of the impact of marital conflict on adolescent adjustment in intact and divorced families: The role of disrupted parenting. *Child Development, 61(4),* 1112–1123.

Feldman, M. A., Case, L., Rincover, A., & Tower, F. (1989). Parent education project III: Increasing affection and responsivity in developmentally handicapped mothers: Component analysis, generalization, and effects on child language. *Journal of Applied Behavior Analysis, 22(2),* 211–222.

Fendrich, M., Warner, V., & Weissman, M. M. (1990). Family risk factors, parental depression, and psychopathology in offspring. *Developmental Psychology, 26,* 40–50.

Feshbach, N. D., & Feshbach, S. (1987). Affective processes and academic achievement. *Child Development, 58(5),* 1335–1347.

Field, T. (1995). Infants of depressed mothers (International Society for Infant Studies). *Infant Behavior & Development, 18,* 1–13.

Field, T., Healy, B., Goldstein, S., & Perry, S. (1988). Infants of depressed mothers show "depressed" behavior even with nondepressed adults. *Child Development, 59,* 1569–1579.

Field, T., Healy, B. T., & LeBlanc, W. G. (1989). Sharing and synchrony of behavior states and heart rate in nondepressed versus depressed mother–infant interactions. *Infant Behavior and Development, 12,* 357–376.

Field, T., & Fogel, A. (Eds.). (1988). *Emotion and early interaction.* Hillsdale, NJ: Lawrence Erlbaum Associates.

Field, T., Fox, N. A., Pickens, J., & Nawrocki, T. (1995). Relative right frontal EEG activation in 3- to 6-month-old infants of "depressed" mothers. Special section: Parental depression and distress:

Implications for development in infancy, childhood, and adolescence. *Developmental Psychology, 31,* 358–363.

Field, T., Pickens, J., Fox, N. A., Nawrocki, T., et al. (1995). Vagal tone in infants of depressed mothers. *Development and Psychopathology, 7,* 227–231.

Fine, G. A. (1987). *With the boys.* Chicago: University of Chicago Press.

Fisher, P. A., & Fagot, B. I. (1993). Negative discipline in families: A multidimensional risk model. *Journal of Family Psychology, 7(2),* 250–254.

Fivush, R. (1991). Gender and emotion in mother–child conversations about the past. *Journal of Narrative and Life History, 1(4),* 325–341.

Flavell, J. H. (1979). Metacognition and cognitive monitoring: A new area of cognitive-developmental inquiry. *American Psychologist, 34,* 906–911.

Fodor, J. A. (1992). A theory of the child's theory of mind. *Cognition, 44,* 283–296.

Forehand, R., Breiner, J., McMahon, R. J., & Davies, G. (1981). Predictors of cross setting behavior change in the treatment of child problems. *Journal of Behavior Therapy and Experimental Psychiatry, 12(4),* 311–313.

Forehand, R., Brody, G., Long, N., Slotkin, J., & Fauber, R. (1986). Divorce/divorce potential and interparental conflict: The relationship to early adolescent social and cognitive functioning. *Journal of Adolescent Research, 1,* 389–397.

Forehand, R., Furey, W. M., & McMahon, R. J. (1984). The role of maternal distress in a parent training program to modify child non-compliance. *Behavioural Psychotherapy, 12(2),* 93–108.

Forehand, R. L., & McMahon, R. J. (1981). *Helping the noncompliant child.* New York: Guilford.

Fox, N. A. (1989). The psychophysiological correlates of emotional reaactivity during the first year of life. *Developmental Psychology, 25,* 364–372.

Fox, N. A. (Ed.). (1994). The development of emotion regulation: Biological and behavioral considerations. *Monographs of the Society for Research in Child Development, 59*(240).

Fox, N. A., & Davidson, R. J. (1986). Taste-elicited changes in facial signs of emotion and the asymmetry of brain electrical activity in human newborns. *Neuropsychologia, 24,* 417–422.

Fox, N. A., & Field, T. M. (1989). Individual differences in preschool entry behavior. *Journal of Applied Developmental Psychology, 10,* 527–540.

Franz, C. E., McClelland, D. C., & Weinberger, J. (1991). Childhood antecedents of conventional social accomplishment in midlife adults: A 36-year prospective study. *Journal of Personality and Social Psychology, 60(4),* 586–595.

Friedman, H. S., Tucker, J. S., Schwartz, J. E., & Tomilson, K. C. (1995). Psychosocial and behavioral predictors of longevity: The aging and death of the "Termites." *American Psychologist, 50,* 69–78.

Frodi, A., Macauley, J., & Thome, P. R. (1977). Are women always less agressive than men? A review of experimental literature. *Psychological Bulletin, 84,* 634–660.

Furey, W. M., & Forehand, R. (1983). Maternal satisfaction with clinic-referred children. *Journal of Behavioral Assessment, 5(4),* 345–355.

Furey, W. M., & Forehand, R. (1986). What factors are associated with mothers' evaluation of their clinic-referred children? *Child and Family Behavior Therapy, 8(1),* 21–42.

Galsworthy, J. (1951). *The man of property.* Harmondsworth, Middlesex, England: Penguin Books.

Garber, J., & Dodge, K. A. (Eds.). (1991). *The development of emotion regulation and dysregulation.* New York: Cambridge University Press.

Gelles, R. J., & Edfeldt, A. W. (1986). Violence towards children in the United States and Sweden. *Child Abuse and Neglect, 10(4),* 501–510.

Gellhorn, E., & Loofbourrow, G. N. (1963). *Emotion and emotional disorders: A neurophysiological study.* New York: Harper & Row.

Gessel, A. (1940). *The first five years of life.* New York: Harper.

Gessel, A. (1946). *The child from five to ten*. New York: Harper.

Gessel, A. (1948). *Studies in child development*. New York: Harper.

Gessel, A. (1956). *Youth: The years from ten to sixteen*. New York: Harper.

Gianino, A., & Tronick, E. Z. (1988). The mutual regulation model: The infant's self and interactive regulation and coping and defensive capacities. In T. M. Field, P. M. McCabe, & N. Schneiderman (Eds.), *Stress and coping across development* (pp. 47–70). Hillsdale, NJ: Lawrence Erlbaum Associates.

Gilmore, J., & Gilmore, E. C. (1978). *Developing the productive child*. Boston: The Gilmore Institute.

Ginott, H. G. (1971). *Between parent and teenager*. New York: Avon Books.

Ginott, H. G. (1975). *Teacher and child*. New York: Avon Books.

Ginott, H. G. (1994). *Between parent and child*. New York: Avon Books. (Original work published 1965)

Goldenberg, I. (1971). Social class differences in teacher attitudes toward children. *Child Development, 42(5),* 1637–1640.

Gordon, T. (1970). *Parent effectiveness training*. New York: Penguin.

Gordon, R. M., & Rosen, A. (1984). Adlerian parent study groups and inner-city children. *Individual Psychology: Journal of Adlerian Theory, Research and Practice, 40(3),* 309–316.

Gottman, J. (1979). *Marital interaction: Experimental investigations*. New York: Academic Press.

Gottman, J. (1981). *Times-series analysis: A comprehensive introduction for social scientists*. New York: Cambridge University Press.

Gottman, J. M. (1983). How children become friends. *Monographs of the Society for Research in Child Development, 48* (2, Serial No. 201).

Gottman, J. M. (1986). The observation of social process. In J. Gottman and J. Parker (Eds.), *The conversations of friends*. New York: Cambridge University Press.

Gottman, J. M. (1993a). The roles of conflict engagement, escalation, or avoidance in marital interaction: A longitudinal view of five types of couple. *Journal of Consulting and Clinical Psychology, 61,* 6–15.

Gottman, J. M. (1993b). A theory of marital dissolution and stability. *Journal of Family Psychology, 7(1),* 57–75.

Gottman, J. M. (1994). *What predicts divorce?* Hillsdale, NJ: Lawrence Erlbaum Associates.

Gottman, J. M. (Ed.). (1996). *What predicts divorce?: The measures*. Mahwah, NJ: Lawrence Erlbaum Associates.

Gottman, J. M. (with J. De Claire). (1997). *The heart of parenting*. New York: Simon and Schuster.

Gottman, J. M., & Katz, L. F. (1989). The effects of marital discord on young children's peer interaction and health. *Developmental Psychology, 25,* 373–381.

Gottman, J. M., & Krokoff, L. (1989). Marital interaction and satisfaction: A longitudinal view. *Journal of Consulting and Clinical Psychology, 57,* 47–52.

Gottman, J. M., & Levenson, R. W. (1985). A valid procedure for obtaining self-report of affect in marital interaction. *Journal of Consulting and Clinical Psychology, 53,* 151–160.

Gottman, J. M., & Levenson, R. W. (1988). The social psychophysiology of marriage. In P. Noller and M. A. Fitzpatrick (Eds.), *Perspectives on marital interaction*. Philadelphia: Multilingual Matters.

Gottman, J. M., & Levenson, R. W. (1992). Marital processes predictive of later dissolution: Behavior, physiology and health. *Journal of Personality and Social Psychology, 63,* 221–233.

Gottman, J., Markman, J., & Notarius, C. (1977). The topography of marital conflict. A sequential analysis of verbal and nonverbal behavior. *Journal of Marriage and the Family, 39,* 461–477.

Gottman, J. M., & Parker, J. (Eds.). (1986). *Conversations of friends*. New York: Cambridge University Press.

Grossman, P., Karemaker, J., & Wieling, W. (1991). Prediction of tonic parasympathetic cardiac control using respiratory sinus arrhythmia: The need for respiratory control. *Psychophysiology, 28(2)*, 201–216.

Grossman, P., Van Beek, J., & Wientjes, C. (1990). A comparison of three quantification methods for estimation of respiratory sinus arrhythmia. *Psychophysiology, 27(6)*, 702–714.

Graudenz, I., Kraak, B., & Haver, D. (1976). Scale to measure child-rearing practices and attitudes of mothers of five to six year old preschool children. *Psychologie in Erziehung and Unterricht, 23(2)*, 70–79.

Graziano, A. M., & Namaste, K. A. (1990). Parental use of physical force in child discipline: A survey of 679 college students. *Journal of Interpersonal Violence, 5(4)*, 449–463.

Greenberg, M., Kusche, D. A., & Speltz, M. (1991). In D. Cicchetti & S. Toth (Eds.), *Rochester Symposium on Developmental Psychopathology* (Vol. 2). New York: Cambridge University Press.

Greenspan, S. I., & Porges, S. W. (1984). Psychopathology in infancy and early childhood: Clinical perspectives on the organization of sensory and affective-thematic experience. *Child Development, 55(1)*, 49–70.

Greven, P. J., Jr. (1973). *Child rearing: Historical sources*. Itasca, IL: F. E. Peacock Publishers.

Grodzinsky, G. M., & Diamond, R. (1992). Frontal lobe functioning in boys with attention deficit hyperactivity disorder. *Developmental Neuropsychology, 8*, 427–445.

Gross, J. A., & Levenson, R. W. (1993). Emotional suppression: Physiology, self-report, and expressive behavior. *Journal of Personality and Social Psychology, 64*, 970–986.

Grossman, P., Karemaker, J., & Wieling, W. (1991). Prediction of tonic parasympathetic cardiac control using respiratory sinus arrhythmia: The need for respiratory control. *Psychophysiology, 28(2)*, 201–216.

Grych, J. H., & Fincham, F. D. (1990). Marital conflict and children's adjustment: A cognitive-contextual framework. *Psychological Bulletin, 108(2)*, 267–290.

Gunnar, M. R. (1989). Studies of the human infant's adrenocortical response to potentially stressful events. *New Directions in Child Development, 45*, 3–18.

Gunnar, M. R., Connors, J., Isensee, J., & Wall, L. (1988). Adrenocortical activity and behavioral distress in human newborns. *Developmental Psychology, 21(4)*, 297–310.

Guralnick, M. J. (1981). Peer influences on the development of communicative competence. In P. Strain (Ed.), *The utilization of classroom peers as behavior change agents* (pp. 31–68). New York: Plenum.

Halberstadt, A. G. (1985). Race, socioeconomic status, and nonverbal behavior. In A. Siegman & S. Feldstein (Eds.), *Nonverbal communication and interpersonal relations* (pp. 227–266). Hillsdale, NJ: Lawrence Erlbaum Associates.

Halberstadt, A. G. (1991). Toward an ecology of expressiveness: Family socialization in particular and a model in general. In R. S. Feldman & B. Rime (Eds.), *Fundamentals of nonverbal behavior* (pp. 106–160). New York: Cambridge University Press.

Halberstadt, A. G., Fox, N. A., & Jones, N. A. (1993). Do expressive mothers have expressive children? The role of socialization in children's affect expression. *Social Development, 2*, 48–65.

Harburg, E., Julius, S., McGinn, N. F., McLeod, J., & Hoobler, S. W. (1964). Personality traits and behavioral patterns associated with systolic blood pressure levels in college males. *Journal of Chronic Disease, 17*, 405–414.

Haviland, J. M., & Kramer, D. A. (1991). Affect-cognition relationships in adolescent diaries: The case of Anne Frank. *Human Development, 34(3)*, 143–159.

Haynes, S. N., Follingstad, D. R., & Sullivan, J. C. (1979). Assessment of marital satisfaction and interaction. *Journal of Consulting and Clinical Psychology, 47*, 789–791.

Heavey, C. L., Layne, C., & Christensen, A. (1993). Gender and conflict structure in marital interaction: A replication and extension. *Journal of Consulting and Clinical Psychology, 61*, 16–27.

Henry, J. P. (1986). Neuroendocrine patterns of emotional response. In R. Plutchik & H. Kellermany

(Eds.), *Emotion, theory and research, Vol 3: Biological foundations of emotion* (pp. 37–607). London: Academic Press.

Henry, J. P., & Meehan, J. (1981). Psychosocial stimuli, physiological specificity, and cardiovascular disease. In A. Weiner, M. Hofer, & A. Stunkard (Eds.), *Brain behavior and bodily disease* (pp. 131–142). New York: Raven.

Henry, J. P., & Stephens, P. M. (1977). *Stress, health, and the social environment.* New York: Springer-Verlag.

Hesiod. (1993). *Words and days.* S. Lombardo (Trans.). Indianapolis, IN: Hackett Publishing Company.

Hetherington, E. M., Cox, M., & Cox, R. (1978). The aftermath of divorce. In J. H. Stevens, Jr. & M. Matthews (Eds.), *Mother–child, father–child relations.* Washington, DC: National Association for the Education of Young Children.

Hetherington, E. M., Cox, M., & Cox, R. (1982). Effects of divorce on parents and children. In M. Lamb (Ed.), *Nontraditional families* (pp. 233–288). Hillsdale, NJ: Lawrence Erlbaum Associates.

Hite, S. (1987). *The Hite report: Women and love—a cultural revolution in progress.* New York: Knopf.

Hochschild, A. R. (1983). *The managed heart: The commercialization of human feeling.* Berkeley, CA: University of California Press.

Hofheimer, J. A., & Lawson, N. (1988). Neurophysiological correlates of interactive behavior in preterm newborns. *Infant Behavior and Development, 11,* 143.

Hollos, M. (1975). Logical operations and role-taking abilities in two cultures: Norway and Hungary. *Child Development, 46(3),* 638–649.

Hollos, M., & Cowan, P. A. (1973). Social isolation and cognitive development: Logical operations and role-taking in three Norwegian social settings. *Child Development, 44,* 630–641.

Holmes, T. H., & Rahe, R. H. (1967). The social readjustment rating scale. *Journal of Psychosomatic Research, 11,* 213–218.

Holroyd, K. A., & Gorkin, L. (1983). Young adults at risk for hypertension: Effects of family history and anger management in determining responses to interpersonal conflict. *Journal of Psychosomatic Research, 27,* 131–138.

Hops, H., Biglan, A., Sherman, L., & Arthur, J. (1987). Home observations of family interactions of depressed women. *Journal of Consulting and Clinical Psychology, 55(3),* 341–346.

Hooven, C. (1994). *The meta-emotion coding system.* Unpublished manuscript, University of Washington, Seattle, WA.

Hooven, C., Gottman, J. M., & Katz, L. F. (1995). Parental meta-emotion structure predicts family and child outcomes. *Cognition and Emotion, 9,* 229–264.

Howes, P., & Markman, J. J. (1989). Marital quality and child functioning: A longitudinal investigation. *Child Development, 60,* 1044–1051.

Huffman, L. C., Bryan, Y. E., Pederson, F. A., & Porges, S. W. (1988). *Infant temperament: Relationships with heart rate variability.* Unpublished manuscript, National Institute of Mental Health, Rockville, MD.

Huffman, L. C., Bryan, Y. E., Pederson, F. A., & Porges, S. W. (1992). *Autonomic correlates of reactivity and self-regulation at twelve weeks of age.* Unpublished manuscript, National Institute of Mental Health, Rockville, MD.

Information Please Almanac. (1992). New York: Houghton Mifflin.

Izard, C. E. (1982). *Measuring emotions in infants and children.* New York: Cambridge University Press.

Izard, C. E., Porges, S. W., Simons, R. F., & Haynes, O. M. (1991). Infant cardiac activity: Developmental changes and relations with attachment. *Developmental Psychology, 27,* 432–439.

Jacobs, S., & Ostfeld, A. (1977). An epidemiological review of the mortality of bereavement. *Psychosomatic Medicine, 39,* 344–357.

Jacobson, N. S., Gottman, J. M., Waltz, J., Rushe, R., & Babcock, N. (1994). Affect, verbal content, and psychophysiology in the arguments of couples with a violent husband. *Journal of Consulting and Clinical Psychology, 62(5)*, 982–988.

Johnson, D. J., & Rusbult, C. E. (1989). Resisting temptation: Devaluation of alternative partners as a means of maintaining commitment in close relationships. *Journal of Personality and Social Psychology, 57(6)*, 967–980.

Jones, O. H. M. (1977). Mother–child communication with pre-linguistic Down syndrome and normal infants. In H. R. Schaffer (Ed.), *Studies in mother–infant interaction*. London: Academic Press.

Jones, O. H. M. (1980). Prelinguistic communication skills in Down syndrome and normal infants. In T. Field, D. Goldberg, D. Stern, & Y. A. Sostek (Eds.), *High-risk infants and children: Interactions with adults and peers*. New York: Academic Press.

Jordan, T. C. (1970). The influence of age and social class on authoritarian family ideology. *Multivariate Behavioral Research, 5(2)*, 193–201.

Kagan, J., Reznick, J. S., & Snidman, N. (1988). The physiology and psychology of behavioral inhibition in children. *Annual Progress in Child Psychiatry and Child Development, 22*, 102–127.

Kagan, J., Reznick, J. S., & Snidman, N., & Gibbers, J. (1988). Childhood derivatives of inhibition and lack of inhibition to the unfamiliar. *Child Development, 59(6)*, 1580–1589.

Kahneman, D. (1973). *Attention and effort*. Englewood Cliffs, NJ: Prentice-Hall.

Karoly, P. (Ed.). (1988). *Handbook of child health assessment: Biopsychosocial perspectives*. New York: Wiley.

Katz, L. F., & Gottman, J. M. (1986). *The meta-emotion interview*. Unpublished manual. University of Washington, Department of Psychology, Seattle, WA

Katz, L. F., & Gottman, J. M. (1991). *The meta-emotion interview*. Unpublished research manual, University of Washington, Department of Psychology, Seattle, WA.

Katz, L. F., & Gottman, J. M. (1993). Patterns of marital conflict predict children's internalizing and externalizing behaviors. *Developmental Psychology, 29(6)*, 940–950.

Katz, L. F., & Gottman, J. M. (1995). *Marital interaction and its effects on mothers and fathers*. Paper presented at the meeting of the Society for Research in Child Development, Indianapolis, IN.

Kellam, S. G. (1994). The social adaptation of children in classrooms: A measure of family childrearing affectiveness. In R. D. Parke & S. G. Kellam (Eds.), *Exploring family relationships with other social contexts* (pp. 147–168). Hillsdale, NJ: Lawrence Erlbaum Associates.

Kerig, P. K., Cowan, P. A., & Cowan, C. P. (1993). Marital quality and gender differences in parent–child interaction. *Developmental Psychology, 29(6)*, 931–939.

Keyes, R. (Ed.). (1992). *Sons on fathers: An anthology*. New York: HarperCollins.

Kiecolt-Glaser, J. K., Fisher, B. S., Ogrocki, P., Stout, J. C., Speicher, C. E., & Glaser, R. (1987). Marital quality, marital disruption, and immune function. *Psychosomatic Medicine, 49*, 13–33.

Kiecolt-Glaser, J. K., Kennedy, S., Malkoff, S., Fisher, L., Speicher, C. E., & Glaser, R. (1988). Marital discord and immunity in males. *Psychosomatic Medicine, 50*, 213–229.

Kliewer, W., & Weidner, G. (1987). Type A behavior and aspirations: A study of parents' and children's goal setting. *Developmental Psychology, 23*, 204–209.

Klinnert, M. D., Emde, R. N., Butterfield, P., & Campos, J. J. (1987). Social referencing: The infant's use of emotional signals from a friendly adult with mother present. *Annual Progress in Child Psychiatry and Child Development*, 26–39.

Klonoff, E. A., & Landrine, H. (1992). Sex roles, occupational roles, and symptom-reporting: A test of competing hypotheses on sex differences. *Journal of Behavioral Medicine, 15*, 355–364.

Kohn, M. (1969). *Class and conformity: A study in values*. Homewood, IL: Dorsey Press.

Kohn, M. (1990). *Social structure and self-direction: A comparative analysis of the United States and Poland*. Cambridge, MA: Blackovich.

Kramer, L., & Gottman, J. M. (1992). Becoming a sibling: "With a little help from my friends." *Developmental Psychology, 28*, 685–699.

Krokoff, L. J. (1984). *A telephone version of the Locke-Wallace test of marital adjustment*. Unpublished manuscript, University of Illinois, Champaign, IL.

Krokoff, L. J. (1987). *Anatomy of negative affect in working class marriages*. Dissertation Abstracts International, 45, 7A. (University Microfilms No. 84-22 109).

Krokoff, L. J., Gottman, J. M., & Haas, S. D. (1989). Validation of a rapid couples interaction scoring system. *Behavioral Assessment, 11*, 65–79.

Krokoff, L. J., Gottman, J. M., & Roy, A. K. (1988). Blue-collar marital interaction and communication orientation. *Journal of Personal and Social Relationships, 5*, 201–221.

Kurdek, L. A. (1991). Marital stability and changes in marital quality in newly wed couples: A test of the contextual model. *Journal of Social and Personal Relationships, 8(1)*, 27–48.

Kurdek, L. A. (1993). Predicting marital dissolution: A 5-year prospective longitudinal study of newlywed couples. *Journal of Personality and Social Psychology, 64*, 221–242.

Kurdek, L. A., & Lillie, R. (1985). Temperament, classmate likability, and social perspective coordination as correlates of parent-rated Type A behaviors. *Journal of Applied Developmental Psychology, 6*, 73–83.

Lacey, J. I. (1967). Somatic response patterning and stress: Some revisions of activation theory. In M. H. Appley & R. Trumball (Eds.), *Psychological stress: Issues in research* (pp. 14–37). New York: Appleton-Century-Crofts.

Ladd, G. W., & Hart, C. H. (1992). Creating informal play opportunities: Are parents' and preschoolers' initiations related to children's competence with peers? *Developmental Psychology, 28(6)*, 1179–1187.

Lakoff, G. (1993). The contemporary theory of metaphor. In A. Ortony (Ed.), *Metaphor and thought* (pp. 202–251). New York: Cambridge University Press.

Lakoff, G., & Johnson, M. (1980). *Metaphors we live by*. Chicago: University of Chicago Press.

Lamb, M. E. (Ed.). (1981). *The role of the father in child development*. New York: Wiley.

Lamb, M. E. (Ed.). (1986). *The father's role: Applied perspectives*. New York Wiley.

Lamb, M. E. (Ed.). (1987). *The father's role: Cross-cultural perspectives*. Hillsdale, NJ: Lawrence Erlbaum Associates.

Lambert, W. E., Hamers, J. F., & Frasure-Smith, N. (1979). *Child rearing values: A cross-national study*. New York. Praeger.

Landis, C., & Hunt, W. A. (1939). *The startle pattern*. New York: Farrar.

Larson, M. C., Gunnar, M. R., & Hertsgaard, L. (1991). The effects of morning naps, car trips, and maternal separation on adrenocortical activity in human infants. *Child Development, 62(2)*, 362–372.

Larson, S. K., & Porges, S. W. (1982). The ontogeny of heart rate patterning in the rat. *Developmental Psychobiology, 15*, 519–528.

Larzelere, R. E. (1993). Response to Oosterhuis: Empirically justified uses of spanking: Toward a discriminating view of corporal punishment. *Journal of Psychology & Theology, 21(2)*, 142–147.

Larzelere, R. E., Klein, M., Schumm, W. R., & Alibrando, S. A. (1989). Relations of spanking and other parenting characteristics to self-esteem and perceived fairness of parental discipline. *Psychological Reports, 64(3, Pt 2)*, 1140–1142.

Leakey, R. E. (1994). *The origin of humankind*. New York: Basic Books.

Levant, R. F. (1988). Education for fatherhood. In P. Bronstein & C. Cowan (Eds.), *Fatherhood today: Men's changing role in the family* (pp. 253–275). New York: Wiley.

Levant, R. F. (1992). Toward the reconstruction of masculinity. *Journal of Family Psychology, 5*, 379–402.

Levant, R. F., & Kelley, J. (1991). *Between father and child*. New York: Penguin.

Levenson, R. W., Carstensen, L. L., & Gottman, J. M. (1994). Influence of age and gender on affect, physiology, and their interrelations: A study of long-term marriages. *Journal of Personality and Social Psychology, 67(1)*, 56–68.

Levenson, R. W., & Gottman, J. M. (1983). Marital interaction. Physiological linkage and affective exchange. *Journal of Personality and Social Psychology, 45,* 587–597.

Levenson, R. W., & Gottman, J. M. (1985). Physiological and affective predictors of change in relationship satisfaction. *Journal of Personality and Social Psychology, 49,* 85–94.

Levi, A. M., Buskila, M., & Gerzi, S. (1977). Benign neglect: Reducing fights among siblings. *Journal of Individual Psychology, 33(2),* 240–245.

Lewak, R. W., Wakefield, J. A., & Briggs, P. F. (1985). Intelligence and personality in mate choice and marital satisfaction. *Personality and Individual Differences, 6,* 471–478.

Linnemeyer, S. A., & Porges, S. W. (1986). Recognition memory and cardiac vagal tone in 6-month-old infants. *Infant Behavior and Development, 9,* 43–56.

Locke, H. J., & Wallace, K. M. (1959). Short marital adjustment and prediction tests: Their reliability and validity. *Marriage and Family Living, 21,* 251–255.

Long, P., Forehand, R., Wierson, M., & Morgan, A. (1994). Does parent training with young noncompliant children have long-term effects? *Behaviour Research & Therapy, 32(1),* 101–107.

Lufi, D., Cohen, A., & Parish, P. J. (1990). Identifying attention deficit hyperactivity disorder with the WISC-R and the Stroop Color and Word Test. *Psychology in the Schools, 27,* 28–34.

Maccoby, E. E. (1980). *Social development.* New York: Harcourt, Brace, & Jovanovitch.

Maccoby, E. E. (1990). Gender and relationships: A developmental account. *American Psychologist, 45(4),* 513–520.

Maccoby, E. E., & Martin, J. A. (1983). Socialization in the context of the family: Parent–child interaction. In E. M. Hetherington (Ed.), *Handbook of child psychology Vol. 4, socialization, personality.* New York: Wiley.

MacDonald, K. (1987). Parent–child physical play with rejected, neglected, and popular boys. *Developmental Psychology, 23(5),* 705–711.

MacDonald, K., & Parke, R. D. (1984). Bridging the gap: Parent–child play interaction and peer interactive competence. *Child Development, 55,* 1265–1277.

MacDougall, J. M., Dembroski, T. M., & Krantz, D. S. (1981). Effects of types of challenge on pressor and heart rate responses in Type A and Type B women. *Psychophysiology, 18,* 1–9.

MacLean, P. D. (1949). Psychosomatic disease and the "visceral brain." Recent developments bearing on the Papez theory of emotion. *Psychosomatic Medicine, 11,* 338–353.

MacLean, P. D. (1970). The limbic brain in relation to the psychoses. In P. Balck (Ed.), *Physiological correlates of emotion.* New York: Academic Press.

Malatesta, C. Z., Culver, C., Tesman, J., & Shepard, B. (1989). The development of emotion expression during the first two years of life. *Monographs of the Society for Research in Child Development* (Serial 219, pp. 1–104). Chicago: University of Chicago Press.

Malatesta, C. Z., & Haviland, J. M. (1982). Learning display rules: The socialization of emotion expression in infancy. *Child Development, 53,* 991–1003.

Malatesta-Magai, C. Z. (1991). Development of emotion expression during infancy. General course and patterns of individual difference. In J. Garber & K. Dodge (Eds.), *The development of emotion regulation and dysregulation* (pp. 49–68). New York: Cambridge University Press.

Margolin, G. (1988). Marital conflict is not marital conflict is not marital conflict. In R. DeV. Peters & Z. McMahon (Eds.), *Social learning and systems approaches to marriage and the family* (pp. 193–216). New York: Brunner/Mazel.

Markham, H. J., & Notarius, C. I. (1987). Coding marital and family in interaction: Current status. In T. Jacob (Ed.), *Family interaction and psychopathology: Theories, methods, and findings.* New York: Plenum.

Martin, I., & Venables, P. H. (1980). *Techniques in psychophysiology.* New York: John Wiley & Sons.

Matthews, K. A., Rakaczky, C. J., & Stoney, C. M. (1987). Are cardiovascular responses to behavioral stressors a stable individuial difference variable in childhood? *Psychophysiology, 24,* 464–473.

Mayer, J. D., & Gashke, Y. N. (1988). The experience and meta-experience of mood. *Journal of Personality and Social Psychology, 55,* 102–111.

McCabe, P. M., Yongue, B. G., Ackles, P. K., & Porges, S. W. (1985). Changes in heart period, heart period variability a, and a spectral analysis estimate of respiratory sinus arrhythmia in response to pharmacological manipulations of the baroreceptor reflex in cats. *Psychophysiology, 22,* 195–203.

McCabe, P. M., Yongue, B. G., Porges, S. W., & Ackles, P. K. (1984). Changes in heart period, heart period variability and a spectral analysis estimate of respiratory sinus arrhythmia during aortic nerve stimulation in rabbits. *Psychophysiology, 21,* 149–158.

Mueller, E., & Brenner, J. (1976). The growth of social interaction in a toddler playgroup: The role of peer experience. *Child Development 48,* 854–861.

Mulhern, R. K., & Passman, R. H. (1981). Parental discipline as affected by the sex of the parent, the sex of the child, and the child's apparent responsiveness to discipline. *Developmental Psychology, 17(5),* 604–613.

Murphy, C. M., & Messer, D. J. (1977). Mothers, infants, and pointing: A study of a gesture. In H. R. Schaffer (Ed.), *Studies in mother–infant interaction.* London: Academic Press.

Myers, H. F., Alvy, K. T., Arrington, A., & Richardson, M. A. (1992). The impact of a parent training program on inner-city African-American families. *Journal of Community Psychology, 20(2),* 132–147.

National Center for Health Statistics. (1993). Advance report of final natality statistics, 1991. *Monthly vital statistics report: Volume 42, No. 3, Suppl.* Hyattsville, MD: Public Health Service.

Nelson, T. O. (Ed.). (1992). *Meta-cognition.* Boston: Allyn & Bacon.

The New York Times. (1994, December 3). Story about a robbery of Mr. Reilly (p. 1.).

Notarius, C., & Markman, H. (1994). *We can work it out.* New York: Putnam.

Nurcombe, B. (1984). An intervention program for mothers of low birthweight infants: Preliminary results. *Journal of the American Academy of Child Psychiatry, 23(3),* 319–325.

O'Keefe, J. L., & Smith, T. W. (1988). Self-regulation and Type A behavior. *Journal of Research in Personality, 22(2),* 232–251.

Ollendick, T. H., & Yule, W. (1990). Depression in British and American children and its relation to anxiety and fear. *Journal of Consulting and Clinical Psychology, 58(1),* 126–129.

Olson, D. R., & Astington, J. W. (1993). Thinking about thinking: Learning how to take statements and hold beliefs. *Educational Psychologist, 28(1),* 7–23.

Olson, D. H., Spengle, D. H., & Russell, C. S. (1979). Circumplex model of marital and family systems I: Cohesion and adaptability dimensions, family types, and clinical applications. *Family Process, 18,* 3–28.

Overton, W. F. (Ed.). (1983). *The relationship between social and cognitive development.* Hillsdale, NJ: Lawrence Erlbaum Associates.

Parke, R. D. (1981). *Fathers.* Cambridge, MA: Harvard University Press.

Parker, J. G., & Asher, S. R. (1987). Peer relations and later personal adjustment: Are low-accepted children at risk? *Psychological Bulletin, 102,* 357–389.

Patterson, C. J., Vaden, N. A., & Kupersmidt, J. B. (1991). Family background, recent life events, and peer rejection during childhood. *Journal of Social and Personal Relationships, 8,* 347–361.

Patterson, G. R. (1982). *Coercive family process.* Eugene, OR: Castalia.

Patterson, G. R. (1993). Orderly change in a stable world: The antisocial trait as a chimera. *Journal of Consulting and Clinical Psychology, 61(6),* 911–919.

Patterson, G. R., Crosby, L., & Vuchinich, S. (1992). Predicting risk for early police arrest. *Journal of Quantitative Criminology, 8(4),* 335–355.

Patterson, G. R., & Forgatch, M. S. (1985). Therapist behavior as a determinant for client noncompliance: A paradox for the behavior modifier. *Journal of Consulting and Clinical Psychology, 53(6),* 846–851.

Patterson, G. R., & Gullion, X. (1971). *Living with children.* Champaign, IL: Research Press.

Patterson, G. R., & Narrett, C. M. (1990). The development of a reliable and valid treatment program for aggressive young children. Special issue: Unvalidated, fringe, and fraudulent treatment of mental disorders. *International Journal of Mental Health, 19(3),* 19–26.

Patterson, G. R., & Stoolmiller, M. (1991). Replications of a dual failure model for boys' depressed mood. *Journal of Consulting and Clinical Psychology, 59(4)*, 491–498.

Pelaez, N. M., Field, T., Cigales, M., & Gonzalez, A., et al. (1994). Infants of depressed mothers show less "depressed" behavior with their nursery teachers. *Infant Mental Health Journal, 15*, 358–367.

Pepler, D. J. (1995). *Results of a study of homeless mothers*. A paper presented at the annual meeting of the Society of Research on Child Development, Indianapolis, IN.

Perret-Clermont, A-N. (1980). *Social interaction and cognitive development in children*. London: Academic Press.

Peterson, J. L., & Zill, N. (1986). Marital disruption, parent–child relationships, and behavior problems in children. *Journal of Marriage and the Family, 48*, 295–307.

Pettit, G. S., Harrist, A. W., Bates, J. E., & Dodge, K. A. (1991). Family interaction, social cognition, and children's subsequent relations with peers at kindergarten. *Journal of Social and Personal Relationships, 8(3)*, 383–402.

Phillips, E. L., Shenker, S., & Revitz, P. (1951). The assimilation of the new child into the group. *Psychiatry, 14*, 319–325.

Pickens, J., & Field, T. (1993a). Attention-getting vs. imitation effects on depressed mother-infant interactions. *Infant Mental Health Journal, 14*, 171–181.

Pickens, J., & Field, T. (1993b). Facial expressivity in infants of depressed mothers. *Developmental Psychology, 29*, 986–988.

Polefrone, J. M., & Manuck, S. B. (1987). Gender differences in cardiovascular and neuroendocrine responses to stressors. In R. C. Barnett, L. Biener, & G. K. Baruch (Eds.), *Gender and stress* (pp. 13–38). New York: The Free Press.

Porges, S. W. (1972). Heart rate variability and deceleration as indices of reaction time. *Journal of Experimental Psychology, 92*(1), 103–110.

Porges, S. W. (1973). Heart rate variability: An autonomic correlate of reaction time performance. *Bulletin of the Psychonomics Society, 1*, 270–272.

Porges, S. W. (1974). Heart rate indices of newborn attentional responsivity. *Merrill-Palmer Quarterly, 20*(4), 231–254.

Porges, S. W. (1976). Peripheral and neurochemical parallels of psychopathology: A psychophysiological model relating autonomic imbalance to hyperactivity, psychopathy, and autism. In H. W. Reese (Ed.), *Advances in Child Development and Behavior, 11*, (pp. 35–65). New York: Academic Press.

Porges, S. W. (1980). Individual differences in attention: A possible physiological substrate. In B. K. Keogh (Ed.), *Advances in special education* (Vol. 2, pp. 111–134). Greenwich, CT: JAI.

Porges, S. W. (1983). Heart rate patterns in neonates: A potential diagnostic window to the brain. In T. M. Field and A. M. Sostek (Eds.), *Infants born at risk: Physiological and perceptual responses* (pp. 3–22). New York: Grune & Stratton.

Porges, S. W. (1984). Heart rate oscillation: An index of neural mediation. In M. G. H. Coles, J. R. Jennings, & J. A. Stern (Eds.), *Psychophysiological perspectives: Festschrift for Beatrice and John Lacey.* New York: Van Nostrand Reinhold.

Porges, S. W. (1985). Spontaneous oscillations in heart rate: Potential index of stress. In P. B. Moberg (Ed.), *Animal stress* (pp. 97–111). Bethseda, MD: The American Physiological Society.

Porges, S. W. (1986). Respiratory sinus arrhythmia: Physiological basis, quantitative methods and clinical implication. In P. Grossman, K. Janssen, & D. Vaitl (Eds.), *Cardiorespiratory and cardiosomatic psychophysiology* (pp. 101–115). New York: Plenum.

Porges, S. W. (1991a). Autonomic regulation and attention. In B. A. Campbell, H. Hayne, & R. Richardson (Eds.), *Attention and information processing in infants and adults* (pp. 201–223). Hillsdale, NJ: Lawrence Erlbaum Associates.

Porges, S. W. (1991b). Vagal tone: An autonomic mediator of affect. In J. Garber & K. A. Dodge (Eds.), *The development of emotion regulation and dysregulation* (pp. 111–128). New York: Cambridge University Press.

Porges, S. W. (1994, October). *Orienting in a defensive world: A Poly-Vagal theory of our evolutionary heritage*. Presidential Address, Society for Psychophysiological Research.

Porges, S. W. (in press). Vagal tone: A physiological marker of stress vulnerability. *Pediatrics*.

Porges, S. W., Arnold, W. R., & Forbes, E. J. (1973). Heart rate variability: An index of attentional responsivity in human newborns. *Developmental Psychology, 8(1)*, 85–92.

Porges, S. W., Bohrer, R. E., Cheung, M. N., Drasgow, F., McCage, P. M., & Keren, G. (1980). New time-series statistic for detecting rhythmic co-occurrence in the frequency domain: The weighted coherence and its application to psychophysiological research. *Psychological Bulletin, 88*, 580–587.

Porges, S. W., & Humphreys, M. M. (1977). Cardiac and respiratory responses during visual search in non-retarded children and retarded adolescents. *American Journal of Mental Deficiency, 82*(2), 162–169.

Porges, S. W., & Raskin, D. C. (1969). Respiratory and heart rate components of attention. *Journal of Experimental Psychology, 81*, 497–503.

Porges, S. W., Doussard-Roosevelt, J. A., & Maita, A. K. (1994). Vagal tone and the physiological regulation of emotion. In N. A. Fox (Ed.), The development of emotion regulation: Biological and behavioral considerations. *Monographs of the Society for Research in Child Development, 59*(240), 167–186.

Porges, S. W., Doussard-Roosevelt, J. A., Portales, A. L., & Suess, A. (1994). Cardiac vagal tone: Stability and relation to difficultness in infants and 3-year-olds. *Developmental Psychobiology, 27*, 289–300.

Porges, S. W., & Doussard-Roosevelt, J. A. (in press). The psychophophysiology of temperament. In J. D. Noshpitz (Ed.), *Handbook of child and adolescent psychiatry*. New York: Wiley.

Porges, S. W., Stamps, L. E., & Walter, G. F. (1974). Heart rate variability and newborn heart rate responses to illumination changes. *Developmental Psychology, 10*(4), 507–513.

Porges, S. W., Walter, G. F., Korb, R. J., & Sprague, R. L. (1975). The influence of methylphenidate on heart rate and behavioral measures of attention in hyperactive children. *Child Development, 46*, 727–733.

Porter, B., & O'Leary, K. D. (1980). Marital discord and childhood behavior problems. *Journal of Abnormal Child Psychology, 8*, 287–295.

Porter, F. L., Porges, S. W., & Marshall, R. E. (1988). Newborn pain cries and vagal tone: Parallel changes in response to circumcision. *Child Development, 59*, 495–505.

Pratt, M. W., Kerig, P. K., Cowan, P. A., & Cowan, C. P. (1992). Family worlds: Couple satisfaction, parenting style, and mothers' and fathers' speech to young children. *Merrill-Palmer Quarterly, 38(2)*, 245–262.

Putallaz, M. (1983). Predicting children's sociometric status from their behavior. *Child Development, 54*, 1417–1426.

Putallaz, M., Costanzo, P. R., & Smith, R. B. (1991). Maternal recollections of childhood peer relationships: Implications for their children's social competence. *Journal of Social and Personal Relationships, 8(3)*, 403–422.

Putallaz, M., & Gottman, J. M. (1981). An interactional model of children's entry into peer groups. *Child Development, 52*, 986–994.

Putallaz, M., & Wasserman, A. (1989). Children's naturalistic entry behavior and sociometric status. A developmental perspective. *Developmental Psychology, 25*, 001–009.

Raine, A., Venables, P. H., & Williams, M. (1990). Relationships between N1, P300, and contingent negative variation recorded at age 15 and criminal behavior at age 24. *Psychophysiology, 27*, 567–574.

Rasmussen, K. L. R., Fellowes, J. R., Byrne, E., & Suomi, S. J. (1988). Heart rate measures associated with early emigration in adolescent male rhesus macaques (*Macaca mulatta*). *American Journal of Primatology, 14*, 439 (abstract).

Ratner, H. H., & Stettner, L. J. (1991). Thinking and feeling: Putting Humpty Dumpty together again. *Merrill Palmer Quarterly, 37(1)*, 1–26.

Raush, H. L., Barry, W. A., Hertel, R. K., & Swain, M. A. (1974). *Communication, conflict, and marriage.* San Francisco, CA: Jossey-Bass.

Rawson, B. (Ed.). (1991). *Marriage, divorce, and children in ancient Rome.* Oxford, England: Clarendon Press.

Redl, F., & Wineman, D. (1951). *Children who hate.* Glencoe, IL: Free Press.

Redl, F. (1966). *When we deal with children.* New York: The Free Press.

Renshaw, P. D., & Asher, S. R. (1985). The study of children's goals: A reply to Gresham's commentary. *Merrill-Palmer Quarterly, 3(1),* 105–109.

Revenstorf, D., Hahlweg, K., Schindler, L., & Vogel, B. (1984). Interaction analysis of marital conflict. In K. Hahlweg & N. S. Jacobson (Eds.), *Marital interaction: analysis and modification* (pp. 159–181). New York: Guilford.

Revenstorf, D., Vogel, B., Wegener, R. Hahlweg, K., & Schindler, L. (1980). Escalation phenomena in interaction sequences: An empirical comparison of distressed and nondistressed couples. *Behavior Analysis and Modification, 2,* 97–116.

Richards, J. E. (1985). The development of sustained visual attention in infants from 14 to 26 weeks of age. *Psychophysiology, 22,* 409–416.

Richards, J. E. (1987). Infant visual sustained attention and respiratory sinus arrhythmia. *Child Development 58,* 488–496.

Roberts, M. W. (1988). Enforcing chair timeouts with room timeouts. *Behavior Modification, 12(3),* 353–370.

Robinson, B. (1977). Sex-typed attitudes, sex-typed contingency behaviors and personality characteristics of male caregivers. *Dissertation Abstracts International, 37,* 5003.

Robinson, B. E., & Hobson, C. M. (1978). Men in day care: You've come a long way buddy. *Child Care Quarterly, 7,* 156–163.

Roe, K. V. (1980). Toward a contingency hypothesis of empathy development. *Journal of Personality and Social Psychology, 39(5),* 991–994.

Rothbart, M. K., Ahadi, S. A., & Hershey, K. L. (1994). Temperament and social behavior in childhood. Special issue: Children's emotions and social competence. *Merrill-Palmer Quarterly, 40(1),* 21–39.

Rothbart, M. K., & Derryberrry, D. (1981). Development of individual difference in temperament. In M. E. Lamb & A. L. Brown (Eds.), *Advances in Development Psychology* (Vol. 1). Hillsdale, NJ: Lawrence Erlbaum Associates.

Rothbart, M. K., & Posner, M. I. (1985). Temperament and the development of self-regulation. In C. L. Hartledge & C. R. Telzrow (Eds.), *The neuropsychology of individual differences: A developmental perspective.* New York: Plenum.

Rubin, L. B. (1976). *Worlds of pain.* New York: Basic Books.

Rusbult, C. E., Johnson, D. J., & Morrow, G. D. (1986). Determinants and consequences of exit, voice, loyalty, and neglect: Responses to dissatisfaction in adult romantic involvements. *Human Relations, 39(1),* 45–63.

Rusbult, C. E., Zembrodt, I. M., & Gunn, L. K. (1987). Exit, voice, loyalty, and neglect: Responses to dissatisfaction in romantic involvements. *Journal of Personality and Social Psychology, 43(6),* 1230–1242.

Rustia, J. G., & Abbott, D. (1993). Involvement in infant care: Two longitudinal studies. *International Journal of Nursing Studies, 30,* 467–476.

Rutter, M. (1971). Parent–child separation: Psychological effects on the children. *Journal of Child Psychology and Psychiatry, 12,* 233–260.

Rutter, M. (1979). Protective factors in children's response to stress and disadvantage. In M. W. Kent and J. E. Rolf (Eds.), *Primary prevention of psychopathology, Vol. 3: Social competence in children* (pp. 49–74). Hanover, NH: University Press of New England.

Rutter, M. (1990). Psychosocial resilience and protective mechanisms. In J. Rolf, A. S. Masten, D.

Cicchetti, K. H. Neuchterlein, & S. Weintraub (Eds.), *Risk and protective factors in the development of psychopathology* (pp. 181–214). New York: Cambridge University Press.

Rutter, M., Yule, B., Quinton, D., Rowlands, O., Yule, W., & Berger, M. (1974). Attainment and adjustment in two geographic areas: Some factors accounting for area differences. *British Journal of Psychiatry, 126,* 520–533.

Sachis, P. N., Armstrong, D. L., Becher, L. E., & Bryan, H. C. (1980). Myelination of the human vagus nerve from 24 weeks postconceptional age to adolescence. *Journal of Neuropathology and Experimental Neurology, 41,* 466–472.

Salovey, P., & Mayer, J. D. (1990). Emotional intelligence. *Imagination, Cognition and Personality, 9,* 185–211.

Scaife, M., & Bruner, J. S. (1975). The capacity for joint attention in the infant. *Nature, 253,* 265–266.

Scaife, J., & Frith, J. (1988). A behaviour management and life stress course for a group of mothers incorporating training for health visitors. *Child Care, Health, and Development, 14,* 25–50.

Schaefer, E. S. (1959). A circumplex model for maternal behavior. *Journal of Abnormal and Social Psychology, 59,* 226–235.

Scull, C. (Ed.). (1992). *Fathers, sons, and daughters.* New York: Putnam.

Schwartz, P. (1994). *Peer marriage.* New York: The Free Press.

Sears, R. R., Maccoby, E. E., & Levin, H. (1957). *Patterns of child rearing.* Evanston, IL: Row Peterson.

Shantz, C. U., & Hartup, W. W. (Eds.). (1992). *Conflict in child and adolescent develoment.* New York: Cambridge University Press.

Shaw, D. S., & Emery, R. E. (1987). Parental conflict and other correlates of the adjustment of school-age children whose parents have separated. *Journal of Abnormal Child Psychology, 15,* 269–281.

Shortt, J. W., Bush, L., McCabe, J. R., Gottman, J. M., & Katz, L. F. (1994). Children's physiological responses while producing facial expressions of emotions. *Merrill-Palmer Quarterly, 40,* 40–59.

Siegman, A. W., & Smith, T. W. (Eds.). (1994). *Anger, hostility, and the heart.* Hillsdale, NJ: Lawrence Erlbaum Associates.

Simons, R. L., Robertson, J. F., & Downs, W. R. (1989). The nature of the association between parental rejection and delinquent behavior. *Journal of Youth & Adolescence, 18(3),* 297–310.

Sirbu, W., Cotler, S., & Jason, L. A. (1978). Primary prevention: Teaching parents behavioral child rearing skills. *Family Therapy, 5(2),* 163–170.

Smith, T. W., & Brown, P. C. (1991). Cynical hostility, attempts to exert social control, and cardiovascular reactivity in married couples. *Journal of Behavioral Medicine, 14(6),* 581–592.

Smolen, R. C., Spiegel, D. A., & Martin, C. J. (1986). Patterns of marital interaction associated with marital dissatisfaction and depression. *Journal of Behavior Therapy and Experimental Psychiatry, 17,* 261–266.

Snyder, J., Dishion, T. J., & Patterson, G. R. (1986). Determinants and consequences of associating with deviant peers during preadolescence and adolescence. *Journal of Early Adolescence, 6(1),* 29–43.

Spock, B. (1957). *Baby and child care.* New York: Pocket Books.

Sroufe, L. A. (1979). The coherence of individual development: Early care, attachment, and subsequent developmental issues. *American Psychologist, 34(10),* 834–841.

Sroufe, L. A. (1984). The organization of emotional development. In K. R. Scherer & P. Ekman (Eds.), *Approaches to emotion* (pp. 109–128). Hillsdale, NJ: Lawrence Erlbaum Associates.

Stanley (a.k.a Wilson), B. J., & Katz, L. (1991). *Vagal tone, gender, and peer relationships of preschool children.* Presentation at the Society for Research in Child Development, Seattle, WA.

Stark, K. D., Kaslow, N. J., & Laurent, J. (1993). The assessment of depression in children: Are we assessing depression or the broad-band construct of negative affectivity? *Journal of Emotional and Behavioral Disorders 1(3),* 149–154.

Starrels, M. E. (1994). Gender differences in parent–child relations. *Journal of Family Issues, 15(1),* 148–165.

Steinhausen, H. (1972). The influence of social class with personality structure and child rearing methods of diabetic mothers. *Zeitschrift fur Psychotherapie und Medizinische Psychologie, 22(1),* 28–39.

Stern, D. N. (1977). *The first relationship.* Cambridge, MA: Harvard University Press.

Stern, D. N. (1985). *The interpersonal world of the infant: A view from psychoanalysis and developmental psychology.* New York: Basic Books.

Stifter, C. A., & Fox, N. A. (1990). Infant reactivity: Physiological correlates of newborn and 5-month temperament. *Developmental Psychology, 26,* 582–588.

Stifter, C. A., Fox, N. A., & Porges, S. W. (1989). Facial expressivity and vagal tone in 5- and 10-month-old infants. *Infant Behavior and Development, 12,* 127–137.

Stoolmiller, M., Duncan, T., Bank, L., & Patterson, G. R. (1993). Some problems and solutions in the study of change: Significant patterns in client resistance. *Journal of Consulting and Clinical Psychology, 61(6),* 920–928.

Sullaway, M., & Christensen, A. (1983). Assessment of dysfunctional interaction patterns in couples. *Journal of Marriage and the Family, 45,* 653–660.

Sullivan, M. W., & Lewis, M. (1989). Emotion and cognition in infancy: Facial expressiveness during contingency learning. *International Journal of Behavioral Development, 12(2),* 221–237.

Tannenbaum, L. E., Forehand, R., & Thomas, A. M. (1990). Adolescent self-reported anxiety and depression: Separate constructs or a single entity. *Child Study Journal, 22(1),* 61–72.

Tavris, C. (1982). *Anger: The misunderstood emotion.* New York: Simon & Schuster.

Telegina, T. L., & Pigarera, M. L. (1992). Correlation between the level of development of intellectual actions and emotional experiences in preschoolers in a play situation. *Journal of Russian and East European Psychology, 30(3),* 45–56.

Thornes, B., & Collard, J. (1979). *Who divorces?* London: Routledge & Kegan Paul.

Tibbits-Kleber, A. L., Howell, R. J., & Kleber, D. J. (1987). Joint custody: A comprehensive review. *Bulletin of the American Academy of Psychiatry and the Law, 15,* 27–43.

Trent, K., & South, S. J. (1989). Structural determinants of the divorce rate: A cross-sectional analysis. *Journal of Marriage and the Family, 51,* 391–404.

Treiber, F. A., Mabe, P. A., Riley, W., & Carr, T. (1989). Assessment of children's Type A behavior: Relationship with negative behavioral characteristics and children and teacher demographic characteristics. *Journal of Personality Assessment, 53,* 770–782.

Tronick, E. Z. (1980). On the primacy of social skills. In D. B. Sawin, L. O. Walker, & J. H. Penticuff (Eds.), *The exceptional infant. Psychosocial risks in infant environment transactions* (pp. 144–158). New York: Brunner/Mazel.

Tronick, E. Z. (1989). Emotions and emotional communication in infants. *American Psychologist, 44,* 112–119.

Tronick, E. Z., & Field, T. (1986). *Maternal depression and infant disturbance: New directions for child development* (Vol. 34). London: Jossey-Bass.

Tronick, E. Z., & Gianino, A. (1986). Interactive mismatch and repair: Challenges to the coping infant. *Zero to Three, 6(3),* 1–6.

Troy, M., & Sroufe, L. A. (1987). Victimization among preschoolers: Role of attachment relationship history. *Journal of the American Academy of Child and Adolescent Psychiatry, 26(2),* 166–172.

Urban, J., Carlson, E., Egeland, B., & Sroufe, L. A. (1991). Patterns of individual adaptation across childhood. *Development and Psychopathology, 3(4),* 445–460.

Van Dyke, C., & Kaufman, I. C. (1993). Psychobiology of bereavement. In L. Temoshok, C. Van Dyke, & L. S. Zegans (Eds.), *Emotions in health and illness: Theoretical and research foundations* (pp. 37–50). New York: Grune & Stratton.

Vincent, J. P., & Friedman, L. C. (1979). Demand characteristics in observations of marital interaction. *Journal of Consulting and Clinical Psychology, 47,* 557–566.

Vincent, J. P., Weiss, R. L., & Birchler, G. R. (1975). A behavioral analysis of problem-solving in distressed and nondistressed married and stranger dyads. *Behavior Therapy, 6*, 475–489.

Vygotsky, L. S. (1962). *Thought and language.* Cambridge: MIT Press.

Waggenheim, J. (1995). Among the promise keepers. *New Age Journal, March/April*, 78–130.

Walden, T. (1991). Infant social referencing. In J. Garber & K. A. Dodge (Eds.), *The development of emotion regulation and dysregulation* (pp. 69–88). New York: Cambridge University Press.

Walker, L. E. (1984). *The battered woman syndrome.* New York: Springer.

Walker, K., Wilson, B., Katz, L., & Gottman, J. M. (in preparation). *Children's physiological recovery from facial expressions of emotion varies with their parents' marital satisfaction.* Unpublished manuscript, University of Washington, Seattle, WA.

Wallerstein, J. S., & Kelly, J. B. (1975). The effects of parental divorce: Experiences of the preschool child. *Journal of the American Academy of Child Psychiatry, 14*, 600–616.

Wallerstein, J. S., & Kelly, J. B. (1980). *Surviving the breakup: How children and parents cope with divorce.* New York: Basic Books.

Watson, D., & Clark, L. A. (1984). Negative affectivity: The dispostion to experience aversive emotional states. *Psychological Bulletin, 96(3)*, 465–490.

Webster-Stratton, C. (1990). Enhancing the effectiveness of self-administered videotape parent training for families with conduct-problem children. *Journal of Abnormal Child Psychology, 18(5)*, 479–492.

Webster-Stratton, C. (1993). *The incredible years: A trouble-shooting guide for parents of children aged 3–8.* Toronto, Ontario: Umbrella Press.

Webster-Stratton, C. (1994). Advancing videotape parent training: A comparison study. *Journal of Consulting and Clinical Psychology, 62(3)*, 583–593.

Wechsler, D. (1974). *Selected papers of David Wechsler.* New York: Academic Press.

Weidner, G., Sexton, G., Matarzzo, J. D., & Periera, C. (1988). Type A behavior in children, adolescents, and their parents. *Developmental Psychology, 24(1)*, 118–121.

Weiner, H. (1977). *Psychobiology and human disease.* New York: Elsevier.

Weiss, R. L., & Summers, K. J. (1983). Marital Interaction Coding System III. In E. E. Filsinger (Ed.), *Marriage and family assessment.* Beverly Hills, CA: Sage.

Wetzel, J. W. (1994). Depression: Women at risk. *Social Work in Health Care, 19(3–4)*, 85–108.

Whalen, C. K., & Henker, B. (1986). Type A behavior in normal and hyperactive children: Multisource evidence of overlapping constructs. *Child Development, 57*, 688–699.

Whitbeck, L. B., Hoyt, D. R., Simons, R. L., & Conger, R. D. Intergenerational continuity of parental rejection and depressed affect. *Journal of Personality and Social Psychology, 63(6)*, 1036–1045.

Whitehead, L. (1979). Sex differences in children's responses to family stress. *Journal of Child Psychology and Psychiatry, 20*, 247–254.

Williams, C. A., & Forehand, R. (1984). An examination of predictor variables for child compliance and noncompliance. *Journal of Abnormal Child Psychology, 12(3)*, 491–503.

Williams, R. B., et al. (1980). Type A behavior, hostility, and coronary atherosclerosis. *Psychosomatic Medicine, 42*, 539–549.

Williams, E., & Gottman, J. M. (1981). *A user's guide to the Gottman-Williams time-series programs.* New York: Cambridge University Press.

Wilson, B. J. (1994). *The entry behavior and emotion regulation abilities of developmentally delayed children.* Unpublished doctoral dissertation, University of Washington.

Wilson, B. J., & Gottman, J. M. (1995). Marital interaction and parenting. In M. H. Bornstein (Ed.), *Handbook of parenting, Vol. 4: Applied and practical parenting* (pp. 33–56). Mahwah, NJ: Lawrence Erlbaum Associates.

Winkler, I., & Doherty, W. J. (1983). Communication styles and marital satisfaction in Israeli and American couples. *Family Process, 22(2)*, 229–237.

Wong, A. K., & Kuo, E. C. Y. (1983). *Divorce in Singapore.* Singapore: Graham Brash (Pte) Ltd.

Yang, B., & Lester, D. (1991). Correlates of statewide divorce rates. *Journal of Divorce and Remarriage, 15*, 219–223.

Yerkes, R. M., & Dodson, J. D. (1908). The relation of strength of stimulus to rapidity of habit formation. *Journal of Comparative Neurological Psychology, 18,* 459–482.

Yogev, S. (1986). Relationships between stress and marital satisfaction among dual-earner couples. *Women and Therapy, 5,* 313–330.

Yongue, B. G., McCabe, P. M., Porges, S. W., Rivera, M., Kelley, S. L., & Ackles, P. K. (1982). The effects of pharmacological manipulations that influence vagal control of the heart on heart period, heart-period variability, and respiration in rats. *Psychophysiology, 19,* 426–432.

Zillmann, D. (1979). *Hostility and aggression.* Hillsdale, NJ: Lawrence Earlbaum Associates.

Author Index

A

Abbott, D., 301
Adler, A., 17
Adorno, T. W., 16
Ainsworth, M. D. S., 11
Akselrod, S., 278
Alibrando, S. A., 25
Allen, B. A., 6
Alvy, K. T., 12, 33
Appel, M. A., 239
Arias, I., 215
Armour, T. E., 6
Arnold, J. E., 29
Arnold, W. R., 323
Arrington, A., 12, 33
Arthur, J., 241
Asher, S., 205
Asher, S. R., 285
Astington, J. W., 6
Averill, J., 236, 237, 249
Avertt, 241
Axelrod, J., 189

B

Babcock, 237
Bank, L., 29
Barclay, D. R., 31, 32
Bardwick, J., 237
Barry, W. A., 215, 238, 265
Barton, K., 215
Baumrind, D., 10, 12
Beach, S. R. H., 215
Becker, W. C., 10, 11
Bell, S. M., 11
Benes, F. M., 288
Berger, A. C., 278
Berger, M., 216
Berkman, L. F., 205
Besag, V. E., 287

Biglan, A., 241
Billings, A., 216
Birchler, G. R., 215, 216
Black, A. E., 12
Blier, M. J., 241
Blier-Wilson, W. L. A., 241
Block, J., 268
Block, J. H., 268
Bloom, B., 205, 217
Bly, R., 295
Bohrer, R. E., 324
Booth, A., 201
Braungart, J. M., 230, 260
Brazelton, T. B., 259
Breiner, J., 29
Breslow, L., 205
Brett, D., 15
Brett, J. M., 293
Briggs, J. L., 259
Briggs, P. F., 215
Drinton-Lee, M. C., 192
Brody, G., 214
Brody, G. H., 12
Broel-Plateris, A., 194
Brooks, L. D., 33
Brown, P. C., 239, 240
Buehlman, K., 3, 195, 253
Bugental, D. E., 259
Burgess, E. W., 193, 215
Burman, B., 205
Bush, L., 169
Buskila, M., 33
Buss, A. H., 270
Butkovsky, L., 230, 260
Bvinelli, D. J., 6

C

Carstensen, L. L., 196, 197, 239
Cassidy, J., 230, 260

Chadwick, B. A., 292
Chase, B. N., 297
Cherlin, A., 190
Chester, R., 194
Cheung, M. N., 324
Christensen, A., 196, 234, 238, 282, 283
Church, P., 29
Cigales, M., 290
Cohen, R. J., 278
Cohn, D. A., 11, 235
Collard, C., 193
Conger, R. D., 12
Cook, J., 209
Corsaro, W., 177
Cotler, S., 32
Cowan, C. P., 10, 11, 214, 215, 230, 234
Cowan, P. A., 10, 11, 214, 215, 230, 234
Cox, M., 214, 216
Cox, R., 214, 216
Crocco, D., 33
Crosbie, J., 186
Crosby, L., 28
Cummings, E. M., 182, 196, 216, 286

D

Davidson, R. J., 277
Davies, G., 29
Davies, P., 182, 196, 216, 286
Day, D. E., 26
de-Boeck, P., 17
DeHaas, P. A., 155
Deley, W. W., 25
Dembroski, T. M., 240
Dennenberg, V. H., 286
DeQuattro, V., 240
Derryberry, D., 270
Dinkmeyer, D., 31
Dishion, T. J., 28
Dixon, S., 259
Dobson, H., 297
Doherty, W. J., 293, 301
Doussard-Roosevelt, J. A., 174, 288
Downs, W. R., 12
Drasgow, F., 324
Dreger, R. M., 215
Dreikurs, R., 15, 17-8
Duncan, T., 29
Dutton, D., 238, 286

E

Easterbrooks, M. A., 214, 215
Edfeldt, A. W., 25
Ekman, P., 7, 242, 260, 262
Emery, R. E., 214, 216

Esler, M., 240
Esters, P., 32

F

Faber, A., 20, 30
Fagot, B. I., 230
Fauber, R., 191, 214
Field, T., 290
Fincham, F. D., 196
Fine, G. A., 178
Fisher, B. S., 205, 241
Fisher, L., 241
Fisher, P. A., 230
Fivush, R., 230
Flavell, J. H., 6
Fodor, J. A., 6
Follingstad, D. R., 216
Forbes, E. J., 323
Forehand, R., 191, 214
Forehand, R. L., 28, 29, 32
Forgatch, M. S., 28
Fox, N.A., 260, 277, 287, 290
Franz, C. E., 17
Frasure-Smith, N., 259
Frenkel-Brunswick, E., 16
Friedman, H. S., 205
Friedman, L. C., 216
Friesen, W. V., 7, 260, 262
Frith, J., 32
Frodi, A., 238
Furey, W. M., 29, 32

G

Galsworthy, J., 190
Gardiner, H., 240
Gaschke, 6
Gelles, R. J., 25
Gerzi, S., 33
Gesell, A., 29
Gianetto, R. M., 259
Gilmore, E. C., 31
Gilmore, J., 31
Ginott, H., 19, 20, 21, 22, 24-5
Glaser, R., 205, 241
Goldenberg, I., 17
Gonzales, A., 290
Gordon, D., 278
Gordon, R. M., 32
Gordon, T., 31, 32
Gorkin, L., 239, 240
Gottman, J., 209
Gottman, J. M., 3, 4, 5, 168, 169, 178, 182, 195,
    196-7, 198, 201, 205, 209, 214, 215,
    216, 217, 218, 224, 233, 234, 237,

238, 239, 241, 242, 253, 258, 264, 277, 282, 287, 289, 301, 302, 325, 327
Graudenz, I., 17
Graziano, A. M., 25
Greven, P. J., Jr., 273
Gross, J. A., 240, 307
Grossman, P., 324
Gullion, X., 28
Gunn, L. K., 194
Gych, J. H., 196

H

Hahlweg, K., 215, 216
Halberstadt, A. G., 259, 260
Hamers, J. F., 259
Harburg, E., 240
Haver, D., 17
Haynes, S. N., 216
Healy, B.T., 290
Heavey, C. L., 196, 234, 238, 282
Hertel, R. K., 215, 238, 265
Heston, T., 292
Hetherington, E. M., 214, 216
Hite, S., 294
Hobson, C. M., 296
Hochschild, A. R., 4, 5
Holmes, T., 29
Holmes, T. H., 205
Holroyd, K. A., 239, 240
Hooven, C., 168
Hops, H., 241
Houts, A. C., 31, 32
Howell, R. J., 294
Howes, P., 215
Hoyt, D. R., 12
Humphreys, M. M., 323
Hunt, W. A., 7

I

Ianotti, R. J., 216

J

Jacobs, S., 241
Jacobson, N. S., 237
Jason, L. A., 32
Johnson, D. J., 194-5
Johnson, M., 7, 312
Jones, N. A., 260
Jordan, T. C., 17
Julius, S., 240

K

Kagan, J., 278
Karemaker, J., 324
Katz, L. F., 3, 4, 5, 168, 169, 195, 214, 224, 233, 234, 253, 287
Kaufman, I. C., 241
Keefer, C., 259
Kelly, J., 31, 267, 300
Kelly, J. B., 216
Kennedy, S., 241
Keren, G., 324
Kerig, P. K., 230
Keyes, S., 268
Kiecolt-Glaser, J. K., 205, 241
Kleber, D. J., 294
Klein, R. E., 25
Kohn, M., 17
Kooy, G. A., 194
Kraak, R., 17
Krantz, D. S., 240
Krokoff, L., 3, 182, 196, 215, 237
Kuo, E. C. Y., 194
Kurdek, L. A., 195

L

Lakoff, G., 7, 306, 311, 312
Lambert, W. E., 259
Landis, C., 7
Larzelere, R. E., 25
Layne, C., 196, 234, 282
Leakey, R. E., 272
LeBlanc, W. G., 290
Lester, D., 193
Levant, R. F., 31, 32, 267, 281, 300; 294.296
Levenson, R. W., 3, 182, 195, 196-7, 201, 216, 237, 239, 240, 241, 258, 301, 307
Levi, A. M., 33
Levin, M., 17
Levine, A. G., 29
Levinson, D. J., 16
Lewak, R. W., 215
Locke, H. J., 193, 215
Long, N., 214
Love, L. R., 259

M

Macauley, J., 238
Maccoby, E. E., 4, 9, 11, 12, 17, 154, 197, 230, 268
MacDonald, K., 230
MacDougall, J. M., 240
MacLean, P. D., 289
Maita, A. K., 288
Malkoff, S., 241
Manuck, S. B., 240

Margolin, G., 205, 216
Markman, H., 196, 215
Martin, C. J., 215
Martin, I., 186
Martin, J. A., 9, 11, 12, 230
Mayer, J. D., 6
Mazlich, E., 20, 30
McCage, P. M., 324
McClelland, D. C., 17
McKay, G., 31
McMahon, R. J., 28, 29
Morrow, J. D., 195
Mulhern, R. K., 230
Murray, J., 209
Myers, H. F., 12, 33

N

Namaste, K. A., 25
Narett, C. M., 29
Nawrocki, T., 290
Notarius, C., 196, 215

O

Ogrocki, P., 205, 241
O'Leary, K. D., 214, 215
Olson, D. H., 215
Olson, D. R., 6
Ostfeld, A., 241

P

Palaez, N. M., 290
Parke, R. D., 229, 229-30, 260
Passman, R. H., 230
Patterson, G. R., 11, 12, 28, 32
Pearson, J., 11, 235
Pepler, D. J., 300
Peterson, J. L., 214
Pickens, J., 290
Plomin, R., 270
Polefrone, J. M., 240
Porges, S. W., 174, 183, 288, 323, 324
Portales, A. L., 174
Porter, B., 214
Pratt, M. W., 230
Putallaz, M., 178, 302

Q

Quinton, D., 216

R

Radke-Yarrow, M., 216
Rahe, R. H., 205

Raine, A., 286
Randall, O., 240
Rausch, H. L., 238, 265
Raush, H. L., 215
Redl, F., 26, 27, 35
Reilly, A. H., 293
Reisine, T. D., 189
Renshaw, P. D., 285
Revenstorf, D., 215, 216
Reznick, J. S., 278
Rice, M., 33
Richardson, M. A., 12, 33
Roberts, M. W., 26
Robertson, J. F., 12
Robinson, B. E., 296
Roe, K. V., 25, 299
Rosen, A., 32
Rosenberg, K. M., 286
Rothbart, M. K., 270
Rothland, J., 241
Rowlands, O., 216
Rubin, L. B., 194
Rusbult, C. E., 194-5
Rushe, R., 209, 237
Russell, C. S., 215
Rustia, J. G., 301
Rutter, M., 214, 216, 221

S

Salovey, P., 6
Sanford, R. N., 16
Scaife, J., 32
Schaefer, E. S., 10
Schindler, L., 215, 216
Schumm, W. R., 25
Schwartz, P., 299
Scwartz, J. E., 205
Sears, R. R., 17
Shaffer, D. R., 12
Shannon, D. C., 278
Sharpley, C. F., 186
Shaw, D. S., 216
Shenk, J. L., 196, 282
Sherman, L., 241
Shortt, J. W., 169, 215
Simons, R. L., 7, 12
Sirbu, W., 32
Skinner, M. L., 28
Slotkin, J., 214
Smith, T. W., 239, 240
Smolen, R. C., 215
Snidman, N., 278
Snyder, J., 28
South, S. J., 192
Spearn, R. C., 33

Speicher, C. E., 205, 241
Spengle, D. H., 215
Spiegel, D. A., 215
Stamps, L. E., 323
Starrels, M. E., 230
Stayton, D. J., 11
Steinhausen, H., 17
Stoolmiller, M., 28
Stout, J. C., 205, 241
Stroh, L. K., 293
Suess, A., 174
Sullaway, M., 283
Sullivan, J. C., 216
Summers, K. J., 215
Swain, M. A., 215, 238, 265
Syme, S. L., 205

T

Tavris, C., 22, 238
Thomas, A. M., 191
Thome, P. R., 238
Thomes, M. M., 215
Thornes, B., 193
Tibbits-Kleber, A. L., 294
Tomarken, A. J., 277
Tomilson, K. C., 205
Trent, K., 192
Tronick, E., 259
Tucker, J. S., 205
Tyson, R., 209

U

Ubel, F. A., 278

V

Van Beek, J., 324
Van Dyke, C., 241
Venables, P. H., 186, 286
Vincent, J. P., 215, 216
Vogel, B., 215, 216
Vuchinich, S., 28

W

Waggenheim, J., 298

Wakefield, J. A., 215
Walker, K., 169
Walker, L. E., 22
Wallerstein, K. S., 216
Walter, G. F., 323
Waltz, J., 237
Webster-Stratton, C., 26, 28
Wegener, R., 215, 216
Weinberger, J., 17
Weiss, R. L., 215
Wetzel, J. W., 241
Whitbeck, L. B., 12
White, J., 209
White, L., 201
White, S., 205, 217
Whitehead, L., 214
Wieling, W., 324
Wientjes, C., 324
Wierson, M., 191
Williams, C. A., 29
Williams, E., 169, 327
Williams, M., 286
Williams, R. B., 240
Wilson, B., 169
Wilson, B. J., 196, 303
Wineman, D., 27
Winkler, I., 301
Wong, A. K., 194

Y

Yang, B., 193
Yogev, S., 215
Young, R. D., 155
Yule, B., 216
Yule, O., 216

Z

Zahn-Waxler, C., 216
Zembrodt, I. M., 194
Zill, N., 214
Zillmann, D., 239
Zweiffer, A., 240

Subject Index

A

Academic achievement
and attention, 106, 130
as developmental outcome, 43
emotion regulation in, 155–156
and gender, 230
and marital discord, 214, 219
and meta-emotion, 155–156,
in meta-emotion theory process model, 165,
172, 179–180
and parental expectations, 41
and parental loss of control, 256
and parenting codes, 157–159
physiological regulation in, 43
in time-2 study, 130, 155–159
Affect
child
coding of, 128
and derogation, 153–154
and facial expression, 127–128, 154,
215, 262–264
and gender, 230–231
and parental meta-emotion, 152–153,
and parenting dimensions, 153–154
and peer relations, 40–41, 100–102, 302
temperament and, 173–174, 270–271
in time-1 study, 127–128
in time-2, 130–131, 152–154
infant
as communication, 110–111
and emotional regulation, 95û96, 97–99,
107–109, 289–290
parental, see also Negative child affect; Facial expressiveness
and child outcomes, 17, 21–22, 40–41
and emotion coaching, 92–93
and marital interaction, 133–135
and marital outcomes, 216
negative, 40–41

parental styles and, 10–12
parenting dimensions and, 10
in research literature, 9–12
Alexythymia, 281, 300
Anger, see also Family response, anger; Emotion metaphors, anger
gender differences in, 237–239
in marital interaction, 196
as negative emotion, 67–68
parental, 141–142, 201
parental, 22–23, 198, 243–249
parental loss of control, 243–249
as parenting variable, 182–183
physical health, 239–240
review of literature, 236–237, 236–241, 242
Annie Stories, 15–16
Attention
and academic achievement, 106, 130
in cognitive development, 106
and emotion regulation, 106, 113
and heart rate variability, 119–121
and peer relations, 111–113
and socio-emotional development, 106
in time-2 study, 130
and vagal tone, 106, 113, 119–121
Authoritarian parenting, 10, 16–18, 297–299
Authoritative parental style, 10
Authoritative/Responsive dimension, 143–144,
220
Autonomic nervous system (ANS), 289–291,
93–97
Autonomic reactivity, 278–279
Awareness
as buffer against marital discord, 221
coding of, 132
and gender, 231
as meta-emotion, 48
in meta-emotion theory process model, 167,
178–181
parental, of child's emotion, 17, 48

B

Balance systems theory, 87, 93–99, 103
Basal vagal tone
  as buffer, 220
  computation of, 238
  and emotion regulation, 183–186
  in meta-emotion theory process model,
    168–170, 183–189
BASE VAGAL, *see* Basal vagal tone
Behavior problems, 12, 28–29
  marital conflict and, 233–235, 286–287, 214
  in time-2, 130–131
  violence as a, 285–287
Buffers, 219–226

C

Cardiovascular reactivity (CVR), *see* Heart rate
    variability
Catecholamines, 96–97, 121, 128, 168
Child development
  and family meta-emotions, 106–116
  and parent training, 31–33, 283
  parental views of, 53–54, 55, 56
  in parenting guides, 29
  stages of, 18
  tasks of, 97–100
Childhood, history of, 88–89, *see also* discipline
Child outcomes, *see also* Academic achieve-
    ment; Affect child; Physical health;
    Attention; Peer relations; Marital
    conflict; Behavior problems
  discipline and, 12–13
  emotion regulation in, 86–87, 93–97,
    99–105, 214–215, 275
  and gender, 230, 233–235
  marital dissolution and, 218–226
  parental styles and, 10–12, 16–17
  parenting dimensions and, 10, 91–93,
    100–103
  parents and, 28–29, 40, 89, 256–258,
    274–275
  temperment and, 270–271
  values as, 23
Coaching
  as buffer, 221
  and child outcomes, 274–275
  and child temperament, 270–271
  coding of, 132
  and cognitive development, 103
  compared to disapproving family response,
    58–59
  compared to dismissing family response, 59
  and criticism, 64
  culture and, 265, 267

  and emotional expressiveness, 259–260
  family style, 49, 115–116
  five steps of, 280
  gender and, 231
  and Ginott, H., 19–20
  and meta-emotion theory process model,
    167, 173–174, 178–181
  and meta-emotions, 48–49, 91–93, 274
  and parent–child interactions, 103–104
  and parenting dimensions, 92–93
  parents and, 41, 59, 63–64, 84–85, 100–102
  and peer relations, 41, 100–102, 115–116
  and regulatory physiology, 275
Coaching family response, 58–57, 59
Coaching parents, and emotional expression,
    259–60
Coding of
  affect, 128
  derogation, 92–93
  directed facial action task, 128
  marital interaction, 126
  meta-emotion, 132–133
  oral history interview, 134–135
  parental loss of control, 242–243
  parent–child interactions, 127, 135–137
  parenting dimensions, 92–93
  peer relations, 129, 137
  Scaffolding/Praising, 92–93
Cognitive development, 43–44, 103, 106
Cognitive meta-emotion variable, 81–82
Cortisol, 104, 128, 168
Cowan and Cowan coding system, 127,
    136–137, 143
Criticism, 21, 64
Culture, 265, 267

D

DELTA VAGAL, *see* Vagal tone, suppression of
Democratic parenting, 17–18
Derogation
  and academic achievement, 157
  as buffer, 220
  and child affect, 153–154
  coding of, 92–93
  and gender, 231–232
  and meta-emotion hypothesis validity,
    143–145
  in meta-emotion theory process model, 167,
    170–173, 175–177, 179
  in parental meta-emotion structure, 89–90,
    87
Directed facial action task, 127–128, 262
Disapproving family response
  anger, 67–70
  compared to coaching, 58–59

sadness, 49–51
Discipline, 12–15, 21, 23–25, 50–51, 68–69, 273, 297–299, *see also* Childhood, history of; Spanking
Dismissing family response
anger, 67, 72–74
compared to coaching, 59
sadness, 51–58
Divorce, *see* Marital dissolution
Dreikurs, R.
compared to Ginott, H., 18, 19–20, 21, 24, 30
and parenting guides, 29, 30–31
Dreikurs program, 15, 17–18

E

Electroencephalogram (EEG) reactivity, 276–278
Emotional awareness of parents, child's emotions, 17
Emotional communication
developmental considerations, 283
and emotion regulation, 114–116
Emotional control
coding of, 133
as meta-emotion, 242–258
Emotional development, 43–44
Emotional expression
and coaching parents, 259–266
during middle childhood, 41, 100–2
and parental meta-emotion, 71–73
review of literature, 259–260
and vagal tone, 268
Emotional intelligence, 101
Emotion coaching, *see* Coaching
Emotion Facial Action Coding System (EM-FACS), 127, 128, 134, 260–261
Emotion metaphors
anger, 311–312
negative, 318–324
positive, 312–313
somewhat positive, 313–314
parents' philosophy
anti-expressing, 319–320
balance, 320–322
pro-expressing, 318
sadness
negative, 309–311
positive, 306–307
somewhat positive, 308
Emotion regulation, *see also* Regulatory physiology
child
and academic achievement, 155–156
and attention, 113

and child outcomes, 287–291
and cognitive development, 103
as Down regulation, 165, 231
middle childhood, 100–102
and emotional communication, 114–116
and language, 113–114
in meta-emotion theory process model, 165, 171, 179–180
parenting and, 106
regulatory physiology, 87, 93–97, 287–291
in time-2, 131
infant, 95–99, 107–109, 289–290
parental, 104, 106, 260–262
Emotion regulation theory, 86–105

F

Facial expressiveness, *see also* Affect
child, 127–128, 215, 262–264
with Directed facial action task, 127–128, 262
and marital interaction, 134
Family response
anger
disapproving, 67–70
dismissing, 67, 72–74
emotion coaching, 74–77
as an emotion philosophy, 79–81
high acceptance but low coaching, 77–79
coaching, 58–67
compared to dismissing or disapproving, 59
Family structure, 291–293
Father–child interactions, *see also* Fathers
and peer relations, 40
related to marital outcomes, 93
with sons, 294–296
and Type A Behavior Pattern (TABP), 121–122
Fathers, *see also* Father–child interactions; Mothers; Parenting
as authoritarian parents, 297–299
and marital dissolution, 293–294
and the Men's Movement, 295, 298–299
meta-emotions of, 140–141, 198
modern role of, 293, 296, 299, 300–301
as variable, 293–301
violence and, 295
Frontal lobes, 288, 289–290

G

Gender, 209–213, 229–235, 239–242, 249–250
Ginott, Haim, 18–26, 29–31, 33–34, 92, 274–275

H

Heart rate variability, 119–121, 128
High acceptance but low in coaching
    anger, 77–79
    sadness, 64–67

I

Infant–caregiver interaction, 94–95, 97–99, 102,
    106, 107–111
Infants, and physiological homeostasis, 97–99
Infant vagal tone
    and emotion regulation, 289–290
    and physiological homeostasis, 97–99
    premature, 95
    and reactivity, 94–95, 97–99
    and risk factors, 118
Infant vagal tone ,suppression, 95–99
Intersubjectivity of infants, 110–111

K

Kahen Affect Coding Systems (KACS), 127,
    135–136
Kahen Engagement and Affect Coding System
    (KEACS), 127, 143–144
Kahen Engagement Coding System (KECS),
    127, 135, 136

L

Language, 113–114
Life space interviewing, 26–28, 35–36, 288,
    289–291
Limbic system, 288, 289–291

M

Marital discord
    buffering children from, 219–226
    and child outcomes, 40, 97, 191, 214–215,
        219, 286–287, 233–235
    conflict resolution and, 215–216, 234
    and life stressors, 215
    and meta-emotion, 198–205
    and physical illness
        child, 97
        parental, 251–252
Marital dissolution
    buffering children from, 219–226
    cascade towards, 217
    and child outcomes, 218–219
    factors in, 193–194
    fathers and, 293–294
    predictors, of, 216

predictors of, 125, 126, 195–197, 216–219
psychological studies of, 194–197
research on, 190–194
sociological studies of, 192–194
Marital interaction
    coding of, 126, 133–134
    and father–child interactions, 93
    and meta-emotion training, 284–285
    and parental affect, 133–134
    and parental loss of control, 251–252,
        254–255
    problem solving in, 133
    in time-1, 133–135
    in time-2, 129–130
Marital satisfaction, 111, 216
    and conflict resolution, 216
    and infant–caregiver interaction, 111
Marital stability, 264–265
Marital variables, and parent loss of control,
    254–255
Marriage
    and conflict resolution, 215–216
    and meta-emotion, 197–205
Meta-emotion
    and academic achievement, 155–156
    and anger, 22, 71–73
    as buffer, 222
    and child negative affect, 152–153
    and child physical illness, 152–153
    coding of, 132–133
    definition of, 6–7
    dimensions of, 48–49
    as emotional control, 242–258
    and emotion coaching, 274
    facial expressiveness, 260–264
    as family patterns, 49–81
    and gender, 209, 229–235
    as loss of control, 242–258
    and marriage, 197–205, 264–265
    parental, 87, 89–93, 140–142, 273–274
    social class and, 265–266
Meta-emotion interview
    coding of, 45, 48, 49
    dimensions, 48–49
    family patterns, 49–81
    outline, 46–48
    qualitative analysis of, 49–81
    validity of, 143–145
Meta-emotion process model
    developmental outcomes for, 163–165
    related to child physiology, 183–189
    results of, 177–181
    structure of, 165–166
    variables for, 165, 167–170, 182–183
Meta-emotion research agenda, 302–305
Meta-emotion structure

and child outcome, 274
definition, 7–8
emotion coaching, 91–93
and family's emotional communication,
     273–274
and marital interacton, 274
and parenting dimensions, 87, 89–93
and physical illness, 130
Meta-emotion study
and child facial expresiveness, 127–128
and Ginott, H., 33–34
hypotheses, 90, 92–93
interview, 45–85, 125–126
laboratory methods, 123–139
marital interaction, 126, 129–130
overview, 123–124, 129
parent–child interactions, 126–127
participant selection, 124–125
peer relations, 129
physiogical assessment, 128
research limitations, 301–302
time-2, 130–131
variable selection, 86–88
Meta-emotion theoretical model
balance systems theory, 93–97
child outcome variables, 87, 93–97, 105,
     285–291, 304
diagram of, 275–276, 302–304
and emotion regulation, 97–100, 105,
     285–291
and emotion regulation theory, 99–100, 304
hypotheses, 92–93, 104–105, 291
limitations of, 301–302
and parent training, 280–283, 304
parenting meta-emotion structure, 91–93,
     276–287, 302
parenting variables, 87, 104–105, 279–285,
     291–301, 304
peer relations in, 100–102, 105, 302
and regulatory physiology, 103–104, 105,
     276–279, 285–289, 303–304
research agenda, 302–304
Meta-emotion training, 280–285, 304
Meta-emotion variables, see Academic achieve-
     ment; Awareness; Coaching; Nega-
     tive child affect; Physical health;
     Physiological regulation
Metaphors, see Emotion metaphors
Middle childhood, 40–41, 100–102, 302
Mothers, 299–300, see also Fathers; Parenting

N

Negative child affect
in meta-emotion theory process model, 171,
     179–181

observed, 137, 180–181, 230
and parents, 152–154, 156
and peer relations, 40, 165

O

Observed negative affect, 137, 180–181, 230
Oral History Interview, 124–125, 134–135, 198,
     252–253

P

Parasympathetic nervous system (PNS), 93–94,
     103–105, 117–121, 128, 138
Parental loss of control, 242–258
and marital variables, 254–255
Parental role
and emotion coaching, 59, 60, 62, 66–67, 76
and emotion dismissing, 57–58
Parent–child interaction, see also Father–child
     interaction
and child regulatory physiology, 275
coding of, 127, 135–137, 143–145
and emotion coaching, 59, 103–104
and Ginott, H., 18, 19–25
meta-emotion study methods, 126–127
and Parental loss of control, 255
and parental meta-emotion structure, 87
and parental style, 10–12
and peer relations, 40, 100–102
Parent Effectiveness Training (PET), 31, 32
Parenting, see also Childhood, history of; Disci-
     pline; Fathers; Mothers; Parenting
     styles
history of, 272–273
research literature on, 9–12
Parenting dimensions, see Derogation; Scaffold-
     ing/Praising; Warmth
Parenting guides, 14–31
compared to research, 14–16
critique of, 30–31
and discipline, 14–15
and Dreikurs, R., 29, 30
and Ginott, H., 29, 30–31
historical traditions, 16–17
and social learning tradition, 28–29
sources of, 29
Parenting styles, 10–12
and discipline, 12–13
meta-emotion training, 284–285
Parenting variables, see Derogation; Authorita-
     tive/Reponsive Parenting
Parents
coaching

attributes of, 84–85
and child peer relations, 41, 100–102
and empathy, 59, 63–64
and Ginott, H., 19–20
Parent training, *see also* individual training programs by name
evaluation of, 31–33
Peer relations
and attention, 111–113
and child affect, 40–41
and coaching, 41, 115–116
coding of, 129, 137, 149
as developmental outcome, 39–41
and marital discord, 40, 41, 97, 214, 219, 233, 234
and meta-emotion theory process model, 170, 173
in middle childhood, 41, 302
and parental expectations, 41
and parental loss of control, 256
and parental meta-emotion, 149–150
and parent–child interactions, 40, 150–151
and physiological regulation, 40
in preschool, 41
and social development, 44
in time-2 study, 130, 150–151
variables, 129
Permissive parental style, 10
Permissive/restrictive parenting dimension, 9–10, 12
Physical illness
child
and meta-emotion theory process model, 164–165, 171, 179–180
as developmental outcome, 43, 205–206
and gender, 230
and marital discord, 97, 164–165, 214, 219
and parental loss of control, 256
and parental meta-emotions, 152–153, 130
and parenting dimensions, 153–154
in time-2 study, 131, 152–154
parental, 104, 239–240, 251–252
Physiological homeostasis, 97–99
Physiological regulation, *see also* Regulatory physiology
and academic achievement, 43
and anger, 239
and gender, 239
and peer relations, 40
Preschool children, 114–115
and peer relations, 41
Preschool children, 10–11, 95, 100, 114–115

R

Rapid Couple Interaction Coding System (RCISS), 126, 133
Rapid Macro peer interaction coding system (R-MACRO), 129, 137, 149
Redl, Fritz, 24, *see also* Life space interviewing
Regulatory physiology
child, 87, 88, 93–105
and emotion regulation, 87, 287–291
and meta-emotion theory process model, 168–170, 173–174, 178–180
and meta-emotion variables, 87
and parent–child interactions, 103
research, 117–122
variables, 105, 138–139
Respiratory sinus arrhythmia (RSA), 94, 118, 138

S

Sadness
coaching family, 58–67
disapproving family response, 49–51
Dismissing family patterns, 51–58
emotion philosophy, 79–81
father's meta-emotions, 141, 198
high acceptance but low in coaching, 64–67
mother's meta-emotions, 141–142, 198
review of literature, 241–242
Scaffolding/Praising
and academic achievement, 157, 159
and child affect, 153–154
coding of, 92
and gender, 231
and meta-emotion hypotheses, 92
and meta-emotion theory process model, 167–168, 175, 178 179
and parental meta-emotion structures, 87, 90
validity as variable, 143–145
Self Esteem Method (SEM), 31–33
Social class, 17, 265–266
Social development, 44, 106, *see also* Peer relations
Social interaction, *see* Peer relations
Social learning tradition, 28–29, 101
Spanking, 24–26, 297
Specific Affect Coding System (SPAFF), 126, 127, 133–134, 137, 198, 261–262
Stress, 96–97, 104, 121, 128, 168, 240–242
Structured Training for Effective Parenting (STEP), 31, 32–33
Sympathetic accelerator, 93, 117, 121–122
Sympathetic nervous system (SNS), 93–94, 96–97, 104–105, 117, 119, 121, 128

T

Temperament, child, 173–174, 270, 271
Time-1 meta-emotion study, 123–129, 132–139
Time-2 meta-emotion study, 129–131, 155–159
Type A Behavior Pattern (TABP), 121–122

U

Urinary endocrine variables, 187–189
Urinary hormones, 97, 104, 128

V

Vagal brake, 93, 117–121

Vagal tone, 289–290, *See also* Basal vagal tone;
      Emotion regulation; Infant vagal
      tone; Physiological regulation
   and attention, 106, 113, 119–121
   as buffer, 222–224
   and cognitive development, 103
   computation of, 118, 323–332
   development of, 118–119
   and emotional expression, 268
   and regulatory processes, 94, 104
   suppression of, 95–99, 119–121, 183–186
Vagus nerve, 93–94, 117, 288–289

W

Warm/cold-hostile parenting dimension, 10,
      11–12
Warmth dimension, 157, 159, 183